From Corporate to Social Media

The corporate and the social are crucial themes of our times. In the first decade of the twenty-first century, both individual lives and society were shaped by a capitalist crisis and the rise of social media. But what marks the distinctively social character of "social media"? And how does it relate to the wider social and economic context of contemporary capitalism? The concept of Corporate Social Responsibility (CSR) is based on the idea that socially responsible capitalism is possible; this suggests that capitalist media corporations can not only enable social interaction and cooperation but also be socially responsible.

This book provides a critical and provocative perspective on CSR in media and communication industries. It examines both the academic discourse on CSR and actual corporate practices in the media sector, offering a double critique that reveals contradictions between corporate interests and social responsibilities. Marisol Sandoval's political and economic analysis of Apple, AT&T, Google, HP, Microsoft, News Corp, The Walt Disney Company and Vivendi shows that media and communication systems in the twenty-first century are confronted with fundamental social responsibility challenges.

From software patents and intellectual property rights to privacy on the Internet, from working conditions in electronics manufacturing to hidden flows of eWaste – this book encourages the reader to explore the multifaceted social (ir)responsibilities that shape commercial media landscapes today. It makes a compelling argument for thinking beyond the corporate in order to envision and bring about truly social media. It will be of interest to students and scholars of media studies, cultural industry studies, sociology, information society studies, organization studies, political economy, business and management.

Marisol Sandoval is a Lecturer at the Department of Culture and Creative Industries at City University London.

Routledge advances in sociology

From Corporate to Social Media

Critical perspectives on corporate social responsibility in media and communication industries

Marisol Sandoval

Routledge
Taylor & Francis Group

LONDON AND NEW YORK

First published 2014
by Routledge
2 Park Square, Milton Park, Abingdon, Oxon OX14 4RN

and by Routledge
711 Third Avenue, New York, NY 10017

Routledge is an imprint of the Taylor & Francis Group, an informa business

British Library Cataloguing in Publication Data
A catalogue record for this book is available from the British Library

Library of Congress Cataloging in Publication Data
Sandoval, Marisol.
From corporate to social media : critical perspectives on corporate social responsibility in media and communication industries / Marisol Sandoval.
pages cm. — (Routledge advances in sociology ; 123)
Includes bibliographical references and index.
1. Social responsibility of business. 2. Mass media—Moral and ethical aspects. 3. Telecommunication—Moral and ethical aspects. 4. Social media—Moral and ethical aspects. I. Title.
HD60.S2475 2014
384.068′4—dc23
2013034768

ISBN: 978-0-415-72256-8 (hbk)
ISBN: 978-1-315-85821-0 (ebk)

Typeset in Times
by Swales & Willis Ltd, Exeter, Devon, UK

Printed and bound in the United States of America by
Edwards Brothers Malloy

For Christian.

Andábamos sin buscarnos pero sabiendo que andábamos para encontrarnos.
Julio Cortazar

Contents

Illustrations

Figures

Tables

Acknowledgement

This research was supported by a DOC scholarship from the Austrian Academy of Sciences.

In short, anything that we can call morality today merges into the question of the organization of the world. We might even say that the quest for a good life is the quest for the right form of politics.

(Adorno 1963/2000: 176)

1 Introduction

The corporate as well as the social are guiding themes of our times. Capitalist crisis and the rise of so-called social media both shaped society and individual lives in the first decade of the twenty-first century: while corporations struggled with decreasing profits, thousands of people lost their homes, their jobs and experienced the brute force of crisis-prone capitalism. At the same time, the online world became a symbol for unprecedented levels of sociality, enabling interaction, communication and cooperation. From user participation in the production of media content, to the rise of online communities and social networks, to so-called "Twitter rebellions and revolutions", online media promised to restore the social in times of increasing individualisation and crisis. But what is the social? What marks the distinctively social character of "social media"? And how does it relate to the wider social and economic context of contemporary capitalism?

Definitions of social media generally focus on sharing, participation and cooperation. Shirky argues that social media "increase our ability to share, to cooperate, with one another, and to take collective action, all outside the framework of traditional institutional institutions and organizations" (Shirky 2008, 20f). Van Dijk stresses that

> The very word "social" associated with media implies that platforms are user centered and that they facilitate communal activities, just as the term "participatory" emphasizes human collaboration. Indeed, social media can be seen as online facilitators or enhancers of *human* networks – webs of people that promote connectedness as a social value.
>
> (van Dijck 2013, 11)

According to boyd the term social media "is often used to describe the collection of software that enables individuals and communities to gather, communicate, share, and in some cases collaborate or play" (boyd 2009). Often used synonymous with the notion web 2.0, most understandings of the term social media highlight the active involvement of users in the production of content, that is user-generated content (O'Reilly 2005; Harrison and Barthel 2009, 157; boyd 2009, 16; van Dijck 2009, 41; Gauntlett 2011, 18; Terranova and Donvan 2013, 297).

The question of how to define social media focuses on qualities such as collaboration, communication, participation and sharing. Following this rhetoric new technologies increase the degree of social interaction and thus make certain media social. Definitions of social media tend to imply that only online media can be social, while other media such as the telephone, newspapers, TV or radio are not. By regarding the sociality of the media as a question of technology, such analyses furthermore remain limited to the level of the technological productive forces. Karl Marx argued that productive forces include labour power, raw materials, and means of production such as technologies and machines (Marx 1867/1990). Productive forces are, however, always embedded within certain relations of production, understood as the social relations that determine how production, distribution and consumption are organized (Marx 1859/1994, 211).

Understandings of social media that neglect the wider social and economic context that encompasses them overlook the level of the relations of production. They therefore are unable to capture the entirety of the social and/or unsocial character of the media today. This book attempts to overcome the narrow focus of the dominant concept of social media by (a) looking at all media industries rather than only online media and by (b) focusing on the specific relations of production within which the media are embedded: in order to determine the degree of sociality in the media system as a whole, it is necessary to look beyond the technological level and to take capitalist relations of production into account. As media in capitalism are primarily provided by private corporations, this requires looking at the corporate organization of the media and at the social impact of a commercial media system.

Truly social media are media that are social both at the level of the productive forces and the relations of production. They thus are not only social in the sense that they enable social interaction, exchange and cooperation (productive forces) but also in the sense that their production, distribution and consumption are compatible with general social well-being (relations of production).

Investigating how exactly such genuinely social media can look like and how to promote their realization requires expanding the debate about social media and to focus on the (un)social character of corporate media. The concept of corporate social responsibility (CSR) seems to be a promising point of departure for such an endeavour: while debates around social media look at the social character of online media as productive forces, the concept of CSR is based on the idea that a socially responsible capitalism is possible and thus suggests that capitalist media corporations can also become socially responsible at the level of relations of production. This book attempts to integrate these two strands of analysis by looking at the potential of CSR to turn corporate media into truly social media.

The idea of socially responsible corporations challenges some of the basic criticisms of capitalism. Critical scholars have characterized capitalism as monstrous, unethical and predatory, rather than good, ethical and social. The monster has been used as a metaphor for unsocial behaviour that undermines and destroys the foundations of society and therefore causes social problems. It is regarded as the antidote and negation of the social and society. In the following I will refer to the metaphor of the monster for pointing at some of the objections against capitalism and contrast it with the idea of CSR, which promises the emergence of ethical corporations and a responsible capitalism. Based on this discussion I highlight the need for and describe the foundations of a critical study of CSR in media and communication industries. Finally I outline important research questions and explain the structure of this book.

Corporate media as monster media?

Throughout the history of capitalism the metaphor of the monster has been used for describing its unethical and destructive tendencies. Annalee Newitz argues that "Capitalist monsters are found in literature and art film as well as commercial fiction and movies. [. . .] the stories fundamental message remains the same: capitalism creates monsters who want to kill you" (Newitz 2006, 3). She stresses that "[T]he history of capitalism can be told as monster story from beginning to end" (Newitz 2006, 12). Not only in popular culture, but also in economic theory the monster appears as a description of and warning against the destructive powers of capital and capitalist social relations. McNally describes "*capitalism* as a monstrous system, one that systematically threatens the integrity of human personhood" (McNally 2011, 3). He highlights that the economic crisis of 2008 triggered the use of metaphors of monsters, zombies and vampires to describe banks, financial markets or global corporations (McNally 2011, 2). However, as McNally points out, accounts that attribute monstrous features only to times of crises, specific corporations, or industries fail to recognize the full extent of the capitalist monstrosity:

> For modernity's monstrosities do not begin and end with shocking crises of financial markets, however wrenching and dramatic these may be. Instead, the very insidiousness of the capitalist grotesque has to do with its invisibility with, in other words, the ways in which monstrosity becomes normalized and naturalized via its colonialization of the essential fabric of everyday-life, beginning with the very texture of corporeal experience in the modern world.
> (McNally 2011, 2)

Similarly Chris Harman argues that "capitalism as a whole is a zombie system, seemingly dead when it comes to achieving human goals and responding to human feelings, but capable of sudden spurts of activity that cause chaos all around" (Harman 2011, 12).

Two of the archetypical monsters of modern Western literature – Frankenstein's monster (1818) and Count Dracula (1879) – were invented in the midst of the rise of industrial capitalism. Mary Shelley's Frankenstein (1818) tells the story of a scientist, who is driven by the ardent desire to create a living being, but as soon as he succeeds, turns away from his creation with fear and abandons it. Warren Montag argues that Mary Shelley's story "is incontestably interwoven" in the history of the rise of a desperate English working class: "it bears witness to the birth of that monster, simultaneously the object of pity and fear, the industrial working class" (Montag 2000, 387). Moretti (1982) interprets the ambivalent relationship between Frankenstein and his monster as the relationship between capital and wage labour: "On the one hand, the scientist cannot but create the monster", like capital cannot but create the proletariat. The proletariat at the same time poses a threat to capital, like the monster threatens Frankenstein: "On the other hand, he is immediately afraid of it and wants to kill it, because he realizes he has given life to a creature stronger than himself and of which he cannot henceforth be free" (Moretti 1982, 69).

While Frankenstein's monster represents the proletariat that capitalism creates, Bram Stoker's Dracula, according to Moretti, represents capital itself. These two monsters embody "two horrible faces of a single society, its *extremes*: the disfigured wretch and the ruthless proprietor" (Moretti 1982, 67). Mark Neocleous argues: "[T]he vampire as monster both demonstrates the capabilities of capital and acts as a warning about it" (Neocleous 2003, 684).

What is essential to the figure of the vampire is the transgression of boundaries between life and death. The vampire is an un-dead creature, dead and alive at the same time (Neocleous 2003, 683f). Melton describes the vampire as "a reanimated corpse that rises from the grave to suck the blood of the living people and thus retain some semblance of life" (Melton 2011, xxx). The vampire in order to keep itself alive needs to suck the life-force out of the living and thus "the vampire's gain is automatically the victim's loss" (Dundes 2002, 27).

The metaphor of the vampire has not only been used in literature. It also repeatedly appears in Karl Marx's descriptions of capital. Marx argued that capital came into the word "dripping from head to toe, from every pore, with blood and dirt" (Marx 1867/1990, 926). He described capital as dead labour: in order to accumulate, capital depends on the labour power of workers, which Marx described as the only source of value (Marx 1867/1990, 270). According to Marx, the capitalist thus exploits the living labour of the worker and turns it into dead labour that is capital.

Marx used the figure of the vampire for illustrating the monstrosity of this process: "Capital is dead labour, that, vampire-like, lives only by sucking living labour, and lives the more, the more labour it sucks" (Marx 1867/1990, 342). This characterisation of capital resembles Bram Stoker's description of the vampire that "can flourish and fatten on the blood of the living. Even more [. . .] his vital faculties grow strenuous, and seem as though they refresh themselves when his special pabulum is plenty" (Stoker 1897, 211).

Marx argued that British industry "vampirelike, could but live by sucking blood" (Marx 1864/2001, 95). Like the vampire depends on human blood, capital depends on human labour power. Marx spoke of capital's "werewolf-like hunger for surplus labour" (Marx 1867/1990, 353), "its insatiable appetite for surplus labour" (Marx 1867/1990, 375), its "vampire thirst for the living blood of labour" (Marx 1867/1990, 367).

Capital resembles the vampire not only because both feed upon the life-force of the living, but also because both continuously expand. In Stoker's novel vampires cannot die, but must go on age after age adding new victims and multiplying the evils of the world. For all that die from the preying of the Undead become themselves Undead, and prey on their kind. And so the circle goes on ever widening, like as the ripples from a stone thrown into the water.

(Stoker 1879, 189)

Like the vampire extends its reach in circles, capital through the cycle of accumulation, continuously turns living labour into capital, which then again exploits living labour to create even more capital:

By turning his money into commodities that serve as the building materials for a new product, and as factors in the labour process, by incorporating living labour into their lifeless objectivity, the capitalist simultaneously transforms values, i.e. past labour in its objectified and lifeless form, into capital, values which can perform its own valorisation process, an animated monster which begins to "work", as if its body were by love possessed.

(Marx 1867/1990, 302)

Like the kiss of the vampire turns a human being into another vampire, capital works as an "animated monster" that turns ever more living labour power into ever more capital. Both capital and the vampire know only one purpose: while capital's single purpose is its constant accumulation, that is, to turn living labour into dead capital (Marx 1867/1990, 253), the only purpose of the vampire is to suck the blood of the living: "as his [count Dracula's] intellect is small and his action based on selfishness, he confines himself to one purpose. That purpose is remorseless" (Stoker 1897, 302). Moretti in this context argues: "Like capital, Dracula is impelled towards a continuous growth, an unlimited expansion of his domain: accumulation is inherent in his nature" (Moretti 1999, 46)

This image of capital as a selfish blood-sucking monster that Marx invoked and that in literature studies served as one interpretation of Dracula, today is contrasted with the image of ethical and responsible corporations. The concept of CSR suggests that the time of ruthless corporations is over. According to this rhetoric, the socially responsible corporation is not preying on the social, but is a responsible corporate actor that contributes to general social well-being.

During the last years the concept of CSR has become increasingly popular among policy makers, academics and companies: in the Conclusions of the Lisbon European Council of March 2000 the European Council made "a special appeal to companies' corporate sense of social responsibility regarding best practices on lifelong learning, work organization, equal opportunities, social inclusion and sustainable development" (European Council 2000, paragraph 39). Since then, the European Commission has published one Green Paper (European Commission 2001) and three Communications (European Commission 2002; 2006; 2011) on CSR; initiated the European Multi-Stakeholder Forum on CSR (2002–2004),[1] and launched the European Alliance for CSR (2006).[2] In the 2011 communication the European Commission highlights that in order to "fully meet their corporate social responsibility, enterprises should have in place a process to integrate social, environmental, ethical, human rights and consumer concerns into their business operations" (European Commission 2011, 6).

In addition to this policy focus on CSR academic research has also paid increasing attention to this issue. The Social Science Citation Index from the start of its records until 1999 recorded 342 publications that contained the words "corporate social responsibility" or "CSR" in the title. Between 2000 and 2012 the number of such publications listed in the index is 2,100.[3] This shows that the interest in CSR as a research topic dramatically increased at the beginning of the twenty-first century. Furthermore CSR has become an important topic for companies. In 2011, 95 per cent of the 250 largest global companies reported their CSR activities (KPMG 2011, 7).

The idea of CSR has also spread within the media and communication business: on its website Microsoft for example highlights that it wants "to help people and businesses throughout the world realize their full potential"[4]; similarly Erikson intends "to improve life for people around the world"[5]; HP aims at making a "positive impact on society and the world"[6]; Disney promises to "Act and create in an ethical manner and consider the consequences of our decisions on people and the planet"[7]; Vivendi commits "to empowering present and future generations to fulfil their need to communicate, nourish their curiosity, develop their talent and encourage intercultural dialogue"[8]; Dell wants "to put technology and expertise to work, where it can do the most good for people and the planet"[9]; Vodafone promises to "Unleash the power of Vodafone to transform societies and enable sustainable living for all"[10]; and Google highlights that "You can make money without doing evil".[11]

These statements suggest that rather than being evil monsters, today's biggest media and communication companies present themselves as ardent servants of the common good. Is capital no longer monstrous? Does CSR turn corporations from evil monsters into social beings? Are the corporate monsters dead and buried or are they only hiding?

A critical analysis of CSR in media and communication industries

Critical theory reminds us to mistrust appearances. Adorno argued that critical theory aims at disenchanting social reality:

> Theory seeks to give a name to what secretly holds the machinery together. The ardent desire for thought, to which the senselessness of what merely exists was once unbearable, has become secularized in the desire for disenchantment. It seeks to raise the stone under which the monster lies brooding.
>
> (Adorno 1957/1976, 68)

In the preface to the first edition of *Capital Volume I*, Marx (1867) stressed the need for independent commissions that investigate working conditions in factories.

He criticized the absence of such commissions in Germany and argued that this absence would mean to "draw the magic cap down over our eyes and ears so as to deny that there are any monsters" (Marx 1867/1990, 91).

Lifting the "magic cap" requires looking beyond company statements at independent investigations in order to find out whether the corporate rhetoric of serving the common good corresponds to actual business practices. Studies that only rely on corporate self-disclosure are unable to determine whether the corporate rhetoric corresponds to actual business practices. Jose and Lee for example stress:

> Since we rely on company self-reports for our information, we report "as it is" as opposed to verifying the accuracy of what companies are reporting. Are companies really doing everything they are reporting? Or are environmental reports a part of the corporate "green-washing agenda?" We cannot answer these questions with absolute certainty.
>
> (Jose and Lee 2007, 319)

In order to find out to what extent the increased talk about CSR indicates a shift towards ethical business conduct or merely serves as a hiding place for the corporate monster, an ideology-critical perspective is necessary.

In taking such an ideology-critical perspective on CSR in media and communication industries, I will contribute to advancing an expanded notion of social media as socially responsible media. Assessing the social implications of media production, distribution and consumption today requires studying the media within their wider, economic, political and cultural context. Based on observations of how information and communication technologies, knowledge, media, etc. are increasingly shaping social structures and practices, some scholars have claimed that we are living in a "media society" (Mettler-Meibom 1994; Croteau and Hoynes 2000; Imhof et al. 2004), a "communication society" (Münch 1995), a "knowledge society" (Böhme and Stehr 1986), an "information society" (Martin 1995; Servaes 2003) a "network society" (Castells 1996).

If, as these concepts suggest, we are entering an age in which information, communication and knowledge become central in various aspects of social life, it is important to ask how these communicative and informational resources are provided. Critical scholars have pointed out that although the societal importance of media and information is rising, contemporary society is still a capitalist society. They developed notions like "digital capitalism" (Schiller 2000), "virtual capitalism" (Dawson and Foster 1998), "high-tech capitalism" (Haug 2003), "cybernetic capitalism" (Robins and Webster 1988), or "global informational capitalism" (Fuchs 2008). The way media and communication are provided today illustrates that capitalist relations of production are prevalent: privately owned companies produce media content and organize access to information and communication content and technology. The question therefore arises whether private companies can provide these essential communicative resources in a way that serves the common good and not merely private profit: are media and communication companies socially responsible?

The investigation of CSR in the media and communication industries that I attempt in the study at hand is guided by an emancipatory research interest. Habermas (1968/1971) distinguished three types of cognitive interest: a technical, a practical and an emancipatory interest. The technical interest characterizes empirical analytical sciences and aims at the production of technically exploitable knowledge (Habermas 1968/1971, 191). The practical interest of historical–hermeneutic sciences wants to create practically effective knowledge (Habermas 1968/1971, 191). Technical and practical knowledge only have a function "to the extent that they are technically exploited or practically efficacious" (Habermas 1968/1971, 196). The third cognitive interest Habermas identifies is an emancipatory interest. Habermas argues that self-reflection has an emancipatory potential as it allows the development of a critical consciousness: "self-reflection of consciousness in its manifestations to the point where the self-consciousness of the species has attained the level of critique and freed itself from all ideological delusion" (Habermas 1968/1971, 55). The "emancipatory cognitive interest" according to Habermas is an interest "in the undoing of repression and false consciousness" and corresponds to a "self-reflective learning process" (Habermas 1968/1971, 347). Emancipation presupposes reflection: "For the pursuit of reflection knows itself as a movement of emancipation" (Habermas 1968/1971, 198). According to Habermas, the emancipatory interest represents the approach of critically oriented studies (Habermas 1968/1971, 308).

The starting point for critical studies is the work of Karl Marx (Rasmussen 1996, 14; Macey 2000, 75; Tjaden 2006, 83). Marxian critique is essentially humanist, it is based on the insight that "man is the highest essence for man", which leads to the "categoric imperative to overthrow all relations in which man is a debased, enslaved, abandoned, despicable essence" (Marx 1844/2007a, 70). Marxist critique is thus directed against all forms of domination and oppression of humans. A central characteristic of Marx's notion of critique is how it relates theory and praxis: on the one hand Marxian critique is both a critique of categories and a critique of social reality. On the other hand Marxian critique is itself both theoretical as well as practical.

The object of a critique includes capitalist ideas and theories as well as societal conditions (Röttgers 1975, 253; Benhabib 1984, 288; Knoche 2002: 104f). As Benhabib points out: "Capital is a critique of the social reality articulated by the discourse of political economy, as well as of this discourse itself" (Benhabib 1984, 288). Furthermore Marx's notion of critique is theoretical as well as practical – it not only seeks to theoretically criticize domination and oppression, but to abolish them. Marx stressed: "In the struggle against that state of affairs, criticism is no passion of the head, it is the head of passion" (Marx 1844/2007a, 66). Ernst Bloch described the relation between theory and praxis that is entailed in Marx's notion of critique as dialectical: "Theory leads to concrete praxis, praxis with its newly emerging contradictions again requires theory" (Bloch 1972, 452 (translation[12])).

Critical theory and contemporary critical political economy have been inspired by Marx's notion of critique and applied and further advanced this concept. Max

Horkheimer in his programmatic article "Traditional and critical theory" (1937), described critical theory as "an essential element in the historical effort to create a world that satisfies the needs and powers of men. [. . .] the theory never aims simply at an increase of knowledge as such. It's goal is man's emancipation from slavery" (Horkheimer 1937/2002b, 246). Critical theory therefore, guided by "the interest of a rationally organized future society" and the "hope of radically improving human existence", "shed[s] critical light on present-day society" (Horkheimer 1937/2002a, 233). Similarly Marcuse in his article "Philosophy and critical theory" (1937) argued that instead of contenting itself with an idealist notion of reason as an issue only of the mind, critical theory aims at realizing reason within society. He stressed:

> If reason means shaping life according to men's free decision on the basis of their knowledge, then the demand for reason henceforth means the creation of a social organization in which individuals can collectively regulate their lives in accordance with their needs.
>
> (Marcuse 1937/1989, 141f)

A critical approach is a normative approach that does not only compile data and describe results, but that interprets their ethical implications. Using a critical approach for studying CSR is important because the concept itself essentially is about normative questions regarding the purpose and goals of the corporation. The idea of CSR suggests that it is possible for corporations to act in a way that contributes to general social well-being. A critical study thus needs to ask whether CSR can fulfil this promise and promote a socially responsible economy and the creation of truly social media.

Research foci and structure

A genuinely social media system is socially responsible in the sense that media production, distribution and consumption satisfy general social needs. The overall aim of this study is to evaluate the potential of CSR to contribute to a achieving a socially responsible media system. The main research question therefore is:

> What do the theory and practice of corporate social responsibility look like in the media and communication industries and to what extent can these two aspects contribute to achieving a socially responsible media and communication system?

This research question focuses on CSR theories, approaches and concepts on the one hand, and on CSR practices on the other hand. Based on the analysis of both, it is possible to discuss how far CSR can contribute to promoting a truly social media system. For that purpose, I analyze CSR concepts and approaches both at a theoretical and an empirical level. In order to study CSR practices, I empirically analyse the CSR activities of media and communication companies.

To answer the main research question I address several sub-questions: conducting a well-founded analysis of CSR theories and practices requires in a first step to explore the meaning of CSR as a theoretical concept. I discuss how different approaches to CSR relate corporate profit goals to social responsibilities.

> How do theories of corporate social responsibility relate corporate profit goals to the social responsibilities of the corporation?

I address this question in Chapter 2 by reviewing the state of the art in CSR theory and constructing a typology of theoretical approaches to CSR. This typology is based on Wolfgang Hofkirchner's (2002, 2003) distinction of four ways of thinking: reductionism, projectionism, dualism and dialectics. I highlight that rather than addressing CSR only from a managerial perspective, the question of CSR should initiate a political reflection about how to establish a socially responsible economy and society.

After the analysis of CSR theories in general, I move on to a more concrete level: CSR in the media and communication industries. I apply the typology constructed in Chapter 2 in order to discuss different approaches to CSR in media and communication companies. The question that guides this analysis is:

> How do theories of the social responsibility of the media relate corporate profit goals to the social responsibilities of media and communication companies?

Before answering this question in Chapter 3, I first suggest a theoretically grounded model of media and communication industries in the twenty-first century that later serves as the basis for selecting companies for the empirical case study. By referring to theories of media ethics, media responsibility, public broadcasting and political economy of media and communication, I subsequently identify reductionist, projectionist, dualist and dialectical ways of describing the relation between profit goals and social responsibilities in the media sector.

Against this theoretical background, I move in the next chapter on to the empirical analysis of CSR in media and communication industries. The overall research question for this empirical study is:

> How do media and communication companies in their CSR approaches and practices deal with conflicts between their economic goals and social responsibilities?

Based on a dialectical perspective on CSR in media and communication industries, this question aims at studying potential areas of conflict between the private interest of companies and the public good in the information age. In Chapter 4, I identify specific empirical research questions that focus on how global media and communication companies approach the topic of CSR (CSR approaches); on how they deal with tensions between their economic goals and their social responsibilities in their business activities (CSR practices); and on identifying challenges and future pathways for media and communication in the twenty-first century (CSR challenges). I suggest a critical content analysis as a method for empirically addressing these topics. The empirical sample consists of eight of the biggest media and communication companies worldwide: Apple, AT&T, Google, HP, Microsoft, News Corporation, Vivendi and The Walt Disney Company.

I argue that the official CSR communication of media companies is a fruitful source for studying CSR approaches and practices. However, taking an ideology critical perspective requires to also consider alternative sources. I therefore decided to test and challenge corporate self-descriptions with descriptions by corporate watchdogs. This comparative analysis allows me to assess the social impact of the practices of media companies and to identify social responsibility challenges for the media and communication sector today.

Based on this methodological framework, I conduct a detailed case analysis of each company, which is documented in Chapters 5–12. Chapter 13 answers the research questions of the empirical study. In Chapter 14 I provide an interpretation and analysis of the results and argue that what underlies social responsibility challenges for media and communication in the twenty-first century is a fundamental conflict between the logic of property and the logic of the common. Finally, a concluding chapter (Chapter 15) brings together the results of the theoretical and empirical study of CSR ideologies and practices in the media and communication industries.

I began this introduction by arguing for the need to expand the debate about social media from a focus on how technologies enable social interaction and collaboration, towards questions of social responsibility in the media system. The concept of CSR puts forward the idea of socially responsible corporations as humane, as ethical, as social actors, and thus opposes the description of capital as unsocial, predatory and monstrous. The question remains: can CSR fulfil what it promises? In putting CSR in media and communication industries under scrutiny this study aims at discussing the prospects, limits, potentials and contradictions of corporate media as genuinely social media.

The framework I adopt for researching CSR ideologies and practices allows taking a critical perspective that on the one hand analyses both theoretical categories and empirical reality, and on the other hand in itself is theoretical as well as practical. The study presented in this book is theoretical as it conducts an academic analysis of CSR in media and communication industries. At the same time it is practical because it attempts to connect its results to actual social struggles by providing not only academic, but also concrete, political conclusions.

Notes

1 EU Multi-Stakeholder Forum on CSR. See: http://circa.europa.eu/irc/empl/csr_ eu_multi_stakeholder_forum/info/data/en/csr%20ems%20forum.htm retrieved on September 5, 2012.

2 European Alliance for CSR. See: http://ec.europa.eu/enterprise/policies/sustainable-business/corporate-social-responsibility/european-alliance/index_en.htm retrieved on September 5, 2012.

3 Search query: "'corporate social responsibility' OR 'CSR'" in the database ISI Web of Knowledge, Social Science Citation Index on September 4, 2012. Retrieved from http://apps.webofknowledge.com.ezproxy.its.uu.se/UA_GeneralSearch_input.do?product=UA&search_mode=GeneralSearch&SID=V23kfp8BbA6gHJHIgiI&preferences Saved= on September 4, 2012.

4 Microsoft. 2011. *Citizenship Report. Introduction.* Retrieved from http://www.microsoft.com/about/corporatecitizenship/en-us/reporting/ceo-intro-letter/ on September 3, 2012.

5 Ericsson. *Corporate Social Responsibility. Corporate Citizenship.* Retrieved from http://www.ericsson.com/hr/about/csr/index.shtml on September 3, 2012.

6 HP. 2011. *Welcome to the HP Global Citizenship Report.* Retrieved from http://www.hp.com/hpinfo/globalcitizenship/commitment/ceoletter.html on September 3, 2012.

7 The Walt Disney Company. *Disney Citizenship. Core Principles. Act.* Retrieved from http://thewaltdisneycompany.com/citizenship on September 3, 2012.

8 Vivendi. *Our Sustainable Development Issues.* Retrieved from http://vivendi-csr-report-2010.production.investis.com/our-sustainable-development-issues?sc_lang=en on September 3, 2012.

9 Dell. *Dell Powering the Possible.* Retrieved from http://content.dell.com/us/en/gen/d/corp-comm/powering-the-possible on September 3, 2012.

10 Vodafone. *Sustainability Vision.* Retrieved from http://www.vodafone.com/content/index/about/sustainability/sustainability_vision.html on September 3, 2012.

11 Google. *Ten Things we Know to Be True.* Retrieved from http://www.google.com/intl/en/about/company/philosophy/ on September 3, 2012.

12 "Die Theorie führt zu konkreter Praxis, die Praxis, mit den in ihr neu hervortretenden Widersprüchen, verlangt wieder Theorie" (Bloch 1972, 425).

2 Corporate social responsibility

Critical perspectives

In 1962, the economist Milton Friedman called the idea that corporations have social responsibilities a "fundamentally subversive doctrine" (Friedman 1962/1982). Some years later, in his article with the programmatic title "The social responsibility of business is to increase its profits" (Friedman 1970/2009), he argued that businessmen are only responsible to shareholders:

> In a free-enterprise, private-property system, a corporate executive is an employee of the owners of the business. He has direct responsibility to his employers. That responsibility is to conduct the business in accordance with their desires, which generally will be to make as much money as possible while conforming to the basic rules of the society.
>
> (Friedman 1970/2009, 75)

Nearly half a century later, in 2011, 95 per cent of the 250 largest global companies reported their CSR activities (KPMG 2011, 7). Has this diffusion of CSR in the corporate world had the "subversive" effect Friedman warned about? Or was Friedman's fear of CSR misleading?

The concept of CSR started to enter the academic debate in the 1950s. Howard Bowen's book *Social Responsibilities of the Businessman*, published in 1953, is generally considered to be the first theoretical exploration in the field of CSR (Carroll 1979; Garriga and Melé 2004; Lee 2008). Bowen took an ethical perspective on examining the relationship between business and society. He defined the social responsibility of the businessman as "the obligations of businessman to pursue those policies, to make those decisions, or to follow those lines of action which are desirable in terms of the objectives and values of our society" (Bowen 1953, 6).

As one of today's leading CSR scholars, Archie B. Carroll (1999), observes, it took until the 1960s for CSR research to begin to expand. In the 1970s definitions became more specific. According to Carroll (1999) from the 1980s onwards the number of new definitions decreased, and research focused on the discussion and measurement of previously developed concepts. In the 1990s the focus of research shifted towards related concepts such as corporate social performance (CSP) or stakeholder theory (Carroll 1999). Ming-Dong Lee highlights that the development of CSR research from the 1950s onwards was not only characterized by a quantitative increase of books and papers published in this field, but also, and more significantly, by a change in the focus of the CSR concept. He highlights that during the 1950s and 1960s CSR was considered an ethical obligation (Lee 2008). In the 1970s the concept of enlightened self-interest became more popular (Lee 2008, 58). The 1980s were characterized by the development of the corporate social performance (CSP) model (Lee 2008, 59), while in the 1990s stakeholder models and strategic management approaches became dominant (Lee 2008, 60). Lee argues that CSR research has "moved from explicitly normative and ethics-oriented arguments to implicitly normative and performance oriented managerial studies" (Lee 2008, 53). This observation suggests that since Friedman's critique the concept of CSR has been integrated in the managerial discourse and adapted to fit the needs of corporations. In order to investigate this further, this chapter aims at understanding what CSR actually means today.

In the following I will first discuss how to approach a typology of CSR theories and then describe four possible ways of thinking about CSR. I conclude with an evaluation of the prospects and limitations of the current debate on CSR.

Towards a typology of CSR approaches

Broadly speaking, there exist two competing assumptions about how the common good can be achieved through and within capitalism: one is based on the principle of laissez-faire and a belief in the self-regulating capacity of the market, while the second stresses the need for government regulation. The origins of the former hypothesis date back to Adam Smith's description of an "invisible hand" that leads self-interested individuals without knowing it to promote the public interest (Smith 1759/1976, 185; 1776/1976, 456). The latter assumption has its origins in the work of John Maynard Keynes, who pointed at the "inadequacy of the theoretical foundations of the laissez-faire doctrine" (Keynes 1936/1967, 339) and argued that it is in the public interest if governments deliberately intervene in certain domains of the economy. Both approaches have found ardent supporters and influence economic theorizing up to today. While supporters of the first view argue that individual self-interested behaviour creates socially desirable outcomes (see for example Hayek 1978, 1982, 1990), advocates of the second view counter that macro-economic policies are necessary to ensure that capitalist economic operations lead to general social well-being (see for example Stiglitz 1994, 2010; Krugman 2007, 2008).

The concept of CSR cuts across both assumptions by positing that corporations, i.e. individual economic actors, have the responsibility to take the social consequences of their behaviour into account. It raises new questions regarding the relation between the corporate and the social. In other words: how are economic goals and social responsibilities of a corporation related to each other? And: what is a socially responsible corporation? Or as Robert King Merton framed it: "Does the successful business try first to profit or to serve?" (Merton 1976, 88 cited in Margolis and Walsh 2003, 281).

The question about how the economic and social goals of the corporation are related has also been an important topic for empirical studies during the last few years. Many empirical investigations have thus tried to find out how acting socially responsibly and maximizing profits affect each other (for a review see Margolis and Walsh 2003; Orlitzky, Schmidt and Rynes 2003). Questions which are addressed in these studies for example are: "Does social performance influence financial performance; does financial performance influence social performance; or, is there a synergistic relationship (either positive or negative) between the two?" (Preston and O'Bannon 1997, 419).

Surprisingly, existing typologies of CSR theories have not considered the relation between economic goals, i.e. generating profit, and social goals, i.e. contributing to general human well-being. The have distinguished CSR approaches based on their focus on different aspects of social reality (Garriga and Melé 2004), the relationship between economics and ethics (Windsor 2006), or between business and society (Preston 1975; Sohn 1982; Secchi 2007). One limitation of existing typologies is that they only include approaches, which explicitly refer to concepts such as CSR, CSP, business ethics etc. This excludes all examinations of the interrelations of business and society that for different reasons refrain from using the mentioned notions. Among them for example are Marxist and other approaches that critically question whether an economy that is based on private, profit-maximizing companies is able to become socially responsible.

In the following section I present a framework for a typology that gives a systematic and comprehensive account of possible ways of approaching the relation between the economic goals and social responsibilities of the corporation. The aim is to examine the state of the art in CSR research and to systematically evaluate its theoretical and normative foundations.

Four ways of thinking about the social responsibility of corporations

A typology that is able to distinguish possible ways of relating the profit goals and social responsibilities of the corporation can be based on a framework of ways of thinking that was introduced by Wolfgang Hofkirchner (2002, 2003). Hofkirchner (2003) distinguishes four possible ways of relating two phenomena with different degrees of differentiation: reductionism, projectionism, dualism and dialectics. Reductionism "reduces the side with the higher degree of differentiation to the side with the lower degree of differentiation" (Hofkirchner, 2003: 133). Projectionism in contrast "takes the higher degree of differentiation as its point of departure and extrapolates or projects from there to the lower degree of differentiation" (Hofkirchner 2003, 133). Dualism separates both phenomena from each other and thus "abandons all relationships between all of them by treating them as disjunctive" (Hofkirchner 2003, 133). Dialectical thinking on the contrary "integrates the lower and the higher degree of differentiation by establishing a relationship between them" and "might be characterized by the following criteria: firstly, both sides of the relation are opposed to each other; secondly, they depend on each other; thirdly, they are asymmetrical" (Hofkirchner 2003, 133).

Applying this typology to the question of how to relate the profit interests and social responsibilities of the corporation requires first of all to decide which of these two phenomena has a higher and which has a lower degree of differentiation. Profit is a goal of a single corporation within the economic sub-system of society. Caring for social issues on the contrary means contributing to the functioning of society as a whole and not just to the success of one of its parts. Doing social good and contributing to the well-being of society can thus be described as a more complex and higher differentiated goal than generating profit and contributing to the well-being of the corporation.

Reductionism, which reduces the higher differentiated phenomenon to the lower differentiated one, sees profit maximization as the primary goal of the corporation. It argues that companies should only engage in social activities if it contributes to achieving this primary goal. Reductionist approaches to CSR reduce the engagement in social activities to a means for advancing profit goals.

Projectionism on the contrary, which projects from the higher differentiated to the lower differentiated side, imposes ethical principles or social considerations onto corporate profit goals. According to this view profit generation should not outweigh any other social responsibilities of the corporation. Projectionist approaches to CSR argue that corporations should generate profit in a socially responsible way.

Dualism treats both phenomena as disjunctive and argues that companies should do both, generate maximum profit and act socially responsible. Dualist approaches separate economic and social goals of the corporation without relating them to each other.

A dialectical view considers how the goal of maximizing profits and the goal of acting socially responsible mutually shape each other. Dialectical approaches to CSR describe the relation between profit goals and social goals as conflictual.

In the following sections I examine reductionist, dualist, projectionist and dialectical approaches in greater detail by discussing some examples.

Reductionism – instrumentalizing the social

Reductionist CSR theories reduce CSR to a means for advancing corporate profit goals. Such approaches stress that CSR is beneficial for businesses through opening up new markets, preventing government regulation, or improving relationships with stakeholders and creating trust in the corporation.

Advocates of a reductionist approach do not question the assumption that the purpose of a corporation is to make as much profit as possible. However, they argue that maximizing profit does not contradict engaging in CSR activities – as long as social issues are addressed in a profitable way. The goal of reductionist CSR approaches thus is to find ways of capitalizing on CSR activities.

One way in which CSR is perceived to be beneficial for business goals is through preventing government regulation. Almeder (1980) for example argues that in terms of reaching business goals, refraining from dealing with social issues is counterproductive. Quite on the contrary, companies would have to make sure that they behave in a way that renders government intervention obsolete:

> Any ardent supporter of the capitalistic system will naturally want to see the system thrive and flourish; and this it cannot do if it invites and demands government regulation in the name of the public interest. [. . .] The only way to avoid such encroaching regulation is to find ways to move the business community into the long-term view of what is in its interest, and effect ways of determining and responding to social needs before society moves to regulate business to that end
>
> (Almeder 1980, 13)

Almeder radically criticizes what he calls the "Friedman doctrine" by emphasizing that its claim that companies should refrain from addressing social problems "will most likely undermine capitalism and motivate an economic socialism by assuring an erosive regulatory climate in a society that expects the business community to be socially responsible in ways that go beyond just making legal profits" (Almeder 1980, 13). According to Almeder companies have to take social issues into account if they want to secure profit in the long run (Almeder 1980, 13).

Some other representatives of a reductionist approach further exaggerate this argument. They highlight that engaging in CSR activities is not only helpful for preventing further regulation but for fostering deregulation and privatization. According to this view social problems should be regarded as "business opportunities" and thus as potential spheres for capital accumulation. Peter Drucker (1984) for example argues that the social problems of the future need to be solved in a profitable way. According to his view, these future problems "can be solved only if seen and treated as opportunities. And the economic realities ahead are such that 'social needs' can be financed increasingly only if their solution generates capital, i.e. generates a profit" (Drucker 1984, 55). In Drucker's view business should be concerned with social issues in a way that allows it to generate profit from dealing with them: "business can discharge its 'social responsibilities' only if it converts them into 'self-interest', that is, into business opportunities" (Drucker 1984, 59). The task would therefore be to privatize domains of social needs. He stresses the necessity to

> create conditions under which a task is outlined by government and under which the means to perform the task are provided either by government (as for instance in the case of the rapidly growing private health care insurance in Britain with reimbursement by the National Health Service) or by "Third Party Payers", but in which the actual performance is done by non-governmental institutions, especially business, and is done locally and on a competitive basis.
>
> (Drucker 1984, 58)

This means that companies should deal with social issues and the necessary money should be provided by private parties or by government. This in fact would mean that government is funding private initiatives that primarily aim at maximizing profits. Public money would thus be turned into private profit. This transformation of public into private wealth is what Drucker calls the "true 'mixed economy' of the future" (Drucker 1984, 58).

Similar to Drucker, Davis also stresses that dealing with social issues can be beneficial for a company's primary task of generating profit. Partly, "the significance of social issues in business success" (Davis 2005, 105), would consist of serving as an indicator for discovering new profitable spheres of investment: "Social pressures often indicate the existence of unmet social needs or consumer preferences. Business can gain advantage by spotting and supplying these before their competitors do" (Davis 2005, 107).

Davis argues for considering social issues in business operations only in so far as they contribute to a company's main aim, that is, the maximization of profits. He highlights that social problems such as high prizes for HIV/AIDS drugs in developing countries, increasing obesity due to unhealthy food and environmental devastation have

> generated value creation opportunities: in the case of the pharmaceutical sector, for example, the growing market for generic drugs, in the case of fast-food restaurants, providing healthier meals; and in the case of the energy industry, meeting fast-growing demand (as well as regulatory pressure) for cleaner fuels such as natural gas.
>
> (Davis 2005, 107)

The argument that companies should try to make profit out of the misery of people is anti-humanist and cynical. Rather than focusing on general human wellbeing these arguments are based on the idea of turning some people's misery into other people's fortune.

Cogman and Oppenheim (2002) have advanced a similar reductionist approach to CSR. Like Drucker and Davis they treat social issues as potentially profitable spheres of investment:

> For some of these companies, however, this spending may well be a source of growth, since many of today's most exciting opportunities lie in controversial areas such as gene therapy, the private provision of pensions, and products and services targeted at low-income consumers in poor countries
>
> (Cogman and Oppenheim 2002, 57)

Cogman and Oppenheim argue that in order to gain access to these "contentious areas" and to use them as spheres of capital accumulation, corporations have to convince society that they are socially responsible. Only if they receive "society's permission" to explore these "contentious business opportunities" it will be possible to "convert the opportunity into a sustainable and profitable market"

(Cogman and Oppenheim 2002, 58). They for example identify human trafficking as a potentially profitable area for future business:

> A black market in human trafficking, for example, has been created by tough immigration restrictions in Europe, but as its need for labour increases, they may be relaxed, thus opening up an opportunity for legitimate organizations seeking to place human resources.
>
> (Cogman and Oppenheim 2002, 61)

This argument embodies the same cynicism and anti-humanism as Davis' (2005) arguments as it seeks to create business advantages from human suffering and at the cost of the most vulnerable members of society.

The described reductionist understandings of CSR recommend dealing with social issues not because they consider it as a moral obligation or social necessity, but because they regard them as potential areas for profit accumulation. Instead of incorporating aspects of social well-being into business operations, this perspective argues for extending the logic of business to all further domains of social life such as education, health care, the pension system, etc. Within the framework of the welfare state, these domains of social welfare were, due to their fundamental importance for social security and inclusion, consciously protected from the competitive logic of the market. The logic of the market is based on the exchange of equivalents and thus always means that access to products and services is restricted to those who have enough resources to afford them and thus is inherently exclusive. Privatization, which means the extension of the market logic on areas that were until then regulated though other mechanisms, thus means an extension of the already existing unequal access to means of economic, social and cultural life. Privatization in the domain of education and health care means that basic social welfare is not guaranteed to every member of society, but only to those who can afford it. In the case of health care, exclusion can literally be a matter of life and death. A private health care system that operates according to market principles thus at the same time means threat of death for the losers, and prospects for profit for the winners of capitalist competition. The idea of solving social problems by imposing on them the competitive logic of markets thus is paradoxical, cynical and anti-humanist.

Other arguments why engaging in CSR activities supports profit interests focus on creating competitive advantages through establishing stakeholder trust and good corporate reputation. Thomas M. Jones (1995) for example argues for an "instrumental theory of stakeholder management". He highlights that companies can benefit financially from having a trustful relationship with their stakeholders (Jones 1995, 422). He argues that taking into account social issues from a business perspective at the first sight might seem to be irrational, but in the long run lies in the self-interest of a company:

> the point of instrumental stakeholder theory is exactly this: manifestations of opportunism may not lead to optimal economic performance. The theory is

intended to explain why certain behaviours heretofore thought to be irrational or altruistic are, in fact, quite compatible with economic success.

(Jones 1995, 429)

In this context Falck and Heblich (2007) point out that "companies have an opportunity to do well by doing good" (Falck and Heblich 2007, 252).

Used well, it [CSR] is a way of actively contributing to the society's basic order and, in doing so, enhancing the company's reputation. From a supply-side perspective, a good reputation is necessary to attract, retain, and motivate quality employees. From a demand-side perspective, a good reputation increases the value of the brand, which, in turn, increases the company's goodwill.

(Falck and Heblich 2007, 248)

Burke and Logsdon (1996) term such an approach strategic corporate social responsibility (S-CSR): "corporate social responsibility (policy, programme or process) is strategic when it yields substantial business-related benefits to the firm, in particular by supporting core business activities and thus contributing to the firm's effectiveness in accomplishing its mission" (Burke and Logsdon 1996, 496).

Many empirical studies have investigated the relationship between a company's financial and social performance. Margolis and Walsh (2003) reviewed empirical studies on the relationship of social and financial performance. They came to the conclusion that studies that show a positive correlation between social and financial performance prevail: "A simple compilation of the findings suggests there is a positive association, and certainly very little evidence of a negative association, between a company's social performance and its financial performance" (Margolis and Walsh 2003, 277). Similarly Orlitzky, Schmidt and Rynes (2003) conducted a meta-analysis of 52 studies on the relation of financial and social performance. They conclude "The results of this meta-analysis show that there is a positive association between CSP [corporate social performance] and CFP [corporate financial performance] across industries and across study contexts" (Orlitzky, Schmidt and Rynes 2003, 423). The results of these empirical studies are likely to influence management decisions. Cochran and Wood (1984) highlight:

If certain actions (classified as socially responsible) tend to be negatively correlated with financial performance of firm, then mangers might be advised to be cautious in this area. If, on the other hand, a positive relationship can be shown to exist, than management might be encouraged to pursue such activities with increased vigour or to investigate the underlying causes of this relationship.

(Cochran and Wood 1984, 42)

Making the decision whether or not to engage in CSR activities dependent on its positive or negative influence on profit means to approach the topic of CSR in a reductionist way. It is reductionist because it only looks at the economic potentials of CSR. Taking care of social issues is reduced to a part of a company's economic and strategic operations. Reductionist approaches to CSR have in common that they treat social issues as an economic and managerial factor that is subject to strategic considerations in the interest of profit maximization.

It is not surprising that many CSR consultancy books for managers are based on reductionist arguments. The consulting literature includes titles such as *When Principles Pay: Corporate Social Responsibility and the Bottom Line* (Heal 2008); *Just Good Business: The Strategic Guide to Aligning Corporate Social Responsibility and Brand* (McElhaney 2008); *CSR Strategies: Corporate Social Responsibility for a Competitive Edge in Emerging Markets* (Urip 2010); *The HIP Investor: Make Bigger Profits by Building a Better World* (Herman 2010); *Green to Gold: How Smart Companies Use Environmental Strategy to Innovate, Create Value, and Build Competitive Advantage* (Esty and Winston 2009). These titles try to establish a connection between profit and CSR that creates the impression of maximizing the former by means of the latter: These titles promise to achieve "bigger profits *by* building a better world", explain how to use "Corporate social responsibility *for* a competitive edge", of how "smart companies" should "*use* environmental strategy" for creating a competitive advantage. A common motif for the instrumental view of social responsibility is also incorporated in the ambiguous meaning of the phrase "good business", which contains the idea of the good as the profitable business. Furthermore, the fact that books that supposedly are about CSR, in their title all use buzzwords for economic success and profit, such as "bottom line", "competitive edge", "competitive advantage", "bigger profits", "make money", highlights their instrumental approach. Following this logic business consultants are also increasingly focusing on CSR and sustainability. Many of them follow an instrumental logic and stress financial benefits and competitive advantages resulting from a good CSR strategy: one example is CSR Consulting Ltd, which promises that CSR has positive effects on "sustainable" growth of the company.[1] Another example is plosion branding that focuses on the integration of CSR in brand development for helping their customers to "gain an edge in the marketplace and create a stronger brand".[2] GoodValues wants to assist companies in "exploiting the opportunities from social and sustainability issues" in order to create competitive advantages.[3] Similarly GoodCorporation Ltd aims at protecting the "most valuable asset" of its clients: "good reputation".[4] The language these consulting firms use for describing their services shows how the ideas of social responsibility and sustainability are appropriated and redefined in accordance with corporate profit interest: "Reputation" is turned into an "asset", "sustainability" becomes a category for "successful economic growth", "sustainability issues" turn into something that can be "exploited", and CSR is treated as a matter of "risks and opportunities" for the firm.

CSR that is pursued under this premise is very likely to be highly selective and superficial. In this sense whether or not a company acts responsibly becomes a matter of calculating cost and benefits. Based on the logic of the arguments described here, it is most likely that companies that follow an instrumental reductionist approach will drop the idea of CSR as soon as cost outweigh benefits, that is, as soon as CSR can only be pursued at the expense of profit. Thus, this way of thinking about CSR might successfully contribute to sustained economic growth, but not to achieving a sustainable society.

For reductionists, CSR is not an end in itself but a means for maximizing profit. CSR is thus conceived as a mere instrument, the use of which is subject to strategic considerations under the primacy of the bottom line. It thus entails what Max Horkheimer (1947/2004) once called "instrumental reason" as the reduction of reason from a means for defining ends, to the "mere regulation of the relation between means and ends" (Horkheimer 1947/2004, 7), to an "executive agency concerned with the how rather than with the what" (Horkheimer 1947/2004, 38). In a similar way, reductionist CSR does not engage in a discussion as to whether ethical and socially responsible behaviour is desirable, it just treats it as an instrument for achieving a given end: profit. The idea of social responsibility is degraded to "a tool, for it derives its meaning only through its connection with other ends" (Horkheimer 1947/2004, 25).

The reductionist approach feeds on the argument that markets are more effective than governments and that their unregulated operation guarantees best possible outcomes not only for business, but for society as a whole. The reductionist version of CSR serves as an ideological underpinning for the neo-liberal desire for the expansion of markets and the search for new spheres of profit accumulation. It thus perverts the idea of social responsibility. Instead of increasing social justice it reinforces inequality and injustice.

Projectionism – idealizing the corporate

Projectionist approaches to CSR regard the corporation as an organization that should contribute to the common good. This view is based on the assumption that profit can be generated in a socially responsible way. Following this approach the profit motive can be tamed through imposing on it certain values and a concern for society and the environment. Thus, profit becomes subordinated to the higher goal of the corporation to contribute to the common good. Corporations should act and generate profit in a way that is beneficial for society in general and not just for the interests of its shareholders.

A projectionist view characterized one of the earliest approaches to CSR: Howard Bowen, whom Carroll called "the Father of Corporate Responsibility" (Carroll 1999, 270), argued that the decisions taken by businessmen have far-reaching consequences and that they therefore are obligated to consider social issues and responsibilities (Bowen 1953). According to this view corporations should act in a way that benefits society.

Some years after Bowen, Frederick (1960) in a similar vein stressed that social responsibility means

> that businessmen should oversee the operation of an economic system that fulfils the expectations of the public. And this means in turn that the economy's means of production should be employed in such a way that production and

distribution should enhance total socio-economic welfare. Social responsibility in the final analysis implies a public posture toward society's economic and human resources and a willingness to see that those resources are used for broad social ends and not simply for the narrowly circumscribed interests of private persons and firms.

(Frederick 1960, 60)

Davis and Bloomstrom (1966) made another early contribution to a projectionist approach when arguing that companies should act in a way that supports the common good instead of only pursuing its business interests:

Social responsibility, therefore, refers to a person's obligation to consider the effects of his decisions and action on the whole social system. Businessmen apply social responsibility when they consider the needs and interest of others who may be affected by business actions. In doing so they look beyond their firm's narrow economic and technical interests.

(Davis and Blomstrom 1966, 12)

In a similar manner, Carroll (1979) argues that CSR means that corporations should fulfil the expectations of society: "The social responsibility of business encompasses the economic, legal, ethical, and discretionary expectations that society has of organizations at a given point of time" (Carroll 1979, 500). He described a pyramid of CSR, which starts with economic responsibilities, followed by legal responsibilities, ethical responsibilities, and the responsibility to be a good corporate citizen (philanthropic responsibility) (Carroll 1991, 42). Carroll argues that the intention of this pyramid is to show that "the total CSR of business comprises distinct components that, taken together, constitute the whole" (Carroll 1991, 42). According to Carroll the four social responsibilities "are not mutually exclusive and are not intended to juxtapose a firm's economic responsibilities with its other responsibilities" (Carroll 1991, 42). He argues that dealing with tensions between these responsibilities is an important managerial task, the goal of which should be to fulfil all of them (Carroll 1991, 42). As a framework for realizing CSR within a corporation Carroll in 1979 suggested the concept of corporate social performance (CSP), which translates the idea of corporate performance to the social sphere. Based on Carroll, Wartick and Cochran (1985) argue that CSP consists of CSR principles, processes and policies (Wartick and Cochran 1985, 758).

Carroll's as well as Wartick's and Cochran's approaches to CSR can be described as projectionist as they subsume profit generation under the "unified whole" of social responsibility. From this perspective corporations should contribute to the common good through generating profit, respecting the law, acting ethically and engaging in discretionary activities.

Another example for a projectionist approach is Edward Freeman's stakeholder approach (1984) and in particular his idea of a "stakeholder capitalism" (Freeman and Phillips 2002). Freeman in his book *Strategic Management. A Stakeholder Approach* (1984) popularized stakeholder theory. The book intended to help managers in dealing with their environment and to assist them in deciding which issues are relevant and which are not (Freeman 1984, 22). From the perspective of this approach a company should try to satisfy the interests of all stakeholders, understood as "any group or individual who can affect, or is affected by, the achievement of a corporation's purpose. Stakeholders include employees, customers, suppliers, stockholders, banks, environmentalists, government and other groups who can help or hurt the corporation" (Freeman 1984, vi). Central to Freeman's definition of stakeholders is the "presumption of equality among the contractors, rather than the presumption in favour of financier rights" (Freeman 1994, 415). According to the stakeholder approach a corporation should still address the interests of shareholders but in a way that does not compromise the needs and interests of other stakeholders. Clarkson (1995) in his application of stakeholder theory argues for a redefinition of the concepts of wealth and values so that they extend beyond economic categories:

> The economic and social purpose of the corporation is to create and distribute increased wealth and value to all its primary stakeholder groups, without favouring one group at the expense of the others. Wealth and value are not defined adequately only in terms of increased share price, dividends, or profits.
>
> (Clarkson 1995, 112)

Freeman, based on his stakeholder approach, developed a model of stakeholder capitalism as opposed to shareholder capitalism. The model of stakeholder capitalism proposes a transformation of capitalism towards the equal recognition of all stakeholders (Freeman 1994; Freeman and Phillips 2002). Freeman and Phillips (2002) stress that the model of stakeholder capitalism is about

> the possibility that business becomes a fully human institution. [. . .] It sets a high standard, recognizes the common sense practical world of global business today, and asks managers to get on with the task of creating value for all stakeholders.
>
> (Freeman and Phillips 2002, 345)

This equal recognition of all stakeholders would also allow for abolishing the separation between business and ethics (Freeman 1994, 1999; Freeman and Phillips 2002). Stakeholder capitalism is conceptualized as a new form of capitalism "that inherently marries business and ethics" (Freeman and Phillips 2002, 345).

Freeman highlights that every management decision and operation at the same time has business-related and ethical implications. The idea of turning business into "a fully human institution" and of abolishing the distinction between business and ethics is similar to Carroll's approach of subsuming financial goals under the concept of social responsibilities. Both approaches are projectionist as they impose ethics and social responsibility onto corporate profit goals.

Another important characteristic of Freeman's version of stakeholder theory that is worth noting is the principle of voluntarism:

Voluntarism means that an organization must on its own will undertake to satisfy its key stakeholders. A situation where a solution to a stakeholder problem is imposed by a government agency or the courts must be seen as a managerial failure.

(Freeman 1984, 74)

Freeman's stakeholder model aims at overcoming the separation between business and ethics and at achieving a more responsible capitalism, by suggesting to managers to voluntarily integrate the demands of all stakeholders into their decisions.

While Freeman advocates pure voluntarism, other representatives of a projectionist approach stress that imposing ethical and social responsibility considerations onto profit generation requires going beyond purely voluntary initiatives. Epstein (1987, 2007) argues that voluntary self-regulation is insufficient. He stresses that "business organizations are not monolithic in nature but have the capacity to manifest the good, the bad, and the ugly" (Epstein 2007, 214). Epstein stresses that within contemporary capitalism there exist several factors that run counter creating "good companies", such as the focus on short-term profit. He argues against a one-sided view of the economy according to which maximizing individual profits automatically brings about the common good (Epstein 2007, 215f). Similar to Freeman, Epstein highlights that companies also have obligations to non-shareholding stakeholders. Both share the idea of establishing more responsible corporations and a more responsible capitalism in general. But while Freeman argues that this should be achieved based on the principle of voluntarism, Epstein argues that voluntary self-regulation is far from enough. He notes that for achieving a "better capitalism" it is indispensable to have responsible companies, effective laws as well as additional instruments such as affinity group regulation, ethical precepts, vigilant and responsible media and civil society (Epstein 2007, 222).

Similarly McInerney stresses that voluntary CSR is insufficient: "voluntary CSR initiatives remain problematic. Properly understood, voluntary CSR measures should supplement not supplant state regulation" (McInerney 2007, 172). He argues that even "if norms such as protecting the environment or human rights are generally valued, taking a purely voluntary approach to promoting compliance with such norms will produce few results" (McInerney 2007, 183) As an alternative McInerney suggest fiscal policy: "fiscal policy, with its ability directly to effect corporate profits, can potentially be much more powerful than CSR, which depends on reputational damage, and any subsequent indirect effects on corporate profits, as its incentive mechanism" (McInerney 2007, 190).

Andreas Georg Scherer and Guido Palazzo (2007) also advocate a shift from "voluntary, business-driven, and case-wise philanthropic acts to a long-term politicized collaboration with governments and civil society actors" (Scherer and Palazzo 2007, 1111). They suggest an approach to CSR that is based on Habermas' concept of "deliberative democracy". This approach "does not aim at utopian and revolutionary alternative to liberal market societies. Instead, the aim is to (re)establish a political order where economic rationality is circumscribed by democratic institutions and procedures" (Scherer and Palazzo 2007, 1097). In a projectionist manner they do not dismiss the profit principle as such but want to subordinate it under the common good. According to Scherer and Palazzo developing a normative approach to CSR requires the exertion of democratic control over corporate decisions:

> A deliberate concept of CSR embeds corporate decision making in processes of democratic will formation. These processes, driven by civil society actors and spanning a broad field of public arenas, establish a democratic control on the public use of corporate power.
>
> (Scherer and Palazzo 2007, 1109)

Measures they suggest for implementing this deliberate concept of CSR include

> developing corporate codes of behaviour in collaboration with critical NGOs [non-governmental organizations], exposing corporate CSR performance to third party control, linking corporate decision making to civil society discourses, and shifting corporate attention and money to societal challenges beyond immediate stakeholder pressure.
>
> (Scherer and Palazzo 2007, 1115)

Representatives of a projectionist approach put forward the idea that CSR is a means for reforming capitalism and reducing its negative social and environmental effects. Projectionism assumes that it is possible to tame the profit motive by imposing ethical norms or social pressure on it. It points at the importance of pursuing non-profit goals but fails to problematize their relation to profit interests. Thus it overlooks capitalist power relations: it does not engage with questions of injustice that arise from the fact that capitalism is always based on the separation of individuals into owners and non-owners of means of production; that this unequal ownership distribution creates an unequal power relation between company managers, owners and shareholders on the one hand and employees, local communities and other stakeholders on the other hand; that the former appropriate the surplus produced by the latter; that as a competitive system capitalism necessarily has to produce winners and losers; that capitalism always has to follow an expansive logic because for its preservation capital has to be constantly accumulated and thus capitalism has to expand, to strive for growth and to permanently find new spheres of accumulation; that those who are not willing to follow the capitalist logic are most likely to lose in the competition and thus will be excluded, etc.

In failing to study the material foundations of capitalist social relations and their effects, projectionists run the risk of explaining problems under capitalism by referring to a lack of morality and social responsibility. The idea that problems of capitalism can be resolved by taming the profit motive through introducing business ethics and CSR overlooks and mystifies the structural immorality of the capitalist system. This moralizing ideology has been a central argument in the context of the 2008 financial crisis. Žižek (2009) highlights the ideological dimension of this argument:

> Over the last several months, public figures from the pope downwards have bombarded us with injunctions to fight against the culture of excessive greed and consumption. This disgusting spectacle of cheap moralization is an ideological operation if there ever was one: the compulsion (to expand) inscribed into a system itself is translated into a matter of personal sin, a private psychological propensity.
>
> (Žižek 2009, 37)

Projectionist approaches to CSR see a necessity to reform capitalism. Projectionists aim at establishing a more "just", "sustainable" or "better" capitalism through the help of business ethics and CSR. They challenge the growth based and profit maximizing logic of capitalism without questioning private property, profit and capital accumulation. The desired changes in the way the economy operates are thus always constrained by the framework of capitalism. This means that projectionists want to reform capitalism, but not transcend it.

According to this view it is possible to resolve the relation between profit and social responsibility through making profit socially responsible by subjecting it to public expectations (Bowen, Davis, Frederick, Carroll), a concern for society as a whole (Davis and Blomstrom), ethical consideration (Freeman), ethics, and laws and civil society control (Epstein, McInerney), or democratic control (Scherer and Palazzo). Following this perspective companies should equally respect the needs and interests of all stakeholders ranging from shareholders to employees to local communities to society in general. However, different stakeholders are likely to have opposing interests. Thus when deciding about corporate strategies, conflicts between different stakeholder groups are likely to arise. Within the framework of a corporation decision power is not equally distributed among the various stakeholders. Owners and managers of a corporation have much more power than for example local communities and are thus more likely to influence corporate decision in way that satisfies their interests. The projectionist idea of realizing equal respect for all stakeholder interests and stakeholder democracy without questioning the framework of a privately owned corporation is idealistic because it ignores actual existing power structures.

Dualism – separating the corporate and the social

Dualist CSR approaches argue that corporations should do both: maximize private profit and do good for society. These two goals, however, remain unrelated: the profit goal and the goal to contribute to the common good are perceived as two separate aims of the corporation. Following a dualist argument, doing good for society is an additional goal that goes beyond the primary goal of profit maximization. This means that dualist approaches do not consider interrelations between the process of maximizing profit and the common good. The concept of philanthropy best exemplifies this approach. Nineteenth century industrialist and philanthropist Andrew Carnegie in a paper known as "The gospel of wealth" (1889) argued that capitalist accumulation has brought about great wealth and progress alongside great inequality:

> We accept and welcome, therefore, as conditions to which we must accommodate ourselves, great inequality of environment, the concentration of business, industrial and commercial, in the hands of a few, and the law of competition between these, as being not only beneficial, but essential for the future progress of the race.
>
> (Carnegie 1889, 655)

Based on this observation Carnegie concludes that instead of changing the social relations that bring about inequality, the wealthy should use their wealth in the best interest of society: Carnegie argued that it is the "duty of the man of Wealth" to use his wealth leading a modest life, to provide for those dependent on him, and

> after doing so to consider all surplus revenues which come to him simply as trust funds, which he is called upon to administer, and strictly bound as a matter of duty to administer in the manner which, in his judgement, is best calculated to produce the most beneficial results for the community.
>
> (Carnegie 1889, 661f)

According to Carnegie the solution to "the problem of the Rich and the Poor" is that

> the millionaire will be but a trustee for the poor; intrusted for a season with a great part of the increased wealth of the community, but administering it for the community far better than it could or would have done for itself
>
> (Carnegie 1889, 664)

Carnegie's view is still present in the views of contemporary philanthropists. George Soros for example stressed: "When I had made more money than I needed for myself and my family, I set up a foundation to promote the values and principles of a free and open society".[5] Philanthropy is based on the idea of generating profit first and then devoting parts of it to promoting the common good. This perspective is willing to accept that profit generation might negatively affect the common good, as long as parts of the profit are afterwards used to do good.

Bill Gates addressed this dualism in the first talk he gave about the work of the Bill and Melinda Gates Foundation. He said that one might find the "idea of mixing the mentality of making money and giving money [. . .] schizophrenic". Gates continued with stressing that in order not to mess up both it's important to keep making profit and doing good separate from each other: "I admit, you've got to be careful not to bring one approach to one thing. If you mix them up you'll going to get it all messed up so I try to keep those two things separate" (Gates

2000). Separating between generating profits and contributing to the common good leads to a strategy of taking with the one hand while giving with the other hand.

Apart from the concept of philanthropic giving, dualist views can also be found in many definitions of CSR. Dualist definitions describe the social responsibility of companies as something beyond the economic goals. According to this view a company should strive for profit and in addition take care of social issues. McGuire (1963) for example stresses: "The idea of social responsibilities supposes that the corporation has not only economic and legal obligations, but also certain responsibilities to society which extend beyond these obligations" (McGuire 1963, 144). Another example is Backman's (1975) definition of CSR, which also stresses that social issues should be addressed in addition to economic goals: "social responsibility usually refers to the objectives and motives that should be given weight by business in addition to those dealing with economic performance (e.g. profits)" (Backman 1975, 2). Similarly Sun, Stewart and Pollard (2010) also stress that CSR goes beyond a company's economic and legal obligations:

> Basically CSR is concerned with corporate attitudes and behaviour towards its responsibility beyond its immediate profit gain and other benefits pursued by its owners, beyond its limited legal obligations and liabilities, and beyond the passive benefits brought from business operations to society.
>
> (Sun, Stewart and Pollard 2010, 5)

The main characteristic of dualist approaches to CSR is that they postpone the socially responsible behaviour to a point after profit goals have already been achieved. How these profit goals are reached and whether reaching them has negative effects on society or the environment is secondary. Žižek (2006) described this reasoning as the ethics of "Liberal Communists" – the chief executive officers (CEOs) of Google, IBM, eBay etc: "According to liberal communist ethics, the ruthless pursuit of profit is counteracted by charity: charity is part of the game, a humanitarian mask hiding the underlying economic exploitation" (Žižek 2006). In "hiding the underlying exploitation", charity and philanthropic giving portray the wealthy as generous benefactors while hiding how the creation of their fortune might have meant other people's misery. Dualist approaches are based on the logic of giving back with one hand what had been before been taken with the other hand.

Dialectics – problematizing the relation between the corporate and the social

Dialectical approaches to CSR problematize the relation between economic goals of a corporation and social responsibilities. Based on a critical analysis of capitalism they argue that profit generation inherently creates social and environmental problems. From this perspective the structural irresponsibility of profit generation can neither be resolved through turning social problems into business opportunities (reductionist CSR) or through imposing ethical norms or a social consciousness on profit generation (projectionist CSR), nor be balanced through charitable giving (dualist CSR approaches). According to this view a more fundamental societal alternative is inevitable in order to create a socially responsible economy and society.

The insight, that profit goals conflict with social goals, is based on Karl Marx's critique of the political economy of capitalism. Marx described capitalism as a system that is based on the division between owners and non-owners of means of production, whereby those who possess means of production exploit the labour power of those who are without property in order to accumulate profit (Marx 1867/1990). This relation of capital and labour lays the foundation for fundamental injustice: "Political economy starts from labour as the real soul of production; yet to labour it gives nothing, and to private property everything" (Marx 1844/2007b, 81). A defining feature of capitalism that Marx highlighted is its constant drive for accumulation. The accumulation of capital which Marx described in the general formula for capital M–C–M' (money–commodity–money plus surplus), does not deliver any use value that satisfies a need, but is an end in itself: "the circulation of money as capital is an end in itself, for the valorization of value only takes place within this constantly renewed movement. The movement of capital is therefore limitless" (Marx 1867/1990, 253). According to Marx, capital accumulation in a first stage requires the investment of capital in order to buy what is necessary for producing commodities: labour time of workers (variable capital) on the one hand, and working equipment like machines and raw materials (constant capital) on the other hand (Marx 1885/1992, 110). Thus, money (M) is used in order to buy labour power as well as machines and resources as commodities (C) that then in a second stage enter the labour process and produce (P) a new commodity (C') (Marx 1885/1992, 118). This new commodity (C') contains more value than the sum of its parts, i.e. surplus value. According to Marx, labour is the source of value and surplus value can only be generated through the specific qualities of labour power as a commodity. Marx argued that labour power is the only commodity "whose use-value possesses the peculiar property of being a source of value, whose actual consumption is therefore itself an objectification of labour, hence a creation of value" (Marx 1867/1990, 270). In a second step the surplus value generated in production, needs to be realized and turned into more money (M') by selling the commodity in the market (Marx 1885/1992, 125). The circuit of capital accumulation can thus be described with the following formula:

$$M \rightarrow C \ldots P \ldots C' \rightarrow M' \qquad \text{(Marx 1885/1992, 110)}$$

As all accumulation of capital is based on the exploitation of labour power, increasing accumulation also means to increase exploitation: "The driving motive and determining purpose of capitalist production is the self-valorization of capital to the greatest possible extent, i.e. the greatest possible production of surplus-value, hence the greatest possible exploitation of labour power by the capitalist" (Marx 1867/1990, 499). Capital's desire to accumulate thus can only be satisfied at the cost of workers. Marx (1867/1976) described several mechanisms through which capital can increase surplus value. Basically it can be increased in two ways: either through extending the total time of work, which means an absolute prolongation of surplus-labour time and thus an increase of surplus-value (absolute surplus-value). Or through increasing intensity and productivity of labour so that more value can be produced during the same time (relative surplus-value): "The production of absolute surplus-value turns exclusively on the length of the working day, whereas the production of relative surplus-value completely revolutionizes the technical process of labour and the groupings into which society is divided" (Marx 1867/1990, 645). As the only way to increase the accumulation of capital consists of increasing the rate of exploitation, the relationship between capital and labour can be described as fundamentally antagonistic: the more capital is accumulated the more labour power is exploited.

While the relation between capital and labour is based on exploitation, the relation between capitalists is structured through competition. Competition forces the individual capitalist, because of the threat of losing his/her business, to join the continuous pursuit of increasing profits and accumulating capital. Marx therefore described competition as a coercive force external to the individual capitalist:

> But looking at the things as a whole it is evident that this does not depend on the will, either good or bad, of the individual capitalist. Under free competition, the immanent laws of capitalist production confront the individual capitalist as a coercive force external to him
>
> (Marx 1867/1990, 286)

According to Callincos the competitive character of capitalism explains why exploitation and accumulation are necessary qualities of capitalism (Callinicos 2003, 36): For avoiding losing in the competition every corporation is forced to follow the logic of increasing productivity and reducing production costs in order to sustain a high level of profit that can partly be reinvested in order to ensure further accumulation. Capitalist competition would make it almost impossible for the individual corporation to resist the logic of exploitation: "A benevolent capitalist who paid his workers wages that broadly correspond to the amount of value that they created would soon find himself out of business" (Callinicos 2003, 37). David Harvey (2010) gives a similar explanation why capitalists constantly need to increase accumulation:

> If I, as a capitalist, do not reinvest in expansion and a rival does, then after a while I am likely to be driven out of business. I need to protect and expand my market share. I have to reinvest to stay a capitalist.
>
> (Harvey 2010, 43)

Likewise, John Holloway (2003) argues that competition forces the individual capitalist to intensify the exploitation of workers:

> The fact that capital is fragmented into many distinct capitalist units (companies), each in competition with the others, each depending for its survival on being able to exploit its workers more effective than the others, means that

capital can never stand still, that it is constantly driven forward to intensify the exploitation of labor.

(Holloway 2003, 231)

Trapped within the forces of competition individual corporations engage in socially irresponsible practices that create problems in all domains of social life. Callinicos for example stresses: "The major problems facing humankind – poverty, social injustices, economic instability, environmental destruction, and war – have the same source, in the capitalist system: the solution to these problems must, accordingly, be a radical one" (Callinicos 2003, 66). Saad-Filho (2003) argues that some contemporary problems of capitalism such as a lack of corporate responsibility and absolute poverty can be solved from within the system, while others are rooted in the way capitalism operates as an economic system (Saad-Filho 2003, 21). Among the latter problems are "unemployment, exploitation of the workforce, economic inequality, the encroachment of work upon free time, systematic environmental degradation, the lack of economic democracy, and production for profit rather than need" (Saad-Filho 2003, 21). Olin Wright in his book *Envisioning Real Utopias* (2010) shows in great detail that a number of contemporary problems are structural problems of capitalism, "generated by the basic structure of capitalism as a system of production with class relations defined by private ownership and propertyless workers, and economic coordination organized through decentralized market exchanges" (Olin Wright 2010, 38).

Form a dialectical perspective, CSR approaches that do not critically questions the profit motive are ideological, because they hide how it inherently creates social and environmental problems. According to this view, a fundamental shortcoming of the concept of CSR is that it never challenges the primacy of profit and the interests of capital (Sklair and Miller 2010, 475). CSR has thus been described as "a deliberate strategy to mystify and obscure the reality of capitalist globalization" (Sklair and Miller 2010, 492), and criticized for functioning as "an ideological 'smoke screen' designed to either soften the image of firms engrossed in the rampant pursuit of profit (at any cost) or a way to deflect attention away from an unsavoury core business model" (Hanlon and Fleming 2009, 938). Treated like this CSR becomes "a commodity and a factor of production" (Hanlon 2008, 159) and thus supports rather than challenges profit maximization. Similarly Shamir highlights that "corporations transform the idea of social responsibility into a marketing device and into a commodity that conceals the power relations that underlie the relationship between global capitalism and social inequality, social harm, and social wrongs" (Shamir 2004, 684). In this context Banerjee stresses that the discourse on sustainability has been "hijacked by corporate interests" (Banerjee 2008, 64). Fleming and Jones (2013, 94) point out that apart from being propaganda CSR, furthermore, is a "parasitical instrument of commodification". If CSR is treated as a productive factor it does not come as a surprise that certain topics are excluded from the debate such employment contracts, 9-to-5 routines of work, inequalities of race, ethnicity and class, business involvement in wars, sweatshop labour, lying in advertising and manipulation (Boje 2008, 9).

The same points of criticism have been raised regarding business ethics in general. Roberts fears "that all this talk of ethics is just that – talk" (Roberts 2003, 250); Boje stresses that it "serves as a shield to hide unethical practice" (Boje 2008, 8), that it forms "ideologies imposed upon the oppressed" (Boje 2008, 19), and constitutes "ideological masks to cover up dirty business and market forces with ethics plaques" (Boje 2008, 19). Roberts in this context talks of an "ethics of narcissus", which means that CSR is used for creating an image of "corporate goodness", while "operational practices remain entirely untouched" (Roberts 2003, 257) and thus serves "only to facilitate 'business as usual'" (Roberts 2003, 257).

Taking into consideration this integration of CSR in the profit maximizing pursuit of business, it has been criticized as being part of the problem instead of the solution to social and environmental problems (Sklair and Miller 2010, 483). Sklair and Miller for example stress that CSR "can be seen as a set of globalizing practices carried out by the four fractions of the TCC [Transnational Capitalist Class] in the interest of capitalist globalization" (Sklair and Miller 2010, 484). Similarly Hanlon emphasizes that "CSR will help to make money from the problems businesses have helped to create, thereby improving shareholder value" (Hanlon 2008, 169). According to these criticisms, CSR functions as a strategy of resistance against all solutions to these problems that might negatively affect corporate profit interests.

Dialectical approaches to CSR thus highlight the necessity of a fundamental critique of the profit motive and of capitalism: Corlett for example takes a dialectical perspective when arguing that "fundamental moral problems with capitalism" exist (Corlett 1998, 103). He highlights that "the private ownership of the means of production is morally wrong because it enables capitalists to extract value from what workers alone produce" (Corlett 1998, 102). The insight that capitalism systematically creates misery and human suffering, limits freedom and is opposed to equality and justice means that from an ethical standpoint it is inevitable to think about societal alternatives to capitalism. In this regard Boje for example stresses that "It is not enough to try to be good and ethical as individuals when it is the systemic processes that must be dealt with" (Boje 2008, 22). In order to establish an ethical and socially responsible economy it thus becomes necessary "to change the whole production and consumption system of global capitalism, and its bedpartners, business and public administration" (Boje 2008, 18). Banerjee stresses that for critically approaching CSR "new questions need to be raised not only about the ecological and social sustainability but of the political economy itself" (Banerjee 2008, 73).

Rethinking political economy in a way that resolves the contradiction between profit and social responsibility requires thinking beyond capitalism. It requires imagining a different economy in which the production of wealth is no longer based on exploitation of workers and the appropriation of private profit. In such an economy economic production would instead aim at increasing general wealth and welfare based on commonly owned means of production, self-determined labour and democratic control over the economy. The sublation of the antagonisms between profit and social responsibility thus consist of an alternative economy and society in which economic and social goals are no longer opposed, but coincide with each other.

The insight that capitalism is inherently socially irresponsible does not mean that the idea of social responsibility needs to be abandoned. Instead it is important to shift the focus of attention from the social responsibility of the corporation to the social responsibility of the economy and to allow thoughts about a social responsibility transcend the boundaries of capitalism.

In the context of economic crisis and social uprisings such as Spain's Indiginados movement, the Occupy movements and protests against austerity in Greece, Jody Dean has argued that "The communist horizon appears closer than it has in a long time. The illusion that capitalism works has been shattered by all manner of economic and financial disaster – and we see it everywhere" (Dean 2012, 21). Hardt and Negri (2009) use the notion of "Commonwealth" for expressing "the need to institute and manage a world of common wealth, focussing on and expanding our capacities for collective production and self-government" (Hardt and Negri 2009, xiii). For Douzinas and Žižek (2010) communism constitutes a new commonwealth:

> Neo-liberal capitalist exploitation and domination takes the form of new enclosures of the commons (language and communication, intellectual property, genetic material, natural resources and forms of governance). Communism, by returning to the concept of the "common", confronts capitalist privatization with a view to building a new commonwealth.
>
> (Douzinas and Žižek 2010, ix)

Eric Olin Wright (2010) argues for socialism as a way of democratizing the economy as well as the state. He defines socialism as

> an economic structure in which social power in its multiple forms plays the dominant role in organizing economic activity, both directly and indirectly through the ways social power shapes the exercise of both state power and economic power. This is the equivalent of arguing for the radical democratization of both the state and economy.
>
> (Olin Wright 2010, 145)

Similarly Callinicos highlights the importance of establishing "a new global economic system based upon social ownership of the main productive resources and democratic planning" (Callinicos 2003, 148). This alternative to capitalism should "meet the requirements of (at least) justice, efficiency, democracy, and sustainability" (Callinicos 2003, 107). These suggestions describe possible ways towards a society that is based on democratic ownership of the means of production and a participatory organization of politics. That in principle achieving a socially responsible economy requires a fundamental transformation of society does not mean that it is impossible to improve the existing system. The idea of social responsibility can thus inspire a vision of an alternative society as well as support reforms that make the existing society more socially responsible. As Olin Wright argues, "emancipatory transformation should not be viewed mainly as a binary shift from one system to another, but rather as a shift in the configuration of the power relations that constitute a hybrid" (Olin Wright 2010, 267). Thus, reforms are necessary that help reduce human suffering and environmental degradation and at the same time improve the conditions for a more radical transformation of society.

Reforms to fight the destruction of the environment and the threat of an ecological catastrophe could for example include binding agreements regarding the reduction of emissions of greenhouse gases and pollution including strong enforcement mechanisms, public investment in the production of renewable energy, well developed and cheap public transport, etc.

Democracy could for example be strengthened through public funding of civil society groups and social movements, more direct forms of political decision making, freely accessible political education, etc. In order to achieve a more democratic workplace it would be important to guarantee workers the right to participate in corporate decision making processes including decisions about wages and working hours and to support worker unions and worker owned cooperatives. Global disarmament is a necessary (but not sufficient) measure for realizing a more peaceful world and for reducing suffering created through wars and political conflict. Instead of spending public money for military purposes it could be redirected to support social movements, public health care provision, education, etc.

Measures to reduce poverty and socio-economic inequality could involve the redistribution of wealth through fiscal policies, the introduction of a guaranteed basic income, worldwide legal minimum wages, worldwide laws against child labour, the reduction of the working week, anti-discrimination laws, abolition of laws that restrict migration, the full cancellation of third world debts, public provision of health care, pensions, education and infrastructure including access to media, information and communication technologies (ICTs) and the Internet.

A necessary measure to reduce the unrestricted power of corporations would be to strengthen state and civil society control over the economy through economic regulations, control of capital flows, nationalization of the banking system, public funding of civil society watchdog organizations and alternative media that report about corporate crimes and wrongdoings around the world, etc.

Furthermore it is important to strengthen those tendencies that entail the potential of going beyond capitalism and contradict the capitalist private property logic and that are based on the idea of the common. Such measures could include the abolition of intellectual property rights and the support of initiatives that strengthen the common such as the open source movement, file-sharing, or Wikipedia. Furthermore, resisting commodification is important for opening up spaces for a culture, which, instead of reproducing existing reality, challenges fantasy and imagination of possible social alternatives.

From a dialectical perspective the idea of a socially responsible economy can be used for criticizing capitalist business practices as socially irresponsible and for inspiring a counter-discourse about economic modes that are more socially responsible and compatible with social and environmental sustainability.

Conclusion

This chapter aimed at answering the question of what constitutes a socially responsible corporation. The answer to this question depends on how the topic of CSR is approached. A responsible corporation can thus be a corporation that maximizes profits (reductionism); a corporation that subordinates its profit interests under the higher goal of general social well-being (projectionism); a corporation that engages in philanthropic giving (dualism); or an illusion that hides the social irresponsibility of capitalism (dialectics). Table 2.1 summarizes the approaches to CSR that were described above.

Reductionist, projectionist and dualist approaches to CSR argue that the problems capitalism has created can be solved within capitalism: either by turning them into business opportunities (reductionism), or by taming capitalism and establishing an ethics of social responsibility (projectionism), or by balancing them through philanthropic activities (dualism).

Table 2.1 Approaches to CSR

Ways of thinking about CSR		*A socially responsible corporation . . .*	*Representatives*
Reductionism	Reduces the social responsibilities to profit goals	. . . maximizes profits and turns social problems into business opportunities	Almeder 1980; Drucker 1984; Jones 1995; Cogman and Oppenheim 2002; Davis 2005; Falck and Heblich 2007
Projectionism	Projects social responsibilities onto profit goals	. . . subjects its profit goals to ethical norms; or the expectations of society; or regulation; or public expectations; or a social and environmental consciousness	Bowen 1953; Frederick 1960; Davis and Blomstrom 1966; Carroll 1979, 1991, 1999; Wartick and Cochran 1985; Freeman 1984, 1999; Freeman and Philips 2002; Clarkson 1995; Epstein 1987, 2007; McInerney 2007; Scherer and Palazzo 2007
Dualism	Separates profit goals and social responsibilities from each other	. . . maximizes profits and gives back to society through philanthropic giving	Carnegie 1889; Gates 2000; McGuire 1963; Backman 1975; Sun, Stewart and Pollard 2010
Dialectics	Describes profit goals and social responsibilities as contradictory	. . . does not exist due to an inherent contradiction between the profit principle and social responsibilities	Sklair and Miller 2010; Hanlon and Fleming 2009; Fleming and Jones 2013; Hanlon 2008; Shamir 2004; Banerjee 2007, 2008; Boje 2008; Roberts 2003; Corlett 1998

Furthermore reductionism and dualism are based on the principle of voluntarism. The reductionist view of CSR remains entirely compatible with liberal and neo-liberal arguments according to which the purpose of the corporation lies in the maximization of its self-interests, i.e. profit. Dualist approaches argue that after profit has been generated parts of it should be employed to serve the common good. From this perspective it remains legitimate that private corporations are left free from government regulation in order to maximize their profits. The decision to engage in philanthropic activities is conceived as merely an ethical, not a legal, obligation.

Projectionist approaches to CSR share with reductionism and dualism the support of a capitalist economy. Representatives of a projectionist approach believe that it is possible to tame the profit motive and to shape profit generation so that it becomes socially responsible. Regarding the question of whether this requires governments to regulate the activities of corporations, projectionists are divided into two camps: one that argues that profit generation needs to become socially responsible while maintaining the principle of voluntarism; and a second one that highlights that taming profit generation and making it socially responsible requires enforcement of stricter regulation. While the former argument is ideologically based on the liberal and neo-liberal advocacy of an unregulated capitalism, the latter changes the focus of CSR towards a Keynesian economic policy of a regulated capitalism.

Dialectical approaches challenge the assumption that CSR can help to create a socially responsible capitalism. That in some cases corporations act "socially responsible" should not distract from looking at the broader picture, which reveals that many of the problems humanity is facing today have been and will continue to be created through the exploitative, expansive, competitive and profit maximizing logic of capitalism. According to this perspective the fundamental contradiction between profit and social responsibility can only be sublated through an alternative mode of economic and societal organization: to reconcile economic and social goals of the economy requires the establishment of a democratic society in which both means of production and the state are democratically controlled.

However, at present this is a minority view and it seems that Friedman's fear that CSR would have "subversive" effects (Friedman 1962/1982) was causeless. On the contrary, the mainstream of the current debate on CSR is based on an unquestioned advocacy of laissez-faire capitalism. Rather than subverting it, CSR tends to strengthen capitalism as it protects its legitimacy. In times in which social movements that are critical of capitalism and corporate globalizations are denouncing irresponsible business practices and corporate crimes, maintaining legitimacy becomes important for many corporate actors. In the context of a crisis of legitimacy CSR can help to maintain the good reputation of corporations as well as capitalism in general.

The mainstream debate on CSR (reductionist, projectionist and dualist approaches) suggests that social and environmental problems of contemporary society can be entirely resolved without calling into question the structural foundations of the present capitalist system. If all problems that contemporary society is facing are solvable within capitalism, looking beyond it becomes obsolete. By taking for granted the existence of capitalist social relations, CSR contributes to the naturalization of capitalism and makes it appear fixed and unchangeable. Thus, Hanlon is right when he asserts that CSR "ensures that subversive alternatives suffer the fate of utopias – they are dismissed as impossible however attractive we find them" (Hanlon 2008, 167). In its present form CSR strengthens capitalist hegemony: "In contemporary global capitalism, ideological naturalization has reached an unprecedented level; rare are those who dare even to dream utopian dreams about possible alternatives" (Žižek 2009, 77). A debate about CSR that does not think beyond capitalism forestalls the question of whether an alternative way of organizing the economy might be more compatible with social and environmental sustainability. It constrains the discussion about what is best for society and not just for corporations and their owners.

This limitation of the dominant CSR debate emphasizes the need for a critical redefinition of the concept that breaks through this ideological naturalization by further advancing a dialectical critique of CSR. Such a critique can be used to establish a counter-discourse that highlights in which respect, despite claims of CSR, capitalism is socially irresponsible. From a dialectical perspective CSR should not be reduced to a managerial question but be discussed on a political level. The task for current politics would be to initiate reforms that on the one hand immediately limit negative social effects of corporate practices and on the other hand improve the conditions for a more fundamental social transformation. For the purpose of initiating such reforms, alliances with the Keynesian stream of projectionist CSR seem fruitful. A dialectical approach to CSR can inspire a critical counter-discourse as well as a political struggle for achieving an alternative, socially responsible economy and society.

Notes

1   CSR Consulting Ltd. See: http://www.csr-consulting.com/
2   Plosion branding. See: http://www.plosionbranding.com/index.htm
3   Goodvalues. See: http://www.goodvalues.co.uk/
4   GoodCorporation. See: http://www.goodcorporation.com/about-us.php
5   GeorgeSoros.com. *Philantropy FAQs*. Retrieved from http://georgesoros.com/faqs/entry/georgesorosphilanthropyisunprecedented/ on August 4, 2012.

3 Social responsibility and the media

The media are often considered to be essential for raising awareness and enabling public debate about CSR. The European Commission in a recent communication on CSR for example states: "The media can raise awareness of both the positive and negative impacts of enterprises" (European Commission 2011, 7). During the last decade several studies investigated how the media report CSR and sustainability issues. Hamilton (2003) for example studied how journalists refer to the term CSR for describing the social, environmental and economic impact of corporations. Dickson and Eckman (2008, 726) analysed how the way media deal with CSR reports, encourages or discourages CSR reporting. Tench, Bowd and Jones (2007) investigated journalists' opinions on CSR, their interests concerning CSR and how companies should communicate with them. Dyck and Zingales (2002), based on an evaluation of several examples, argue that "media do play a role in shaping the public image of corporate managers and directors and in so doing they pressure them to behave according to societal norms" (Dyck and Zingales 2002, 5).

The fact that existing research largely focuses on how the media report the social responsibilities of other companies and industries results in two main blind spots: first, most studies of CSR and the media neglect that media today are mostly organized as companies themselves. Capitalist relations of production shape the media and communication system: privately owned companies produce media content and organize access to information and communication content and technology. The media are part of what Leslie Sklair (2001) termed the Transnational Capitalist Class (TCC). What is missing are studies that look at the social responsibilities of corporate media themselves. Second, an exclusive focus on how CSR is represented in media reports means reducing the media to the level symbols, meaning and text. This narrow focus not only neglects the media's responsibilities regarding their employees and the environment but furthermore overlooks that today's media landscape extends far beyond content and depends on the production of ICTs, software design and telecommunication infrastructure. Looking at the responsibility of the media only in terms of content misrepresents the reality of the contemporary media and communication system.

In order to overcome these blind spots it is necessary to expand the study of the social responsibility of the media and to address the question of whether private companies can provide media content as well as other essential communicative resources in a way that serves the common good and not merely private profit: are media and communication companies socially responsible?

This chapter will lay the theoretical foundation for the empirical study of this question (see Chapters 4–6). In a first step it is necessary to come to a definition of media and communication industries that is suitable for the twenty-first century. In a next step I apply the typology of CSR theories that was constructed in the previous chapter to the question how the corporate profit goals and social responsibilities of the media are related. Finally, I conclude with a brief summary and an outlook onto the empirical study of CSR in media and communication industry.

Media and communication industries – in search of a definition

The aim of this chapter is to identify relevant media and communication industries today. The starting point for such an endeavour are concepts such as creative industries (Caves 2000; Hartley 2005), network media industries (Winseck 2011), information industries (Chon et al. 2003; Noam 2009), cultural industries (Garnham 1987/1997; Hesmondhalgh 2007; Miège 2011), media industries (Compaine and Gomery 2000; Croteau and Hoynes 2000; Albarran 2010), telecommunications, information, media and entertainment (TIME) industries (Winter 2006), or media and communication industries (Arsenault 2011).

These concepts differ in regard to which industries are included. Introductions to media economics for example in their presentation of media industries tend to focus on media content production (Croteau and Hoynes 2006; Compaine and Gomery 2000). Likewise Harry Pross' classic distinction of three types of media focuses on different types of content media: Harry Pross in 1972 distinguished primary, secondary and tertiary media. Primary media (Pross 1972, 145) have in common that the relation between sender and receiver is not technically mediated. Secondary media (Pross 1972, 145) are those media that require a technical device for sending a message but not for its consumption (e.g. newspapers, flyers etc.). Tertiary media (Pross 1972, 224) require technical devices both for sending as well as for receiving a message (e.g. radio, telephone, TV, etc.).

The focus on media content is also present in recent accounts of media industries. Dwayne Winseck for example defines "network media industries" as "core and emergent public communications media that migrate around various distribution networks and media platforms and devices" (Winseck 2011, 3), which according to Winseck includes the 10 largest media and Internet industries: television, Internet access, newspapers, books, films, magazines, music, radio, Internet advertising, and video games (Winseck 2011, 3). Telecommunications as well as the ICT sector would be closely related but not part of the network media industries.

This separation of a core media industry and other associated industries is similar to Garnham's (1987/1997) description of cultural industries. For Garnham the term "cultural industries" refers to those institutions of our society which employ the characteristic modes of production and organization of industrial corporations to produce and disseminate symbols in the form of cultural goods and services, generally, although not exclusively, as commodities.

(Garnham 1987/1997, 55)

This definition focuses on media content industries. Garnham, however, similar to Winseck, notes that these media content-industries are connected to media technology and distribution industries (Garnham 1987/1997, 55).

Likewise, David Hesmondhalgh defines "cultural industries" as those industries that "deal primarily with the industrial production and circulation of text" (Hesmondhalgh 2007, 12). These are broadcasting, film industries, the content aspects of the Internet industry, music industries, print and electronic publishing, video and computer games, advertising and marketing (Hesmondhalgh 2007, 12f). For Hesmondhalgh these industries form an economic sector because they all produce symbolic artefacts and compete for the same resources: consumer income, advertising revenue, consumption time, and skilled creative and technical labour (Hesmondhalgh 2007, 13). Similar to Garnham and Winseck, Hesmondhalgh also mentions some "borderline cases" which would be related to, but, however, not part of the cultural industries. These are sport, fashion, consumer electronics and the cultural industry, hardware as well as software (Hesmondhalgh 2007, 14).

While the concept of cultural industries usually focuses on those sectors that are concerned with the production of symbols, meaning and text, that is, media content industries, the concept of creative industries is broader. Hartley (2005, 5) argues that the concept of creative industries relates to the convergence of creative arts and cultural industries in the context of the spread of ICTs. Caves (2000, 1) defines creative industries as those industries that supply

goods and services that we broadly associate with cultural, artistic, or simply entertainment value. They include book and magazine publishing, the visual arts (painting and sculpture), the performing arts (theatre, opera, concerts, dance), sound recordings, cinema and TV films, as well as fashion and toys and games.

This understanding of creative industries extends beyond the production of media content and includes other cultural artefacts such as fashion and toys. The concept of creative industries has also been used in the context of information society policy. In 1998 the UK Department for Culture Media and Sports (DCMS) in a Creative Industries Mapping Document identified 13 creative industries: advertising, antiques, architecture, crafts, design, fashion, film, leisure software, music, performing arts, publishing, software, TV and radio (DCMS 1998). In 2001 the DCMS slightly revised the list of creative industries: advertising, architecture, art and antiques market, crafts, design, designer fashion, film and video, interactive leisure software, music, performing arts, publishing, software and computer services, television and radio (DCMS 2001).

While definitions of cultural industries usually focus on the production of texts and symbols (Garnham 1987/1997; Hesmondhalgh 2007), the concept of creative industries puts an emphasis on the creativity involved in a specific production process (DCMS 1998, 2001; Caves 2000; Hartley 2005).

Pratt (2006) argues that precisely because of this focus on creativity, the concept of creative industries would lose its analytical value as "it would be difficult to identify a non-creative industry or activity" (Pratt 2006, 33). The concept of cultural industries would be more meaningful as it relates to the production of cultural objects and not to creativity as such (Pratt 2006, 33). In line with this argument, Hesmondhalgh and Pratt (2006) argue that in order to avoid a too broad definition of cultural industries it would be necessary to focus on outputs: "A more sensible option is to recognise that the main interest in such industries is the symbolic, aesthetic and, for want of a better term, artistic nature of their output" (Hesmondhalgh and Pratt 2006, 6). Flew (2011, 19) points out that a too broad definition of creative industries would fail to recognise the specifics of cultural production.

Nicholas Garnham (2006) in a critical discussion of the concept of creative industries argues that the shift from using the notion of cultural industries to the notion of creative industries needs to be understood in the context of information society policies. Garnham argues that the "creative industry" would serve a specific political purpose that is related to a redrawing of boundaries between cultural policy and industrial and economic policy (Garnham 2006, 15f). The main policy implication of the rhetoric of creative industries is their construction as an important economic growth sector. Garnham highlights that this argument can only be maintained by including the software sector as part of creative industries (Garnham 2006, 26). This broad, creativity- and artist-centred notion of creative industries according to Garnham helped to justify a shift in cultural policy from ensuring access to culture to introducing stronger copyright protections and thus exclusion from cultural products (Garnham 2006, 26).

As this comparison of the cultural industry and the creative industry concepts shows, the latter's focus on creativity transcends the media and communication sector and includes all industries for which creativity is an essential productive capacity. The former makes an effort to keep the concept of cultural industries limited to those industries that are essentially concerned with the production of media content. The creative industries concept focuses on the characteristics of the production process, while the notion of cultural industries is centred on the outcome of cultural production.

The concept of creative industries seems too broad to be useful for constructing a model of media and communication industries. The fact that creativity is important in various different industries makes it difficult to define clear boundaries. The criterion of creativity thus is not precise enough to grasp the distinctive qualities of media and communication industries. The notion of cultural industries on the other hand seems rather narrow. Its focus on symbols, meaning and text tends to neglect those industries that produce media technology, which is essential for media production, distribution and consumption. For most media types, such as TV, radio, online media, and even the print media, media technology is essential for at least one stage in the process of production, distribution or consumption. Media technologies range from production technologies such as the video equipment to consumption technologies such as TV sets and DVD players to distribution technologies such as cable networks to the computer as a universal technology for media production and consumption. Which technologies are available and used essentially shapes media content. Stuart Hall (1973/2006) in his encoding/decoding model pointed out that what shapes the meaning of a message are not only frameworks of knowledge and relations of production, but also the technical infrastructure. Furthermore it is important to remember that the etymological meaning of the word medium refers to "a middle ground" or an "intermediate agency".[1] As Eli M. Noam (2009) correctly points out "the term connotes not just content but the means of its delivery. A medium is a way to distribute content; it is not content per se" (Noam 2009, 47). Noam furthermore stresses that media convergence makes it necessary to go beyond a narrow definition of the media industry that is limited to media content (Noam 2009, 47).

In approaching a definition of media and communication industries it therefore seems necessary to not only focus on media content but start looking at media technology as well. Bernard Miège (2011) made an attempt to extend the cultural industries concept into this direction. His distinction of four types of cultural commodities also includes technical devices needed for consumption. Based on the criterion of "reproducability" Miège identifies four types of cultural commodities. Type 1 are reproducible commodities which can be reproduced without the involvement of informational workers, such as technical devices that are needed for accessing cultural and informational products. Type 2 includes all reproducible commodities that require the involvement of cultural workers in their production, such as books, disks and films. Type 3 are semi-reproducible products that are produced by artists and in which reproduction is technically or socially limited, such as limited reproductions of fine arts. Type 4 are those cultural commodities that are produced by artists and can not be reproduced and therefore are not part of the cultural industry, such as unique pieces of art (Miège 2011, 86).

Amelia Arsenault (2011, 106f) identifies six media and communication industries: converged communication infrastructure, hardware and software, gaming, telecoms, Internet content and multi-media. She points out that as a result of concentration and convergence companies often belong to more than one of these industries (Arsenault 2011, 107). Arsenault's classification includes media technology and distribution industries but remains imprecise regarding content producing industries. While online media content and multi-media are included, traditional media content industries seem to be missing.

Carsten Winter argues that the convergence of telecommunications, information, media and entertainment has lead to the emergence of a TIME (telecommunications, information, media, entertainment) sector (Winter 2006, 23). Through TIME convergence a new type of digital network media has emerged that breaks with the traditional linear communication model and allow users to take part in all moments of the communication process, production, allocation, reception and usage of mediated communication (Winter 2006, 24). Digital network media would expand the typology suggested by Pross (1972) by a quartiary media segment, which would depend on software and transmission technology, so-called client–server technologies (Winter 2006, 24). Winter's contribution is important as it illustrates the importance of looking at newly emerging media sectors; however, it does not provide a complete classification of media and communication industries.

A promising starting point for developing such a classification is the concept of information industries. Eli M. Noam (2009, 45f) in his study of media concentration in America identified 100 information industries and grouped them into four sectors: first, mass media including print and publishing, music, film, electronic retail distribution and programming networks; second, information technology including hardware and software; third, telecommunications including telecom services and equipment; and fourth, Internet industries. Similarly Chon et al. (2003, 142) distinguish between three information industries: content production-related services, content delivery-related services and data-processing services.

The presented concepts offer some useful elements for a definition of media and communication industries that is suitable for the twenty-first century. However, none of these definitions is explicitly based on a systematic media and communication model. The industries they identify therefore are often incomplete or overlapping. Constructing a systematic model can help to identify all media and communication industries that are relevant today. Such a model can be based on the classic distinction of three economic spheres: production, distribution and consumption (Marx 1857/2004, 129). In this context Manfred Knoche (2005) argues that considering these three spheres is important for understanding the development of media technologies (Knoche 2005, 46). He therefore distinguishes between means of production and investment, means of distribution and means of consumption. The same model can be used for constructing a model of how media production, distribution and consumption takes place in contemporary society and that shows which industries are involved in these processes. Figure 3.1 is divided into

- the sphere of production in which media content is produced and (technically) encoded,
- the sphere of distribution which (technically) organizes the transport of media messages from producers to consumers and
- the sphere of consumption in which media messages are (technically) decoded and consumed.
- In addition the sphere of prosumption is introduced as a feature of online media industries.

The model represented in Figure 3.1 on the one hand describes five different ways of how media content circulates through these different stages, and on the other

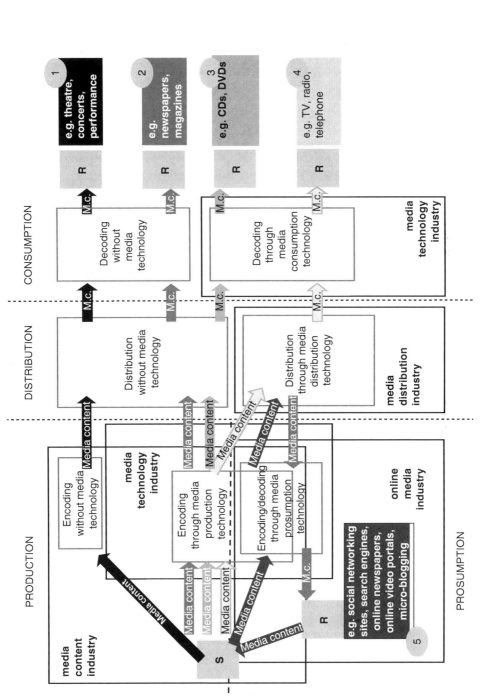

Figure 3.1 A model of media types and media and communication industries.

hand shows which industries are involved in making these communications flows possible.

Figure 3.1 describes five different ways of how media content can be produced, distributed and consumed.

- In the first case no media technology is involved for production, distribution, or consumption. This involves all kinds of live performances in which content is transported through acoustic or visual codes. Examples of this type of media are music concerts, theatre shows, dance performances, etc.
- In the second case media technology is used for encoding content, but distribution and consumption is possible without media technology, as is the case with all print media.
- In the third case media technology is needed for both encoding and decoding of media content; distribution, however, takes place without the involvement of media technology. Media of this type such as CDs, DVDs etc. require a non-mediated physical movement from the producer to the consumer.
- In the fourth case all stages of the media production, distribution and consumption processes are based on media technology. Examples of this type of media are the telephone as well as radio and television.
- With computers and the Internet a fifth way of circulating media content has emerged, which allows the use of the same media technologies for both production and consumption of media content. These technologies can therefore be called media prosumption technologies. Based on these technologies a more interactive way of producing media content has emerged in which all users have the technological means to not only consume but also produce media content. This marks the emergence of the prosumer (Toffler 1980; Fuchs 2008).

Following Pross' (1972) typology of media types, case 1 corresponds to primary media, case 2 to secondary media, and cases 3 and 4 to tertiary media. As Pross only considered production and consumption he could not distinguish between media that are distributed via media technology such as broadcasting and the telephone, and those that require physical transport such as CDs and DVDs. Case 5 can be described as quartiary media that have emerged during the last couple of decades.

However, Figure 3.1 does not only describe different types of media, it most importantly shows which industries are involved in making these various ways of circulating media content possible:

- *Media content industry*: The first important industries are those that are concerned with the production of media content. This includes all kinds of content production from theatre or musicals, to print media production, to music recording and film production.
- *Media technology industry*: In most cases, except for live performances, some kind of technical encoding is necessary before media content can reach its audience. This technology ranges from the printing press, to microphones,

photo cameras and film equipment to computers. In some cases the technically encoded media content again needs to be technically decoded for being
consumed. These media consumption devices for example include CD, DVD
and mp3 players, TV and radio sets and increasingly also mobile phones
and computers. The production of media encoding and decoding technology
forms an important industry that frames the production and consumption of
media content. Some of these encoding and decoding technologies are hardware products with built-in software such as CD players, video cameras, or
TV sets. Other products, in particular mobile phones and computers, require
additional software. Hardware and software products have different qualities.
While the former is a physical product, the latter is a non-physical knowledge
product. After software has been programmed it can potentially be used by
an unlimited number of people. Hardware on the contrary needs to be constantly reproduced. These differences in the nature of the product also create
differences for the business model of hardware and software industries: while
hardware companies sell physical products, software companies sell licences
that for a certain amount of time grant access to knowledge. Because of these
fundamental differences it seems appropriate to treat the hardware and software industries as two different segments of the media technology industry.

- *Media distribution industry*: Another industry that is essential in the media
circulation process is the media distribution industry. Figure 3.1 shows that
in the case of live performances, print media, CDs, DVDs, etc. distribution
takes place without media technology; in the case of telephone, broadcasting
and the Internet media distribution technology such as cables, radio and satel-
lite, or other telecommunication technologies are necessary for transporting
media content form producers to consumers.

- The online media industry is depicted as a separate industry as it takes media
production and consumption to a new level. Computer and Internet technologies allow going beyond the boundaries between media producers and consumers and make prosumption possible. The concept of prosumption, which
Alvin Toffler introduced in *The Third Wave* (1980), is today usually used for
describing the fact that on the Internet users can act both as consumers and
producers of media content. Christian Fuchs argues, that "In the Internet each
receiver is a possible transmitter, a prosumer. It is technologically based on
a decentralized network that forms a polydirectional medium of interaction
where many-to-many communication can take place" (Fuchs 2008, 240)

The fact that the same technology can be used both for production and consumption, and prosumption therefore becomes possible, does not mean that
every online communication is necessarily is a form of prosumption. Much
Internet content is still produced by professional content producers, who also
have the means to advertise their content, which therefore is likely to be more
visible on the net. However, the technical possibility has transformed traditional media. Not only are most media (except live performances, see type 1
in Figure 3.1) now available online, the Internet also alters their functionality
by adding elements of prosumption: online newspapers, radio and TV, music

and film offers include comment functions and other interactive and community features. All media content can be easily shared and discussed online. Furthermore new media models have emerged that almost entirely depend on content production by consumers such as (mirco)blogging sites, search engines, social networking and file-sharing sites.

In this section five media and communication industries have been identified: media content industries, media technology industries including hardware as well as software industries, media distribution industries and online media industries. As Knoche (1999, 155) highlights cross-sectoral concentration processes in the media sector are leading to the economic convergence of different media industries. It is thus important to note that despite the fact that the identified industries are structurally and functionally different from each other, one company might be active in more than one of them. Furthermore these different industries are also connected and both economically and functionally dependent on each other and thus form a joint media and communication complex. The following section takes a look at existing research about the corporate social responsibilities of these sectors.

Approaching the social responsibility of the media

The study of the social responsibilities of media and communication companies has long been neglected by CSR research. In fact, it was mainly consultancy groups and media companies themselves that initiated the first discussions on this topic. In 2001 several British media companies created the Media CSR Forum, which aims at discussing, developing and promoting CSR and sustainability for the media sector. Its members are media organizations such as the BBC, Reed Elsevier, News International, Sky, Yell, the Guardian Media Group and Virgin Media.[2]

Another effort to develop a CSR framework for media companies was made by SustainAbility, UNEP and Ketchum (2002). In a report they argued that media are not only important for raising awareness on CSR issues but also have to implement CSR and sustainable development principles into their own practices (SustainAbility, UNEP and Ketchum 2002, iii). In 2004 SustainAbility together with the WWF issued a second report, which focused on the media's responsibility in regard to content (Sustainability and WWF 2004, i). In 2009 the Doughty Centre for Corporate Responsibility together with the German Centre for Corporate Citizenship issued a report about corporate responsibility and the media. The study author David Grayson argues that the responsibilities of media companies are connected to the following areas: editorial policy and freedom of expression, privacy and public decency, advertising, and duty to educate and inform (Grayson 2009, 14–16).

This brief outline shows that industry and consultancy actors made some efforts to identify areas of the social responsibilities of media companies. However, to develop a more systematic and critical account of CSR in media companies, looking into academic work in this area seems necessary.

To present different approaches to the social responsibility of the media in a systematic way, I will apply the typology of CSR theories that I constructed in Chapter 2. The description of reductionist, projectionist, dualist and dialectical approaches to CSR is thus again based on Hofkirchner's (2002, 2003) distinction of four ways of thinking. The questions that guide the description of approaches to the social responsibility of the media are: what characterizes socially responsible media? How are the economic goals and social responsibilities of the media related to each other?

- Reductionist approaches reduce social responsibilities to business opportunities and highlight how engaging in CSR activities can benefit the business goals of media companies.
- Projectionist approaches stress that commercial media can become socially responsible if their operations are guided by values. They highlight that in order to meet their social responsibilities media need to adhere to ethical principles, rules and guidelines.
- Dualist approaches describe economic goals and social responsibilities as disjunct and thus treat the economic goals and social responsibilities of the media separate from each other.
- Dialectical approaches highlight that economic interests and social responsibilities mutually shape and contradict each other. They argue that in order to become truly socially responsible media need to be freed from the necessity to be commercially successful.

In the following I discuss these approaches by referring to some examples.

Reductionism – social responsibility as strategic advantage

Reductionist accounts of the social responsibility of the media focus on highlighting how social issues can be approached in ways that benefit business interest. Anke Trommershausen (2011) takes a reductionist perspective that aims at showing how addressing emerging challenges in the area of communication and culture can be turned into strategic opportunities for companies (Trommerhausen 2011, 27). Based on Carsten Winter's (2006) concept of the TIME industries, she analysed CSR in telecommunications, information and media (TIM) companies.

Trommershausen argues that challenges for TIM(E) companies that result from the emergence of digital network media (Trommershausen 2011, 28) and the convergence of industries (Trommershausen 2011, 119–123) can be turned into strategic opportunities for TIM(E) companies: the challenge of ensuring access would create potentials for entering new markets (Trommershausen 2011, 171–174); the challenge of changing stakeholder relations would entail the potential for successfully managing stakeholders by individualizing relations to stakeholders through digital media (Trommershausen 2011, 174–178); the challenge of enabling the constitution of a public sphere would yield long term strategic potentials if TIM(E) companies ensured a secure and fair access to digital media

products and services and thereby meet their responsibility as citizens in a dig-
italized world (Trommerhausen 2011, 179–181); the challenge of corporate
responsibility management could result in competitive advantages if professional
corporate responsibility management and control strategies were established
(Trommershausen 2011, 182).

Trommershausen argues that strategic potentials can be realized if corporate
responsibility strategies focus on the core business of a company, which in the case
of TIM(E) companies lie in the area of communication and culture (Trommershausen
2011, 181). Instead of CSR she therefore suggests the notion of "corporate responsibility for communication and culture" (Trommershausen 2011, 30).

Trommershausen's approach to CSR in media and communication companies
is based on a corporate logic according to which business goals are more important than social responsibilities: "Alongside general normative demands on the
social responsibility for companies, the fundamental managerial and competitive orientation must not be regarded as secondary" (Trommershausen 2011, 182
(translation[3])). Trommershausen continues

> In order to actually generate this competitive advantage, the realization and
> control within the scope of a strategic management of Corporate Respon-
> sibility is necessary. Only that way it becomes possible to exploit strategic
> potentials and test them with respect to a Return on Corporate Responsibility
> based on the Business Case.
>
> (Trommershausen 2011, 182 (translation[4]))

The notion of a "return on corporate responsibility" takes the economic reduction of the idea of social responsibility to its extreme – instead of contribution to
the common good, responsible behaviour is supposed to yield a financial return.
By focusing on the question of how emerging social challenges in the realm of
communication and culture can be turned into strategic business opportunities,
Trommershausen continues the instrumental rhetoric of a strategic CSR (S-CSR)
(Burke and Logsdon 1996, 496) and applies it to the realm of communication and
culture.

Apart from its instrumentality, another limitation of Trommershausen's
approach is its exclusive focus on the media's responsibilities for communication
and culture. She argues that media convergence has fundamentally altered the
media landscape and led to the emergence of the TIM(E) sector and digital network media, which, according to Trommerhausen, include hardware such as PCs,
notebooks, mobile phones as well as web 2.0 media such as weblog and wikis
(Trommershausen 2011, 33). The hardware industry is an example that perfectly
illustrates that working conditions and environmental destruction are important
issues for the media and communication sector.[5] Trommerhausen, despite pointing at the growing importance of the hardware sector, ignores these issues when
arguing that the particular social about the responsibility of TIM(E) companies is
their responsibility for communication and culture. This exclusive focus on communication and culture fails to grasp the whole spectrum of social responsibilities

of the media and communication sector. CSR strategies that are based on such a reductionist approach are thus likely to be highly selective and will ignore social problems if addressing them contradicts business goals. The main beneficiaries of a reductionist approach to the social responsibility of the media are the owners of media corporations.

Projectionism – ethics in a commercial media system

Projectionist approaches are based on the assumption that in order to be socially responsible, media should meet the expectations of society. Following this view responsible media, despite their commercial organization, need to embody certain moral values. Projectionist approaches become manifest in ethics codes for journalism and media.

In 1956 Siebert, Peterson and Schramm described a social responsibility theory of the press as one of *Four Theories of the Press.* Apart from the social responsibility theory, Siebert, Peterson and Schramm (1956) distinguished three further theories of the press: an authoritarian, a libertarian, and a soviet-communist (Siebert, Peterson and Schramm 1956). Their description of the social responsibility theory bears characteristics of a projectionist approach: it is based on the assumption that the commercial organization of media needs to be balanced by a strong ethical awareness.

The development of ethics codes for the media reflected the theory of social responsibility (Siebert, Peterson and Schramm 1956, 85). Ethics codes are based on a projectionist approach to social responsibility, which suggests that commercial media can be socially responsible if they adhere to certain ethical rules. The American Society of Newspaper Editors developed the earliest of these codes in 1923. It defined seven principles of sound journalistic practice: responsibility, freedom of the press; independence; sincerity, truthfulness, accuracy; impartiality; fair play; and decency (American Society of Newspaper Editors 1923). Similarly, the report *A Free and Responsible Press* (1947) by the Commission on the Freedom of the Press, known as the Hutchins Commission, identified five requirements for the press: it would be the task of the press (1) to give a truthful, comprehensive and intelligent account of current events and their context; (2) to function as a forum for the exchange of comment and critics; (3) to give a representative picture of the constituent groups in society; (4) to represent and clarify the goals an values of society; and (5) to facilitate full access to current knowledge (Commission on Freedom of the Press 1947, 20–27).

These are early examples of ethics codes for journalism, which even today primarily target print media (Harris 1992, 63). Print media are based on a commercial, profit-oriented business model. Although in many countries print media receive some public subsidies, their income mainly relies on advertising revenue. The aim of ethics codes is that media, despite their commercial organization, meet their social responsibilities.

Journalistic ethics codes "provide working journalists with statements of minimums and perceived ideals" (Elliott-Boyle 1985/1986, 25). These standards specify ideal journalistic behaviour in respect to ethical issues of journalistic practices, which include "freedom, objectivity, truth, honesty, privacy" (Belsey and Chadwick 1992, xiii). Such codes have been adopted both by countries and individual media companies (Harris 1992, 62). Himelboim and Limor argue that journalistic ethics codes are designed to define the role of journalists in society (Himelboim and Limor 2011, 76).

Several studies analysed the content of these codes (Bruun 1979; Jones 1980; Laitila 1995; Himelboim and Limor 2011) as well as their implementation and impact (Harris 1992; Boeyink 1994; Fink 1995). Himelboim and Limor (2011) for example conducted a content analysis of 262 media ethics codes from press councils, media conglomerates, media organizations and professional journalist organizations in 94 countries. They found that the most commonly mentioned journalistic roles are "distributing information", "commitment to public interest", "commitment to the public's right to know", and "promote pluralism in media" (Himelboim and Limor 2011, 82). Laitila (1995) analyzed 31 journalistic ethics codes from 29 European countries (Laitila 1995, 529). Most common principles were truthfulness, protection of integrity and independence of journalists, responsibility of journalists for forming public opinion, fairness, protection of sources, and freedom of expression (Laitila 1995, 539). Clement Jones (1980) studied journalistic ethic codes from 50 countries around the world. He found that most codes emphasized integrity, truth and objectivitiy as important journalistic qualities (Jones 1980, 83).

Irrespective of their particular content a main problem regarding voluntary ethics codes is that they contain guidelines for journalists without sufficiently considering how economic realities hamper the implementation of these guidelines. Print media, like all commercial media, are profit-oriented companies and dependent on advertising income. Journalists are either directly employed or work freelance for these companies. Market pressure thus also affects journalists who are employed by or want to sell their work to media companies. McQuail for example points out that codes of ethics provide some normative guidelines, which, however, cannot always be applied in actual journalistic practices (McQuail 2010, 172).

Codes that simply demand from journalists to protect sources, be truthful and fair (Laitila 1995), to ensure integrity, truth and objectivity (Jones 1980, 83), or to commit to the public's right to know (Himelboin and Limor 2011, 82) treat ethical behaviour as the individual responsibility of journalists. A focus on journalists and their (un-)ethical behaviour also characterizes many textbooks on media ethics. Christians et al. in their widely used book on *Media Ethics* (2001) for example focus on moral duties of media practitioners. They argue, media practitioners have a duty to themselves, to their clients, to their organization or firm, to professional colleagues and to society (Christians et al. 2001, 22) and therefore need to be able to "make defensible ethical decisions" (Christians et al. 2001, 2). Plaisance in his introduction to *Media Ethics* (2009) describes the "credibility gap and the ethics scandals that plague our media system" as a moral failure of media professionals (Plaisance 2009, xvi). He argues that the key to an ethical media system are media practitioners that are well trained in the field of journalistic ethics (Plaisance

2009, xvii). Kieran (1998) stresses that it is crucial that journalists are aware of the responsibilities that are connected to their profession:

> The intelligibility and rationality of the practices and activities of news journalists themselves depend upon recognizing journalism's internal goal, informing the public about significant events in the world, and this goal requires journalists to strive to be impartial and thus objective.
>
> (Kieran 1998, 35)

Awareness of journalists regarding their role in society is certainly important, even if commonly assumed journalistic standards such as impartiality and objectivity are questionable. It can for example be doubted whether objectivity can ever be achieved. Every decision about which topics to write about, which sources to consult, and even which words to use for describing reality involves some subjective judgement. Apart from debates about the content of ethical guidelines for journalists, it is furthermore doubtful that ethical commitments of individual journalists are enough for achieving a socially responsible media system. The projectionist belief that commercial media can become socially responsible through imposing ethical behaviour guidelines on them is both individualistic and idealistic and likely to overlook existing economic pressures and necessities. In a commercial media system journalism is a business and media companies that strive for a profit have to abide the demands of the market, which can contradict journalistic ethics.

Some contributors to the field of media ethics recognize this shortcoming. McManus for example stresses: "Major American journalism ethics codes, however, not only fail to examine the corporate profit motive, most don't even recognize its existence" (McManus 1997, 13). He argues that journalism ethics needs to consider potential conflicts between journalists and shareholders, advertisers, sources, consumers, government, parent corporations, media firms, or pressure groups (McManus 1997, 13f). Similarly Richards highlights that debates around journalistic ethics fail to sufficiently take corporate realities into account (Richards 2004, 123). Richards points out that media ethics can learn from business ethics and management studies. He particularly suggests the stakeholder model as a promising starting point (Richards 2004, 125). McQuail in this context suggests the following: "Improving the status of professional associations of media workers and encouraging education and self-regulation are more appropriate avenues to follow and can help to provide a counterweight to the extremes of commercial motivation and to multinational conglomerates" (McQuail 1997, 527).

These approaches acknowledge that commercial pressures can hamper the implementation of ethical standards within a media company. However, their conclusion from this observation is not that commercialism promotes unethical behaviour and therefore should be criticized. Instead they argue for developing more thorough modes of ensuring ethical conduct. Their argument remains projectionist as it suggests taming the profit motive through mechanisms such as industry associations, ombudsmen, advisory boards, etc. as a sufficient measure for keeping journalism ethical and socially responsible.

Dualism – commercial success and ethical behaviour

Dualist approaches to CSR treat the economic interests and social responsibilities of the media as separate from each other. Altmeppen's (2011) concept of "media social responsibility" exemplifies this approach. It is based on a distinction between journalism and media. Both would be functionally and structurally different organizational entities. They would, however, co-operate since journalism would produce the content that is distributed via the media (Altmeppen 2011, 248). According to Altmeppen journalism selects topics and creates content that can be distributed via the media. Journalism itself would neither have the means for distributing content nor for paying for its own costs. In Altmeppen's view journalism is no business model. It would depend on media organizations that ensure its funding and distribute its products (Altmeppen 2011, 249). Media organizations on the contrary would generate money through the distribution of content. This would allow them to pay for journalism and the production of media content (Altmeppen 2011, 249). Treating media and journalism as structurally and functionally different entities establishes a dualism between economic goals and social responsibility: media generate profit, journalism is ethical. According to Altmeppen journalism should aim at fulfilling its social responsibility or producing relevant news content, while media companies should primarily aim at generating profit (Altmeppen 2011, 259).

The analytical distinction between journalism and media for identifying social responsibilities is questionable. In fact both are operating together: journalistic production requires financial resources, and media organizations cannot make money without journalism. Neither of the two is able to operate without the other, which creates strong mutual dependencies. A dualism between content (journalism) and organizational form (media) that assumes that media is a business model while journalism is not, runs the danger of seeing journalism as independent of market pressures. Furthermore Altmeppen's claim that journalism would be no business model is questionable. Altmeppen himself argues that "media 'pay' a 'price' to journalism for its creation of informative, topical content" (Atmeppen 2011, 258 (translation[6])). This shows that the business model of journalism is selling media content to media companies. Media companies receive the money from advertising clients. Those who pay for journalism in fact are advertisers. What Altmeppen conceptualizes as media is just the administrative intermediary that organizes the sale of advertisements. It is exactly this double role of media content companies, as both profit-oriented economic entities and providers of media content, which challenges the media's ability to meet its social responsibilities. An approach that is based on a distinction between media and journalism misses this double role and resulting challenges.

Dialectics – the social irresponsibility of commercial media

Dialectical approaches stress that economic goals and social responsibilities of the media mutually shape each other. From this perspective the economic success and profitability of media companies have consequences that impair their social responsibility. On the other hand, socially responsible media that resist commercial mechanisms and market pressures are likely to suffer from a lack of resources and visibility.

Streams of media studies that – without referring to the notion of CSR – have always stressed the importance of considering interrelations between the economic organization of the media and their social and cultural roles and responsibilities are critical theory and the political economy of media and communication.

Karl Marx pointed out that the press has the important social role of serving as a public watchdog. According to Marx the press should be "the public watchdog, the tireless denouncer of those in power, the omnipresent eye, the omnipresent mouthpiece of the people's spirit that jealously guards its freedom" (Marx 1849/1959, 231[7]). Marx furthermore argued that the press should be partial for the oppressed: "it is the duty of the press to come forward on behalf of the oppressed in its immediate neighbourhood" and "to undermine all the foundations of the existing political state of affairs" (Marx 1849/1959, 234[8]). He at the same time recognized that in order to fulfil its important social role, the press needs to be organized in a non-commercial way: "The primary freedom of the press lies in not being a trade" (Marx 1842/1976, 71[9]).

Following Marxian thinking, critical political economy of media and communication departs from the insight that media have a double role in society: they on the one hand are profit-oriented corporations and on the other hand have certain special social and cultural responsibilities. Murdock and Golding point out: "The obvious starting point for a critical political economy of mass communication is the recognition that the mass media are first and foremost industrial and commercial organizations which produce and distribute commodities" (Murdock and Golding 1997, 3f). However, they at the same time recognize that media also have an important ideological role. Murdock and Golding continue: "It is this second ideological dimension of mass media production which gives it its importance and centrality and which requires an approach in terms not only of economics but also of politics" (Murdock and Golding 1997, 4f).

Several critical political economists have highlighted this double role of the media as both economic actors and producers of cultural resources. Oscar Gandy highlights: "The media are seen to have an economic as well as an ideologic dimension" (Gandy 1997, 100). Manfred Knoche (2002) stresses that commercial mass media fulfil four central functions for capitalism: first, mass media realize profits for the media industry itself. Second, they contribute to the realization of profits of other industries by advertising and promoting commodities. Third, capitalist media help to legitimize capitalism and to establish a consumerist climate. Fourth, they contribute to the regeneration and reproduction of labour (Knoche 2002, 106–107). Whereas the first two functions describe media as economic actors, the second two functions relate to the ideological character of capitalist mass media.

Based on this recognition of the double role of media and communication, critical political economists highlight that understanding the media's effects in society requires studying them within the wider context of capitalism. Mosco stresses that critical political economy decentres the media: "Decentering the media means viewing systems of communication as integral to fundamental economic, political, and other material constituents" (Mosco 2009, 66). Herman and McChesney point out the necessity of considering global capitalism or understanding the social role of media: "Only by understanding global corporate capitalism's social and political implications can we possibly make sense of the global media's important social and political role" (Herman and McChesney 1997, 10). Similarly Garnham emphasizes that understanding the capitalist mode of production and its core characteristics such as waged labour and commodity exchange is essential for the study of cultural practices (Garnham 1998, 611). Knoche points out that a critique of the political economy of the media needs to focus on the relationship between media and capitalist society (Knoche 2002, 105). Murdock stresses that critical political economy investigates how "central dynamics of capitalism, and the shifting balances between markets and public provision [. . .] facilitate, comprise or block the building of a truly democratic common culture" (Murdock 1997, 93f).

These statements illustrate that that studying the interrelation between the economic dimensions of media and communication on the one hand, and their social and cultural responsibilities on the other hand, is at the heart of a critical political economy of the media. Based on this orientation critical political economists highlight how economic mechanisms and pressures that are at play in a commercial media system impair the ability of the media to meet their social responsibilities. From this perspective, commercial media are socially irresponsible because their need and desire to generate profit negatively affects economic and cultural production as well as the distribution of media and communication products.

Economic production – media commodities and a culture of exploitation

Golding and Murdock highlight that "the media are first and foremost industrial and commercial organizations" (Golding and Murdock 1973, 207). In a commercial media system, media products are produced as commodities. The production of commodities requires the exploitation of labour power. Fuchs highlights "Media as commodities contain surplus values produced by their non-owners. The goal of the overall process is the self-expansion of money, that is, the accumulation of capital" (Fuchs 2011a, 146).

Nicholas Garnham (1986/2006) argues that surplus in the media industry can either be created by selling media as commodities (e.g. CDs), or by integration of the media industry in the accumulation processes of other industries through advertising (Garnham 1986/2006, 224). Dallas Smythe showed that in the case of the advertising media business model the commodity that is sold by the media is their audience (Smythe 1977/1997, 440). He therefore talks of the "audience commodity" and describes the time that recipients use for consuming media products as working time because "In 'their' time which is sold to the advertisers workers (a) perform essential marketing functions for the producers of consumers' goods and (b) work at the production and reproduction of labour power" (Smythe 1977/1997, 440). Christian Fuchs (2009a, 2010) applied Smythe's model of the audience commodity to the Internet and particularly the so-called social media. He stresses that on social media sites, prosumers are productive workers because they create media content and usage data that is sold in order to generate profit. Thus, the productive labour of prosumers is exploited for purposes of capital accumulation (Fuchs 2010, 191). Thus, fulfilling their role of realizing profits for the media industry (Knoche 2002, 106) requires commercial media to exploit the labour power of media workers and/or media (prod)users.

Cultural production – media ideologies and a culture of conformity

Producing media as commodities affects the cultural aspect of media production. In 1947 Horkheimer and Adorno highlighted that the market mechanisms, i.e. the mechanisms of supply and demand, result in mass deception, the creation of uniformity, conformism and the elimination of every thought on resistance and the "constant reproduction of the same thing" (Horkheimer and Adorno 1947/1997, 134). The reason for that is that market mechanisms ensure that cultural products that do not conform, cease to exist: "Not to conform means to be rendered powerless" (Horkheimer and Adorno 1947/1997, 133). This would create a culture of uniformity and identity: "In the culture industry this imitation finally becomes absolute. Having ceased to be anything but style, it reveals the latter's secret: obedience to the social hierarchy" (Horkheimer and Adorno 1947/1997, 131).

Critical media scholars have shown in detail which myths and ideologies corporate media are promoting (see for example Schiller 1997; McChesney 2004). Edward Herman and Noam Chomsky pointed out how the commercial orientation of the media influences the content of media products. In their propaganda model they identify five news filters that show how "money and power are able to filter out the news fit to print, marginalize dissent, and allow the government and dominant private interests to get their messages across to the public" (Herman and Chomsky 1988, 2). According to this view media tend to exclude everything that does not promise economic success or that questions the corporate model on which today's media's existence rests and thereby establish a culture of conformity.

Distribution – unequal access to media and communication and a culture of exclusion

Exclusion of the deviant is just one way how exclusion works in a corporate media system. Exclusion of those who cannot buy access rights is another way.

The circulation of media and communication products as commodities has as a consequence that only those who can afford to buy these commodities are granted access to media and communication. Critical political economists have shown that trends towards deregulation and privatization, while expanding the possibilities for profit generation, weaken the accessibility of information and communication resources. Nicholas Garnham (1983) for example points out that privately owned information rather serves private profit than the public good: "What we are witnessing is a struggle to turn all information into private property and therefore a source of private profit rather than claimed development of a system to provide information widely and cheaply to all" (Garnham 1983, 19f). Vincent Mosco in the context of the deregulation of the media sector, especially telecommunications, pointed at changes in how the US government sees information: "It no longer tends to see information as a public good and a right of citizenship. Market power, not the need for political democracy, increasingly determines access to communication resources" (Mosco 1994, 117). He therefore speaks of a "class division" between those who can afford access to media and communication and those who cannot (Mosco 1988, 12). One major consequence of the corporate dominance of the media and communication sector is that that access to these resources becomes more unequal.

These divisions of "the digital 'haves' from the 'have-nots'" reflect income inequalities and occur both within and between nations (Murdock and Golding 2002, 122). The fact that in a corporate media system media access becomes structured by income, fetters the empowering potential of media and communication: "the media's embrace by the corporate structure of capitalism has distorted their potential contribution to informing and empowering citizens in an effective democratic structure" (Murdock and Golding 2002, 124).

Herbert Schiller and Anita Schiller (1988) point out that turning access to information into a privilege for those who can afford it threatens the democratic process:

> Transforming information into a saleable good, available only to those with the ability to pay for it, changes the goal of information access from egalitarian to a privileged condition. The consequence of this is that the essential underpinning of a democratic order is seriously damaged. This is the ultimate outcome of commercializing information throughout the social sphere.
>
> (Schiller and Schiller 1988, 154)

Christian Fuchs highlights that the ability to communicate freely is essential for human beings:

> Denying humans to communicate is like denying them to breathe fresh air; it undermines the conditions of their survival. Therefore the communicative commons of society should be available for free (without payment or access requirements) for all and should not be privately owned by a class.
>
> (Fuchs 2011a, 336)

He furthermore highlights that the privatization of the commons, by limiting the ability of individuals to engage in creative production through restricting access to communication and knowledge, also limits positive development of society: "The commercially restricted availability of knowledge limits human self-development and thereby the positive development of society by restricting the creative capacities that emerge when humans engage with the intellectual products of others" (Fuchs 2011a, 338). Through restricting access to media and communication products, commercial media foster exclusion in society and hamper the creation of a democratic common culture.

Based on this brief overview of the research field of the critical political economy of communication, one can conclude that a dialectical perspective on the social responsibilities of the media emphasizes that business interests of media companies tend to undermine the creation of a socially responsible media system: In order to be economically successful, corporate media need to produce media and communication products as commodities that are based on the exploitation of labour power of employees and/or media users; need to produce media content that meets the preferences of the majority and that creates advertising friendly climate; and need to enforce the exclusion from media and communication products and technologies in order to be able to accumulate profit. Commercial media are thus creating a media culture that is based on exploitation, conformity and exclusion.

The ideas advanced by dialectical approaches to the social responsibility of the media are embodied in a real existing alternative to the commercial media model: public broadcasting. The European model of public service broadcasting emerged in Great Britain before World War II (Seneviratne 2006, 26), partly due to the necessity to regulate the limited transmission capacity (McQuail 2010, 177). The birth of public broadcasting coincides with the creation of the British Broadcasting Corporation, the BBC, as a non-commercial public monopoly in 1926 (Seaton 2003, 111; Seneviratne 2006, 26). The establishment of the BBC was based on the conviction that the full potentials of broadcasting could only be achieved if it is "governed by social and not financial priorities" (Seaton 2003, 113). The model of public service broadcasting thus entailed the insight that in order to be able to meet its social responsibilities broadcasting needed to be free from the need to generate profit.

McQuail highlights that in most countries "public service broadcasting refers to a system that is set up by law and generally financed by public funds (often a compulsory license paid by households) and given a large degree of editorial and operating independence" (McQuail 2010, 178). The World Radio and Television Council identified four basic principles of public broadcasting: universality, diversity, independence and distinctiveness (World Radio and Television Council 2001, 11–13). McChesney defines public service broadcasting as

> nonprofit and noncommercial, supported by public funds, ultimately accountable in some legally defined way to the citizenry, aimed at providing a service to the entire population, and one which does not apply commercial principles as the primary means to determine its programming.
>
> (McChesney 1997)

Public broadcasting thus is based on the idea that freedom from commercial necessities allows the production of media products as public goods; the production of media content independent from market pressures; and the making of media products universally accessible. However, since the 1980s the public broadcasting model has been increasingly put under pressure. Seneviratne argues that the deregulation of the broadcasting sector in the 1980s challenged public broadcasting as from then on it had to compete with private broadcasting (Seneviratne 2006, 27). According to McChesney the main reason why public service broadcasting is on the decline is that the increasing acceptance of the neo-liberal belief in the superiority of the self-regulation of the market also occurs in the field of media (McChesney 1997). Murdock and Golding describe the weakening of public service broadcasting as "the most obvious, and distinctly European, feature of media marketization" (Murdock and Golding 1999, 125).

Collin Sparks (1995) points out that what created a crisis of public service broadcasting in the UK was not the introduction of commercial broadcasting channels, which had already happened in the 1950s, but regulatory changes that were initiated by the 1990 UK Broadcasting Act. Between 1954 and 1992 a strong regulatory framework existed, which for example obliged the privately owned Independent Television (ITV) companies to produce a certain amount of socially valuable programmes and to pay a levy that was used for funding public broadcasting (Sparks 1995, 326f). Sparks argues that the UK Broadcasting Act from 1990 eroded this strong regulatory framework and increased economic pressure. According to Sparks it was the starting point for the crisis in public broadcasting in the UK, which consists of a "shift from a public service system towards a commercial system in which there remains a public service element" (Sparks 1995, 340).

Due to the fact that the model of public broadcasting has been weakened by neo-liberal deregulation, the privatization process and the triumph of market ideologies, public broadcasting stations in Europe today have to compete with numerous private radio and television companies and are thus no longer free from market pressures. With the decline of the public service broadcasting model the success of the commercial media becomes complete. The question of how commercial mechanisms affect the social responsibilities of the media in their everyday operations, and what consequences this has for media and communication in the twenty-first century thus becomes ever more pressing.

Conclusion

I began this chapter by outlining a definition of the media and communication industries, which includes media content, media hardware, media software, media distribution technology and the online media sector. Today, the media and communication business is a highly profitable industry. There are 14 media and communication companies among the top 100 companies in the Forbes ranking of the 2000 biggest public companies worldwide.[10] In 2010 these 14 media and communication companies generated a total profit of 157 billion USD, which amounts to 16.5 per cent of the total profits of the top 100 companies. After financial services (30.4 per cent of total profits of the Forbes 100) and oil and gas (21.92 per cent of the total profits of the Forbes 100) they therefore form the third most profitable sector within the 100 biggest companies worldwide.[11] For comparison, the amount of profits these 14 companies made in 2010 is similar to the annual income of countries such as Hungary, with a gross domestic product of 129 billion USD; New Zealand, with a gross domestic product of 140 billion USD, or Peru, with a gross domestic product of 153 billion USD.[12]

This data suggests that the media and communication sector is one of the economically most important sectors. However, looking at company assets provides a different perspective. In terms of assets the financial sector is by far the dominant one, and in 2010 media and communication companies only controlled 0.56 per cent of the assets of Forbes' top 100 companies.

Overall the financial industry thus is the dominant economic sector and the economic importance of media and communication industries should not be overestimated. Nevertheless the provision of media and communication obviously is a highly profitable business. The question therefore arises as to how far this business success is compatible with meeting the social responsibilities of media and communication. Are media and communication companies socially responsible? Do they provide media and communication in a socially responsible way?

In approaching these questions, I reviewed reductionist, projectionist, dualist and dialectical approaches to the social responsibility of media and communication. Table 3.1 summarizes their main characteristics. One observation was that most discussions about media ethics and responsibility focus on media content production only. Such accounts of social responsibility in the media sector thus contribute to what critical scholars have described as "digital sublime" (Mosco 2004) or "technological sublime" (Maxwell and Miller 2012, 7). These concepts highlight that there are certain myths and utopian ideals attached to media, communication and computer products. The material impact media and communication have on society and the environment often remains hidden behind the perceived immateriality of symbols, content, meaning and text. Maxwell and Miller in this context highlight that "The way technology is experienced in daily life is far removed from the physical work and material resources that go into it" (Maxwell and Miller 2012, 7). Looking at the social responsibility of the media only in terms of media content contributes to the technological sublime as it overlooks the various ways in which contemporary media and communication industries have an impact on work, the environment, politics, power, technological innovation, social inclusion/exclusion, etc.

Based on the broad definition of media industries this study deliberately wants to go beyond this limitation. This seems necessary because if anything indicates that we are living in an "information age", it is not primarily the importance of media content but of the way technologically mediated information, communication, and co-operation, telecommunications, computers, mobile phones, etc., shape the way people work, live, play, interact, create, learn, etc.

I argued that reductionist approaches to the social responsibility of the media focus on how engaging in CSR activities yields strategic business advantages. Projectionist approaches believe that commercial media can embody ethical principles in their operations, while dualist approaches fail to recognize any

Table 3.1 Approaches to the social responsibility of the media

Ways of thinking about the social responsibility of the media		Socially responsible media . . .	Representatives
Reductionism	Reduces social responsibilities to profit goals	. . . address social challenges while turning them into strategic business opportunities	Trommershausen 2011
Projectionism	Projects social responsibilities onto profit goals	. . . resist commercial pressures towards irresponsible behaviour by basing their operations on ethical principles and guidelines	American Society of Newspaper Editors 1923; Commission on Freedom of the Press 1947; Christians et al. 2001; Kieran 1998; McManus 1997; Richards 2004; Bardoel and d'Haenens 2004; McQuail 1997
Dualism	Separates profit goals and social responsibilities from each other	. . . simultaneously are economically successful commercial companies and socially responsible	Altmeppen 2011
Dialectics	Describes profit goals and social responsibilities as contradictory	. . . are undermined by commercial pressures. In order to become truly socially responsible creating a non-commercial media system is necessary	Marx 1842/1976, 1749/1959; Murdock and Golding 1997, 1999, 2002, 2005; Golding and Murdock 1973; Gandy 1997; Mosco 1988, 1994, 2009; Herman and McChesney 1997; Murdock 1997; Fuchs 2009a, 2010, 2011a; Garnham 1983, 1986/2006; Smythe 1977/1997; Herman and Chomsky 1988; Schiller and Schiller 1988; Horkheimer and Adorno 1947/1997

interrelations between economic goals and needs and social responsibilities of the media. A dialectical approach is necessary in order to grasp the complex character of the commercial media reality today. The perspective of a critique of the political economy of media and communication, which decentres the media and regards "systems of communication as integral to fundamental economic, political, and other material constituents" (Mosco 2009, 66), seems the most promising for empirically researching the social responsibilities of media and communication in the context of contemporary capitalism. Furthermore this approach allows identifying and studying areas of conflict between the private interest of companies and the public good in the information age.

Based on this perspective I will analyse in the following chapters the CSR communication of global media and communication companies and thereby focus on how they approach the topic of CSR; how they deal with tensions between their economic goals and their social responsibilities; and finally identify challenges and future pathways for media and communication in the twenty-first century.

Notes

1 Online Etymology Dictionary. Medium. Retrieved from http://www.etymonline.com/index.php?allowed_in_frame=0&search=medium&searchmode=none on March 5, 2011.
2 Media CSR Forum. *Who we are*. Retrieved from http://mediacsrforum.org/home.php on March 5, 2011.
3 "Neben allgemeinen normativen Ansprüchen an die gesellschaftliche Verantwortung von Unternehmen darf deren grundsätzlich betriebswirtschaftliche und wettbewerbsorientierte Ausrichtung keinesfalls als zweitrangig angesehen werden" (Trommershausen 2011, 182).
4 "Um diesen Wettbewerbsvorteil tatsächlich generieren zu können, ist die Umsetzung und Kontrolle im Rahmen eines strategischen Managements der Corproate Responsibility notwendig. Nur so können die strategschen Potenziale tatsächlich genutzt und hinsichtlich eines Return on Corporate Responsibility durch den Business Case geprüft werden" (Trommershausen 2011, 182).
5 The European project makeITfair for example has shown in numerous reports that on the one hand unacceptable working conditions exists in the supply chain of media hardware companies and that on the other hand the improper disposal of electronic products creates fundamental threats for human health and the environment. See: http://makeitfair.org/en?set_language=en
6 "Medien 'zahlen' dem Journalismus einen 'Preis' für die Lieferung informativer, aktueller Inhalte" (Altmeppen 2011, 258).
7 Translation: Marxists.org: http://www.marxists.org/archive/marx/works/1849/02/07.htm accessed on March 5, 2011.
8 Translation: Marxists.org: http://www.marxists.org/archive/marx/works/1849/02/07.htm accessed on March 5, 2011.
9 Translation: Marxists.org: http://www.mlwerke.de/me/me01/me01_066.htm accessed on March 5, 2011.
10 These companies are: AT&T (ranked 14), Vodafone (27), IBM (31), Telefonica (31), China Mobile (34), Hewlett Packard (42), Apple (47), Nippon Telegraph and Tel (48), Microsoft (50), Verizon (64), France Telecom (74), Cisco Systems (87), America Movil (88), Deutsche Telecom (92). *Forbes Magazine*. 2011. *The Biggest Public Companies*

2010. Retrieved from http://www.forbes.com/global2000/#p_1_s_arank_All_All_All on June 17, 2011.

11 The media and communication sector in this figure is comprised of the following industries: telecommunications, computer services, computer hardware, software and programming, communication equipment.

12 IMF. 2011. World Economic Outlook Database, April 2011. Retrieved from http://www.imf.org/external/pubs/ft/weo/2011/01/weodata/index.aspx on March 20, 2012.

4   Towards a critical empirical case study of CSR in media and communication industries

In this chapter I develop a framework for a critical empirical study of CSR in the media and communication industries. The general purpose of this study is to investigate how companies deal with conflicts between their economic goals and social responsibilities, and to what extent the way corporations understand and practice CSR can contribute to achieving a social, i.e. a socially responsible, media and communication system for the twenty-first century.

One possible way to gain more insights into CSR approaches, practices and particular challenges for media companies is the study of their CSR communication. CSR codes and reports for a corporation are a means to inform customers, potential employees, shareholders, the media, non-governmental organizations (NGOs), etc. about how its business practices are justifiable in social and ecological terms. These documents thus provide a valuable source for finding out how a company wants to present itself as socially responsible. However, these documents are publicly available and part of the strategic communication of a company. Thus, their value for research is not to gain insights about internal conflicts, debates and decisions related to CSR, but to shed light on how a company aims to be seen by the public. Kaptein notes: "A code clarifies the objectives the company pursues, the norms and values it upholds and what it can be held accountable for" (Kaptein 2004, 13). Carasco and Singh (2003) mention five reasons that lead companies to use CSR codes: enhancement of corporate reputation, information of stakeholders about their ethical commitment, creation of corporate culture and operationalization of values, avoiding fines and sanctions, and development of universal standards that go beyond national law (Carasco and Singh 2003, 72). What is written in CSR reports thus on the one hand provides insights into how companies try to construct themselves as socially responsible and at the same time creates certain standards against which companies can be held accountable.

In the following sections I discuss how to best approach the analysis of CSR reporting in order to contribute valid and meaningful knowledge about social responsibility in the media and communication sector. I will first give an overview of existing studies on CSR reporting and highlight some major shortcomings of existing research on that topic. Based on this literature review I will proceed with specifying research questions. In a next step I suggest and operationalize critical content analysis as a research method.

Studying CSR reporting

Chapter 3 illustrated that CSR in the media industry has not been a popular research topic. It is thus not surprising that only a few empirical studies about CSR reporting of media companies exist. Jiran Hou and Bryan H. Reber (2011) conducted a content analysis of the CSR reports of the 10 largest US media companies. They found that 9 of the 10 companies disclosed CSR information, 7 companies reported on environmental protection, 8 companies disclosed information about their community relations, 7 companies stressed that they try to foster diversity, 3 companies reported on their employee relations, 4 companies referred to human rights and 6 companies mentioned media related CSR activities (Hou and Reber 2011, 167f). Anke Trommershausen (2011) conducted a qualitative content analysis of CSR reports of 12 media companies. Trommershausen argued that the studied media companies would partly make use of strategic potentials that emerge in the context of a corporate responsibility of communication and culture. In particular telecommunications and information companies would recognize media-specific corporate responsibilities, such as fostering digital inclusion, and use them in their CSR strategies (Trommershausen 2011, 292).

Studies about how media companies report about CSR are rare. However, the analysis of corporate self-disclosure is a popular method within CSR research in general. Existing studies on CSR reporting differ in various respects: first, regarding the chosen object of investigation, second, regarding the topics of analysis, third, regarding employed research methods, and fourth, regarding the goal of analysis.

- In respect to the object of investigation there exist four approaches: first, studies that focus on a specific CSR topic, such as environmental reporting (Jose and Lee 2007, 311). Second, studies which investigate a specific industry (Chaudhri and Wang 2007). Third, studies which chose the largest corporations worldwide as their research objects (Abbott and Monsen 1979; Carasco and Singh 2003; Kaptein 2004; Morhardt 2009). Fourth, and the majority, studies which analyse a specific country or the comparison between countries (Gray, Kouhy and Lavers 1995; Adams, Hill and Roberts 1998; Maignan and Ralston 2002; Perrini 2005; Hartman, Rubin and Dhanda 2007; Golob and Bartlett 2007; Nielsen and Thomsen 2007).
- Regarding the topics of analysis the prevailing focus lies on the identification of CSR themes mentioned in reports (see for example Abbott and Monsen 1979; Gray, Kouhy and Lavers 1995; Carasco and Singh 2003; Kaptein 2004; Perrini 2005; Jose and Lee 2007; Chaudhri and Wang 2007; Hartman, Rubin and Dhanda 2007). Some other studies try to identify rhetorical patterns within corporate reports (Maignan and Ralston 2002; Nielsen and Thomsen 2007; Castelló and Lozano 2011). Others investigate the motivations that drive managers to compile CSR reports (Wilmshurst and Frost 2000; Spence 2007)
- The method that is most frequently used for analysing corporate reporting is quantitative content analysis (see for example Abbott and Monsen 1979; Svales 1988; Gray, Kouhy and Lavers 1995; Maignan and Ralston 2002;

Carasco and Singh 2003; Kaptein 2004; Perrini 2005; Jose and Lee 2007; Chaudhri and Wang 2007; Hartman, Rubin and Dhanda 2007; Morhardt 2009). An exception is a study by Nielsen and Thomsen (2007) that was based on Critical Discourse Analysis. Some other studies used surveys (Wilmshurst and Frost 2000) or interviews with managers in order to learn more about the motivations behind and practices of writing CSR reports (Spence 2007; Castelló and Lozano 2011).

- The goal of most studies on CSR reporting is purely descriptive. They show which topics appear in CSR reports and highlight differences between countries and regions. As Morhardt argues, the aim of most studies is documentation: "The main purpose of most of these studies is simply documentation of the types and quantity of sustainability reporting done by various subsets of companies at the time of the study" (Morhardt 2009, 437). Many studies on CSR reporting do not even attempt to explain the wider implication of their research, e.g. regarding the usefulness and effectiveness of CSR. Such research does not answer some of the most pressing questions in this field, such as for example whether CSR actually goes beyond image improvements and cosmetic reforms, or whether the current form of voluntary self-reporting is reasonable or a more regulation centred approach is necessary.

Based on these insights on the current state of the study of CSR reporting, in the next section I define research questions that will guide the study at hand.

Research questions

The research questions of this study focus on three main topics: the way companies conceptually approach CSR, potential gaps between CSR rhetoric and CSR practices, and particular social responsibility challenges for media and communication in the twenty-first century. For each of these areas I identified research questions that intend to overcome shortcomings of existing CSR research.

CSR approaches

In the light of the dominance of quantitative studies of CSR reporting (see for example Abbott and Monsen 1979; Svales 1988; Gray, Kouhy and Lavers 1995; Maignan and Ralston 2002; Carasco and Singh 2003; Kaptein 2004; Perrini 2005; Chaudhri and Wang 2007; Jose and Lee 2007; Hartman, Rubin and Dhanda 2007; Morhardt 2009) an important task is to investigate not only which CSR topics companies address but how they conceptualize the concept of CSR. The number of studies that have taken a more qualitative approach is relatively low. Castelló and Lozano (2011) analysed 93 reports from 25 companies. They could identify 17 themes, which they grouped into three rhetorical strategies: strategic, institutional and dialectic (Castelló and Lozano 2011, 17): "strategic rhetoric seeks pragmatic legitimacy based on a firms economic rationale; institutional rhetoric, by contrast refers to cognitive legitimacy; while dialectical rhetoric aims to establish moral legitimacy" (Castelló and Lozano 2011, 24). They found a dominance of strategic and institutional rhetoric but a trend towards the growing importance of dialectical rhetoric (Castelló and Lozano 2011, 23). Maignan and Ralston (2002) analysed 400 corporate websites of US and Europe based corporations and identified differences in the structure of argumentation (Maignan and Ralston 2002, 511). Nielsen and Thomsen in their analysis of the CSR disclosure of six Danish companies were interested in the self-presentation of these companies, their reporting strategies, dominant concepts and discourses (Nielsen and Thomsen 2007, 26). They identified two types of discourses: "the public discourse on social responsibility and the business discourse on profit maximization or strategy" (Nielsen and Thomsen 2007, 39).

As I have argued earlier the difference between different theoretical approaches to CSR results from different views on how to relate profit goals on the one hand and social and environmental responsibilities on the other hand. There exist four possible ways of relating these two dimensions: reductionism, projectionism, dualism, or dialectics (see Chapter 2). Departing from this typology of theoretical CSR approaches the question remains as to how far these approaches are present in corporate understandings of CSR. I hypothesize that while it is likely to find reductionist, projectionist and dualist descriptions, a dialectical approach is not to be found in company reports since it challenges the very idea that profit-oriented companies can ever become socially responsible. This study wants to increase understanding of how CSR is understood and conceptualized in the corporate world by asking which CSR narratives and approaches media and communication companies use, and in which way they thereby relate profit goals and social responsibilities. The first research question therefore is:

> RQ 1: Which justifications and narratives do media and communication companies use in their reports for describing their commitment to CSR? How is the relation between economic goals on the one hand and social and ecological goals on the other hand represented in the CSR reports of media and communication companies?

CSR practices

Thus far hardly any attempts have been made to compare corporate self-descriptions regarding CSR with descriptions by others. One exception is Bartkus' and Glassman's study that compared corporate mission statements with the KLD social issues rating (Bartkus and Glassman 2008, 211). One main criticism of CSR is that it remains limited to corporate communication strategy for image improvement and does in fact not have any or only limited effects regarding the sustainability of actual business practices (Roberts 2003, 257; Boje 2008, 9; Hanlon and Fleming 2009, 938). Considering this criticism the fact that the study of CSR reports has thus far mainly relied solely on corporate self-reporting is surprising. Taking into account how others evaluate the degree of responsibility or irresponsibility of particular business practices allows challenging corporate self-description and adding the dimension of ideology to the study of CSR reporting. By comparing corporate self-descriptions and descriptions by others it might become possible to gain some insights into the truthfulness, completeness and limits of corporate self-reporting. Such an approach can be used to reveal which issues companies do not report about, whether reports contain distorted, varnished or wrong descriptions of business practices and how companies react to criticism. The aim of considering not only corporate self-reporting but a variety of alternative sources is to arrive at a more nuanced and multifaceted picture about CSR reporting practices. For this purpose I focus on three main aspects: first, it is important to learn more about the economic context in which CSR activities are pursued. It is interesting to know how a company's CSR activities relate to a company's business model, to its economic success, to the particular market it operates in etc. Considering this economic context allows for a more integrated discussion of CSR, which avoids discussing a company's CSR activities in isolation from its economic activities. Second, it is necessary to find out if there exists any criticism of the business practices of a particular company that questions its social responsibility. In a third step it becomes possible to investigate how controversial topics are presented in corporate self-descriptions and whether and how companies react to criticism. Research questions 2–4 are:

> RQ 2: Which business models do media and communication companies have and what does the economic situation of companies and sectors within the media and communication business look like?

> RQ 3: What criticisms of business practices of media companies exist?

> RQ 4: How do companies discuss controversial topics in their CSR reports and respond to criticism regarding their social and/or environmental impact?

CSR challenges

Only a few empirical accounts of CSR reporting of media and communication companies exist (Hou and Reber 2011; Trommershausen 2011). While both the degree of theoretical discussion and the number of empirical studies of CSR in the media sector is low, scholars agree that media companies have certain special responsibilities that go beyond those of other industries (Media CSR Forum 2008; Tommershausen 2011). In addition this view is also common among media professional as a study by Gulyás (2009) shows. The results of a survey conducted among UK media professionals showed that almost 90 per cent of the respondents "agreed that media firms share CSR issues with companies in other industrial sectors, but that they also hand some extra media-specific issues" (Gulyás 2009, 660).

While identifying certain CSR topics that are particularly relevant for media industries is certainly an important starting point, this study aims at going deeper into the analysis by indentifying not only CSR topics, but specific social responsibility challenges for the media sector in the twenty-first century. Identifying social responsibility challenges for media and communication companies requires analysing both self-descriptions of media companies as well as descriptions and criticisms by independent corporate watchdogs. Based on these different and probably partly conflicting descriptions it might be possible to tease out which social responsibilities of media companies are particularly important and how far companies are able to meet them. Research question 5 therefore is:

> RQ 5: What are particular challenges for a socially responsible media and communication system in the twenty-first century?

Not all of these five research questions can be answered by analysing CSR reports. The research design and the selection of research question are intended to analyse the CSR approaches and practices of media and communication companies from different perspectives. Research questions 1 and 4 will be addressed based on an analysis of CSR reports; addressing research question 3 requires additional research into information provided by corporate watchdogs; research question 2 furthermore requires including financial company reports and industry statistics. Research question 5 will be answered based on the assessment of all of these sources (see Table 4.1).

The critical study of documents

To answer these research questions, this study will rely on the analysis of documents in the form of CSR reports, annual company reports, research reports, NGO reports, media reports, etc. Several authors have highlighted the relevance of documents for social research (Prior 2003, 2004, 2008; Atkinson and Coffey 2004; Wolff 2004; Punch 2005, 184–186; Jupp 2006). Prior notes that although documents are key sources for social scientific inquiry, their use is seldom described in methods literature (Prior 2008, 230). She proposes content analysis as a fruitful method for studying documents: "The most straightforward approach to document content involves the adoption of some form of content analysis" (Prior 2008, 230).

Victor Jupp (2006) has advanced the idea of critical document analysis. According to Jupp "Critical analysis is characterized by not taking for granted what is being said in a document and what is often assumed to be 'knowledge'" (Jupp 2006, 289). As such explanations that are put forward in documents should be challenged and alternative explanations sought (Jupp 2006, 284). Jupp stresses that the critical analysis of documents does not follow a standardized procedure: "The method does not exhibit the formal protocols of quantitative content analysis (categorizing, coding, counting), but is a critical reading of texts aimed at uncovering how problems are defined, what explanations are put forward and what is seen as the preferred solution" (Jupp 2006, 284).

Taking a critical approach to the study of CSR reporting can help to overcome the limitation to descriptive analysis in the study of CSR reporting. It allows questioning of corporate self-descriptions and assessment of how far they adequately represent actual corporate practices.

Table 4.1 Research foci, questions and objects of analysis

Research foci	Research questions	Object of analysis
CSR approaches	RQ 1: Which justifications and narratives do media and communication companies use in their reports for describing their commitment to CSR? How is the relation between economic goals on the one hand and social and ecological goals on the other hand represented in the CSR reports of media and communication companies?	CSR reports
CSR practices	RQ 2: Which business models do media and communication companies have and what does the economic situation of companies and sectors within the media and communication business look like?	Industry statistics and financial company reports
	RQ 3: What criticisms of business practices of media companies exist?	Reports by corporate watchdogs
	RQ 4: How do companies discuss controversial topics in their CSR reports and respond to criticism regarding their social and/ or environmental impact?	CSR reports
CSR challenges	RQ 5: What are particular challenges for a socially responsible media and communication system in the twenty-first century?	CSR reports Reports by corporate watchdogs Industry statistics and financial company reports

Critical social research

Critical theory is first and foremost known for its critical studies about various aspects of social life that are analysed in the context of a capitalist society. Drawing on the work of Karl Marx, representatives of the so-called Frankfurt School established a philosophically grounded framework for a critical theory of society.

Based on the work of Max Horkheimer, Theodor W. Adorno and Herbert Marcuse its main characteristics can be described as follows: critical theory is based on dialectical thinking that rejects one-dimensional logic and conceives social phenomena as complex and dynamic; it considers social relations that lie behind mere appearances and analyses social phenomena in the context of societal totality; it is characterized by an humanist orientation, an interest in human emancipation and the desire to create a society without domination and oppression in which all human beings can live a self-determined life; and it perceives social structures and phenomena as historically specific results of human practice and therefore as changeable (Marcuse 1937/1989; Horkheimer 1937/2002a, 2002b; Adorno 1962/1976).

Despite its philosophical roots and the high importance given to theory building critical theory never rejected empirical social research (Adorno 1972/1995, 538). Adorno points out that Marx's and Engels' work contained rich empirical evidence (Adorno1972/1995, 540). Examples are Marx's descriptions about the working day in first volume of *Capital* (1867/1990) and Engels' work on *The Condition of the Working Class in England* (1892/2009). Adorno argued that he considered it highly necessary to foster studies that combine theory and empirical research: "what should be fundamental, namely the combination of empirical investigations with theoretically central questions, has—despite isolated attempts—not yet been achieved" (Adorno 1957/1976, 83).

However, Adorno at the same time was highly critical of the way empirical research was approached and executed. He therefore stressed the necessity of approaching empirical research in a critical, theory driven way and to adapt empirical methods for this purpose: "empirical methods can be functionally redirected – to use that expression – to provide a critical, empirical perception of society, albeit one that presupposes theory" (Adorno 1968/2002, 140). He pointed out that the Frankfurt School's critique has been directed against blind empiricism and not against empirical research as such: critical theory wants to

> defend experience against empiricism, to develop a less restricted, less narrow and reified notion of experience. Aim of the controversy is not yes or no to empirical research, but the interpretation of empirical research itself, particularly the so-called empirical methods.
>
> (Adorno 1972/1995, 545f (translation[1]))

Among the representatives of the Frankfurt School it was mainly Adorno himself, who in a debate with Karl Popper, which became known as the positivism dispute in German sociology (Adorno 1969/1976), clarified some implication of critical theory for empirical research. Based on Adorno's work, in the following I briefly highlight some important elements of critical social research.

- *Critique of society*: In his contribution to the positivism dispute Adorno argued against a positivist notion of critique, which merely focuses on the "reformulation of contradictory statements for the sake of consistency in the scientific realm" (Adorno 1962/1976, 115). He argued that "Such logicity, by shifting the real substance, can become false" (Adorno 1962/1976, 115). Critical theory on the contrary would not seek to eliminate contradictions but regard them as an expression of antagonistic social relations as part of the "structural constitution of society itself" (Adorno 1962/1976, 115). Critique for Adorno should never be reduced to a merely formal critique of categories but needs to aim at the material critique of society: "The critical path is not merely formal but also material. If its concepts are to be true, critical sociology is, according to its own idea, necessarily also a critique of society" (Adorno 1962/1976, 114). Adorno argued that critical theory adheres to a certain "desire for disenchantment. It seeks to raise the stone under which the monster lies brooding" (Adorno 1957/1976, 68), while on the contrary, "sociological research into facts opposes such a desire" (Adorno 1957/1976, 68).

Critical social research thus is based on an understanding of critique as the critique of society. Integrating this critical perspective into the realm of empirical research requires embedding it into theory.

- *Theory-drivenness*: Another important characteristic of critical social research for Adorno was that it is guided by theory: "Empirical social research ought to dismiss completely the superstition that research must begin like a *tabula rasa*, where the data that are assembled in an unconditioned manner are prepared" (Adorno 1957/1976, 82). For Adorno the benefits of empirical research can only unfold in the context of theory: "Critical social research wants to make empirical research finally fully productive through deciphering it theoretically" (Adorno 1972/1995, 545 (translation[2])). This theory for Adorno on the one hand is necessary for identifying relevant research questions and generating hypotheses and on the other hand is needed for interpreting results. Critical theory provides a rich resource for developing a critical, theoretical background as well as for the critical interpretation of empirical data.

- *Dialectical thinking*: According to Adorno complex dialectical thinking is necessary for conducting critical social research. He argued that dialectics "simply represents a more logical way of thinking" (Adorno 1968/2002, 83). Dialectical thinking would be essential for interpreting facts critically instead of just accepting their existence. Therefore for Adorno "the real sin of positivism is to cut off this logic of thought, this advance of a theory driven logic by its own inner necessity, in favour of a naïve and stubborn adherence to immediate facts" (Adorno 1968/2002, 83).

- *Primacy of the object over the method*: One of Adorno's main points of criticism of positivist social research is that it would foster a "primacy of the method over the object" (Adorno 1957/1976, 73). He argued that positivist studies often place too much emphasis on questions of reliability and viability at the expense of the suitability of the research instrument for answering the questions of interest (Adorno 1968/2002, 73). He criticizes the "overvaluation of method as such, for the sake of its reliability, in isolation from any interest in specific subject matter" (Adorno 1968/2002, 75). According to Adorno this obsession with methodological questions constitutes a form of instrumental reason because the method, "the instruments or means of thought have become independent of the purposes of thought, have become reified" (Adorno 1968/2002, 76).

Primacy should be given to the actual research interests, and methods as an instrument should be designed in a way that allows gaining most substantial insights into these specific topics: "they should be so used that they take on emphasis from the meaning of the subject matter, rather than making themselves independent of it" (Adorno 1968/2002, 73).

• *Critical interpretation and ideology critique*: The way data are interpreted probably marks the most decisive difference between positivist and critical social research. Adorno emphasizes the importance of regarding empirical facts as the final source of truth: "facts in society are not the last thing to which knowledge might attach itself, since they themselves are mediated through society" (Adorno 1962/1976, 112).

Habermas pointed out that social research therefore does not limit itself to collecting facts and discussing their technical or practical application (Habermas 1968/1971, 191), but instead follows an emancipatory interest (Habermas 1968/1971, 198, 347) and interprets them based on critical theory. The insight that facts are not the definite source for understanding society leads social research that is inspired by critical theory to interpret them in the context of the totality of society. Societal totality on the one hand includes fundamental social structures and principles, which Adorno called social objectivity (Adorno 1972/1995, 544). On the other hand it includes not yet realized social potentials. Marcuse argues: "All such distinctions take place and change within the framework of the totality of society. This framework itself is never transcended, not even in concepts such as essence and potentiality" (Marcuse 1936/1968, 83). Placing empirical facts in the context of societal totality thus means analysing them in relation to (a) social objectivity and (b) not yet achieved societal possibilities:

a)   Empirical facts and social objectivity. Facts as they are collected through empirical research are not pure and absolute but only exist in and are shaped by a specific social context. Adorno therefore stressed that facts found through empirical investigation are conditioned by society: "The given, the facts which, in accordance with its methods, it encounters as something final, are not themselves final but rather are conditioned" (Adorno 1957/1976, 84f).

This does not mean that empirical facts are irrelevant for critical research. But only by analysing facts within the context of social structures empirical social research can generate substantial knowledge about society. Adorno argued: "The confrontation of subjective opinions with those objective moments, results in something more essential then the tabula-rasa-method, for which opinion is king, like the seller supposedly is on the market" (Adorno1972/1995, 545 (translation[3])).

Empirical facts are a means for uncovering ideological operations within society: "since even ideologies, necessary false consciousness, are a part of social reality with which anyone who wishes to recognize the latter must be acquainted" (Adorno 1957/1976, 85). When comparing subjective opinions with objective social structures social research enters the realm of ideology critique:

> The differences which thereby emerge between social objectivity and the consciousness of the subjectivity, no matter in what form this consciousness may be generally distributed, mark a place at which empirical social research reaches knowledge of society—the knowledge of ideologies, of their genesis and of their function.
>
> (Adorno 1957/1976, 83)

Knowledge about society includes knowledge about the operation of ideologies.

b) Empirical facts and societal possibility. Critical theory also does not consider social reality as absolute and unchangeable. Considering the tension between the existing (*das Bestehende*) and the possible is one important characteristic of critical thinking. From the perspective of critical theory what exists is not necessarily what is right. Marcuse argued that through relating what exists to what is possible critique becomes possible: "Measured against their real potentialities, the facts reveal themselves to be the 'bad' manifestations of a content which must be realized by doing away with these manifestations in opposition to the interests and powers connected with them" (Marcuse 1936/1968, 71).

A critical interpretation of empirical results thus needs to consider their historical character and analyse empirical reality not just as what it is but as what it could be: "It must dissolve the rigidity of the temporally and spatially fixed object into a field of tension of the possible and the real: each one, in order to exist, is dependent upon the other" (Adorno 1957/1976, 69). Critical social research thus also regards facts as an indicator for the possible. According to Adorno, critical social research "perceives in the facts themselves the tendency which reaches out beyond them. That is the function of philosophy in empirical social research" (Adorno 1957/1976, 85). For Adorno a dialectics of theory and empirical research is necessary for adequately grasping both essence and appearance: "If the task of a theory of society is to relativize critically the cognitive value of appearance, then conversely it is the task of empirical research to protect the concept of essential laws from mythologization" (Adorno 1957/1976, 84).

The fact that critical empirical research questions facts and interprets them in the light of social objectivity and social possibility means that critical empirical research always entails a moment of ideology critique. The term ideology has been widely used in different ways. The following excursus shall therefore contribute to clarifying the meaning of the concept of ideology.

Ideology and its critique

The notion of ideology has been defined in various different ways (for a discussion see Herkommer 2005; Eagelton 2007; Rehmann 2008). Sebastian Sevignani (2009, 29) points out that two different ways of approaching the topic of ideology exist: some theorists are interested in the question how ideology is generated (e.g. Gramsci; Laclau and Mouffe), others are more concerned with the content of ideology and ideological consciousness (e.g. Lukács and the representatives of the Frankfurt School). According to Herkommer (2005, 32), the most important division within the theory of ideology can be drawn between a broad and a narrow notion of ideology: while the former defines ideology as worldview, the latter considers ideology as false consciousness.

Similarly Karl Mannheim distinguished a particular and a total understanding of the term ideology: as a particular concept the term ideology is used to describe the ideas of an opponent as "more or less conscious disguises of the real nature of a situation, the true recognition of which would not be in accord with his interests" (Mannheim 1929/2002, 49). The total conception on the other hand refers "to the ideology of an age or of a concrete historico-social group" (Mannheim 1929/2002, 49). According to Mannheim all knowledge is socially determined and therefore it would be "hardly possible to avoid this general formulation of the total conception of ideology according to which the thought of all parties in all epochs is of an ideological character" (Mannheim 1929/2002, 69). Adopting a general formulation of the total conception of ideology would transform the theory of ideology into the sociology of knowledge (Mannheim 1929/2002, 69).

Adorno criticized the total conception of ideology because it would neutralize its critical edge:

> But the so-called total concept of ideology, and the elimination of the distinction between true and untrue, does not correspond to the classical doctrine of ideologies, if one might call it that. It represents a degenerate form of the latter. It allies itself with the attempt to blunt the critical edge of that doctrine and to neutralize it to a branch in the domain of science.
>
> (Adorno 1962/1976, 115)

Similarly also Horkheimer, in his discussion of Mannheim's concept of ideology, argued against a general notion of ideology: "If all thought as such is to be characterized as ideological, it becomes apparent that ideology, just like 'particularity', signifies nothing other than inadequacy to eternal truth" (Horkheimer 1930/1995, 145). For critical theorists such as Adorno, Horkheimer and Marcuse the possibility of a distinction between truth and falseness therefore is essential for the concept of ideology. Marcuse highlighted "in contrast to all other theories, materialist theory, precisely by virtue of its guiding interest, advances a claim of truth for which value-free positivism affords absolutely no basis" (Marcuse 1936/1988, 77). The concept of ideology of the Frankfurt School entails a claim of truth and is connected to the antagonistic reality of capitalism. Their understanding of ideology therefore is not just "particular" in the sense of denoting the ideas of any opponent (Mannheim 1929/2002, 49), but normative and based on a distinction between objective truth and falseness.

Representatives of the Frankfurt School defined ideology as "false consciousness" (Marcuse 1962/1978, 324). Their understanding of ideology was dialectical – being at the same time true and false. Adorno described ideology as "a consciousness which is objectively necessary and yet at the same time false, as the intertwining of truth and falsehood, which is just as distinct from the whole truth as it is from the pure lie" (Adorno 1972, 189). For Adorno, false consciousness would be objectively necessary because the falseness would not just be a matter of thinking, but a matter of reality that would be false from a normative perspective. At the same time the values an ideology refers to, such as freedom or equality, could be true in a normative sense, while false in assuming that they are already realized. Adorno calls this the dialectical problem of ideology: "ideologies are indeed false consciousness but not only false. [. . .] They can be true 'in themselves,' as the ideas of freedom, humanity, and justice are, but still they present themselves as though they were already realized" (Adorno 1972, 198).

Similarly Georg Lukács described the notion of "false consciousness" as twofold dialectically determined. On the one hand false consciousness would be subjectively right as it reflects the specific social life context of individuals but at the same time would be objectively wrong (Lukács 1923/1971, 50). The dialectics of false consciousness now means that at the same time it is wrong at the subjective level because it fails in fulfilling its own goals, and right on the objective level as it contributes to the realization the aims of society:

> On the other hand, we may see the same consciousness as something which fails subjectively to reach its self-appointed goals, while furthering and realising the objective aims of society of which it is ignorant and which it did not choose.
>
> (Lukács 1923/1971, 50)

This dialectic of false consciousness also characterized Karl Marx's discussion of ideology. In "The German ideology" Marx described material life processes as the roots of ideological thinking: "we set out from real active men, and on the basis of their real life-process we demonstrate the development of the ideological reflexes an echoes of this life-process" (Marx 1846/2004, 47). Thus for Marx the falseness of thinking is a consequence of the falseness of being: "In all ideology men and their circumstances appear upside-down as in a camera obscura, this phenomena arises just as much from their historical life-process

as the inversion of objects on the retina does from their physical life-process"
(Marx 1846/2004, 47).

For Marx, ideology, however, is not only created though the experience of a
false life process but also through the intellectual force of the ruling class, which
possesses the means for advancing and promoting certain ideas that are in its own
interest:

> The ideas of the ruling class are in every epoch the ruling ideas, i.e. the class
> which is the ruling material force of society, is at the same time its ruling
> intellectual force. The class which has the means of material production at its
> disposal, has control at the same time over the means of mental production,
> so that thereby, generally speaking, the ideas of those who lack the means of
> mental production are subject to it.
>
> (Marx 1846/2004, 64)

From this critical conception of ideology its capacity to stabilize the status quo
and to secure the interest of the ruling class through creating subjective identification with an objectively wrong social system is central. False consciousness
adapts to the status quo and generates a belief in its rightness. Marcuse highlighted the stabilizing role of ideology for the capitalist system: "In the advanced
areas of industrial society an 'inner' identification with the system exists even for
the 'disadvantaged, a positive thinking and acting, which deeply protects those
societal institutions" (Marcuse 1962/1978, 326 (translation[4]).

Because of this stabilizing quality of false consciousness, from the perspective of critical theory the critique of ideology becomes essential. Adorno conceptualizes ideology critique as an immanent critique that reveals the inability
of capitalist society to meet its own values and standards: ideology critique

> is the negation defined in the Hegelian sense, the confrontation of the spir-
> itual with its realization, and has as its presupposition the distinction of the
> truth or falsity of the judgment just as much as the requirement for truth in
> that which is criticized.
>
> (Adorno 1972, 191)

From the perspective of Mannheim's sociology, ideology just refers to the social
determination of all knowledge, independent of the question of whether a certain
social reality and the consciousness, which is based on it, is true or false. Based on
this general understanding of ideology, ideology critique becomes obsolete. From
the perspective of critical theory on the contrary, ideology is a notion of critique.
It is used to denote those ways of thinking that conceal the falseness of capitalist
social relations and thereby help to stabilize them. The critique of ideology therefore is essential: "The dissolution of ideology as an alteration of reflexive disposi-
tions of the ruled class is not in itself the political action that sublates domination,
but it is one element in the learning process that could lead to it" (Ritsert 1972,
97 (translation[5]).

Critical content analysis

The method I have chosen in order to study the CSR reporting of media and communication companies is based on content analysis. Mayring notes that "The goal of content analysis is the systematic examination of communicative material" (Mayring 2004, 266; see also Wright 1986, 125; Berg 2001, 240; Julien 2008, 120; Babbie 2010, 333).

Krippendorff defines six components of content analysis (Krippendorff 2004, 83) which would be "undoubtedly present in qualitative research as well, albeit less explicitly so" (Krippendorff 2004, 87). These six components are: unitizing, sampling, recording/coding, reducing data, abductively inferring contextual phenomena, narrating. According to Hsieh and Shannon (2005, 1285) the execution of a qualitative content analysis involves the following steps: formulating research questions, selecting a sample, defining categories, outlining the coding process and coder training, implementing the coding process, determining trustworthiness, analysing results.

Qualitative content analysis, which aims at explicating content and structures of meaning of a text, seems to be a suitable tool for answering the research question of this study. However, it lacks the critical intent, which is an important element of the study at hand. In this section I therefore attempt to contribute to further developing qualitative content analysis into a critical content analysis (CCA).

Jürgen Ritsert (1972) made such an attempt when proposing to use content analysis as a method for ideology critique. He acknowledged that Kracauer (1952/1953) in his critique of quantitative content analysis made an important contribution to freeing content analysis from its positivist guise and developing an approach to content analysis that is more open for the examination of context, latent meaning and singular cases. However, he argued that the strict rejection of a quantitative approach would be counterproductive for a critical endeavour. According to Ritsert an ideology-critical content analysis should also include frequency counting if this seems useful for a specific purpose (Ritsert 1972, 27f). Since Ritsert's work on this topic in the 1970s, hardly any attempts have been made for advancing content analysis as a critical research method.

Following Ritsert a starting point for such an endeavour is not to focus on the distinction between qualitative and quantitative content analysis but to instead develop a CCA. Based on the characteristics of critical social research that I described above, it is possible to define some elements of CCA:

- *Critique of society*: CCA is critical in the sense described in "Critical social research" above. This means that it examines the workings of oppression and domination in society and tries to find ways to overcome them in order to establish a society in which domination ceases to exist and all human potentials can be realized. This critical intent guides the research process from the stage of planning a research design, to selecting a research sample, choosing categories and units to the final interpretation of results.

- *Theory-drivenness*: CCA is embedded within a strong theoretical framework. In this study the theory-drivenness was achieved by using the theoretical discussion of CSR theories (Chapter 2) and the role of media in society (Chapter 3) as a foundation for the empirical study.
- *Dialectical thinking*: CCA uses dialectical thinking as a guiding principle. This avoids linear, one-dimensional thinking and instead regards social phenomena as complex and contradictory. It for example allows the identification of both negative and positive potentialities, truth and falseness in a certain phenomenon. In conducting a content analysis dialectical thinking can help to deal with contradictions found in a text and to interpret them in relation to an antagonistic social reality. Ritsert (1972) argued that an ideology-critical content analysis should expect to find contradictory levels and contexts of meaning (Ritsert 1972, 88).

   Furthermore it is important to conceive the relation between text and social reality in a dialectical way. This idea is also an important element of critical discourse analysis: Fairclough and Wodak argue that "we can only make sense of the salience of discourse in contemporary social processes and power relations by recognizing that discourse constitutes society and culture as well as being constituted by them" (Fairclough and Wodak 1997, 273). By recognizing that the texts and ideas that are manifested in them are an expression of society and at the same time contribute to the shaping of society, it becomes evident that they are an important source for critical social research.

- *Primacy of the object over the method*: CCA avoids methodological fetishism by adapting research methods in order to best suit the research object. For this study giving the object of study primacy over the method meant adapting the framework of content analysis in order to best fit the research question. This on the one hand was achieved by giving content analysis a critical edge. On the other hand this also required transcending the boundaries of a classical content analysis, challenging the analysed texts (company CSR reports) by comparing them to alternative sources. The comparison between corporate self-descriptions and description by others creates room for critique and matches the ideology-critical intent of critical social research. It reflects the intent of critical social research of looking behind subjective accounts of reality. Including various sources and shifting between different vantage points in analysing CSR reports provides CCA with the necessary basis for a critical interpretation of results.

- *Critical coding and interpretation*: The critical intent in CCA is also reflected in the process of coding texts and interpreting results. A critical approach to content analysis requires interpreting the results of the coding process in the context of social totality. This requires looking at the context of (a) social objectivity and the (b) social possibility:

   a) *Texts and social objectivity*: Conducting a CCA requires analysing text in the context of contemporary society. This means that a CCA does not entirely rely on the subjective and context-based content found in a specific text but analyses a text in the light of theory and other empirical facts. In this study this has been achieved by challenging the content of the analysed texts (CSR reports of media and communication companies) with other texts and with empirical context data (see Table 4.1).

The goal of the study at hand thus is not to simply find out what companies write about CSR but to reveal what corporate accounts of CSR might tell about the current phase of capitalist society and the dominant commercial media and communication system.

b) *Texts and societal possibility*: CCA does not stop with revealing the social meaning of texts but also evaluates these results in the light of social actuality and social potentiality. This means that for critical social research it is not enough to identify and describe certain social phenomena but crucial to reveal their repressive and/or emancipatory potentials. An important question for critical social research thus is in how far a certain social phenomenon, which could be described through empirical research, stabilizes domination in society and/or advances human emancipation and self-determination. Critical social research not only describes what certain social phenomena are, but what they could be. It therefore tries to identify elements within them that point towards their actual potentials and therefore could be a starting point for emancipatory transformation.

The following section describes how this approach of a CCA can be operationalized for the study of CSR reports of media and communication companies.

Operationalization: a CCA of CSR reporting

The planning of a CCA can resort to methodological guidelines for qualitative content analysis (Mayring 2000, 4–6; 2010, 60; Krippendorff 2004, 83; Hsieh and Shannon 2005, 1285). Essential tasks therefore are the selection of a sample and the definition of units and categories. For the purpose of this study furthermore it is necessary to describe the selection of alternative sources that will be used for challenging corporate self-descriptions. The following sections thus describe the sampling process, the selection of alternative sources, and the definition of units and categories.

Sampling

The sampling process consisted of two phases: first, I chose the companies to be included in this study. Second, I decided to select one CSR topic for each company that could be studied in detail based on an analysis and comparison of corporate self-descriptions as well as watchdog descriptions. Both the selection of cases and the selection focus areas are described below.

Selection of cases

The CSR reports of the leading worldwide media and communication companies make up the parent population of this study. There are two main reasons for choosing the biggest worldwide media companies: first, these companies in economic terms are the most successful media companies in the world. It is important to examine how this economic success relates to social and ecological responsibility. Due to their success the leading companies are furthermore likely to be considered as role models for smaller media companies that try to compete with larger ones. A second reason why studying the largest media companies seems particularly relevant is that due to their leading market position their practices also have huge impacts all over the world (Jose and Lee 2007, 311).

For these reasons the way the biggest media and communication companies are approaching and practicing CSR has strong political significance. The practices of large global corporations are likely to indicate how media and communication will develop in the twenty-first century. The sampling method of focusing on the cases that have the strongest political significance has been described as "sampling politically important cases" (Miles and Huberman 1994, 28; Patton 2002, 241; O'Leary 2004, 110; Teddlie and Tashakjori 2009, 344; Mertens 2010, 323). According to Teddlie and Tashakkori sampling politically important cases "is a strategy that involves selecting politically significant or sensitive cases for a research study" (Teddlie and Tashakkori 2009, 344).

A ranking that is frequently used for identifying the biggest companies in a region or an industry is the Forbes lists of biggest public companies (Abbott and Monsen 1979; Jose and Lee 2007; Bartkus and Glassman 2008). Every year *Forbes Magazine* publishes a list of the 200 leading companies worldwide. The companies are ranked according to assets, sales, profit and market value. Forbes compiles its annual ranking by adding up the scores in each of these four categories.[6]

Based on the Forbes 2000 ranking for the year 2010 I identified the three biggest companies for each of the media and communication industries that I described in Chapter 3. Table 4.2 shows which companies I identified for each sector.

I decided to select the biggest company of each of the five media sectors described in Table 4.2. Selecting one company from each sector covers the whole media and communication industry. Choosing the largest companies makes it possible to give a comprehensive picture of CSR reporting and CSR practices in market leading companies in the media and communication business. The initial sample thus consisted of five media and communication companies.

The available time resource for completing this study allowed the inclusion of three more companies, which I selected based on purposive random sampling. Purposive random sampling means cases are selected randomly from a population that was deliberately chosen based on a non-probability sampling strategy (Morgan 2008, 725). The advantage of using this technique is to create further sample credibility. Miles and Huberman stress that purposive random sampling "adds credibility to sample when potential purposeful sample is too large" (Miles and Huberman 1994, 28). Using a random generator I selected three companies from all second and third largest companies in the specified five media and communication sectors (in total 10 companies).[7] The randomly chosen companies were News Corporation, Apple and Vivendi.

Table 4.2 Biggest media and communication companies

Sector	Three biggest companies[1]
Media content sector	Walt Disney (Forbes rank 110) Vivendi (146) News Corporation (149)
Hardware sector	Hewlett Packard (42) Apple (47) Cisco (87)
Software sector	Microsoft (50) Oracle (107) SAP (248)
Telecommunication sector	AT&T (14) Vodafone (27) Telefónica (21)
Online media sector	Google (120) Yahoo (584) Baidu (1103)

Source: Data based on *Forbes Magazine*. 2011. *The World's Biggest Public Companies. 2010.*
Retrieved from http://www.forbes.com/global2000/#p_1_s_arank_All_All_All on June 17, 2011.

Note
1 According to Forbes 2000 ranking for 2010 (ranking published in April 2011).

The final sample thus consisted of eight media and communication companies (Table 4.3).

I analysed all CSR reports the selected companies had published up to 2011 and that were available online. Two companies – Google and News Corp – did not provide regular CSR reports. I decided not exclude these companies, because the fact that some of the leading media companies do not report on CSR issues should not be ignored. In the case of Google it turned out that a variety of information

Table 4.3 Final sample

Sector	Company
Media content	Walt Disney Vivendi News Corp
Hardware	Hewlett Packard Apple
Software	Microsoft
Telecommunications	AT&T
Online media	Google

Source: Data based on *Forbes Magazine*. 2011. *The World's Biggest Public Companies. 2010.*
Retrieved from http://www.forbes.com/global2000/#p_1_s_arank_All_All_All on June 17, 2011.

about the company's philosophy and policies was available online that very much resembled the CSR reports and policies of other companies. It therefore was used as source of information on the company's CSR approach and activities. Table 4.4 lists all reports that were included in the coding process.

Selection of focus areas

After deciding which companies to include in the study I selected one CSR focus area for each company. The sampling method I used for selecting a focus area for each case (company) was critical case sampling. According to Patton (2002, 54) "critical cases are those that can make a point quite dramatically or are, for some reason, particularly important in the scheme of things". Miles and Huberman (1994, 28) argue that critical case sampling "permits logical generalizations".

Table 4.4 Sample CSR reports and websites

Company	CSR reports
Apple	2006 Final Assembly Supplier Audit Report
	2007 Driving Change. Supplier Responsibility Progress Report
	2008 Supplier Responsibility. Progress Report
	2009 Supplier Responsibility. Progress Report
	2010 Apple Supplier Responsibility. Progress Report
AT&T	2006 Social Responsibility Report
	2007 Connecting With People, Everywhere They Live and Work – AT
	2007/2008 AT&T Citizenship and Sustainability Report. Connecting for a Sustainable Future
	2008 AT&T Citizenship and Sustainability Report. Connecting for a Sustainable Future
	2009 AT&T Citizenship and Sustainability Report. Connecting for a Sustainable Future
	2010 Meet the Possibility Economy – 2010 AT&T Sustainability Report
Google	Website information:
	Company Overview
	Corporate Information
	Google Green
	Google.org
	Google Culture
	Google Investor Relations
	Google Competition
	Google Philosophy
	Google Privacy Principles
	Google Ads in Gmail
	Google Advertising and Privacy
	Google Personalized Ads
	Google Privacy Policy
	Google Privacy Policy for Ads

HP	2001 Social and Environmental Responsibility Report
	2002 Global Citizenship Report
	2003 Global Citizenship Report
	2004 Global Citizenship Report
	2005 Global Citizenship Report
	2006 Global Citizenship Report
	2007 Global Citizenship Report
	2008 Global Citizenship Report
	2009a Global Citizenship Report
	2009b Changing the Equation – The Impact of Global Citizenship in 2009 and Beyond
	2010a A Connected World – The Impact of HP Global Citizenship in 2010 and Beyond
	2010b A Connected World – The Impact of HP Global Citizenship in 2010 and Beyond
Microsoft	2003 Citizenship Report
	2004 Global Citizenship Report
	2005 Citizenship Report
	2006 Partners in Innovation – Citizenship Report
	2007/2008 Citizenship @ Microsoft
	2009 Corporate Citizenship @ Microsoft – Addressing Societal Needs in the Global Community
	2010 Citizenship Report
	2011 Citizenship Report
NewsCorp	2011 Standards of Business Conduct
The Walt Disney Company	2000 Enviroport
	2001 Enviroport
	2002 Enviroport
	2003 Enviroport
	2004 Enviroport
	2005 Enviroport
	2006 Enviroport
	2007 Enviroport
	2008 Corporate Responsibility Report
	2009 Corproate Responsibility. Interim Update
	2010 Corproate Citizenship Report
	Code of Conduct for Manufacturers.
	Labor Standards FAQ
Vivendi	2002 Report – Our Economic, Social and Environmental Responsibility
	2003 Sustainable Development Report
	2004/2005 Sustainable Development Report
	2005/2006 Sustainable Development Report
	2006/2007 Sustainable Development Report
	2008 Activity and Sustainable Development Report
	2009 Activity and Sustainable Development Report
	2010 Activity and Sustainable Development Report

Among all possible CSR topics the most critical ones for media and communication companies are those that are directly related to their business models. If in market-leading companies, which are analysed within this study, CSR issues are found that are directly linked to the specific ways of generating profit in the media and communication business, these are likely to also occur in other companies that pursue the same media and communication business models. Focusing on topics that lie at the very foundation of the media and communication business model thus provides the most valuable and logically generalizable insights into CSR in the media and communication business. For each company in the sample (see Table 4.3) I selected a focus area that characterizes the business model of the specific company:

- Apple is a successful producer of computer hardware. The case of Apple illustrates one pressing social issue in the context of hardware production: *labour rights*. During 2010 and 2011 news media around the world reported on suicides and bad working conditions at Apple's contract manufacturer's in China.[8] For the hardware industry in general, and Apple in particular, a critical CSR issue certainly is under which conditions highly profitable high tech products are manufactured.
- AT&T makes a profit by selling access to Internet and telephone networks. AT&T in the US operates 61,433 network access lines and has 95,536 wireless customers (AT&T SEC filings. 10-k form 2010). 96.3 per cent of its revenue is based on these two business segments (AT&T SEC filings. 10-k form 2010). Central to the provision of Internet access is the question of whether all online content should be treated equally, or if internet service providers such as AT&T should be allowed to prioritize data if users are willing to pay for faster transportation. The idea of treating all data equally is called *net neutrality*. The question of whether to abandon net neutrality has been a controversial discussion in the US. As AT&T is a main provider of the services that are affected by net neutrality it is important to investigate how AT&T deals with this socially important and at the same time controversial issue.
- Google's revenues in 2010 were 29.3 billion USD, 96 per cent of which was generated through advertisements (Google SEC filings. 10-k form 2010). Creating personalized ads requires the collection of user data that is stored in databases. In the context of such a business model the topic of *privacy* is central. An important question is how far Google can adequately protect users from potential dangers connected to surveillance and data mining.
- HP, like Apple, is one of the most important players in the hardware industry. Unlike many other media sectors such as the media content industry, the hardware sector is concerned with the production of physical products such as computers, photo cameras, hard drives, printers, mp3 players, etc. Since the production of these products requires the extraction and manufacturing of natural resources, it has a substantial impact on the environment. 52.8 per cent of HP's revenues are based on the sale of computers, printing devices and printing supplies (HP SEC filings. 10-k form 2010). Computers

and printing devices, and especially ink cartridges and toners, contain toxic substances that pose a substantial threat to human health and the environment, especially if these products are not disposed properly. The example of HP illustrates that apart from labour rights, a second critical case for the hardware business is the question of how to deal with toxic *waste* and the potential threats to humans and the environment.

- Microsoft's profit is almost entirely based on vending software (Microsoft SEC filings. 10-k forms 1994–2011), which presupposes strong intellectual property protection and *software patents*. The legitimacy of software patents is contested: advocates of free and open source software argue that if the source code is openly accessible and everybody is allowed to participate in the improvement of software the result will be much better than if only one company has the monopoly on designing software. In terms of social responsibility it thus needs to be investigated how Microsoft deals with the topic of *software patents*.

- News Corp owns TV channels and newspapers around the world that supply millions of people with their daily news and entertainment. Arsenault and Castells estimate that News Corp today reaches around 75 per cent of the global population (Arsenault and Castells 2008, 491). This symbolic power can be used in different ways. How News Corp deals with this power certainly highlights one important dimension of the social responsibility of media companies. How News Corp deals with its symbolic power in the generation of *media content* was therefore selected as the critical case.

- The Walt Disney Company is known all over the world for its movies and TV series for kids and families. However, Disney has developed a strategy to exploit the popularity of its movie characters in various different ways. This strategy includes Disney theme parks, Disney books, Disney toys, Disney furniture, Disney clothes, etc. Disney has brought the strategy of cross-promotion to perfection. Janet Wasko therefore states: "Indeed, the Disney company has developed the strategy so well that is represents the quintessential example of synergy in the media/entertainment industry" (Wasko 2001, 71).

Nonetheless, content production is still more important in financial terms: in 2010 Disney generated a revenue of 23.9 billion USD based on its media networks and studio entertainment business, while revenues from theme parks and consumer products amounted to 13.4 billion USD (Disney SEC filings. 10-k form 2010). However, 13.4 billion USD – the amount of money Disney creates from offering products and services that further exploit stories and characters from its movies and series – is still very high.

The content of Disney's movies and its ideological implications have already been widely studied (see for example Dorfman and Mattelart 1975; Bell, Haas and Sells 1995; Sardar 1996; Byrne and McQuillan 1999; Ward 2002; Brode 2005; Giroux and Pollock 2010). It therefore seems important to draw attention to a more hidden aspect of the Disney business

Table 4.5 Final sample including focus areas

Sector	Companies (Forbes ranking)	Focus areas
Media content	Walt Disney (110)	Working conditions in the supply chain
	Vivendi (146)	Peer-to-peer file-sharing
	News Corp (149)	Media content
Hardware	Hewlett Packard (42)	e-Waste
	Apple (47)	Working conditions in the supply chain
Software	Microsoft (50)	Software patents
Telecommunications	AT&T (14)	Net neutrality
Online media	Google (120)	Privacy

model – its cross-promotional consumer products business. This seems particularly important because the Walt Disney company in its CSR communication prides itself as being "the world's largest licensor" of manufactured goods (DI_CSR 2008, 5; DI_CSR 2010, 5) as well as the largest children's book publisher (DI_CSR 2008, 5; DI_CSR 2008, 8). Most of these products are manufactured in low wage countries such as China. It is an interesting question as to whether Disney, the company that in its movies creates joyful stories with happy ends and pleasurable fantasy worlds, can in reality ensure adequate *working conditions* in its supply chain.

- Vivendi owns the biggest recording company in the world: Universal Music Group (UMG) (Music and Copyright 2011). During the last decade illegal music file-sharing has constantly challenged the music industry. The industry's response was to threaten file-sharers with draconian penalties and to file lawsuits against file-sharing facilitators that often ended with the shutdown of *file-sharing* platforms. It is thus an important question as to how Vivendi reacts to the peer-to-peer *file-sharing* challenge and whether this reaction meets the criteria of social responsibility.

Table 4.5 summarizes the final sample of companies and respective focus areas.

The goal of this study is to test and challenge the way companies describe their business practices in these areas based on criticism from corporate watchdogs.

Supplementary sources

It is one of the central aims of this CCA to challenge corporate self-reporting with descriptions by corporate watchdogs (RQ 3). Corporate watchdogs in this context are understood as all individuals, academics, groups or organizations that observe and critically report on corporate behaviour.

Table 4.6 shows the corporate watchdogs that were used as a starting point for gathering alternative information about the behaviour of the selected companies and their implications for social responsibility.

Table 4.6 Corporate watchdogs

Corporate watchdogs	
CorpWatch	http://www.corpwatch.org/
Corporate Accountability International	http://www.stopcorporateabuse.org/
Multinational Monitor	http://www.multinationalmonitor.org/
Corporate Crime Reporter	http://www.corporatecrimereporter.com/
Transnational Corporate Observatory	http://www.transnationale.org/
No Sweat	http://www.nosweat.org.uk/
SwedWatch	http://www.swedwatch.org
Somo	http://somo.nl/
DanWatch	http://www.danwatch.dk
FinnWatch	http://www.finnwatch.org/
GermanWatch	http://www.germanwatch.org/
SACOM	http://sacom.hk/
Responsible Shopper	http://www.greenamerica.org/programs/responsibleshopper/
Corporate Watch	http://www.corporatewatch.org
Ethical Consumer	http://www.ethicalconsumer.org/
Corporate Crime Reporter	http://corporatecrimereporter.com/
Center for Corporate Policy	http://www.corporatepolicy.org/index.htm
Corporate Crime Daily	http://corporatecrime.wordpress.com/
Corporate Europe Observatory	http://www.corporateeurope.org/
China Labour Watch	http://www.chinalaborwatch.org/
Greenpeace	http://www.greenpeace.org
Global Witness	http://www.globalwitness.org/
Global Trade Watch	http://www.citizen.org/trade/
Human Rights Watch	http://www.hrw.org/
Institute for Global and Human Rights	http://www.globallabourrights.org/
Fair Labour Association	http://www.fairlabor.org/

Corporate media watchdogs	
Fairness and Accuracy in Reporting	http://www.fair.org/index.php
Free Press	http://www.freepress.net/
Media Access Project	http://www.mediaaccess.org/
Center for Creative Voices in Media	http://www.creativevoices.us/
Reclaim the Media	http://www.reclaimthemedia.org/
Media Watch	http://www.mediawatch.com/
Media Matters Action Network	http://mediamattersaction.org/
Center for Media and Democracy's PR Watch	http://www.prwatch.org/
Computer Professionals for Social Responsibility	http://cpsr.org/
makeITfair	http://makeitfair.org/en?set_language=en
Electronic Frontier Foundation	https://www.eff.org/
Privacy International	https://www.privacyinternational.org/
Privacy Rights Clearinghouse	https://www.privacyrights.org/
Google Watch	http://www.google-watch.org/
CleanIT	http://www.clean-it.at/

These sources were used to identify criticism of the business practices of the selected companies. If necessary I used further sources in order to find specific facts and to deepen information about a particular issue. These additional sources were mainly alternative media such as Mother Jones, AlterNet and Democracy Now; established media such *The New York Times*, *The Guardian*, the BBC and CNN; academic writings; as well as additional information that is provided by the companies themselves such as annual financial reports, blog entries or press releases.

Apart from challenging corporate self-descriptions with criticism raised by corporate watchdogs, another aim of this CCA was to place the analysis of corporate CSR activities in a broader context such as a company's history, its economic situation and development and its future business aims and strategies (see RQ 2 and RQ 5). Sources for gathering this context information were mainly financial reports published by the companies themselves. Important sources of information were official SEC filings, which all public companies in the US have to compile and publish every year. They contain key financial data about a company as well as the company's assessment of its market situation, its competitors and future business goals. For gathering context information regarding media and communication markets I used data provided by market analysts such as NetMarketshare, Gartner, International Data Corporation (IDC), Columbia Institute of Tele-Information (CITI) and Nielsen. Moreover media reports served as an additional source. To sum up: the supplementary sources that were used for this study included:

- Corporate watchdogs (RQ 3, RQ 5).
- Established and alternative online news media (RQ 3, RQ 5).
- Annual reports of companies (RQ 2, RQ 5).
- Corporate SEC filings (RQ 2, RQ 5).
- Websites of market analysts (RQ 2, RQ 5).

Definition of units, dimensions and categories

For analysing the corporate self-descriptions of the selected media and communication companies (RQs 1, 4, 5) I chose a combination of deductive and inductive category generation. This combined approach allowed me to derive categories based on theoretical insights, and to generate new categories based on the material of analysis. The following categories were chosen:

- *RQ 1* deals with the CSR approaches of media and communication companies. Identifying different ways of defining CSR was a major aim of the theoretical part of this study. The result of Chapter 2 was a typology of reductionist, projectionist, dualist and dialectical approaches. To address the question of how companies approach the topic of CSR, a deductive approach therefore seemed the most promising. It allowed me to investigate in how far approaches that were found in CSR theory also are present in corporate CSR accounts. The categories for the dimension "CSR approach" thus were "reductionism", "projectionism", "dualism" and "dialectics". These four options are based on theoretical considerations (see Chapter 2); for ensuring comprehensiveness, the option that a company has no CSR approach was included as a fifth category.

- *RQ 4* deals with the question of how media companies respond to criticism raised by corporate watchdogs. Here the categories were generated inductively based on the analysis of CSR reports and will thus be presented in the results section (see Chapter 13).
- *RQ 5* aims at identifying CSR challenges for media and communication companies. Categories for this research question were generated inductively. In addition to the content analysis of CSR reports, reports from corporate watchdogs, financial company data and industry statistics were used to identify one main challenge for each company in the chosen focus area. CSR challenges were defined as those topics that showed disagreement between companies and corporate watchdogs and that pointed towards a conflict between a company's business model and its social responsibilities.

Before the start of coding it is not only important to define categories but also to define coding and context units (Krippendorff 2004, 97). For the purpose of this study themes seemed the most suitable coding units. Ritsert argues that: "'Themes' (motifs) can be regarded as statements (explanations) on a circumstance or as interrelated structures of meaning" (Ritsert 1972, 56 (translation[9])). Using thematic coding units requires the definition of certain themes. The coding units then are all parts of a text that contain this theme. They can be of varying length (one sentence, one paragraph, one chapter, etc.). The context unit that was chosen for this study is an entire CSR report. This means coding units were categorized in the context of an entire report. The following themes were used as coding units:

- *RQ 1*: For addressing research question 1 the thematic unit was "CSR approaches". I included all passages that contained conceptual statements on a company's CSR approach and/or reasons or justifications that explain why a company engages in CSR activities in the coding.
- *RQ 4*: For addressing research question 4 the thematic unit was "CSR practices". I coded all passages that contained information about a company's activities that affect the CSR areas that were pre-selected for each company (net neutrality for AT&T, working conditions in the supply chain of Apple and Disney, e-waste for HP, the open source movement for Microsoft, media content for News Corp, and peer-to-peer music file-sharing for Vivendi).
- *RQ 5*: For research question 5 the thematic unit again was "CSR practices" in the chosen focus area (net neutrality for AT&T, working conditions in the supply chain of Apple and Disney, e-waste for HP, the open source movement for Microsoft, media content for News Corp, and peer-to-peer music file-sharing for Vivendi).

Table 4.7 summarizes categories, dimensions and coding units for each research question.

Table 4.7 Summary of dimensions, categories and coding units

	RQ 1		
Dimension	*Categories*	*Description*	*Coding unit*
CSR approach	Reductionism	Reductionist arguments emphasize benefits of CSR for the bottom line, e.g. - CSR helps to increase shareholder value - CSR is important for economic success - CSR is important for economic "sustainability"	*Thematic* All passages that: - contain conceptual statements on a company's CSR approach or - contain reasons or justifications that explain why a company engages in CSR activities.
	Projectionism	Projectionist arguments emphasize that profit should be generated in a way that is compatible with a company's social and environmental responsibilities, e.g. - Business operations are guided by values - Business operations aim at contributing to the positive development of society and/or the environment - Business operations serve the common good	
	Dualist	Dualist arguments emphasize that companies can simultaneously reach their economic goals and contribute to the common good, e.g. - CSR simultaneously benefits corporate profits and society - Acting responsibly equally includes reaching profit goals and social goals - Economic success and social responsibility are equally important company goals	
	Dialectical	Dialectical arguments emphasize contradictions between the profit motive and social goals, e.g. - The profit motive entails mechanisms that threaten the sustainable development of society and the environment	

		- The profit motive entails mechanisms that lead to socially irresponsible behaviour - Profit generation has immoral implications	
	No CSR	No CSR communication (reports, documents, statements, press releases, etc.) available	

RQ 4

Dimension	Categories	Description	Coding unit
Reaction to criticism	Categories for this dimension were generated inductively and are presented in the results section (see Chapter 13)	"Reaction to criticism" describes the way how each company responds to watchdog criticism regarding its corporate practices, either - directly by explicitly referring to watchdog criticism, or - indirectly by presenting the company's own assessment of an issue that is subject to watchdog criticism without explicitly referring to this criticism	*Thematic* All passages that: deal with the company's activities regarding one of the following areas: - net neutrality (AT&T) - working conditions in the supply chain (Apple and Walt Disney) - privacy (Google) - e-waste (HP) - software patents (Microsoft) - media content (News Corp) - file-sharing (Vivendi)

RQ 5

Dimension	Categories	Description	Coding unit
CSR challenges	Categories for this dimension were generated inductively and are presented in the results section (see Chapter 13)	"CSR challenges" for each area are those topics that: - show disagreement between companies and corporate watchdogs - point towards conflicts between a company's business model and its social responsibilities.	Thematic All passages that: deal with the company's activities regarding of the following areas: - net neutrality (AT&T) - working conditions in the supply chain (Apple and Walt Disney) - privacy (Google) - e-waste (HP) - software patents (Microsoft) - media content (News Corp) - file-sharing (Vivendi)

Conclusion

This chapter has described the process of generating a methodological framework for the study of CSR reporting of media and communication companies. Based on the characteristics of critical social research I suggested a CCA as a suitable method. CCA is characterized by a material understanding of critique as the critique of capitalist society, dialectical thinking, the primacy of the research object over the method and critical coding that considers context, latency, singularity and presence as well as a critical interpretation that relates the content of texts to social objectivity and social possibility.

This study goes beyond traditional qualitative content analysis because it explicitly follows a critical intent and for that reason includes alternative sources, based on which the texts that are studied – corporate self-descriptions – can be challenged with critical viewpoints. The main aim of this study is not to find out what companies write in their CSR reports but whether the way corporations understand and practice CSR can contribute to achieving a socially responsible media and communication system. To answer this question it is insufficient to exclusively rely on corporate claims about the responsibility of their business practices. Therefore the special feature of the research design described in this chapter is that CSR claims of companies are confronted with critique from corporate watchdogs.

By grasping the tension between corporate self-descriptions and critique from corporate watchdogs important insights can be gained in regard to CSR approaches, practices and challenges:

- *CSR approaches*: The research design of this study focuses on corporate approaches to CSR. However, using additional sources such as information provided by corporate watchdogs also allows insights into civil society perspectives on how responsible business practices of media companies do and should look like. It thus it includes both the "corporate" and the "social" perspective in the issue of CSR.
- *CSR practices*: In regard to CSR practices the advantages of this comparative approach is that it entails an ideology-critical perspective that allows the uncovering of whether companies hide irresponsible practices, ignore criticism, euphemize their business practices, etc. It thereby allows the assessment of whether corporate CSR strategies are mere rhetoric or in fact render business practices more responsible.
- *CSR challenges*: By analysing controversies and the different viewpoints of companies and corporate watchdogs it becomes possible to identify those issues that pose the most fundamental challenge to CSR in the media and communication sectors. These challenges are those issues that are highly important from a social perspective but at the same time hard to achieve from a corporate perspective.

In the following chapters I present the detailed case studies of Apple, AT&T, Google, HP, Microsoft, News Corporation, The Walt Disney Company and Vivendi. All cases studies follow the same structure: I begin with a brief description of the company, followed by an analysis of corporate self-descriptions in CSR reports. I continue with a discussion of watchdog criticism and controversies concerning the social or environmental impact of the respective company's business practices. Finally, I summarize main results in a conclusion.

Notes

1 "Uns lockt es, die Erfahrung gegen den Empirismus zu verteidigen, einen minder eingeschränkten, minder engen und verdinglichten Begriff von Erfahrung zuzubringen. Ziel der Kontroverse is nicht in Ja oder Nein zur Empirie, sondern die Interpretation von Empirie selber, zumal der sogenannten empirischen Methoden" (Adorno 1972/1995, 545f).

2 "Die kritische Sozialforschung möchte die Empirie durch ihre theoretische Entschlüsselung erst ganz produktiv machen" (Adorno 1972/1995, 545).

3 "Die Gegenüberstellung der subjectiven Meinungen mit jenen objektiven Momenten ergibt wesentlicheres als die tabula-rasa-Methode, für die die Meininung König ist, wie angeblich der Käufer auf dem Markt" (Adorno1972/1995, 545).

4 "In den fortschrittenen Gebieten der Industriegesellschaft ist heute bei den 'Benachteiligten' eine 'innere' Identifizierung mit dem System vorhanden, ein positives Denken und Handeln, welchesdie gesellschaftlichen Insitutionen in einer tiefen Dimension schützt" (Marcuse 1962/1978, 326).

5 "Die Auflösung von Ideologien als Änderung von Reflexionsbestimmungen bei der beherrschten Klasse ist noch nicht die Herrschaft aufhebende politische Tat, aber sie ist ein Moment in jenem Lernsprozeß, der dazu führen könnte" (Ritsert 1972, 97).

6 *Forbes Magazine*. 2011. *Global 2000. Methodology*. Retrieved from http://www. forbes.com/2011/04/20/global-2000-11-methodology.html on June 17, 2011.

7 Every company was assigned a number. Subsequently three numbers were chosen, using zufallsgenerator.net

8 See for example: *The New York Times*. 2010. *String of Suicides Continues at Electronics Supplier in China*. By David Barboza on May 25, 2010. Retrieved from http://www.nytimes.com/2010/05/26/technology/26suicide.html on October 24, 2011.

9 "'Themen' (Motive) können als Aussagen (Ausführungen) über einen Sachverhalt oder als zusammenhängende Sinnstrukturen gelten" (Ritsert 1972, 56).

5 Apple

Dirty computers?

Steve Wozniak, Steve Jobs and Ronald Wayne founded Apple in 1976 (Linzmayer 2004, 6). However, it was not until the mid-2000s that Apple joined the elite of the most profitable companies in the world. In 2005 Apple's profits for the first time exceeded 1 billion USD and during the following years continued to increase rapidly until they reached 41.7 billion USD in 2012 (Apple SEC filings. 10-k form 2012), which made Apple the second most profitable company in the world.[1] Between 2000 and 2012 Apple's profit on average grew 39.2 per cent each year[2] (Apple SEC filings. 10-k form 2012).

Furthermore *Fortune Magazine*, for six years in a row (2008–2013), has ranked Apple the most admired company in the world.[3] However, in 2010 strong criticism of Apple's supply chain management was raised after several workers committed suicide at one of the company's supplier factories in China. This chapter will therefore look behind the brand, and put working conditions in Apple's supply chain under scrutiny.

CSR approach

The publication of Apple's first supplier responsibility document was a reaction to ongoing criticism of the company's business practices in its supplier factories. It starts with the following sentence: "In the summer of 2006, we were concerned by reports in the press alleging poor working and living conditions at one of our iPod final assembly suppliers in China" (Apple_SR 2006, 1). The document summarizes the results of Apple's audits of 11 supplier factories. From then on, Apple started to publish annual *Supplier Responsibility Progress Reports*, which document the results of factory audits. They contain hardly any general information on how Apple approaches the idea CSR and tries to implement it in its business practices. In fact, Apple's conceptual statements on social responsibility are largely limited to the following phrase:

> Apple is committed to the highest standard of social responsibility in everything we do. We are dedicated to ensuring that working conditions are safe, the environment is protected, and employees are treated with respect and dignity wherever Apple products are made.
>
> (Apple_SR 2006, 4; for similar statements
> see also 2007, 3; 2008, 3; 2009; 3; 2010, 3)

Apple does not try to justify its engagement in CSR activities. Neither does it provide any narrative that relates the company's engagement in CSR to certain values or to an honest concern for society and the environment.

Apple's CSR communication is limited both in scope and in profundity. It is largely a reaction to criticism from media and social movements. However, Apple praises itself for having installed a social responsibility training programme for teaching managers and production workers in its supplier factories how to ensure good working conditions. Until 2010 more than 300,000 workers and 6,000 supervisors and managers have been trained within this programme (Apple_SR 2010, 5). In the 2009 *Supplier Responsibility Progress Report* Apple quotes a manger on what he has learned during the training programme: "I learned that social responsibility training can add value not only to society but also to my company" (Apple_SR 2009, 7). This statement reflects an instrumental approach to CSR and might give a glimpse of the content of Apple's social responsibility courses.

Controversies: labour rights

In May and June 2010 many major Western media reported a series of suicides at factory campuses in China. The factories, at which 17 young workers jumped to death[4] belong to the Taiwan-based company Hon Hai Precision Industry Co. Ltd, better known as Foxconn, which is a major supplier for computer giants such as Apple, Hewlett-Packard, Nokia and Sony Ericsson (FinnWatch, SACOM and SOMO 2011, 8). For some weeks, Western media were looking behind the surface of bright and shiny computer products. They reported about bad working conditions and desperate workers at factories, which are supplying Western brands with computer devices that are sold to millions of customers. For example, *The New York Times* wrote *String of Suicides Continues at Electronics Supplier in China*[5]; the BBC reported on *Foxconn Suicides: 'Workers Feel Quite Lonely'*[6]; and *The Guardian* headlined *Latest Foxconn Suicide Raises Concern over Factory Life in China.*[7]

However, these suicides only are the tip of the iceberg. For several years NGOs have stressed that computers, mp3 players, game consoles, etc. are often produced under miserable working conditions. Far away from shopping centres and department stores, workers in developing countries are producing these products during 10 to 12 hour shifts, a minimum of six days a week for at best a minimum wage. Apple's suppliers are no exception. I will in the following refer to major criticism regarding working conditions at Apple's contract manufacturers before as well as after the suicides, and discuss Apple's response to these allegations.

A history of labour rights violations

In 2004 the Institute for Contemporary Observation (ICO), FinnWatch and the Finnish Export Credit Agency (ECA) pointed at problems due to precarious employment contracts at the Shenzhen Foxconn campus (ICO, Finnwatch and ECA 2005, 17). One year later the Dutch non-profit centre SOMO investigated the

Foxconn factories in Shenzhen. SOMO found: "On average, a worker that works 27 days a month and 10–11 hours a day will receive about RMB 1000 a month including all the subsidies and OT [overtime] compensation" (SOMO 2005b, 26). In 2005 1000 RMB were equivalent to about 100 EUR or 120 USD. Food from Monday until Friday and lodging was subsidized by the factory (SOMO 2005b, 27). Workers at Foxconn complained that during the peak season they would not receive a single day off in four months (SOMO 2005b, 15).

Furthermore unbearable working conditions were documented in particular in respect to Apple's production line at Foxconn: in 2008 FinnWatch, SACOM and SOMO monitored buildings C03 and C04 of Foxconn's Shenzhen campus, in which 2,800 workers at 40 assembly lines were producing iPhones (FinnWatch, SACOM and SOMO 2009, 35). The findings included:

- Employees had to work compulsory excessive overtime of up to 120 hours per month. According to Chinese labour law monthly overtime must not exceed 36 hours per month (FinnWatch, SACOM and SOMO 2009, 37).
- Wages corresponded to the legal minimum wage of around 980 yuan (FinnWatch, SACOM and SOMO 2009, 36), which workers, however, perceived as too low to cover their basic living expenses (FinnWatch, SACOM and SOMO 2009, 44). Some workers reported that during the training period overtime on weekends was unpaid (FinnWatch, SACOM and SOMO 2009, 37)
- Strict disciplinary measures were in place at the factory. No personal belongings were allowed in the factory and procedures of how to start work and how to leave the shop floor were strictly regulated. Workers reported that if asked how they felt they had to shout: "Fine! Very fine! Very, very fine!" (FinnWatch, SACOM and SOMO 2009, 38). Talking, giggling, and crossing legs was forbidden while sitting at the assembly line. Talking could be punished with shop floor cleaning (FinnWatch, SACOM and SOMO 2009, 38). Wage reductions were used as a disciplinary measure (FinnWatch, SACOM and SOMO 2009, 38).
- A labour union existed, but workers did not know about it (FinnWatch, SACOM and SOMO 2009, 38).

It is important to note that Foxconn is in fact not the only Apple supplier that keeps violating labour rights:

- In 2007 SOMO interviewed workers at five Apple supplier factories in China, the Philippines and Thailand (SOMO 2007, 19f). Workers in all investigated factories reported that their wages were too low to cover their living expenses (SOMO 2007, 21). SOMO found that in one factory workers had to work up to 80 hours per week; in four of five investigated factories total working hours exceeded 60 hours per week. At three factories this overtime was compulsory (SOMO 2007, 22).
- In 2010 SACOM investigated United Win, a subsidy of Wintek Corporation, which produces Apple products. Between July 2009 and early 2010, 47 United Win workers were hospitalized because of being poisoned with

n-hexane (SACOM 2010b, 2). The poisoned workers were using n-hexane for cleaning iPhone touchscreens (SACOM 2010b, 2).

These findings show that years before the suicides occurred in 2010, corporate watchdogs were well aware of labour rights violations and had also informed Apple about these deficiencies.

Desperate workers

In 2010, 18 workers at different Foxconn campuses attempted to commit suicide, 14 of them died after jumping from buildings (FinnWatch, SACOM and SOMO 2011, 8). After this series of suicides and the resulting media attention, Foxconn announced the raising of wages by 20 per cent. Furthermore safety nets were installed in order to prevent more suicides. Various NGOs in 2010 and 2011 conducted follow-up research in order to assess the reported wage rises and improvements of working conditions. In the following I briefly summarize the results of independent watchdog investigation of Apple's contract manufacturers after 2010.

- *Wages*: In a 2010 investigation of Apple's production line at Foxconn's Shenzhen campus FinnWatch, SACOM and SOMO found that Foxconn increased wages for workers that were working at the factory for more than six months to 2,000 Yuan a month starting from October 2010. However, only an estimated 50 per cent of the workforce actually works in this factory for more than six months (FinnWatch, SACOM and SOMO 2011, 28). Furthermore the wage increases only applied to Shenzhen and not to newly established upcountry factories to which Foxconn is increasingly relocating its production (FinnWatch, SACOM and SOMO 2011, 8). An investigation conducted by SACOM in 2011 confirmed that Foxconn increased wages, but at the same time cancelled food and housing subsidies. This means that despite Foxconn's claims, there was no actual wage increase (SACOM 2011a, 6). Foxconn was not paying a living wage.
    Figure 5.1 shows substantial gaps between actual wages and a living wage that is high enough to cover expenses for food, housing, clothes, education, social security and health care for a family, and allow for some savings
- *Working hours*: Connected to the problem of low wages is the problem of long working hours. Workers very often depend on the extra money they receive for overtime work because their regular wages are too low (FinnWatch, SACOM and SOMO 2011, 29). According to FinnWatch, SACOM and SOMO, in 2010 excessive compulsory overtime at Apple's production line at Foxconn Shenzhen was still the same as in 2008; the situation changed after June 2010. From then on workers were granted one day off per week and overtime was reduced from 120 hours to between 75 and 80 hours per month, which still exceeds the legal maximum of 36 hours (FinnWatch, SACOM and SOMO 2011, 29).

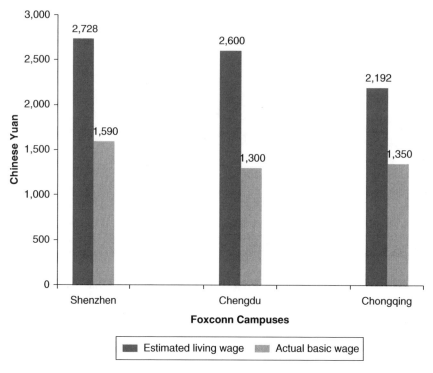

Figure 5.1 Actual basic wages in comparison to estimated living wages at three Foxconn campuses.

Source: SACOM 2011a, 6, 9.

Likewise SACOM in its 2011 investigation of Foxconn campuses in Shenzhen, Chengdu and Chongqing found that in order to earn enough money to cover basic living expenses, workers had to work overtime. One 19-year-old interviewee who was producing iPhones at Guanlan, Shenzhen stated:

> We do not have much overtime work this month. Our department has 3 shifts a day now. I can only receive a basic salary at CNY 1600 this month. It's really not enough for a living but I believe the 8-hour shift is just a temporary measure for the low season.
>
> (Worker quoted in SACOM 2011a, 9)

The situation was worst in Chengdu, which is exclusively producing for Apple: here the gap between an actual and a living wage was highest (see Figure 5.1) and workers worked between 80 and 100 hours per month – the longest working hours of all investigated factories (SACOM 2011a, 10).

- *Disciplinary measures*: FinnWatch's, SACOM's and SOMO's research conducted in 2010 showed that disciplinary measures at Foxconn were less strict after the suicides in 2010 than they were in 2008. However, security checks at toilets still existed and workers still had to collectively reply "Fine! Very fine! Very, very fine!" when asked how they felt (FinnWatch, SACOM and SOMO 2011, 31).

   SACOM (2011a) also found harsh and humiliating management methods at the Foxconn campus in Chengdu. New workers for example had to participate in military training, which only consisted of lining up and standing. Furthermore workers had to stand for up to 14 hours per day. During breaks they sat on the floor often without talking to each other because they were too exhausted. If workers made mistakes they had to write confession letters to their supervisors and sometimes even read them loud in front of the other workers. Supervisors were under pressure too. If one of the workers they were supervising made a mistake they had to face punishment themselves (SACOM 2011a, 16f).

- *Health and safety*: SACOM's investigation furthermore revealed an alarming occupational health and safety situation at the Foxconn campus in Chengdu. SACOM found poor ventilation, insufficient protection equipment and noisy workplaces. Workers were using chemicals, without knowing whether they were harmful. At the milling and the polishing department – in which the iPads' aluminium cover is polished until it is untarnished and shiny – workers were constantly breathing in aluminium dust. Several workers were suffering from a skin allergy after working with glue-like substances without wearing gloves (SACOM 2011a, 14). Shortly after SACOM's report was published, an explosion at the polishing department at Chengdu killed 3 workers and left 15 injured (SACOM 2011b, 1). SACOM's research also shows that at the Foxconn subsidiary, Futaihua Precision Electronics, workers were exposed to chemicals without adequate protection equipment. Some workers suffered from allergies. Toxic n-hexane was used for cleaning products (SACOM 2011b, 7).

- *High work pressure and psychological problems*: Working conditions at Apple's contract manufactures not only threaten the physical health of workers but also cause psychological problems. FinnWatch's, SACOM'S and SOMO's 2010 investigation revealed that workers suffered from social isolation because they were not allowed to talk during work and had to share their dormitories with workers from different production lines. They therefore neither got to know their immediate colleagues nor their roommates (FinnWatch, SACOM and SOMO 2011, 30; see also SACOM 2011a, 12f). SACOM's (2011a) research shows that machines at Foxconn's factories have to run 24/7. Therefore some workers always had to remain on the shop floor during meal breaks. These continuous shifts require workers to skip meals. One worker complained:

   The machines in our department are in operation 24/7. If some colleagues go out for dinner, then the workers who stay in the workshop have to take care of 3 machines at the same time. It is hard work but we do not have additional subsidy for that. Workers can only have dinner after the work shift ends. Continuous shift occurs everyday.

(Worker quoted in SACOM 2011a, 11)

Similarly SACOM in 2011 found that social life at Foxconn is deprived. Workers do not have time for any free time activities. Their life consists of working, eating and sleeping. Often they do not even find enough time to sleep. When asked what they would like to do on holiday most interviews said that they would like to sleep (SACOM 2011a, 12).

Apple's response

Apple has been hesitant in responding to the criticism raised by NGOs. FinnWatch, SACOM and SOMO in 2009 and in 2011 asked Apple for a reaction to their findings. Apple never replied (FinnWatch, SACOM and SOMO 2009, 40; 2011, 33; SACOM 2011b, 1).

While Apple leaves critical NGO reports mostly uncommented, it provides information on its own factory audits on the company website. The main argument that characterizes Apple supplier responsibility documents is that in the majority of cases working conditions at supplier factories are good and that whenever violations of Apple's Code of Conduct (CoC) occur, Apple cooperates with the respective supplier in order to ensure improvement (Apple_SR 2006–2010). Apple stresses that its auditing programmes ensure that "products are produced under socially and environmentally responsible conditions" (Apple_SR 2010, 13). The company emphasizes that due to its audits continuous improvements are being made. The 2009 report for example highlights: "In general, annual audits of final assembly manufacturers show continued performance improvements and better working conditions" (Apple_SR 2009, 15; see also Apple_SR 2010, 15).

However, even Apple's own audits of contract manufacturers reveal high non-compliance rates in regard to fundamental issues such as wages and working hours. The non-compliance rate in regard to payment of at least minimum wages and transparent wage calculations was 46 per cent in 2007, 41 per cent in 2008, 35 per cent in 2009 and 30 per cent in 2010. Although these figures show an improvement, it still means that a large number of workers in Apple's supplier factories are paid below the legal minimum. Considering that even the legal minimum is often below a living wage, these numbers are even more troubling. Apple's figures on working hours give a similar picture. In 2007 workers in 82 per cent of all monitored factories had to work more than 60 hours per week. This non-compliance rate dropped to 59 per cent in 2008, and to 54 per cent in 2009, before it increased again to 69 per cent in 2010. These results confirm that the majority of workers have to work excessive overtime while producing Apple's products. Despite low levels of compliance in regard to working hours and wages (see above) Apple claims that treatment of workers is "fair" in more than 90 per cent of all monitored factories (Apple_CR 2007–2010).

While Apple does not usually disclose the names of the facilities it is auditing, in the 2010 report the company responded to the suicides at Foxconn. Apple highlighted that it is "disturbed and deeply saddened to learn that factory workers were taking their own lives at the Shenzhen facility of Foxconn" (Apple_SR 2010, 18). Apple stressed that as a reaction to the suicides it launched "an international search for the most knowledgeable suicide prevention specialists - particularly those with experience in China – and asked them to advise Apple and Foxconn" (Apple_SR 2010, 18). Based on a survey among 1,000 Foxconn workers, face to face interviews with workers and managers, an individual investigation of each suicide and an evaluation of Foxconn's response to the suicides the expert team concluded that Foxconn dealt with the suicides in an appropriate way and that "Foxconn's response had definitely saved lives" (Apple_SR 2010, 19). Suggestions for further improvement were only made regarding the training of hotline and care centre stuff (Apple_SR 2010, 19).

The measures taken by Apple and the improvement suggested by the "most knowledgeable suicide prevention specialists" seem rather limited. They do not include any improvement of working conditions, which according to different labour rights groups had been bad for many years (SOMO 2005b; FinnWatch, SACOM and SOMO 2009, 2011; SACOM 2011a,b). The anti-suicide team's findings suggest that the suicides had nothing to do with working conditions at Foxconn. A study conducted by China Labour Watch (2010c) shows different results. On May 17, 2010 China Labour Watch asked 25 Foxconn workers about what they believed were the reason for the suicides of Foxconn workers. Seventeen said that high pressure at work was the main reason. Five workers argued that lacking a sense of community at Foxconn had led to the suicides. Three workers doubted that the reasons for the deaths actually were suicides (China Labour Watch 2010c).

In commenting on the suicides at Foxconn Steve Jobs said: "It's a factory, but they have restaurants and movie theatres. They've had some suicides and attempted suicides. They have 400,000 people there. The rate is under what the US rate is, but it's still troubling".[8] The fact that suicides also occur somewhere else does not make those at Foxconn any less problematic. It is cynical to point out that Foxconn has movie theatres and restaurants, while not mentioning low wages, health risks and extremely long working hours. Considering this reaction, it is not surprising, albeit alarming, that after the suicides, working conditions remained similarly as bad as before:

> While Apple commends the measures taken by Foxconn to improve working conditions, SACOM finds predicaments of workers remain. Workers always have excessive and forced overtime in order to gain a higher wage. Workers are exposed to dust from construction site and shop floor without adequate protection. Even worse, they are threatened by potential harm of occupational diseases in various departments.
>
> (SACOM 2011a, 2)

As another response to the labour rights crisis at Foxconn campuses, in January 2012 Apple announced that it, the first electronics company, had joined the Fair Labour Association (FLA). In February 2012 the FLA audited three Foxconn factories in Guanlan, Longhua and Chengdu in China. This audit shows that major violations of labour rights at Foxconn campuses still persist (FLA 2012). The FLA summarizes the results of the audit as follows: "FLA found excessive overtime and problems with overtime compensation; several health and safety risks; and crucial communication gaps that have led to a widespread sense of unsafe working conditions among workers".[9]

It is doubtful whether the measures Apple is taking for avoiding such violations and for improving working conditions at its suppliers will lead to any significant improvements. Apple stresses that if violations are detected, the respective factory is requested to develop a correction plan, the implementation of which will be monitored within 90 days (Apple_SR 2007, 5; 2008, 5; 2009, 14). Apple's assessment also relies on self reporting – suppliers have to submit regular reports on several key performance indicators, which are used to "evaluate how a supplier's performance has changed over the previous quarters, and we can compare their results with those of similar suppliers" (Apple_SR 2006, 5; 2007, 14). However, Apple does not provide any concrete information on measures included in these correction plans.

In fact, training is the only solution Apple is proposing for addressing work place issues (Apple_SR 2007, 13; 2008, 13, 15; 2009, 4; 2010, 5). Apple stresses: "Education that raises awareness of social responsibility is a critical factor for sustained performance" (Apple_SR 2007, 12). Until 2010, 300,000 workers had undergone training on social responsibility and labour rights (Apple_SR 2010, 5).

This focus on training suggests that the existence of bad working conditions is the fault of a lack of management skills at the suppliers, and has nothing to do with Apple. Apple presents itself as a benevolent saviour that is bringing knowledge to developing countries. At no point does Apple mention how much money it is paying for the production of its products in these supplier factories and whether this amount is enough for ensuring adequate working conditions.

The lower the price for labour, the higher the profits for Apple as well as Foxconn. It is no secret that the very reason why companies like Apple outsource their production to developing countries is cheap labour (SOMO 2005a, 22). Foxconn is itself a profitable corporation. Its profits in 2010 were 2.45 billion USD.[10] However, Foxconn remains largely dependent on orders from consumer brands such as Apple. FinnWatch, SACOM and SOMO describe this situation as follows:

> These companies often drive down the price they pay their suppliers, which then makes the suppliers less or no longer profitable. To get back in the game, suppliers reduce costs, often at the cost of workers, violating labour laws in the process.
> (FinnWatch, SACOM and SOMO 2009, 44)

Competition between contract manufacturers such as Foxconn is also high, which is why profit rates can often only be achieved by keeping costs low (SOMO 2005a, 41). The losers in this corporate race for profit are the workers.

Measures to improve the life of workers in Apple's supplier factories would require paying workers more money for less working time and therefore would pose a significant threat to Apple's and Foxconn's profits. This obviously is not in Apple's interest.

As the second most profitable company[11] in the world, Apple could afford to spend more money on the manufacturing of its products, even if this would significantly lower its profits. According to calculations made by Kraemer, Linden and Dedrick, Apple in 2010 kept 58.5 per cent of the sales price of an iPhone, the costs of materials amounted to 21.9 per cent of the sales prize, while only 1.8 per cent was spent on labour costs for final assembly in China. For the iPad, Chinese labour costs amounted to 2 per cent, input materials to 31 per cent and Apple's profits to 30 per cent of the sales price (Kraemer, Linden and Dedrick 2011, 5). The less Apple has to spend on paying wages the higher the company's profits.

In its marketing campaigns Apple presents its products as technological marvels without history.[12] They divert attention away from the fact that underpaid Chinese workers are producing these products during 10 to 12 hour shifts at least six days a week, in exhausting and repetitive working procedures, while jeopardizing their health. Once displayed on posters, magazines and TV spots, iPad, MacBook and co. have lost any trace of the conditions under which they were produced.

Conclusion

The conditions in Apple's supply chain do not remain uncontested. For several years NGOs and labour rights activists have been protesting against Apple tolerating unbearable working conditions in its supplier factories. For example on May 7, 2011 an international day of action against unacceptable treatment of workers was held. Make IT Fair, a project of a group of European corporate watchdog organizations, under the slogan "Time to bite into a fair Apple; Call for sustainable IT!" organized protest events throughout Europe.[13,14]

Furthermore workers themselves are engaging in protest actions. For example on January 15, 2010, 2,000 workers at United Win, the factory in which n-hexane poisonings occurred, organized a strike (SACOM 2010b, 1). On November 15, 2011 several thousand workers from the Foxconn facility in Foshan were protesting against low wages.[15] Such protests are not without risks for factory workers. In 2011 during an investigation at Foxconn's Zhengzhou factory some interviewees told SACOM about workers being dismissed after attempting to strike (SACOM 2011b, 10). In January 2011 the police arrested around 20 workers at another Foxconn facility while protesting against miscalculation of wages (SACOM 2011a, 8).

However, the scope of these protests is limited in comparison to the systematic abuse of workers that takes place throughout the electronics industry. Apple is not the only hardware company that fails to resolve the problem of unacceptable working conditions in its supplier factories. Sweatshop-like working conditions can be found throughout the industry. SOMO for example stresses:

Research done for SOMO in China and the Philippines shows that computers are produced under endemic overtime, while a lack of unions and barriers to organizing means that the workers cannot negotiate improvements. Workers are hired on short term contracts for years, blacklisted and subjected to discriminatory application processes.

(SOMO 2005a, preface)

The main reason why most computer companies have relocated their production to China and other low wage countries is to reduce costs. Apple stresses that competition in the computer industry is high "The Company is confronted by aggressive competition in all areas of its business" (Apple SEC filings. 10-k form 2010). The industry would furthermore be characterized by strong price pressure: "Over the past several years, price competition in these markets have been particularly intense" (Apple SEC filings. 10-k form 2010). These conditions reinforce the need for cheap labour. Capitalist globalization and capital mobility allow companies to exploit cheap labour wherever they find it. Violations of labour rights and extreme exploitation of workers are thus not a merely moral problem of a specific company, such as Apple, but relate to the way capitalism operates as an economic system. Capitalism is characterized by the competition of private companies that strive for maximum capital accumulation. If one company decides not to participate in this price competition it is unlikely that it can survive in the market. The conditions in factories in low wage countries are an example that shows that capitalism has not been able to overcome de-humanized work and to create a good life for all.

Karl Marx in 1844 in the *Economic Philosophic Manuscripts* described the alienation of workers as his/her labour becoming an external object that "exists outside him, independently, as something alien to him" (Marx 1844/2007b, 70). The more life the worker puts into his/her product, the more alienated s/he becomes: "The worker puts his life into the object; but now his life no longer belongs to him but to the object. [. . .] The greater this product, the less is he himself" (Marx 1844/2007b, 70). Workers have put their labour power into Apple's products while producing them. Many workers left their families, gave up their free time and their health for producing these products, which they will never be able to own. The finished products, although containing the workers' energy and labour, suddenly are out of their reach. Workers are inside Apple's products, but at the same time insurmountably separated from them. One worker form Foxconn's Guanlan facility in Shenzhen expressed this condition of alienation as follows: "Though we produce for iPhone, I haven't got a chance to use iPhone. I believe it is fascinating and has lots of function. However, I don't think I can own one by myself" (Worker quoted in SACOM 2011a, 19).

Notes

1 *Forbes Magazine. The World's Biggest Public Companies.* Retrieved from http://www.forbes.com/global2000/#page:1_sort:4_direction:desc_search:_filter:All%20industries_filter:All%20countries_filter:All%20states on April 24, 2013.

2 Compound annual growth rate (CAGR).
3 *Fortune*. 2013. *World's Most Admired Companies*. Retrieved from http://money.cnn.com/magazines/fortune/most-admired/ on April 24, 2013.
4 *Wired Magazine*. 2011. *1 Million Workers. 90 Million iPhones. 17 Suicides. Who's to blame?* By Joel Johnson on February 28, 2011. Retrieved from http://www.wired.com/magazine/2011/02/ff_joelinchina/all/1 on October 23, 2011.
5 *The New York Times*. 2010. *String of Suicides Continues at Electronics Supplier in China*. By David Barboza on May 25, 2010. Retrieved from http://www.nytimes.com/2010/05/26/technology/26suicide.html on October 24, 2011.
6 BBC. 2010. *Foxconn Suicides: Workers Feel Quite Lonely*. May 28, 2010. Retrieved from http://www.bbc.co.uk/news/10182824 on October 24, 2011.
7 *The Guardian*. 2010. *Latest Foxconn Suicide Raises Concern over Factory Life in China*. By Tania Branigan on May 17, 2010. Retrieved from http://www.guardian.co.uk/world/2010/may/17/foxconn-suicide-china-factory-life on October 24, 2011.
8 Steve Jobs. 2010. Quoted in *The Telegraph*. 2010. *Foxconn Suicides Rate is lower than in the US, say's Apple's Steve Jobs*. Retrieved from http://www.telegraph.co.uk/technology/steve-jobs/7796546/Foxconn-suicide-rate-is-lower-than-in-the-US-says-Apples-Steve-Jobs.html on October 31, 2011.
9 FLA. 2012. *Foxconn Investigation Report*. Retrieved from http://www.fairlabor.org/report/foxconn-investigation-report on April 10, 2012.
10 *Fortune*. 2011. *Global 500*. Retrieved from http://money.cnn.com/magazines/fortune/global500/2011/snapshots/11204.html on October 24, 2011.
11 *Forbes Magazine*. *The World's Biggest Public Companies*. Retrieved from http://www.forbes.com/global2000/#page:1_sort:4_direction:desc_search:_filter:All%20industries_filter:All%20countries_filter:All%20states on April 24, 2013.
12 In 2011 for example Apple advertised the iPad as "Amazingly thin and light" as a "Technology so advanced, you'll forget it's even there". Apple. 2011. Retrieved from http://www.apple.com/ipad/ on October 25, 2011.
13 SOMO. 2011. *Time to Bite Into a Fair Apple. Call for Sustainable IT! Join Action Day on May 7th*. Retrieved from http://somo.nl/events-en/time-to-bite-into-a-fair-apple-call-for-sustainable-it-join-action-day-on-may-7th on October 27, 2011.
14 A video that documents one campaign activity can be watched. Retrieved from http://www.youtube.com/watch?v=kaiXni3h2Ug&feature=player_embedded on October 27, 2011.
15 M.I.C. Gadget. 2010. *More Problems With Foxconn; Workers Protest Against Their Wages*. Retrieved from http://micgadget.com/9620/more-problems-with-foxconn-workers-protest-against-their-wages/ on October 27, 2011.

6   AT&T

Internet censor?

AT&T Inc has a complex company history. Today's AT&T is the outcome of a number of mergers and acquisitions in the aftermath of the dissolution of the original AT&T Corporation. The origins of the original AT&T company date back to 1877 and the formation of the Bell Telephone Company. In 1899 the Bell Telephone Company was transferred to AT&T, which had until then had been one of its subsidies. The AT&T Corporation for many decades held a de facto monopoly on telecommunications in the US. However, in 1974 the US Department of Justice filed an antitrust lawsuit against AT&T, which was resolved with a settlement in 1982. On January 1, 1984 AT&T was spilt up into seven regional telecommunications companies, commonly referred to as Baby Bells.[1] Today's AT&T company is the result of a merger of one these Baby Bells and its former parent company AT&T: the Southwestern Bell Corporation, which in 1995 changed its name to SBC Communications Inc, acquired AT&T Corporation and again changed its name to AT&T Inc.[2] In 2006 AT&T Inc. acquired another Baby Bell, BellSouth.[3]

Today, AT&T Inc. is the largest telecommunications company in the world. In 2010 its profits amounted to 20.18 billion USD (AT&T SEC filings. 10-k form 2010) and *Forbes Magazine* ranked it as the 14th biggest company in the world.[4]

CSR approach

AT&T published its first CSR report in 2006, followed by four further reports until 2010. In these reports AT&T seems to aim at creating a balance between presenting itself as a responsible company with good business sense – as good but also rational: two different lines of argument can be identified in AT&T's CSR communications – one based on a dualist logic of creating benefits for society and the company, and another one that highlights the instrumental value of CSR for the bottom line.

The dualist rhetoric is manifested in statements that express AT&T's aims of contributing to both, building a better company and a better world. CEO Randall Stephenson highlights in the 2007/2008 report: "we work to build a better company [. . .] and create a better world and more sustainable future" (AT&T_CSR 2007/2008, 5). Similarly AT&T in the 2008 report writes: "Working together, we'll build a better company, a better world and a more sustainable future" (AT&T_CSR 2008, 3). A statement from the 2009 report contains the essence of a dualist view on CSR as being beneficial for society and business interests: "We use the term citizenship and sustainability (C&S) to talk about these efforts – and to describe a way of doing business that benefits both our company and society" (AT&T_CSR 2009, 10). This idea of creating shared values represents a dualist understanding of CSR as a means for satisfying both social needs and business interest.

In attempting to create credibility regarding the company's CSR commitment, AT&T refers to a long history of social responsibility: "AT&T has enjoyed a long history as one of the world's leading communications companies. Since our company was created, we have dedicated ourselves to satisfying customers, enriching stockholders and meeting the needs of society" (AT&T_CSR 2006, 1; see also 2007/2008, 5; 2008, 3).

The 2008 report furthermore contains a sustainability and citizenship timetable (AT&T_CSR 2008, 10f), which lists everything AT&T considers as a proof of its social concern: from introducing an employee benefits programme in 1913, to their efforts in enabling long distance calls to enable communication between soldiers and their families in World War II, to the launch of an environment programme in 1995 and the acquisition of 105 alternative-fuel vehicles in 2008, to name just a few.

Despite these references to a long history of social and environmental responsibility, more instrumental arguments can also be found in AT&T's CSR reports. Several statements in AT&T CSR communications reveal a reductionist logic in which business benefits and competitive advantages are described as the main reason for engaging in CSR activities. In 2007 AT&T for example points at positive effects of good citizenship for business growth, stability, and product innovation: "At AT&T, we believe that good citizenship spurs growth, creates stability and triggers new opportunities to help the world communicate" (AT&T_CSR 2007, 3). Likewise AT&T uses the concept of sustainable development in a reductionist sense as sustained business growth: "our business wouldn't be sustainable without the continued innovation that brings to life new business models and products" (AT&T_CSR 2009, 6). Given this understanding of sustainability the motto of the AT&T's CSR communication "Connecting for a Sustainable Future" seems to refer to sustainable business success, rather than to the sustainable development of society.

Furthermore the way AT&T selects its CSR focus areas is highly instrumental: AT&T argues that no company is able to focus on all relevant CSR issues and that therefore a decision has to be made "about where it can direct its resources and realize maximum benefit" (AT&T_CSR 2007/2008, 48). AT&T therefore tries to select "issues that combine business relevance, stakeholder importance and the ability to act in a meaningful way" (AT&T_CSR 2007/2008, 48). The company introduced a "strategic materiality assessment" to identify the most important CSR topics. This assessment combines two factors: "importance to stakeholders" and "influence on business success" (AT&T_CSR 2007/2008,51).

Those issues that score the highest in both domains mark AT&T's focus areas (AT&T_CSR 2007/2008, 51). AT&T assessed the category "importance to stakeholders" based on reports and statements from governments, media, customers, NGOs, socially responsible investors, etc. For assessing the category "business relevance" AT&T conducted interviews with senior executives (AT&T_CSR 2007/2008, 48).

AT&T first did this assessment in 2007/2008 and repeated it in 2010. The issues that ranked highest in both domains in 2007/2008 were "company energy use, privacy and data security, employee diversity, innovation" (AT&T_CSR 2007/2008, 51). In 2010 these issues were "company energy use", "innovation", "network reliability", "customer privacy" and "data security and diversity" (AT&T_CSR 2010, 75).

This way of identifying CSR issues is highly instrumental. It not only shows AT&T which issues directly influence business success, but also which CSR issues are the most important for customers. Addressing the former issues are those that are core to business success, while addressing the latter issues creates additional advantages because it allows the company to develop a good reputation in those areas that are most relevant to civil society in general and customers in particular. Of course some issues are ranked low in one of the two areas or even in both areas. Issues ranked lowest in both areas were "packaging", "water usage", "ozone depleting emissions", "mobile theft" (AT&T_CSR 2007/2008, 51) in 2007/2008 and "compensation benefits", "working hours and wages", "offshoring", "outsourcing" (AT&T_CSR 2010, 76) in 2010. Issues that scored highest in regard to importance for stakeholders and at the same time lowest in influence on business success were "network recycling" and "waste reduction" in 2007/2008 (AT&T_CSR 2007/2008, 51) and "hazardous waste reduction", "content protection", "network equipment recycling", "conflict minerals" and "customer products recycling" in 2010 (AT&T_CSR 2010, 76). These issues remain outside AT&T's focus area, no matter how important they might be from the perspective of society or the environment. Using the criterion of "influence on business success" from the outset removes all issues that might limit business success from AT&T's CSR agenda.

Controversies: net neutrality

AT&T is one the leading companies that provide access to telecommunications and Internet networks to people throughout the US. According to the Columbia Institute of Tele-Information (CITI), in 2011 AT&T controlled 39.5 per cent of the US wireline Internet market, followed by Verizon with a market share of 24.7 per cent (CITI 2011a). The US Internet access market is highly concentrated, with AT&T being the biggest player.

AT&T and a handful of other companies thus have large amounts of power over telecommunications in the US. Civil society groups, most prominently Free Press, highlight the need to restrict the power of these companies. They campaign for the importance of an open and accessible Internet and call for regulation that forces Internet Services Providers to fulfil this responsibility. In recent years this controversy has unfolded in regard to the concept of net neutrality. The media reform group Free Press, which aims at protecting net neutrality, defines it as follows: "Net Neutrality means that Internet service providers may not discriminate between different kinds of content and applications online. It guarantees a level playing field for all websites and Internet technologies".[5] They emphasize the importance of net neutrality for protecting the openness of the Internet: "The loss of Net Neutrality would end this unparalleled opportunity for freedom of expression".[6]

During the past years net neutrality was subjected to a contested policy formation process in the US. After having defined the principles of net neutrality in 2005, the Federal Communications Commission (FCC) in 2009 attempted to enact stronger net neutrality regulation, including the possibility of stricter enforcement (FCC 2009). However, due to strong corporate pressure the proposed rules were substantially weakened (FCC 2010) until they came into effect on November 20, 2011.[7] In fact, many observers called the final rules a victory for AT&T. *The New York Times* for example highlighted that "the new rules are, at best, net semi-neutrality" and that they would "afford more wiggle room to wireless providers like AT&T and Verizon".[8] In the following I summarize AT&T's arguments against net neutrality and confront them with the concerns of net neutrality advocates.

AT&T's arguments against net neutrality regulation

AT&T does not mention the topic of net neutrality in its CSR communications. However, on several occasions the company has publicly highlighted that it rejects the idea of net neutrality. Jim Cicconi, AT&T's Senior Executive Vice President-External and Legislative Affairs, for example stated: "AT&T has consistently opposed any FCC [Federal Communication Commission] regulation of Internet services or facilities. This is still our strong preference today".[9]

AT&T was at the forefront of the lobbying process against net neutrality. The company for example was a member of the "Hands Off the Internet" campaign, a coalition of net neutrality opponents.[10] AT&T made great efforts to influence the FCCs' policy on net neutrality. Jim Cicconi claimed in 2011 that the FCC and its attempt to enforce net neutrality was influenced by the ideas of AT&T's "opponents", which "were in many cases truly bad, and radical, ideas".[11]

> In October of 2009, some of these bad ideas found their way into a proposed net neutrality rule at the FCC. AT&T, and the entire industry, strongly opposed this proposal. It created a high degree of market concern, and needless to say a very bad climate for investment.[12]

Furthermore, in a letter to all the company managers Jim Cicconi urged them to tell the FCC that they opposed net neutrality.[13] In the following I briefly summarize AT&T's anti-net neutrality arguments as they can be found in this letter to employees and in several postings on the AT&T Public Policy Blog, letters to the FCC and other documents.

- *The net was never neutral*: One of AT&T's arguments against net neutrality is that the Internet thus far has been flourishing without any regulation that enforced net neutrality. According to AT&T net neutrality regulation would mean an unnecessary and harmful government intervention into a well functioning market. AT&T argues: "Why disrupt a market that works so well".[14]

  By arguing that net neutrality has not existed in the past AT&T refers to a method called "differentiated service code point", DiffServ. DiffServ allows users to flag different data packages and to define which of them should be given priority within a user's Internet traffic (AT&T 2010, 1f). Packages a user might choose for prioritization for example are those that require a fast Internet connection and function best without interruption such as voice or streaming services.

  In 2010 in a blogpost on AT&Ts website[15] the company's Vice President for Federal Regulatory Affairs Hank Hultquist, who represents the company at the FCC, stressed that he would prefer the term "quality of service" over "paid prioritization". He argued that through DiffServ "paid prioritization of Internet traffic is widely available to businesses today" and calls those who oppose paid prioritization, such as Free Press, the "Church of Extreme Net Neutrality (CoENN)".[16]

- *Regulation is harmful*: AT&T's arguments against net neutrality are rooted in the belief that markets automatically produce best results and regulation is always a burden that hampers optimum outcomes for companies, consumers and society: "The market is working for consumers. Don't burden it with unnecessarily harmful regulations".[17] According to this view, the wireless and broadband industry works well and brings investment and jobs to the USA and should therefore not be "burdened" by regulation.[18] AT&T makes clear that its opposition to Internet regulation is not limited to the topic of net neutrality: "Obviously, AT&T's strong preference would be for the FCC [Federal Communication Commission] to refrain from any regulation in the Internet space".[19]

- *Net neutrality threatens jobs and infrastructure*: Furthermore AT&T argues that net neutrality poses a threat to the improvement of broadband infrastructure because it would "halt private investment in broadband infrastructure".[20] In a letter to the FCC, AT&T demands that

    > the Commission should reject calls from Free Press and others to ban or significantly restrict the provision of paid prioritization services, which would be contrary to the goals of innovation, investment, and growth, and contrary to the interests of small, medium-sized, and minority-owned businesses.[21]

- *Net neutrality hampers the spread of broadband Internet access*: According to AT&T's logic, it is only possible to provide comprehensive broadband access if network companies are using their bandwidth capacity in an effective way. Net neutrality would render this impossible.[22] Especially in regard to mobile Internet, traffic management according to AT&T is a technical necessity. In a blogpost on August 13, 2011[23] AT&T argued, that "wireless is simply different". As wireless broadband is challenged through a "struggle between capacity and demand" it would be essential to allow dynamic traffic management without restrictions through net neutrality regulation. This would require "protecting wireless broadband networks from onerous new net neutrality regulations". Finally AT&T highlights that creating an exception for wireless broadband from net neutrality rules would be necessary for ensuring "continued growth of the industry".[24]

- *Large Internet corporations are the main beneficiaries of net neutrality*: AT&T also argues that net neutrality would first and foremost benefit large Internet corporations, because they would not have to pay for delivering their service to their customers. According to AT&T net neutrality would allow Google, Facebook, Yahoo!, etc. to use broadband services for free. Former AT&T CEO Edward Whitacre in an interview with *Bloomberg Businessweek* explained why he considers the "free-riding" of large corporations a problem:

> Now what they would like to do is use my pipes free, but I ain't going to let them do that because we have spent this capital and we have to have a return on it. So there's going to have to be some mechanism for these people who use these pipes to pay for the portion they're using. Why should they be allowed to use my pipes? The Internet can't be free in that sense, because we and the cable companies have made an investment and for a Google or Yahoo! or Vonage or anybody to expect to use these pipes [free] is nuts![25]

AT&T's arguments against net neutrality do not remain uncontested. Advocates of net neutrality try to show that a dismissal of net neutrality would fundamentally change the way the Internet works today.

The case for net neutrality regulation

Efforts to protect net neutrality are connected to the "Save the Internet" campaign,[26] which was created by the media reform group Free Press.[27] Net neutrality advocates argue that without net neutrality the Internet would structurally privilege powerful economic and political actors and compromise the online visibility of those who cannot pay for it. In the following I present their counter-arguments against AT&T's anti-net neutrality claims.

- *The Internet has flourished because of net neutrality*: AT&T's argument that the Internet has flourished thus far without net neutrality misrepresents the history of the Internet. Tim Berners Lee, inventor of the www for examples stresses: "There have been suggestions that we don't need legislation because we haven't had it. These are nonsense, because in fact we have had net neutrality in the past".[28] Quite contrary to AT&Ts claims, the development and the success of the Internet has been based on an egalitarian structure that does not privilege any provider of online content, services and application through technical mechanisms. Vinton Cerf, who because of his involvement in the development of the Transmission Control Protocol (TCP) and Internet Protocol (IP) is known as one of the founding fathers of the Internet,[29] stresses that the Internet from its very beginning was based on the principles of neutrality, openness and the "overarching rationale that no central gatekeeper should exert control over the Internet" (Cerf 2009, 18.2). At a hearing at the US Congress Cerf emphasized the danger that would result if Internet providers are no longer bound by net neutrality rules: "Allowing broadband carriers to control what people see and do online would fundamentally undermine the principles that have made the internet such a success".[30] In contrast to AT&T, these Internet pioneers argue that it was due to net neutrality that the Internet could flourish.

Free Press has strongly contested AT&Ts argument that DiffServ technology constitutes a form of paid prioritization and therefore would illustrate the absence of net neutrality rules in the past. Free Press argues that DiffServe is a useful, user-driven method for traffic management that is free of charge.[31] In contrast to DiffServe, paid prioritization would mean that customers could pay internet service providers (ISPs) for privileging their content through slowing down other content.[32] Vinton Cerf in this context warned not to confuse net neutrality with legitimate traffic management "Some people have mistakenly claimed that sustaining openness means preventing legitimate network management or service offerings from ISPs" (Cerf 2009, 18.2). While net neutrality does not mean to prohibit all forms of traffic management, it does mean that ISPs are not allowed to take money for privileging the content of one provider over the content of any other.

- *Market logic is harmful*: AT&T claims that regulations would harm the Internet market.[33] This argument is questionable – even from a pro-market perspective: as Derek Turner from Free Press highlights, without net neutrality AT&T and other ISPs could require all providers of online content to pay fees for having their content delivered to potential users. This would not only mean that using the Internet would become more expensive or even unaffordable for non-profit organizations but also for new businesses. From this perspective net neutrality regulation protects the market instead of destroying it (Turner 2009, 9).

Furthermore it is questionable whether leaving telecommunications to the logic of markets is desirable. The development of the US mobile wireless market for example clearly shows that market logic leads to concentration: while in 1984 the four largest mobile phone providers together controlled 27.9 per cent, in 2011 the largest four companies control 95.9 per cent of the market (CITI 2011b). "Free" competition and market logic have thus resulted in rapid concentration processes that have placed a huge amount of power over an extremely important infrastructure in the hands of just a few corporations. Without net neutrality regulation these companies would acquire even more power.

- *Net neutrality creates incentives for investment*: AT&T argues that net neutrality regulation would reduce investments in this sector. Free Press points out that quite the contrary net neutrality would require ISPs to expand their infrastructure in order to be able to serve all potential customers (Turner 2009, 3). Without net neutrality these investments would not be necessary because ISPs could profit from keeping capacities limited, creating artificial scarcity and instead offering paid prioritization services to those who can afford them (Turner 2009, 3).

  A study based on game-theoretical modelling confirms this argument: "The incentive for the broadband service provider to expand under NN [net neutrality] is mostly higher than the incentive to expand when the principle of NN is abolished" (Cheng, Bandyopadhyay and Guo 2011, 75). Free Press furthermore argues that AT&T itself has in the past invested heavily in the expansion of infrastructure, despite net neutrality rules (Turner 2009, 7).

  Moreover, AT&T is an extremely profitable company that can afford maintenance and further development of broadband infrastructure. AT&T's financial records show continuous economic growth (AT&T SEC filings. 10-k forms 1993–2010): from a loss of 849 million USD in 1993, AT&T's profits climbed to 20.2 billion USD in 2010. During this period its revenues increased from 10.7 billion USD to 124.3 billion USD and in terms of total assets AT&T today is 11 times richer than it was in 1993. For comparison, AT&T's 2010 profits of 20.18 billion USD are more than double the gross domestic product of Mozambique, a country with almost 23 million inhabitants, which in 2010 was 9.9 billion USD.[34] Amounting to 268.5 billion USD, AT&T's total assets are higher than Egypt's 2010 gross domestic product of 218.5 billion USD, a country with more than 80 million inhabitants.[35]

  Given these numbers AT&T's arguments that net neutrality would threaten investment seems extremely implausible. It is not net neutrality that poses a threat to future investment, but AT&T's profit considerations. AT&T's argument that net neutrality would threaten jobs and the development of infrastructure seems to be both a threat to the government to cut investments if regulators decide against AT&T's interests and an excuse for cutting jobs and investments.

- *Net neutrality is a precondition for equal access*: AT&T argues that its bandwidth capacities are limited and it would therefore be necessary to prioritize certain Internet content. Again, the question how much bandwidth is available is not a question of net neutrality regulation being in place or not. It solely depends on AT&T's willingness to expand its infrastructure instead of keeping it artificially scarce.

  AT&T's claim that "wireless is different"[36] is, however, not too surprising. The wireless segment is becoming increasingly important for AT&T's profits. The number of AT&T'S wireless customers more than quadrupled from 19.7 million subscribers in 2010 to 95.5 million customers in 2010 (AT&T

SEC filings. 10-k form 2010). In 2010 income from the wireless segment made up 43 per cent of AT&T'S total revenues of 124.3 billion USD (AT&T SEC filings. 10-k form 2010).

Avoiding net neutrality regulation for wireless Internet for AT&T means protecting one of its most important business segments from regulation that might fetter profit accumulation. Without net neutrality rules AT&T could for example raise its income through charging providers of mobile Internet content for fast delivery of their content.

- *Society is the main beneficiary of net neutrality*: One of AT&T's arguments against net neutrality is that these rules would allow large corporations to use their network for free. First of all this argument neglects that Internet access is not free today. Consumers are paying for accessing the content and services they want to use. Turner from Free Press has points out that consumers only pay for Internet access because they want to use specific services: "consumers don't place value on the connection; they place value on the content delivered by that connection" (Turner 2009, 3). AT&T's argument that anybody would use the company's infrastructure for free is therefore not true.

  However, it is true that companies such as Amazon, eBay or Google advocate net neutrality.[37] As net neutrality protects these companies from paying additional fees, it is not surprising that they are in support of such a regulation. This, however, does not mean that they are its main beneficiaries. Companies such as Google and Amazon are highly profitable and could afford to pay fees for prioritizing their services. Individual bloggers, NGOs, civil society organizations, alternative media, protest groups, social movements, etc. on the contrary often have only limited financial resources and could therefore not afford prioritization. This means that in an Internet without net neutrality financially powerful actors could distribute their services much faster than others. In such an Internet, power would further shift away from the public to financially powerful corporations. Thus it is not true that the main beneficiaries of net neutrality are corporations. On the contrary it is society, including individuals, NGOs, protest groups, alternative media, etc., which net neutrality protects from a further expansion of corporate power and control.

To sum up: AT&T's arguments are flawed. AT&T follows its own private profit interests and tries to present them as the universal interests of society. AT&T's arguments against net neutrality ignore the fact that the Internet has thus far been protected through net neutrality regulations; miss the difference between net neutrality and network management; follow a one-dimensional market logic that denies that markets do not automatically create best results for everybody, but instead lead to concentration of power and to inequality; use net neutrality regulation as an excuse for not investing in infrastructure and for cutting jobs; and confuses the beneficiaries and losers of net neutrality regulation.

One loser of net neutrality regulations certainly is the profit of AT&T and other internet service providers because it prohibits them from charging additional money for prioritizing Internet traffic. Without net neutrality AT&T could, instead of spending money for further developing broadband infrastructure, generate more profit through distributing existing bandwidth capacity among providers of Internet content by establishing fast lanes for those who pay extra money and slow lanes for those who do not. It seems that the real reason why AT&T opposes net neutrality is that it considers it a fetter to further profit maximization.

Conclusion

In its CSR communication AT&T alternates between a dualist and a reductionist rhetoric. At AT&T the selection of CSR focus areas is based on a so-called "strategic materiality assessment", which defines those topics as most relevant that score high both in regard to relevance for business success and relevance for stakeholders. Social and environmental issues that might contradict business success are thus excluded from AT&T's CSR agenda.

The topic of net neutrality is not even included in AT&T's materiality assessment. Considering the importance this topic has had in policy debates regarding the telecommunications sector during the last few years, this neglect seems surprising.

AT&T's opposition to net neutrality is problematic from a social responsibility perspective. Critical media scholars and civil society groups highlight that the abolition of net neutrality would threaten online content and access to the Internet. Lessig and McChesney in this context point out:

> A handful of massive companies would control access and distribution of content, deciding what you get to see and how much it costs. Major industries such as health care, finance, retailing and gambling would face huge tariffs for fast, secure Internet use – all subject to discriminatory and exclusive deal-making with telephone and cable giants.
>
> (Lessig and McChesney 2006)

For individuals, non-profit organizations, alternative media, protest groups, etc. it would on the contrary become even more difficult to distribute content online. This would further increase the dominance of corporate and mainstream media content and marginalize alternative and oppositional content.

These threats are not hypothetical. There have already been instances in the past where AT&T has discriminated against local public access TV channels. In its TV offerings AT&T created a generic channel for all public access stations instead of putting each on an individual channel. This created less visibility for public access stations. The complexity of the process of navigating through this bundled channel further restricted the accessibility of these alternative media stations. [38,39]

A technically egalitarian structure is an important precondition for realizing an accessible Internet. However, technical equality is not enough. Even with net neutrality rules being in place, the Internet is not completely neutral. Those who have the resources to advertise and regularly update their content and services are likely to receive greater visibility. For alternative media projects, individual bloggers or protest groups it is often much more difficult to attract a large online audience than it is for established corporate media. A look at the Alexa ranking of the 500 top sites on the web reveals that most frequently accessed sites belong to large media corporations.[40] Without technical net neutrality economic censorship on the Internet would reach an unprecedented level and a few ISPs could function as gatekeepers.

Net neutrality thus is a necessary but not a sufficient condition for the emergence of an open, egalitarian and accessible public sphere on the Internet. The debate on net neutrality thus has important implications for the future of the Internet. Given the social importance of this topic, AT&T's neglect to discuss it in its CSR communication seems problematic.

Notes

1 CNN. 2001. *The Story of Ma Bell.* Retrieved from http://money.cnn.com/2001/07/09/deals/att_history/index.htm on December 1, 2011.

2 AT&T. *A Brief History.* Retrieved from http://www.corp.att.com/history/history5.html on December 2, 2011.

3 *The New York Times.* 2006. *AT&T to Buy Bell South, Creating Telecom Giant.* Retrieved from http://www.nytimes.com/2006/03/05/business/05cnd-phone.html on December 1, 2011.

4 *Forbes Magazine.* 2011. *Global 2000 Leading Companies. AT&T.* Retrieved from http://www.forbes.com/companies/att/ on June 17, 2011.

5 Free Press. *Save the Internet Campaign. FAQs.* Retrieved from http://www.savetheinternet.com/faq on December 5, 2011.

6 Free Press. *Save the Internet Campaign. FAQs.* Retrieved from http://www.savetheinternet.com/faq on December 5, 2011.

7 *The Washington Post.* 2011. *FCC Net Neutrality Official 20 Nov; Lawsuit Expected to Follow.* By Cecillia Kand. Retrieved from http://www.washingtonpost.com/blogs/post-tech/post/fcc-net-neutrality-official-nov-20-lawsuits-expected-to-follow/2011/09/22/gIQARXdWoK_blog.html on December 8, 2011.

8 *The New York Times.* 2010. *F.C.C. Approves Net Rules and Brace for Fight.* By Brian Stelter. Retrieved from http://mediadecoder.blogs.nytimes.com/2010/12/21/f-c-c-approves-net-rules-and-braces-for-fight/ on December 9, 2011.

9 Cicconi, Jim. 2011. *AT&T's Cicconi on Net Neutrality Before Congressional Hearing.* AT&T Public Policy Blog. Retrieved from http://attpublicpolicy.com/government-policy/atts-cicconi-on-net-neutrality-before-congressional-hearing/ on December 5, 2011.

10 Hands Off the Internet. *Member Organizations.* Retrieved from http://web.archive.org/web/20080704184836/http://www.handsoff.org/blog/member-organizations on December 3, 2011.

11 Ciccioni, Jim. 2011. *AT&T's Cicconi on Net Neutrality Before Congressional Hearing.* AT&T Public Policy Blog. Retrieved from http://attpublicpolicy.com/government-policy/atts-cicconi-on-net-neutrality-before-congressional-hearing/ on December 5, 2011.

12 Cicconi, Jim. 2011. *AT&T's Cicconi on Net Neutrality Before Congressional Hearing.* AT&T Public Policy Blog. Retrieved from http://attpublicpolicy.com/government-policy/atts-cicconi-on-net-neutrality-before-congressional-hearing/ on December 5, 2011.

13 AT&T Letter to Managers. 2009. Retrieved from http://www.freepress.net/files/Cicconi_0.jpg on December 5, 2011.

14 AT&T Letter to Managers. 2009. Retrieved from http://www.freepress.net/files/Cicconi_0.jpg on December 5, 2011.

15 Hultquist, Hank. 2010. *The Danger of Dogman*. AT&T Public Policy Blog. Retrieved from http://attpublicpolicy.com/government-policy/the-danger-of-dogma/ on December 7, 2011.

16 Hultquist, Hank. 2010. *The Danger of Dogma*. AT&T Public Policy Blog. Retrieved from http://attpublicpolicy.com/government-policy/the-danger-of-dogma/ on December 7, 2011.

17 AT&T Letter to Managers. 2009. Retrieved from http://www.freepress.net/files/Cicconi_0. jpg on December 5, 2011.

18 AT&T Letter to Managers. 2009. Retrieved from http://www.freepress.net/files/Cicconi_0. jpg on December 5, 2011.

19 AT&T Blog Team. 2010. *AT&T Statement on Proposed FCC Rules to Preserve an Open Internet*. Retrieved from http://attpublicpolicy.com/government-policy/att-statement-on-proposed-fcc-rules-to-preserve-an-open-internet/ on December 5, 2011.

20 AT&T Letter to Managers. 2009. Retrieved from http://www.freepress.net/files/Cicconi_0. jpg on December 5, 2011.

21 AT&T. 2010. Letter to the FCC on August 30, 2010. Retrieved from http://fjallfoss.fcc. gov/ecfs/document/view?id=7020910396 on December 5, 2011.

22 AT&T Letter to Managers. 2009. Retrieved from http://www.freepress.net/files/Cicconi_0. jpg on December 5, 2011.

23 Marsh, Joan. 2011. *Wireless is Different*. AT&T Public Policy Blog. Retrieved from http://attpublicpolicy.com/government-policy/wireless-is-different/ on December 5, 2011.

24 Marsh, Joan. 2011. *Wireless is Different*. AT&T Public Policy Blog. Retrieved from http://attpublicpolicy.com/government-policy/wireless-is-different/ on December 5, 2011.

25 Whitacre, Edward. 2005. Interview with *Bloomsberg Businessweek* on November 7, 2005. Retrieved from http://www.businessweek.com/magazine/content/05_45/b3958092.htm on December 5, 2011.

26 Save the Internet. *About*. Retrieved from http://www.savetheinternet.com/about on December 7, 2011.

27 Save the Internet. *About*. Retrieved from http://www.savetheinternet.com/about on December 7, 2011.

28 Berners Lee, Tim. 2006. *Net Neutrality: This is Serious*. Retrieved from http://dig. csail.mit.edu/breadcrumbs/node/144 on December 12, 2011.

29 *The New York Times. Laurels for Giving the Internet its Language*. Retrieved from http://www.nytimes.com/2005/02/16/technology/16internet.html on December 7, 2011.

30 Cerf, Vinton. 2010. Cited in *The Economist*. 2010. *A Virtual-counter Revolution*. Retrieved from http://www.economist.com/node/16941635 on December 7, 2011.

31 Free Press. 2010. Letter to the FCC. Retrieved from http://fjallfoss.fcc.gov/ecfs/document/view?id=7020910396 on December 5, 2011.

32 Free Press. 2010. Letter to the FCC. Retrieved from http://fjallfoss.fcc.gov/ecfs/document/view?id=7020910396 on December 5, 2011.

33 AT&T Letter to Managers. 2009. Retrieved from http://www.freepress.net/files/Cicconi_0. jpg on December 5, 2011.

34 International Monetary Fund. 2011. *Gross Domestic Product Mozambique*. Retrieved from http://www.imf.org/external/pubs/ft/weo/2011/01/weodata/weorept.aspx?pr.x= 80&pr.y=15&sy=2009&ey=2016&scsm=1&ssd=1&sort=country&ds=.&br=1&c=68 8&s=NGDPD&grp=0&a= on December 12, 2011.

35 International Monetary Fund. 2011. *Gross Domestic Product Egypt*. Retrieved from http://www.imf.org/external/pubs/ft/weo/2011/01/weodata/weorept.aspx?pr.x=71&pr. y=9&sy=2009&ey=2016&scsm=1&ssd=1&sort=country&ds=.&br=1&c=469&s=N GDPD&grp=0&a= on December 12, 2011.

36 Marsh, Joan. 2011. *Wireless is Different*. AT&T Public Policy Blog. Retrieved fro http://attpublicpolicy.com/government-policy/wireless-is-different/ on December 5, 2011.

37 Google et al. 2009. Letter to the FCC. Retrieved from http://voices.washingtonpost.com/
    posttech/NN%20Letter%20of%20Support%20to%20Chairman%20Genachowski%20
    final%201019.pdf on December 9, 2011.
38 Democracy Now. 2009. *AT&T Accused of Discriminating Against Local Public Access
    Channels*. Retrieved from http://www.democracynow.org/2009/3/9/at_t_accused_of_
    discriminating_against on December 3, 2011.
39 Illinois Coalition for Justice, Peace & the Environment. 2010. *Bring AT&T to Justice
    for Discrimination*. Retrieved from http://icjpe.org/actions/Bring-AT-T-to-justice-for-
    discrimination on December 3, 2011.
40 Alexa. 2011. *Top Sites*. Retrieved from http://www.alexa.com/topsites/global on
    December 12, 2011.

7   Google
Evil spy?

Larry Page and Sergey Brin founded Google in 1998.[1] In the early 2000s Google's profit started to multiply and the company began to continuously expand its business. Some of Google's biggest acquisitions include the purchase of the photo sharing platform Picasa in 2004,[2] the mobile phone software provider Android in 2005 for 50 million USD,[3] YouTube in 2006 for 1.65 billion USD,[4] the email software Postini in 2007 for 625 million USD,[5] DoubleClick, purchased in 2008 for 3.1 billion USD,[6] AdMob mobile advertising for 750 million in 2009,[7] and in 2011 the online biding platform for selling ads Admeld for 400 million USD[8] as well as Motorola for 12.5 billion USD,[9] Google's most expensive purchase thus far.

Google's popularity among Internet users and its economic success have inspired books such as *The Google Story* (Vise 2005), *Planet Google* (Stross 2008), *The Google Way* (Girard 2009) or *What Would Google Do?* (Jarvis 2009). Some authors have argued that Google heralds a new way of doing business in the twenty-first century. Girard in *The Google Way* (2009) for example argues that Google was the first to build a "management model for the knowledge economy" and that Google is a "new enterprise archetype" (Girard 2009, 2). Jarvis calls Google "the first post-media company" (Jarvis 2009, 5) that operates "by new rules of a new age" (Jarvis 2009, 3).

In this chapter I will take a closer look and Google's business model and discuss its implications for the social responsibility of new media organizations.

CSR approach

Google does not provide a comprehensive CSR report. The company only uses the notion of CSR in regard to its philanthropic activities. Google writes: "Since its founding, Google has been firmly committed to active philanthropy and to addressing the global challenges of climate change, education and poverty alleviation".[10] Google Green and Google.org detail Google's philanthropic CSR activities. On Google Green, Google reports about its efforts in promoting environmental sustainability.[11] Google.org focuses on the theme of "technology driven philanthropy". Within its Google.org programme Google carries out charity and in-kind donations projects, offers volunteer work by Google employees, and operates several projects that intend to "find engineering solutions to global challenges such as climate change, clean energy and global health".[12] Google.org projects for example include Google Flu and Google Dengue Trends, which estimate the frequency of occurrence of these illnesses in specific countries or regions based on related search requests.[13] This focus on philanthropy suggests a dualist orientation of Google's CSR strategy that regards generating profit and giving back to society as two separate corporate goals.

However, Google's rhetoric of how it positively contributes to society goes far beyond that. Throughout its websites, Google presents itself as a company with strong corporate principles and values as well as a thorough corporate philosophy. Google states that its mission is "to organize the world's information and make it universally accessible and useful".[14] Without framing it as CSR, Google's descriptions of its business conduct resemble a projectionist approach to CSR that stresses that profit is generated in a socially responsible way. Google's *Code of Conduct* starts with the phrase "Don't be evil".[15] This corporate credo according to Google applies to how Google employees behave towards users, customers, towards other employees and also requires them to respect the law and to behave "honourably" in general.[16] In order to avoid being "evil" Google has established a variety of principles and policies including a *Code of Conduct*,[17] a 10 point Google philosophy,[18] five privacy principles,[19] 10 design principles,[20] six software principles,[21] a no pop-up policy[22] and a security policy.[23]

This projectionist rhetoric of being a company in which business activities are inherently socially responsible for example becomes evident in Google's descriptions of its corporate culture as playful, open, non-hierarchical and collaborative. Google highlights that what characterizes all its offices around the world are expressions of local culture, dogs, bicycles, lava lamps, massage chairs, large inflatable balls, laptops everywhere, shared offices and huddle rooms for "Googlers", yoga, dance classes, pool tables, pianos, video games, grassroots employee groups on various interests such as meditation or wine tasting, healthy food and break rooms with free snacks and drinks.[24] These descriptions of its corporate culture resemble what has been described as the post-bureaucratic workplace (see for example Kjonstad and Willmott 1995; Maravelias 2003; Hodgson 2004), in which labour relations become more flexible, networked, participatory and less hierarchical. Maravelias (2003, 549) states: "It is argued that, whereas bureaucracies are built on distinct splits between work and leisure, reason and emotion, pleasure and duty, etc., post-bureaucracies are all of a piece."

Google obviously plays with the blurring of boundaries between work and play. This also means that the boundaries between working time and free time tend to collapse. While the reasons to leave the workplace become fewer, the level of identification with the company becomes higher. A playful workplace is a creative workplace. Google has understood well how to foster the realization of the creative potentials of its employees that are key to its success. It stresses: "Our commitment to innovation depends on everyone being comfortable sharing ideas and opinions".[25]

One far-reaching measure Google takes is that it allows its engineers and developers to devote 20 per cent of their working time to their own projects.[26] Google stresses that this working environment allows them to attract the best employees and has resulted in profitable business projects: "We offer our engineers '20-percent time' so that they're free to work on what they're really passionate about. Google Suggest, AdSense for Content, and Orkut are among the many products of this perk".[27] This shows that Google profits financially from the "free time" it grants its employees.

Despite colourful sofas, sports facilities, free snacks and flexible working hours Google ultimately remains a workplace and a company with profit goals. It creates an environment that at the same time allows the unleashing and capturing the creative potentials of its employees. "Googlers" use their innovative human capacity for inventing useful software solutions, which Google appropriates and turns into profitable business opportunities.

In terms of CSR rhetoric Google's philanthropic activities are based on a dualist reasoning, while the company's descriptions of its corporate culture, values and business model follow a projectionist approach.

Controversies: online surveillance

Despite its commitment to not being evil, during the last few years corporate watchdogs have criticized Google's business practices. Christian Fuchs (2011b) in an article on the political economy of Google summarizes the major points of criticism that have been raised in the academic debate about Google: the company monopolizes the search engine market, provides a distorted and incomplete picture of reality, contributes to an unequal distribution of attention on the Internet, advances ideology, is opaque in regard to its search mechanism, contributes to Internet censorship and curtails human capacities (Fuchs 2011b). One theme that can be found in most critiques of Google is that its business model threatens the privacy of users. In the following I will summarize the key arguments of Google's critics regarding privacy violations, discuss how this relates to Google's business model and to Google's claim of doing business without being evil, and finally point out some of the risks related to surveillance online.

Online privacy

Siva Vaidhyanathan stresses that Google's privacy policy is "pretty much a lack-of-privacy policy" (Vaidhyanathan 2011, 84). Tene emphasizes: "Google's access to and storage of vast amounts of personally identifiable information create a serious privacy problem" (Tene 2008, 3). Tatli raises concerns that "Google with its huge index size threatens our privacy" (Tatli 2008, 51). Zimmer argues that the model of "search 2.0", which combines search infrastructure with web 2.0 applications, leads to "the concentrated surveillance, capture, and aggregation of one's online intellectual and social activities by a single provider" (Zimmer 2008). Maurer et al. in a research report on dangers and opportunities posed by large search engines stress "Google is massively invading privacy" (Maurer et al. 2007, 5).

Furthermore corporate watch organizations have also criticized the way Google collects and handles user information. In 2007 Privacy International (PI) for example, in an evaluation of the privacy practices of the largest Internet based companies, ranked Google at the bottom of list and described it as being "hostile to privacy".[28] After the European Commission approved Google's acquisition of DoubleClick in 2008, PI raised fundamental concerns that this merger would further compromise the protection of user data. Simon Davies, director of PI stated:

> This single reprehensible action by the Commission represents this decade's greatest threat to online privacy. The EU will rue the day that it allowed a near monopoly market to be controlled by this company. Online privacy will now be a hostage to fortune, inevitably suffering death from a thousand cuts. [29]

Similarly Google-watch.com calls Google a "privacy time bomb"[30]; Privacy Rights Clearinghouse (PRC) in 2004 criticized Google's Gmail privacy policy which permitted Google to scan the content of email and to store emails even if an account has been deleted[31]; Corporate Watch in 2008 highlighted shortcomings of the privacy policy for Google's Internet browser Google Chrome[32]; Google Monitor criticized Google for tracking Internet traffic, scanning emails and having default setting that allow for maximum data collection.[33] Google Monitor argues: "Google's targeted advertising business model is no 'privacy by design' and no 'privacy by default'".[34] Google Monitor in this statement points at the reason for the threat Google's practices pose to user data: its advertising based business model.

The web 2.0 business model

So-called web 2.0 or social media companies such as Google grant users to access products and services for free, while generating profit through selling space for advertisements (Sandoval 2012).

The money, which Google turns into its profit, does not come from its users but from advertisers. In a FAQ section on its Investor Relations webpage Google makes it clear that advertisers, not users, are its customers: "Our customers are over one million of advertisers, from small businesses targeting local customers to many of the world's largest global enterprises".[35]

Advertisers pay for receiving access to relevant consumer groups, which they can target with personalized ads. Personalized ads can be based on a variety of information about consumers such as demographics, personal interests, web usage behaviour, previous purchases, etc. As they are tailored to the needs and interests of specific individuals or groups they are supposed to be more effective than mass advertisements. Darren Charters for example states: "The ability to continually tailor Internet advertising to the interests of a user is an advance on previous advertising mediums and represents an opportunity to develop a competitive advantage in the industry" (Charters 2002, 243).

Google's initial business model focused on licensing search engine services to websites. In 2000 the company shifted to an advertising-based business model. Google's first offering to advertisers was called "Premium Sponsorship": advertisers could place text based ads on the Google website that matched different search queries. The price for these ads depended on how often the ad was displayed. Soon Google introduced AdWords, a web-based self-service offering for advertisers to place targeted ads on Google's websites. In 2002 the pay per display model was changed to a pay per click model (Google SEC filings. 10-k form 2004, 21). Furthermore Google created its AdSense program, which allows advertisers to display ads not only on the Google website but also directly on other websites that are part of the so-called "Google Network" (Google SEC filings. 10-k form 2004, 22).

Today, AdWords not only allows the display of ads on websites but also includes them in online videos, television and radio broadcasting (Google SEC filings. 10-k form 2009, 8). Advertisers using Google's AdWords can enter keywords, based on which their targeted ads are shown to users (Google SEC filings. 10-k form 2009, 9). Google has further diversified its AdSense offerings, which apart from AdSense for search and AdSense for content now include: Google AdSense for Domains, Google AdSense for Mobile, Google AdSense for Mobile Applications, Google AdSense for Video, Google AdSense for Feeds, Google AdSense for Games and Google Television Ads (Google SEC filings. 10-k form 2009, 11f). The fees advertisers have to pay to Google today are either calculated based on a pay per click or on a pay per impression model (Google SEC filings. 10-k form 2010, 25). Table 7.1 gives a brief overview of Google's current advertising services.

Table 7.1 Google's advertising services

AdWords	Text-based targeted ads that are displayed next to related search results or content on websites of Google and Google Network members.
AdSense	A program that allows members of the Google Network to display matching ads from Google's AdWords customers on their websites.
Google Display	Includes interactive video, text and image-based ads that are displayed on various Google and Google Network websites.
DoubleClick	Offers ad-serving technology and services to publishers and advertising agencies that allows them to create personalized ads and to display them across the web.
YouTube video advertising	Ads that are integrated into YouTube videos.
Google Mobile Advertising	Provides advertising solutions that are particularly suitable for mobile devices, for example click-for-call ads, which include a phone number in the ad text that can be instantly called.
Google local advertising	A service that is specifically targeted to help local businesses to advertise their offerings to people that are present in a specific local area.

Source: Google SEC filings. 10-k form 2010, 4.

For providing these advertising products Google collects, stores and combines masses of data about each and every user. When users use any of Google's services they have to agree to its privacy policy which details what information Google is allowed to collect and how it uses it.[36]

Google's privacy policy lists various kinds of user information that is collected.[37] Basically, Google stores three types of information about its users: first of all, Google collects information that users provide themselves when creating a Google account, using Google services, services of websites that are affiliated with Google and third party applications. Second, Google stores cookies on the computers of users that automatically collect and store information such as search queries, unique application number, location information, log information such as IP address, browser type, language, date and time of usage, etc. The third type of information Google collects and stores is the content of emails and messages. According to its privacy policy Google is allowed to store content of messages that are sent to Google as well as associated data such as phone number and email address.[38] What Google does not mention in its privacy policy is that it furthermore scans the content of all emails of a user's Gmail account to create personalized ads. In a statement on ads in Gmail Google writes "In Gmail, ads are related to the content of your messages".[39] Google's privacy policy applies to Gmail services; no additional Gmail privacy policy exists. The fact that this policy does not mention that Google is allowed to use email content for creating personalized ads shows that it is incomplete and deceives users.

Google's privacy policy remains fairly unspecific regarding how user data is used. It states that once collected, the information is used for providing and further developing Google's services, including advertising and for protecting "the rights or property of Google or our users".[40] In a section called "Information sharing" Google furthermore stresses that it only "shares" individual personally identifiable information under specific circumstances such as to affiliated companies that handle this information on Google's behalf, if the user has opted-in for passing on his/her data, or if it is necessary for the protection of Google's rights and property.[41]

The Privacy Policy for Google Ads and the Google Display Network is a bit more specific about which user data is used for advertising purposes. Personalized ads on Google Search on Google's AdSense for search partners is based on "recent search queries, the language we believe you prefer when performing your search, and log information, including cookie and device information, IP address, browser type, operating system and the date and time of your request".[42]

Considering the multiplicity of Google's products and services – ranging from various search engines to the video sharing platform YouTube, Gmail email services, the social networking site Orkut, the image sharing service Picasa, iGoogle, the browser Google Chrome, Android mobile applications, GoogleDocs, Google Maps to Google translate – the range of data Google can collect about its users is enormous. Through its Google Network Partners and cookies placed on the computer of users Google is able to monitor large parts of an individual's Internet usage. Surveilling emails, recoding search queries and monitoring which content a user consumes, which videos s/he watches, which programs s/he downloads, which ads s/he clicks on, which shops s/he visits, with whom s/he interact online, etc. provides Google with a lot of personal details about every individual user ranging from political opinions to music and movie taste, travels, job situation, personal relations, hobbies, interests, social relationships to health conditions and illnesses. Christian Fuchs argues that Google collects personal, ecological, technological, economic, political and cultural user information, which is generated through cognitive, communicative and co-operative activities on Google's websites (Fuchs 2011b).

As a default setting personalized advertising is activated for all Google services. However, Google provides some opportunities for opting-out (based on Google's Ads Preference Manager,[43] Advertising Cookie Opt-Out Plugin,[44] Google Dashboard,[45] or via the Network Advertising Initiative[46]). But opting out often involves a complex procedure that requires users to navigate through several pages until finally the opt-out button appears. Furthermore, even if users choose to opt-out they will continue to receive ads that fit search results and website contents, only user demographics, interests, etc. will no longer be used to personalize these ads.

Doing business without being evil?

According to Google's descriptions of its business model, it is advantageous for everybody: Google provides users with free services and relevant advertising, gives advertisers the opportunity to advertise their products and thereby generates money for further innovation. Google highlights

> One of the things that makes Google search especially valuable is that it's completely free. So, how does Google make money and continue to drive constant innovation? We give advertisers the opportunity to place clearly-marked ads alongside our search results. We strive to help people find ads that are relevant and useful, just like our results.[47]

The statement neglects that Google's advertising based business model also is extremely successful in terms of the maximization of Google's private profits.

In 2001 Google's profits amounted to 7 million USD. In 2010 the company's profits had multiplied by 1,215 times, reaching 8.5 billion USD (Google SEC filings. 10-k forms 2004–2010). Similarly Google's assets increased around 688 times from 84 million USD in 2001 to 57.85 billion USD in 2010 (Google SEC filings. 10-k forms 2004–2010). Google accumulated this enormous amount of money mainly by selling user data to advertisers and through allowing them to place targeted ads on Google's and its partners' websites. Google in 2010 derived 96 per cent of its profits from advertising. From 2004 until 2007 it was 99 per cent.

Following Google's corporate rhetoric these profits have been generated "without being evil": point six of Google's 10 point corporate philosophy states that Google believes that "you can make money without being evil".[48] Google stresses that despite its business being based on advertising it wants to serve all users, not only advertisers. According to Google its business model is not evil because ads always match search results and/or website content and therefore are "relevant" to what users want to find, because Google does not show any disturbing flash pop-up ads and always separates ads from search results, and finally because search results and ranking are never manipulated for advertising purposes.[49]

Throughout its webpages and corporate information Google repeats that personalized ads are also beneficial for users. Google for example stresses: "Our goal is to provide Gmail users with ads that are useful and relevant to their interests".[50] The fact that Google scans the email content of its Gmail users would ensure that users are shown "interesting" ads: "Gmail will better predict which ads may be useful to you. For example, if you've recently received a lot of messages about photography or cameras, a deal from a local camera store might be interesting".[51] Cookies according to Google allow improvement of the "relevance" of ads as part of an improved user experience: "cookies to improve your online experience, including the display of more relevant ads".[52] It would furthermore reduce the total amount of ads that are shown to a user: "When we personalize ads based on your searches and clicks on Google and Gmail, we can actually show you fewer ads that better match your interests".[53]

Risks of online surveillance

In contrast to Google's claim that its business model creates only advantages for its users, its practices of collecting, storing and selling access to user data entails a number of risks for Internet users.

- *Surveillance of Internet users*: The mix of Google's own services and its network of advertising partners allows Google to collect a variety of information about the life of its users. According to Alexa.com between September 24, 2011 and November 24, 2011, 49.2 per cent of all Internet users visited Google.com,[54] 31.7 per cent visited YouTube.com[55] and 12.8 per cent visited Blogger.com.[56] These are only the statistics for Google's most poplar webpages. The net of Google's services extends far beyond that. Twenty per cent of the 100 most popular websites belong to Google.[57] This means that Google has access to the data of large numbers of Internet users. The collected data is stored in huge, searchable databases. These databases often include information that can identify an individual personally such as IP address, name, address or birthday. Users lose control over these data and how they are used. As described above, Google stresses that it only hands on personally indentifying information under specific circumstances.[58] However, even information that is as such not personally identifiable can potentially reveal the identity of a person if it is combined in the right way. There are various ways in which it could be used to the disadvantage of individuals: political disadvantages for example could result from surveillance of a person's political worldviews, employer surveillance might negatively affect an individual's professional and economic life, knowledge about a person's health condition could lead to disadvantages regarding health or life insurances, etc.

In 2013 documents were revealed according to which the US National Security Agency (NSA) can access the systems of Google and other Internet companies such as Facebook.[59] As part of the so-called Prism program NSA officials are allowed collect and store a variety of data about Internet users including search histories, content of emails, or live chats.[60] Google officially refutes these allegations,[61] even though US President Barack Obama confirmed the existence of the surveillance scheme.[62] This example illustrates how widespread the use of user data stored in Google's databases can be and how difficult it is for users to maintain control over their personal information.

- *Commodification of user data*: Google's advertising based business model turns personal information into a tradable commodity. Google sells this information to advertisers and potentially to any other interested buyer. In 2010 the *Wall Street Journal* reported on a leaked Google strategy paper from 2008. In this confidential document Google discusses the different possibilities of making use of user data. Apart from using it for targeted advertising the document considerers a second way of using data in a profitable way: "Google can build a data exchange / trading platform allowing individual data owners to transact with others directly, or openly sell data to any bidder".[63] This statement clearly shows that Google considers data about individuals as a commodity, as something that can be owned, bought and sold.

- *Commercialization of the Internet*: By showing ads on all of its websites and those of its Advertising Network Members Google contributes to creating a commercial online culture. The omnipresence of advertising turns the Internet into a commercialized space in which different companies compete for the attention and finally for the money of users.

- *Enforcement of a consumer culture*: Extensive advertising does not only contribute to the commercialization of the Internet but also reinforces a consumer culture in general. As a consequence users are permanently confronted with and annoyed by ads for consumer goods and services. Google states that scanning the content of emails, monitoring online behaviour, and recording search terms is beneficial for users because this allows Google to deliver relevant, interesting and useful ads (see for example[64,65]). This assumes that when people look for information, write emails or interact with friends all they are are looking for is more products to buy and consume. The business model of Google and other web 2.0 companies is based on connecting all activities to matching consumer products. In such a culture, no matter which activities people pursue or which interests they have, there will not only be a matching commodity but also an ad for it.

- *Manipulation*: For personalized sales strategies to be successful, marketing campaigns need to create the illusion that individuality and authenticity can be achieved by buying certain consumer products. Contemporary sales strategies thus rest on the surveillance and categorization of consumers as well as on an ideology that ties individuality to specific consumption patterns. Mass media play an in important role in disseminating this ideology. In this context Mathiesen has coined the notion of the synopticon. He points out that "synopticism, through the modern mass media in general and television in particular, first of all directs and controls or disciplines our consciousness" (Mathiesen 1997, 230). The idea behind personalized advertising is to make marketing more effective, that is, to convince more people to buy certain products and services. Controlling the behaviour of consumers, that is, to make them buy certain commodities and services, also requires controlling their mind. No matter whether successful or not, the aim of (personalized) advertising is to manipulate consumer, that is, to make them behave in a certain way. Allmer highlights that the goal of economic surveillance is to "control economic behaviour of people and coerce them to produce or buy specific commodities" (Allmer 2012, 140). Surveillance and manipulation are two complementary strategies for influencing consumer behaviour.

- *Discrimination and social sorting*: Oscar Gandy has coined the term "panoptic sort" to describe the categorization based on specific criteria. In the economic realm the panoptic sort means that individuals are categorized "according their perceived value in the marketplace and their susceptibility to particular appeals" (Gandy 1993, 2). Similarly David Lyon uses the concept of "social sorting" for highlighting the "classifying drive of contemporary surveillance" (Lyon 2003, 15).

  For the purposes of personalized marketing individuals are grouped according to their perceived value as customers for certain products. Gandy highlights that the panoptic sort "is a discriminatory technology that allocates options and opportunities on the basis of those measures and the administrative models that they inform" (Gandy 1993, 15). Grouping individuals according to their susceptibility to specific products is likely to result in discrimination of those people who do not fit into any solvent consumer group. The result could be that advertising financed online services are primarily designed to suit the needs of those who are the most attractive to advertisers. The ability to use databases for grouping individuals according to different characteristics could potentially be used for various kinds of discrimination for example based on gender, sexual orientation, class, ethnicity, illnesses, political orientation, etc.

- *Exploitation of Internet prosumers*: Because of the double role of web 2.0 users as consumers as well as producers they have been characterized as produsers or prosumers (Bruns 2007; van Dijck 2009, 41; Fuchs 2009b; see also Toffler 1980). Christian Fuchs has argued that realizing profit out of personalized advertising constitutes a form of exploitation of prosumers (Fuchs 2010). Fuchs points out that on web 2.0 sites, users are productive workers because they create media content and usage data that builds the basis for generating profit. Without this content, web 2.0 sites would not be attractive to users, and the owners of these sites would therefore be unable to sell user data for advertising purposes and no profit could be generated. Advertising on web 2.0 platforms is only rewarding for advertisers if the site's users form an attractive demographic audience of potential consumers. Thus only if a platform has enough users, will advertisers be willing to buy space for ads. User data can only be sold if enough users leave their information on the site. This shows that without the work done by users who produce and upload content, it would be impossible to generate profit. Thus the owners of web 2.0 platforms exploit the labour power of users in order to satisfy their profit interests.

While Google claims that it does business without harming anybody, watchdogs point out that Google's business model is based on user surveillance and the reinforcement of consumerism. It has negative effects on individuals and society ranging from commercialization of the Internet and commodification of user data to manipulation, discrimination and exploitation of individuals.

Conclusion

Google does not use the notion of CSR. Nevertheless it presents itself as a company that is concerned about the impact it has on its environment. The company is known for its slogan "Don't be evil".[66] According to its self-description this motto guides Google's relations with its employees and users, as well as its role in society. Google, as a relatively young media company, presents itself as a new type of business organization that has never done anything immoral and whose business is beneficial for everybody. In particular CSR activities and reports, it seems, are not necessary as the company is "not evil" anyway. According to Google's corporate narrative users benefit from both good search results and personalized advertising; advertisers benefit from detailed user data; and society benefits from structured access to knowledge and information. What Google doesn't report is how it benefits itself from its business model: between 2001 and 2010 on average it grew by more than 100 per cent each year and reached 8.5 billion USD in 2010 (Google SEC filings. 10-k forms 2004–2010).

Google's actual customers are advertisers. Nevertheless Google needs its users. Without users, there would be no reason for advertisers to purchase Google's products. Google's success thus also depends on providing services that are valuable to users. Its various search products assist Internet users around the world in finding relevant information online. Nevertheless Google at the same time takes advantages of the data users provide while using Google's services.

The disadvantages Google's business model creates for users and society have no space in its corporate narrative and do not fit into the image of a non-evil company. Paul Buchheit, one of Google's first employers and the developer of Gmail as well as Google's AdSense, suggested the company's motto "Don't be evil". In an interview he explained some of the background of this slogan: "It's also a bit of a jab at a lot of the other companies, especially our competitors, who at that time, in our opinion, were kind of exploiting the users to some extent" (Buchheit 2008, 170). It is interesting that the assumption behind the slogan is that exploiting users is evil. With the term "exploiting" Buchheit refers to the practice of hiding advertisements as regular search results. However, also without faking search results Google's advertising-based business model exploits users. Users give their data to Google for free; Google sells them to advertisers for a high profit.

Notes

1 Google. *Company Overview*. Retrieved from http://www.google.com/intl/en/about/corporate/company/ on November 17, 2011.
2 *The New York Times*. 2004. *Google Buys an Online Photo Manager*. Retrieved from http://www.nytimes.com/2004/07/14/business/technology-google-buys-an-online-photo-manager.html on January 21, 2012.
3 Gizmodo. 2011. *Google's Biggest Acquisitions so Far*. Retrieved from http://www.gizmodo.com.au/2011/08/googles-16-biggest-acquisitions-so-far-and-what-happened-to-them/ on January 21, 2012.
4 *The New York Times*. 2006. *Google to Acquire YouTube for $1.65 Billion*. Retrieved from http://www.nytimes.com/2006/10/09/business/09cnd-deal.html on January 21, 2012.
5 Bloomsberg. 2007. *Google Agrees to Purchase Postini for $625 Million*. Retrieved from http://www.bloomberg.com/apps/news?pid=newsarchive&sid=arhI.l5SlRyw on January 16, 2012.
6 *Wall Street Journal*. 2010. *Google Agonizes on Privacy as Ad World Vaults Ahead*. Retrieved from http://online.wsj.com/article/SB1000142405274870330970457541355385 1854026.html#project%3DGOOGLEDOCS1008%26articleTabs%3Darticle on January 21, 2012.
7 *Bloomsberg Businessweek*. 2009. *Google Buys AdMob in Bid to Boost Mobile Ads*. Retrieved from http://www.businessweek.com/the_thread/techbeat/archives/2009/11/google_buys_adm.html on January 21, 2012.
8 *Financial Times*. 2011. *Google Purchases AdMeld for $400m*. Retrieved from http://www.ft.com/intl/cms/s/0/d3a10f0e-9613-11e0-8256-00144feab49a,s01=1.html#axzz1eMvwPrEF on January 21, 2012.
9 Gizmodo. 2011. *Google's Biggest Acquisitions so Far*. Retrieved from http://www.gizmodo.com.au/2011/08/googles-16-biggest-acquisitions-so-far-and-what-happened-to-them/ on January 21, 2012.
10 Google. *Corporate Social Responsibility*. Retrieved from http://www.google.com/intl/zh-CN/corporate/responsibility_en.html on November 20, 2011.
11 Google Green. Retrieved from http://www.google.com/green/ on November 17, 2011.
12 Google.org. Retrieved from http://www.google.org/index.html on November 17, 2011.
13 Google.org. Retrieved from http://www.google.org/index.html on November 17, 2011.
14 Google. *Company Information*. Retrieved from http://www.google.com/intl/sw/corporate/ on November 17, 2011.
15 Google. *Code of Conduct*. Retrieved from http://investor.google.com/corporate/code-of-conduct.html on November 18, 2011.
16 Google. *Code of Conduct*. Retrieved from http://investor.google.com/corporate/code-of-conduct.html on November 18, 2011.
17 Google. *Code of Conduct*. Retrieved from http://investor.google.com/corporate/code-of-conduct.html on November 18, 2011.
18 Google. *Philosophy*. Retrieved from http://www.google.com/about/company/philosophy/ on November 17, 2011.
19 Google. *Privacy Principles*. Retrieved from http://www.google.com/intl/en/policies/privacy/principles/ on November 17, 2011.

20 Google. *Design Principles*. Retrieved from http://www.google.com/intl/sw/corporate/ux.html on November 17, 2011.

21 Google. *Software Principles*. Retrieved from http://www.google.com/intl/en/about/company/software-principles.html on November 17, 2011.

22 Google. *No Pop-Ups*. Retrieved from http://www.google.com/intl/sw/corporate/nopopupads.html on November 17, 2011.

23 Google. *Security Policy*. Retrieved from http://www.google.com/intl/sw/corporate/security.html on November 17, 2011.

24 Google. *Our Culture*. Retrieved from http://www.google.com/intl/en/about/corporate/company/culture.html on November 17, 2011.

25 Google. *Our Culture*. Retrieved from http://www.google.com/intl/en/about/corporate/company/culture.html on November 17, 2011.

26 Google. *The Engineer's Life at Google*. Retrieved from http://www.google.com/intl/en/jobs/lifeatgoogle/englife/index.html on November 18, 2011.

27 Google. *The Engineer's Life at Google*. Retrieved from http://www.google.com/intl/en/jobs/lifeatgoogle/englife/index.html on November 18, 2011.

28 Privacy International. 2007. *Consultation Report. Race to the Bottom?* Retrieved from http://www.privacyinternational.org/issues/internet/interimrankings.pdf on January 21, 2012.

29 Privacy International. 2008. *Privacy International Response to European Commission Approval of the Google-Doubleclick Merger*. Retrieved from https://www.privacyinternational.org/article/privacy-international-response-european-commission-approval-google-doubleclick-merger on January 21, 2012.

30 GoogleWatch.com *And Then We Were Four*. Retrieved from http://www.google-watch.org/bigbro.html on January 21, 2012.

31 Privacy Rights Clearinghouse. 2004. *Google's New Email Service, Gmail, Under Fire for Privacy Concerns*. Retrieved from https://www.privacyrights.org/ar/GmailAGadvisory.htm on January 21, 2012.

32 Corporate Watch. 2008. *Google's New Spy*. Retrieved from http://www.corporate-watch.org/?lid=3134 on January 21, 2012.

33 Google Monitor. 2010. *What Private Information Google Collects*. Retrieved from http://www.googlemonitor.com/wp-content/uploads/2010/05/Google%20Privacy%20Fact%20Sheet.pdf on January 21, 2012.

34 Google Monitor. 2011. *Google's No Privacy by Design Business Model*. Retrieved from http://googlemonitor.com/2011/googles-no-privacy-by-design-business-model/ on January 21, 2012.

35 Google. *Corporate Governance*. Retrieved from http://investor.google.com/corporate/faq.html#toc-customers on November 19, 2011.

36 Google's privacy policy applies to all Google services except for Positini. In addition to this policy Google has a privacy policy for Google ads and the Google display network. Furthermore for some services such as Google+, YouTube, Blogger, Orkut, Picassa, etc. Google provides a service-specific privacy notice that applies in addition to its main privacy policy (Google. *Privacy Policy*. Version October 20, 2011. Retrieved from http://www.google.com/intl/en/policies/privacy/ on November 19, 2011.)

37 Google. *Privacy Policy*. Version October 20, 2011. Retrieved from http://www.google.com/intl/en/policies/privacy/ on November 19, 2011.

38 Google. *Privacy Policy*. Version October 20, 2011. Retrieved from http://www.google.com/intl/en/policies/privacy/ on November 19, 2011.

39 Google. *Ads in Gmail*. Retrieved from https://mail.google.com/support/bin/answer.py?answer=6603&hl=en on November 18, 2011

40 Google. *Privacy Policy*. Version October 20, 2011. Retrieved from http://www.google.com/intl/en/policies/privacy/ on November 19, 2011.

41 Google. *Privacy Policy*. Version October 20, 2011. Retrieved from http://www.google.com/intl/en/policies/privacy/ on November 19, 2011.

42 Google. *Privacy Policy for Google Ads and the Google Display Network*. Retrieved from http://www.google.com/intl/en/privacy/ads/privacy-policy.html on November 20, 2011.

43 Google. *Ad Preference Manager*. Retrieved from https://www.google.com/settings/u/0/ads/preferences/?hl=en#optout on November 18, 2011.

44 Google. *Cookie Opt-Out Plugin*. Retrieved from http://www.google.com/ads/preferences/html/intl/en/plugin/ on November 18, 2011.

45 Google. *Dashboard*. Retrieved from https://accounts.google.com/ServiceLogin?service=datasummary&passive=900&continue=on November 18, 2011.

46 Network Advertising Initiative. *Opt-Out of Behavioural Advertising*. Retrieved from http://www.networkadvertising.org/managing/opt_out.asp# on January 21, 2012.

47 Google. *Competition. About Ads*. Retrieved from http://www.google.com/competition/howgoogleadswork.html on November 18, 2011.

48 Google. *Philosophy*. Retrieved from http://www.google.com/about/company/philosophy/ on November 17, 2011.

49 Google. *Philosophy*. Retrieved from http://www.google.com/about/company/philosophy/ on November 17, 2011.

50 Google. *Ads in Gmail*. Retrieved from https://mail.google.com/support/bin/answer.py?answer=6603&hl=en on November 18, 2011.

51 Google. *Ads in Gmail*. Retrieved from https://mail.google.com/support/bin/answer.py?answer=6603&hl=en on November 18, 2011.

52 Google. *Advertising and Privacy*. Retrieved from http://www.google.com/intl/en/policies/privacy/ads/ on November 19, 2011.

53 Google. *Ads on Google*. http://www.google.com/support/websearch/bin/answer.py?answer=1634057&hl=en on November 19, 2011.

54 Alexa. *Top Sites. Google.com* Retrieved from http://www.alexa.com/siteinfo/google.com on January 24, 2012.

55 Alexa. *Top Sites. YouTube.com* Retrieved from http://www.alexa.com/siteinfo/youtube.com on January 24, 2012.

56 Alexa. *Top Sites. Blogger.com* Retrieved from http://www.alexa.com/siteinfo/blogspot.com on January 24, 1012.

57 Alexa.com *Top Sites*. Accessed from http://www.alexa.com/topsites on January 24, 2012.

58 Google. *Privacy Policy*. Version October 20, 2011. Retrieved from http://www.google.com/intl/en/policies/privacy/ on November 19, 2011.

59 *The Guardian*. 2013. *NSA Prism Program Taps in to User Data of Apple, Google and Others*. By Glenn Greenwald and Ewen MacAskill on June 7, 2013. Retrieved from http://www.guardian.co.uk/world/2013/jun/06/us-tech-giants-nsa-data on July 19, 2013.

60 *The Guardian*. 2013. *NSA Prism Program Taps in to User Data of Apple, Google and Others*. By Glenn Greenwald and Ewen MacAskill on June 7, 2013. Retrieved from http://www.guardian.co.uk/world/2013/jun/06/us-tech-giants-nsa-data on July 19, 2013.

61 Larry Page. 2013. *What The . . . ?* Google Official Blog on June 7, 2013. Retrieved from http://googleblog.blogspot.co.uk/2013/06/what.html on July 19, 2013.

62 *The Guardian*. 2013. *Facebook and Google Insist They Did Not Know of Prism Surveillance Program*. By Dominic Rushe on June 8, 2013. Retrieved from http://www.guardian.co.uk/world/2013/jun/07/google-facebook-prism-surveillance-program on July 19, 2013.

63 *Wall Street Journal*. 2010. *Google Agonizes on Privacy as Ad World Vaults Ahead.* Retrieved from http://online.wsj.com/article/SB100014240527487033097045754135 53851854026.html on January 21, 2012.

64 Google. *Ads in Gmail*. Retrieved from https://mail.google.com/support/bin/answer. py?answer=6603&hl=en on November 18, 2011.

65 Google. *Competition. About Ads*. Retrieved from http://www.google.com/competition/ howgoogleadswork.html on November 18, 2011.

66 Google. *Code of Conduct*. Retrieved from http://investor.google.com/corporate/code-of-conduct.html on November 18, 2011.

8 HP

Hazardous products?

William R. Hewlett and David Packard founded HP in 1939. The company became officially incorporated in 1947 and went public in 1957.[1] Among HP's most important mergers and acquisitions are the purchases of Compaq Computer Corporation in May 2002 (HP SEC filings. 10-k form 2003) and of the IT company Electronic Data Systems in 2008.[2] *Forbes Magazine* for the year 2010 ranked HP the largest hardware company and the 42nd biggest public company worldwide.[3] HP in September 2011 controlled 41 per cent of the worldwide hardcopy peripherals market[4] and in October 2011 was the leading PC vendor with a market share of 17.7 per cent.[5]

CSR approach

Since its first CSR report in 2001, HP has extensively reported on its CSR activities in yearly reports. For the years 2009 and 2010 HP published additional CSR documents, which contain further background information about the company's CSR engagement.

HP is not only a powerful industry leader, but also a company with a well-established CSR reporting practice. Its CSR approach combines projectionist, dualist and reductionist arguments. Projectionist arguments in HP's CSR communication highlight a deep concern about how the company's practices affect society. In 2001 HP for example writes: "It has become commonplace for companies to say they are committed to being good corporate citizens. At Hewlett-Packard, this is more than a slogan; it has been at the heart and soul of our global operations for 60 years" (HP_CSR 2001, 5). In addition, HP emphasizes that its economic power obliges the company to act socially responsible. CEO Léo Apotheker in his letter to the company's 2010 CSR report for example stresses: "We're also using our position as the world's largest information technology (IT) company to help address some of society's most pressing challenges" (HP_CSR 2010a, 4). HP stresses that it is deeply concerned about meeting its social responsibilities and that CSR therefore is integrated into the company's business strategy. In the 2010 CSR report HP for example states: "Global citizenship is integral to HP's business strategy. It helps shape decisions about where and how we apply our technologies, influence, and expertise to make the greatest positive impact on the world around us" (HP_CSR 2010a, 3). HP's commitment to social responsibility includes highly ambitious goals such as to "improve the lives of people throughout the world" (HP_CSR 2001, 1), "improve society" (HP_CSR 2010a, 7) and to "create a better world" (HP_CSR 2010a, 5). These statements are projectionist as they highlight that the company's business practices are guided by values and a concern for society.

Such projectionist arguments are supplemented with a dualist rhetoric that points out that business goals and social responsibility can be achieved in parallel. HP stresses that it is working towards the twofold goal of being successful in economic terms as well as being a responsible "corporate citizen": "We want to be the world leader — not only in our market and financial performance but in our global citizenship activities as well" (HP_CSR 2007, 4). Chairman and CEO Carly Fiorina in 2002 for example pointed out that attempting to be a profitable company and to make a contribution to society at the same time is part of the company's history:

> HP has always been a company that is thoughtful about its role in the world. Our co-founder, Dave Packard, put it best when he wrote that "many assume, wrongly, that a company exists simply to make money [. . .] the real reason HP exists is to make a contribution". Today, the idea that HP exists to make both a profit and a contribution to society is still the foundation of everything we do.
>
> (HP_CSR 2002, 1)

These passages clearly illustrate a dualist CSR approach: building shareholder value and making a contribution to society are presented as two parallel goals. According to these statements HP aims at becoming an industry leader both in respect to economic as well as social and environmental standards.

At the same time a third, reductionist, rhetoric is present in HP's CSR communications. In some passages HP argues that being a responsible corporate citizen is beneficial for achieving profit goals. Reductionist statements justify the company's CSR activities through referring to positive effects for the bottom line. In the 2002 report HP stressed that HP's corporate citizenship also provides an opportunity for entering new markets. Carly Fiorina highlighted that HP's efforts for reducing the digital divide is in fact a preparatory activity for creating new markets for HP products:

> Engaging in these markets is not just the right thing to do, it's the smart thing to do. As representatives of an industry whose goods are affordable for just 10 percent of the world's population, we have to acknowledge that growth will come from markets that are underserved today. In other words, it is entirely in our interests to apply technology to economic development because not only will this help empower millions of people to benefit from the digital age – it will also help create a new generation of ideas, employees and customers for HP.
>
> (HP_CSR 2002, 1)

Similarly Mark Hurd in 2010 stressed the potential of the company's low carbon initiatives for developing new markets: "Developing solutions for the low-carbon economy offers tremendous potential to reinvent or create entirely new markets" (HP_CSR 2010a, 3).

Debra Dunn, Senior Vice President of Corporate Affairs and Global Citizenship, writes in the 2004 report that HP regards CSR as a business opportunity: "In the 21st Century, global citizenship is not just a corporate responsibility, but also a prime business opportunity to grow our company in new ways" (HP_CSR 2004, 5). She considers corporate citizenship as an investment: "Some see this work as charity, philanthropy, or an allocation of resources that could better be donated by share-owners themselves. But to us, it is a vital investment in our future, essential to our top-line and bottom-line business success" (HP_CSR 2004, 5). In the 2004 report Dunn again makes a reference to the one of the company's founders, Dave Packard. While in 2002 Carly Fiorina highlighted that Packard's vision was to make both a profit and a contribution, Dunn argues that the company's founders wanted to build shareholder value by making a contribution:

> In his memoirs, Dave Packard recalled an industry conference he was invited to address in the 1940s. He took the opportunity to assert his belief that build-ing long-term shareowner value didn't simply require focusing on making a profit, but making a contribution.
>
> (HP_CSR 2004, 5)

This argument is reductionist as it describes "making a contribution" as a means to increase shareholder values. In this context CEO Mark Hurd in 2006 speaks of HP's corporate citizenship programme as a "hidden component" of the com-pany's business success: "The way we see it, global citizenship and business success go hand in hand. In fact, global citizenship is the 'hidden component' in HP products – embedded in our design and engineering, including acces-sibility, energy efficiency and recycling" (HP_CSR 2006, 3). In particular, HP argues that corporate citizenship investments strengthens HP's business through enabling it to meet customer expectations, making sure that HP main-tains access to markets through complying with regulations, being essential to the company's competitiveness, attracting and retaining qualified employees, fostering stakeholder dialogue especially with NGOs, building a good reputa-tion and trust, reducing business risks, saving costs and inspiring innovation (HP_CSR 2010a, 8f).

HP oscillates between a projectionist, a dualist and a reductionist justifica-tion for engaging in CSR activities. It presents its CSR engagement as an honest concern for its business practices' impact on society (projectionism), as a way of doing business that allows it to at the same time achieve profit goals and make a contribution to society (dualism) and as a means for building shareholder values (reductionism). The extensive amount of CSR reports HP has produced during the last decade as well as the efforts the company makes in describing its CSR com-mitment as a company tradition and honest concern, combined with statements that highlight the instrumental business benefits of CSR suggests that HP regards CSR as a means for creating competitive advantages through good reputation.

However, HP has been criticized for insufficiently addressing the problem of e-waste. In the following section I will discuss some controversies regarding this topic.

Controversies: e-waste

Protecting the environment has always been presented as a key element of HP's CSR activities. In the company's first CSR report CEO Carly Fiorina promised: "Environmental protection is a complex undertaking, but the laws of nature are simple. We will provide leadership on the journey to an environmentally sustainable future, with efficient products and creative recycling systems" (HP_CSR 2001, 1). Every year HP's CSR reports have a section that describes the company's environmental policies, and achievements as well as future goals. These sections mainly focus on the topics energy and emissions, waste and recycling, as well as sustainable design.

HP highlights its progress in regard to its environmental performance through measures such as voluntary purchases of renewable energy (8 per cent of total electricity use in 2010) (HP_CSR 2010a, 48) or the recent opening of a new data centre in Wynyard, UK which sources 10 per cent of its electricity from wind power (Greenpeace 2011a, 33). However, HP has a strong environmental impact for example in terms of greenhouse gas emissions. In 2009, the year in which the information HP disclosed is the most comprehensive,[6] HP in total emitted 8,116,800 tonnes of carbon dioxide (CO_2) (HP_CSR 2009a, 47). This is as much as 3,556,880 average cars in the EU emit during one year.[7]

Apart from high greenhouse gas emissions, one major problem for the whole electronics industry is e-waste. HP is no exception – as a market leader in the printing and copying as well as the PC segment, HP is also a major producer of e-waste. Due to the fact that most electronic products contain toxic substances the consequences of irresponsible treatment of e-waste can be devastating for human health and the environment. According to estimates by the United Nations Environment Programme (UNEP) every year 40 million tonnes of e-waste are produced worldwide (UNEP 2009a, 1). Producers of computer hardware have a major influence on reducing these risks through sustainable design and responsible recycling of generated waste. Hardware producers such as HP can influence how many toxic substances e-waste contains, how much e-waste is generated and that e-waste is adequately disposed of. In the following I will point out the watchdog's criticism regarding the toxic components contained in HP's products, discuss the related problem of toxic e-waste and the possibilities for avoiding, recycling and reusing e-waste.

Toxic products

In 2005 Greenpeace called HP "a prime example of a dirty electronics company" that "has done little to eliminate hazardous materials in its products" (Greenpeace

2005a). The Electronics TakeBack Coalition in 2010 ranked the HP's recycling practices with a C- on a scale ranging from A (best) to F (worst).[8] In 2006 Greenpeace found high concentrations of toxic substances in HP products. Among the substances found were flame-retardant polybrominated diphenylethers (PBDE) chemicals and the heavy metal, lead (Greenpeace 2006a, 109). According to the US Environmental Protection Agency evidence exists that PBDE has toxic effects on the human liver, the thyroid and neurodevelopment.[9] The high levels of PBDEs in HP products are even more alarming because HP in its CSR communications claimed to have eliminated PBDEs several years ago (Greenpeace 2006b). This claim can be found in HP's CSR reports up to today. In its 2010 report HP published a timeline that suggested that PBDEs had been eliminated from its products in the early 1990s. The inconsistency of information raises doubts as to the accuracy of information provided by HP. The timeline furthermore still includes the goal of stopping the use of polyvinyl chloride (PVC) and brominated flame retardants (BFRs) in HP products by the end of 2009. According to Greenpeace this commitment was not fulfilled (Greenpeace 2009, 32).

Greenpeace's research shows that HP's products still contain various hazardous substances and that the information provided regarding the toxicity of its products is inconsistent. Many of the substances contained in electronic products are toxic to nature, microorganisms, animals and humans: the heavy metal, lead, for example is a "multi-organ system toxicant" that even at low exposure levels can cause damage to nervous systems, blood systems, kidneys and children's brain development.[10] Another dangerous heavy metal that can be found in computer products is mercury, which can cause permanent damage to the human nervous system.[11] As it accumulates in living organisms such as fish humans can ingest it through the food chain (BAN and SVTC 2002, 9). Cadmium is a toxic element that accumulates in human kidney's and in human bones.[12] Barium can cause brain swelling, muscle weakness, and damage the heart, liver and spleen. Hexavalent chromium can damage human cells (BAN and SVTC 2002, 9), and beryllium can cause lung cancer (BAN and SVTC 2002, 10). Toners of laser printers contain the pigment carbon black, which can cause cancer if it is inhaled (BAN and SVTC 2002, 10).

In order to prevent such toxic substances from entering the environment it is not only important to avoid these substances as far as possible but furthermore to reduce the amount of e-waste that can potentially cause a danger to the environment and human health.

Toxic waste

In its CSR reports HP makes a distinction between non-hazardous and hazardous waste. Non-hazardous waste is defined as "paper, pallets, used electronic equipment (e-waste), metals, and packaging" (HP_ CSR 2010a, 88). HP, however, does not specify which products are included in the hazardous waste category. Figure 8.1 shows how many tonnes of waste HP itself has generated through its operations every year from 2005 to 2010.

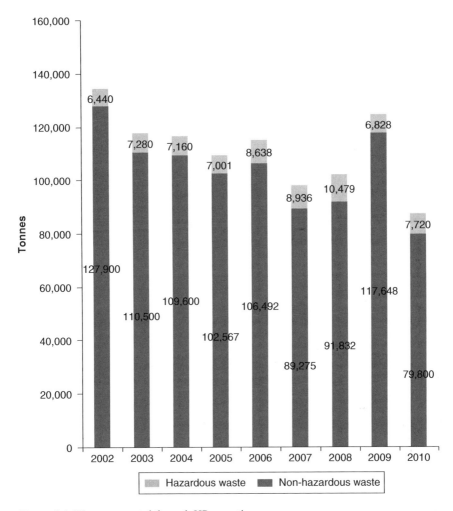

Figure 8.1 Waste generated through HP operations.

Source: HP_CSR 2002–2010.

The waste that is produced through HP's operations is only minor in comparison to the waste generated through the use of HP's products. HP does not report how much waste is generated through the use of its products. However, HP discloses the total weight of products that are returned every year for reuse and recycling (see Figure 8.2).

HP presents the increasing amount of reused and recycled material as progress. Increasing the amount of recycled products is also one of HP's CSR goals (HP_CSR 2010a, 119). In terms of reducing negative impacts of waste for humans and the environment, this goal is misleading: an increased amount of recycled

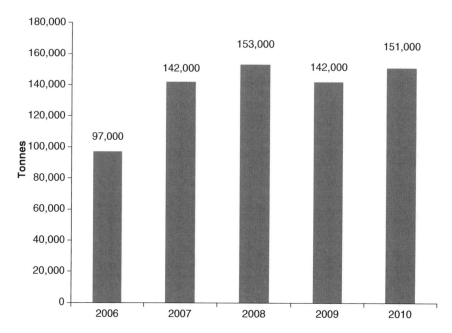

Figure 8.2 HP's total reuse and recycling.

Source: HP_CSR 2006–2010.

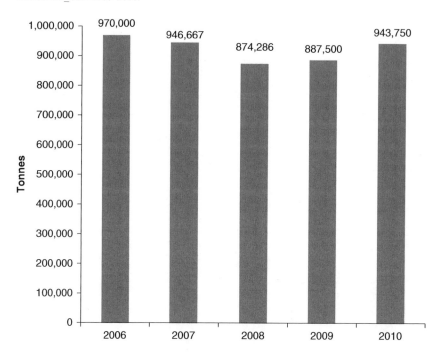

Figure 8.3 Waste generated from HP products.

Source: own calculation based on HP_CSR 2006–2010.

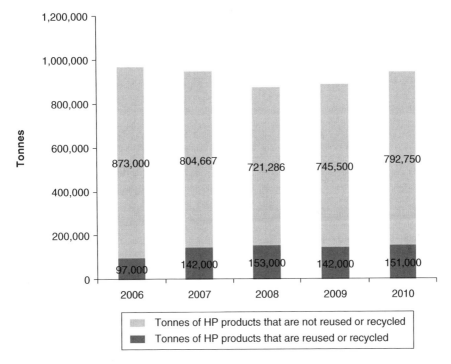

Figure 8.4 Reuse and recycling of HP products.

Source: own calculation based on HP_CSR 2006–2010.

products does not necessarily mean that there is less waste dumped into landfills or incinerated. This is only the case if the amount of recycled products relative to the total discarded products, that is, the recycling rate, is rising.

Since 2006 HP has been reporting an annual reuse and recycling rate that shows the share of used HP products that are reused or recycled. It is calculated by comparing the total weight of products returned to recycling with the total weight of products sold seven years earlier (HP_CSR 2010a, 81). This rate has increased from 10 per cent in 2006 to 15 per cent in 2007, to 17.5 per cent in 2008 and then decreased again to 16 per cent in 2009 as well as 2010 (HP_CSR 2006–2010). Based on the reuse and recycling rate and the total amount or reused and recycled HP products (see Figure 8.2) it is possible to calculate the total amount of waste generated through HP's products (Figure 8.3) as well as the total amount of HP products that are not returned for reuse and recycling (Figure 8.4).

These figures show that every year around 900,000 tonnes of HP products are discarded. It is unclear what exactly happens to the more than 700,000 tonnes of discarded HP products that are not reused or recycled. They might be part of the so called "hidden flow of e-waste" that is incinerated, stored in a landfill or often also illegally exported to non-*Organisation for Economic Co-operation and Development* (OECD) countries (Greenpeace 2008, 9).

According to Greenpeace every year 8.7 million tonnes of e-waste is produced in the EU. Only 25 per cent of this amount is collected and treated. The remaining 75 per cent or 6.6 million tonnes constitute the hidden flow of e-waste (Greenpeace 2008, 9). Waste that is not collected often ends up in the informal recycling sector. The recycling methods used in the informal sector often endanger human health and the environment (Greenpeace 2008, 11). Necessary infrastructure for adequate treatment of hazardous waste is most often not available in developing countries. Workers in informal "recycling" sectors suffer from immense health problems ranging from cuts and coughs to headaches, rashes and burns to infertility, miscarriage, tumours, endocrine diseases and birth defects (DanWatch 2011, 6).

According to UNEP electronic products can contain up to 60 elements, some of which are hazardous, that can be valuable for reuse. Due to ineffective recycling techniques, limited take-back programmes and illegal export of e-waste to developing countries, these resources often cannot be extracted for reuse (UNEP 2009a, 6). At the same time improper waste management results in an uncontrolled release of hazardous substances (UNEP 2009a, 12).

The EU has responded to the problem off hidden flows of e-waste with a directive on Waste from Electrical and Electronic Equipment (WEEE), which laid a legal foundation for the principle of producer responsibility, according to which producers are responsible to "provide at least for the financing of the collection, treatment, recovery and environmentally sound disposal of WEEE from private households deposited at collection facilities" (European Commission 2003, Art. 8.1). In order to confront the problem of exports of e-waste from rich to poor nations, several states in 1989 adopted the Basel Convention on the Control of Transboundary Movements of Hazardous Wastes and their Disposal. The convention aims at reducing hazardous waste as well as minimizing its export especially to developing countries.[13] It has, however, not been ratified by the USA.[14]

Despite existing regulation, export of e-waste to developing countries is still common. Often the export of e-waste takes place under the disguise of exporting still functioning second-hand electronic products that are sold to developing countries. In most cases these products end up on landfills, either because they are already broken when they arrive or they are still used for some time and inadequately disposed of afterwards.

Products of all major computer brands can be found at landfills in developing countries. In 2005, the Basel Action Network (BAN) conducted a study on e-waste imports to Lagos, Nigeria. At the time of this study every month around 400,000 broken computers and monitors were arriving in Nigeria, among them products of all the major computer brands including HP, Dell, Apple, IBM, Sony and Toshiba (BAN 2005, 37). Similarly Greenpeace reported having found disposed products of these computer brands on waste dumps in Guiyu, China (Greenpeace 2005b, 2007).

Reusing, recycling and avoiding toxic waste

The fact that HP's recycling programme is not comprehensive makes it likely that HP's products are inadequately disposed of. Greenpeace in its most recent *Guide to Greener Electronics* which ranks HP as number 1, critically notes that where HP "scores relatively poorly is e-waste, where it needs to expand its take-back programme for consumers in countries without legislation" (Greenpeace 2011b, 1). In 2010 HP had hardware recycling programmes in 49 and cartridge recycling programmes in 54 countries (HP_CSR 2010a, 78). Take-back programmes are particularly poor in most African, Asian and Latin American countries.[15] The only African country in which HP provides recycling opportunities for laser jet and inkjet cartridges is South Africa. In India HP offers only 15 hardware recycling centres, which are located in nine cities.[16] Inkjet and laserjet cartridges in India can be returned at 1 of 24 HP offices in 11 cities.[17] Furthermore HP's recycling programmes do not cover all products. On its website HP lists 21 different models of inkjet cartridges and 14 models of laserjet toner bottles that are excluded from the recycling programme: HP states that these products "cannot be recycled through the HP Planet Partners program".[18]

Apart from the limits of HP's recycling programme, HP's business model in general is not a waste avoiding one. HP's printer business is largely based on the idea of selling printers at cheap prices and generating income through selling ink cartridges. AlterNet therefore called HP's printer cartridges an "e-waste disaster"[19]: HP's most popular printer on Amazon.com is the HP Deskjet 1000 printer. It ranks in the bestseller list at 7 in the category "printers" and in the bestseller at 1 in the category "inkjet printers".[20] The printer costs 38.95 USD. The black cartridge is sold at 14.99 USD and the tri-colour cartridge at 19.99 USD. According to HP the black cartridge allows printing of up to 190 pages[21] and the tri-colour cartridge prints up to 165 pages.[22] HP does not remanufacture ink cartridges or provide refilling options. On its website HP states that this policy is due to the lower printing quality of refilled cartridges.[23] A refilling model, however, could contribute to avoiding waste and would therefore be more sustainable than a model that is based on disposable cartridges with a short lifespan that has to be replaced frequently.

While this business model of selling products with short lifespans threatens human health and the environment, in terms of profit it has proven beneficial for HP. HP's profits, revenue, and assets since 1993 have shown a clear upward trend (HP SEC filings. 10-k forms 1993–2010): Between 1993 and 2010 HP multiplied its profits by 7.4 times from 1.2 billion to 8.8 billion USD, its revenues by 6.2 times from 20.3 to 126 billion USD, and HP's assets 7.4 times from 16.7 to 124.5 billion USD.

On several occasions Greenpeace has protested against the hazardous HP products and the company's inadequate recycling programmes. Greenpeace activists have for example dumped toxic HP e-waste in front of HP's office in Geneva (Greenpeace 2005b). After HP broke its promise to eliminate BFRs and PVC plastics from its computers by the end of 2009, Greenpeace painted the 11,500 square feet message "Hazardous Products" on the roof of HP's headquarter in Palo Alto, California.[24]

Conclusion

The fact that HP provides an extensive amount of CSR communication indicates that presenting itself as a company with a social and environmental consciousness is a priority for HP. HP's CSR communications combine projectionist, dualist and reductionist statements.

The way watchdogs evaluate HP's actions to reduce its environmental impact through phasing out toxic substances from its products and installing take-back programmes is ambivalent. During the last few years HP has been both ranked as one of the worst and as one of the best companies in regard to the issue of e-waste. In *Newsweek*'s 2011 ranking of the greenest companies, HP was ranked second among the 500 largest US companies[25] and 15th among the 500 largest companies worldwide.[26] While in 2005 and 2009 Greenpeace strongly criticized HP for failing to reduce toxic substances in their products (Greenpeace 2005a[27]), HP has managed to climb from the penultimate place (ranked 16) in March 2009 (Greenpeace 2009) to be ranked 1 in Greenpeace's 2011 *Guide To Greener Electronics* (Greenpeace 2011b).

This apparent improvement suggests that HP is actively addressing watchdog criticism. In its CSR reports HP explicitly stresses that it co-operates with NGOs in order to reduce its environmental impact. Nevertheless at a more basic level HP's business interests conflict with the development of sustainable IT products. HP's profits are based on selling hardware products, which often contain toxic materials, with short lifespans at affordable prices. Another major problem of the way HP deals with the problem of e-waste is the insufficient provision of take-back options, especially in developing countries where legal requirements are less strict. It is thus likely that HP's products are disposed of in inappropriate ways and pose a threat to human health and the environment. The real challenge would be to develop more sustainable and probably less profitable products.

Notes

1 HP. *HP Timeline*. Retrieved from http://www8.hp.com/us/en/hp-information/about-hp/history/hp-timeline/hp-timeline.html on November 6, 2011.
2 HP. 2008. *News Release. HP to Acquire EDS*. Retrieved from http://www.hp.com/hpinfo/newsroom/press/2008/080513a.html on November 6, 2011.
3 *Forbes Magazine*. 2011. *The World's Biggest Public Companies. 2010*. Retrieved from http://www.forbes.com/global2000/#p_1_s_arank_All_All_All on June 17, 2011.
4 IDC. 2011. *Growth in Worldwide Hardcopy Peripherals Market Slows in Second Quarter Despite Strong Results in Emerging Markets, According to IDC*. Retrieved from http://www.idc.com/getdoc.jsp?containerId=prUS23022511 on November 13, 2011.
5 Gartner. 2011. *Gartner Says Worldwide PC Shipments Grew 3.2 Percent in Third Quarter of 2011*. Retrieved from http://www.gartner.com/it/page.jsp?id=1821731 on November 13, 2011.
6 For the year 2009 HP disclosed information on CO_2 emissions from operations, employee travel, product manufacturing and product transport (HP_CSR 2009a, 47).

7 This calculation is based on the following assumptions: according to estimates from the United Nations Environment Programme (UNEP), private cars in the EU on average emit 163g of CO_2 per km (UNEP 2009b, 95). According to the European Automobile Manufacturers' Association, cars in Europe on average travel 14,000 km per year (European Automobile Manufacturer's Association. 2010. *Vehicles in Use*. Retrieved from http://www.acea.be/news/news_detail/vehicles_in_use/ on November 11, 2011). The annual CO_2 emissions per car thus are 2,282,000g, which equals 2,282 tonnes. HP in 2009 emitted 8,116,800 tonnes of CO_2 (HP_CSR 2009a, 47).

8 Electronics TakeBack Coalition. 2010. *Recycling Report Card*. Retrieved from http://www.electronicstakeback.com/hold-manufacturers-accountable/recycling-report-card/ on November 12, 2011.

9 US Environment Protection Agency. 2010. *Polybrominated diphenylethers (PBDEs)*. Retrieved from http://www.epa.gov/oppt/pbde/ on November 11, 2011.

10 United Nations Environment Programme. *Lead and Cadmium*. Retrieved from http://www.unep.org/hazardoussubstances/LeadCadmium/tabid/29372/Default.aspx on November 10, 2011.

11 United Nations Environment Programme. *Reducing Risk from Mercury*. Retrieved from http://www.unep.org/hazardoussubstances/Mercury/tabid/434/Default.aspx on November 10, 2011.

12 United Nations Environment Programme. *Lead and Cadmium*. Retrieved from http://www.unep.org/hazardoussubstances/LeadCadmium/tabid/29372/Default.aspx on November 10, 2011.

13 Basel Convention. *Text of the Convention*. Retrieved from http://www.basel.int/TheConvention/Overview/TextoftheConvention/tabid/1275/Default.aspx on November 6, 2011.

14 Basel Convention. *Parties to the Basel Convention*. Retrieved from http://www.basel.int/Countries/StatusofRatifications/PartiesSignatories/tabid/1290/Default.aspx#13 on November 6, 2011.

15 HP. *Product Recycling*. Retrieved from http://www8.hp.com/us/en/hp-information/environment/product-recycling.html on November 13, 2011.

16 HP. *Recycling India*. Retrieved from http://h20423.www2.hp.com/program/suppliesrecycling/in/en/hardware/resource/collection-centres.pdf on November 13, 2011.

17 HP. *Recycling Information*. Retrieved from http://h20423.www2.hp.com/program/suppliesrecycling/in/en/supplies/index.asp on November 13, 2011.

18 HP. *HP Supplies Recycling*. Retrieved from http://h30248.www3.hp.com/recycle/supplies/non_returnable.asp?_cc=us on November 13, 2011.

19 AlterNet. *HP's Printer Cartridges Are an E-Waste Disaster – Does the Company Really Care?* Retrieved from http://www.alternet.org/environment/65945/hp%27s_printer_cartridges_are_an_e-waste_disaster_—_does_the_company_really_care/?page=2 on November 15, 2011.

20 Amazon.com. *Bestsellers in Computer Printers*. Retrieved from http://www.amazon.com/Best-Sellers-Electronics-Computer-Printers/zgbs/electronics/172635/ref=zg_bs_unv_e_3_3071697011_2 on May 28, 2013.

21 HP. *Home & Home Office Store*. Retrieved from http://www.shopping.hp.com/product/CH561WN%2523140?landing=supplies&category=ink_toner&family_name= on May 28, 2013.

22 HP. *Home & Home Office Store*. Retrieved from http://www.shopping.hp.com/en_US/home-office/-/products/Ink_Toner_Paper/HP-Ink/CH562WN?HP-61-Tri-color-Ink-Cartridge on May 28, 2013.

23 HP. *The Truth About Remanufactured Ink and Toner Cartridges*. Retrieved from http://www.hp.com/sbso/product/supplies/remanufactured-ink-toner.html?jumpid=ex_R295_go/suppliesreliability on November 15, 2011.

24 Cnet. 2009. *Greenpeace Wars With HP*. Retrieved from http://news.cnet.com/8301-1001_3-10297357-92.html on November 12, 2011.

25 *Newsweek*. 2011. Green Ranking. US Companies. Retrieved from http://www. thedailybeast.com/newsweek/features/green-rankings/2011/us.html on November 10, 2011.
26 *Newsweek*. 2011. *Green Rankings. Global Companies*. Retrieved from http://www.thedailybeast.com/newsweek/features/green-rankings/2011/international.html on November 10, 2011.
27 Cnet. 2009. *Greenpeace Wars With HP*. Retrieved from http://news.cnet.com/8301-1001_3-10297357-92.html on November 12, 2011.

9 Microsoft

Knowledge monopoly?

Bill Gates and Paul Allen founded Microsoft in 1975. In the 1980s Microsoft started licensing the so-called disc operating system (DOS) to IBM, which a few years later was followed by the Windows operating system (Geisst 2006, 197). In 2010 Microsoft was the leading software company and the 50th largest company in the world with 89,000 employees.[1] Its main business areas are: the Windows operating systems, server offerings such as Microsoft SQL and Windows Azure, online services including Bing and MSN, software and computer programs, entertainment devices such as the gaming console Xbox, Windows phones, PC gaming software and online games (Microsoft SEC filings. 10-k form 2010). With the acquisition of the popular Internet telephony service Skype in 2011, Microsoft added a new segment to its business activities. The 8.5 million USD deal was approved by the US Federal Trade Commission in June, and by the European Commission in October 2011.[2]

CSR approach

Microsoft uses the label "corporate citizenship" for its CSR communications. On its corporate citizenship website Microsoft provides a broad range of information regarding its CSR activities including CSR reports for the years 2003 to 2011.

Starting from the first CSR report in 2003, Microsoft's CSR approach has been centred on the following mission: "Microsoft's mission is to enable people and businesses throughout the world to realize their full potential" (MI_CSR 2003, 1). This idea of realizing human potentials can be found in all subsequent CSR reports (MI_CSR 2004, 10; 2005, 2; 2006, 2; 2007/2008, 5; 2009, 2; 2010, 8; 2011, 6). Microsoft describes itself as "a values-driven company, motivated by its mission to help people and businesses realize their potential" (MI_CSR 2004, 74). This focus and these values as guiding principles of the company's business practices illustrate the projectionist orientation of Microsoft's CSR approach. Its values, that according to Microsoft's CSR communication are an integral element of the company's mission and business practice, are documented in an extensive set of guidelines, codes and policy documents: "At Microsoft, everything we do is guided by corporate values, codes of conduct, and company policies" (MI_CSR 2006, 2).

Microsoft stresses that through its business it wants to improve the life of people around the world. The following extract from the 2004 report's "executive welcome" from Steve Ballmer and Bill Gates illustrates the broad orientation of Microsoft's CSR approach:

> Whether we're working with community-based organizations and NGOs in China to increase employment opportunities for unskilled migrant workers, partnering with law enforcement officials in Canada to develop a customized system that helps the police fight computer-facilitated crimes against children, collaborating in Latin America with the Organization of American States and its affiliate The Trust for the Americas to help people with disabilities gain the skills they need to start their own businesses and find employment, or working with leading companies and community organizations in Europe on a grants program to help small and medium-sized enterprises improve productivity through technology, our commitment is the same: to make it possible for people to use technology to improve their lives.
>
> (MI_CSR 2004, 4)

Microsoft presents itself not only as being a values-driven company that aims at realizing human potentials, but also a successful, but local, company: "While Microsoft, by many measures, could be considered the world's most successful software company, it is also a local company and a neighbour in every country and community where Microsoft employees live, work, and do business" (MI_CSR 2004, 5). Despite its global business activities, Microsoft is aware of its local importance:

> As the world's largest software company—with more than 90,000 employees in over 100 countries—Microsoft has an important role to play in helping to advance social and economic opportunities in the communities where we work, live and do business.
>
> (MI_CSR 2009, 4)

According to Microsoft's CSR communications, the needs of various stakeholders should be satisfied equally with shareholder's profit interest:

> we must demonstrate, more than ever before, that Microsoft is a business that behaves with integrity in all interactions with customers, partners, shareholders, consumers, and governments – all the many different stakeholders whose trust we must continue to earn and honour.
>
> (MI_CSR 2004, 19)

This statement again entails a projectionist approach as it highlights that Microsoft designs its business practices in a way that takes into account the interests of all stakeholders. Microsoft stresses that in order to contribute to the common good it needs to align business operations and citizenship efforts: "Microsoft believes that it can make the greatest contribution to society when its business operations and citizenship efforts are closely aligned" (MI_CSR 2007/2008, 2). As part of this strategy one of Microsoft's focus area regarding CSR is "responsible business practices": "Finally, in addition to thinking about the effects of what we do as a business, we remain firmly committed to thinking about the effects of how we do business, with a strong commitment to responsible business practices" (MI_CSR 2010, 3).

Despite Microsoft's focus on "responsible business practices", the company in the past has been strongly criticized for attempting to build a monopoly, eliminate competitors and undermine potential alternatives to Microsoft's proprietary software model. How this criticism relates to Microsoft's CSR rhetoric will be discussed in the next section.

Controversies: software patents

Large parts of the executive welcomes and mission statements of Microsoft's CSR communications could almost make the reader believe that s/he is reading a report from a charitable organization, with the goal of providing software in order to contribute to the full development of human potentials and to improve the lives of individuals around the world. What Microsoft's CSR communications largely ignore is that Microsoft actually is the most profitable software company in the world.[3,4] All financial measures show that Microsoft has been rapidly growing since the 1990s. Microsoft's assets in 2011 amounted to 108.7 billion USD and its profits were 23.2 billion USD, which in both categories means a 20-fold increase in comparison to 1994 (Microsoft SEC filings. 10-k forms 1994–2011). Microsoft's revenues in 2011 amounted to 69.9 billion USD and thus were 15 times higher than in 1994 (Microsoft SEC filings. 10-k forms 1994–2011).

This multiplication of Microsoft's assets, revenues and profits and the maintenance of its status as the world's leading software company has not been achieved through charity, but through business practices that have been strongly criticized for violating antitrust laws and for attempting to repress the realization of the full potentials of free and open source software (OSS). Critics point out that through these practices Microsoft is creating a knowledge monopoly. I will now look at Microsoft's legal disputes in regard to antitrust laws, the company's changing attitude towards the free and open source movement and its policy regarding software patents.

Violations of antitrust laws

On May 18, 1998 the US Department of Justice (DOJ) filed an antitrust lawsuit against Microsoft. The DOJ argued that the bundling of Microsoft's browser Internet Explorer with the Windows operating system was an attempt to hamper the use of the Netscape Internet browser and to thereby strengthen Window's monopoly power (Economides 2001, 10).

On April 3, 2000 the court convicted Microsoft for violating antitrust laws, stressing "that Microsoft maintained its monopoly power by anticompetitive means and attempted to monopolize the Web browser market".[5] After an appeals court in 2001 overturned this ruling, Microsoft and the Justice Department finally agreed on a settlement in which Microsoft agreed on some restriction of its conduct. According to this agreement Microsoft for example had to make technical interfaces available to competitors and was no longer allowed to use its market power for restricting computer manufacturers in using or offering products from Microsoft's competitors.[6] Microsoft furthermore violated European antitrust laws. In 2004 the company was fined 497 million EUR because of keeping software protocols secret, a practice that hindered interoperability with non-Microsoft products.[7] Because Microsoft did not take sufficient steps towards interoperability it was again fined 280.5 million EUR in 2006.[8]

Considering these antitrust lawsuits, it is not surprising that in its CSR communications Microsoft tries hard to confront the image of being a company that by all means wants to secure its monopoly market position. Starting from its first CSR report in 2003 Microsoft put great emphasis on its awareness regarding "responsible leadership". In 2006 Microsoft for example highlights:

> We ensure integrity, transparency, and social accountability in our business practices, whether complying with the laws of the countries where we do business, supporting industry standards, adhering to the highest ethical and environmental practices, or making sure our products interoperate well with those of other companies — including our competitors.
>
> (MI_CSR 2006, 5; see also MI_CSR 2004, 18; 2009, 7)

Microsoft also refers to past and ongoing legal disputes in Europe as well as the US. In 2004 Microsoft stressed that in order to ensure antitrust compliance the company had introduced standardized licences and royalty rates for PC manufacturers, and granted developers access to Windows interfaces necessary for developing applications (MI_CSR 2004, 21; see also MI_CSR 2005, 17; 2006, 55).

However, Microsoft contests the European Commission's verdict in its 2004 CSR report: "We contest the conclusion that European competition law was infringed and will defend our position" (MI_CSR 2004, 15). In its 2005 report, however, Microsoft stresses that its attempt to achieve a settlement with the European Commission was unsuccessful and it now would aim at full compliance with antitrust laws (MI_CSR 2005, 16). Despite this commitment the European Commission in 2006 again fined Microsoft because of violations of competition laws. This subsequent verdict is not mentioned in Microsoft's CSR communications.

In this context of antitrust lawsuits and repeated accusations of Microsoft's "anticompetitive" behaviour, Microsoft's emphasis on its willingness to co-operate with competitors can be interpreted as a strategy to actively confront the company's monopoly image. Microsoft's main strategy for demonstrating its willingness to engage in competition has been to show a commitment towards interoperability (MI_CSR 2004, 13; 2005, 10; 2006, 44; 2009, 12; 2010; 2011) – a lack of which had been the reason for the European Commission's antitrust lawsuits against Microsoft. Interoperability means to design software products in a way that makes them compatible with products from other companies. Given the statements found in the company's CSR communications it seems obvious that Microsoft wants to present itself as a company that is willing to co-operate in order to develop the best possible software solutions that help individuals around the world "to develop their full potential". However, this rhetoric does not correspond to the way in which Microsoft dealt with the emerging free and open source and software (FOSS) movement.

Free and open source software as a challenge for Microsoft

Both the free software as well as the open source movement are based on the idea that the source code of software should be accessible and modifiable in order to enable collaborative work on and improvement of software. According to the definition given by the Free Software Foundation, free software means that the source code can be viewed and modified and software can be redistributed free of charge.[9] The Open Source Initiative refers to 10 criteria that define OSS, including the right to redistribute it for both commercial and non-commercial purposes, the free accessibility of source code as well as the right to modify it.[10]

While the definitions of free software and open source hardly differ from each other, what distinguishes these movements is why they think that source code should be open, modifiable and freely distributable: while advocates of the open source movement argue this is important in order to improve software, the free software community emphasizes the value of freedom. Richard Stallman, a prominent figure in the free software community, therefore described the difference as follows: "Open source is a development methodology; free software is a social movement".[11]

Microsoft considered the emergence of the free software and open source movement as a major threat to its monopoly market position. Looking at statements made by Microsoft executives in the late 1990s and early 2000s reveals the company's intention to secure its monopoly and thereby maximize profits.

In 1998, two internal Microsoft strategy documents on the topic of open source were leaked. They provide insights into Microsoft's attitude towards open source and free software. In these so-called Halloween documents Microsoft stressed that it considered OSS a threat to the company's revenues: "OSS poses a direct, short-term revenue and platform threat to Microsoft" (Halloween Document I 1998). Microsoft was afraid of the potential development of alternative software, which would make it possible to bypass Microsoft's monopoly position:

> Linux poses a significant near-term revenue threat to Windows NT Server in the commodity file, print and network services businesses. [. . .] In the worst case, Linux provides a mechanism for server OEMs [Original Equipment Manufacturers] to provide integrated, task-specific products and completely bypassing Microsoft revenues in this space.
>
> (Halloween Document II 1998)

This quote illustrates that Microsoft considered OSS as powerful enough to challenge the company's monopoly position. Furthermore Microsoft admitted that the open source model including the free exchange of ideas and co-operation for the production of software creates benefits that cannot be achieved through a proprietary licensing model such as Microsoft's: "Additionally, the intrinsic parallelism and free idea exchange in OSS has benefits that are not replicable with our current licensing model and therefore present a long term developer mindshare threat" (Halloween Document I 1998). Microsoft clearly acknowledges that Linux has advantages in comparison to Windows. According to the second Halloween document, "Linux's (real and perceived) virtues over Windows NT include": customization, availability and reliability, scalability and performance, as well as interoperability (Halloween Document II 1998).

These advantages of OSS over Microsoft's proprietary software and the resulting threat for its revenues, for Microsoft were reason enough for taking measures in order to "deny OSS projects entry into the market" (Halloween Document I 1998). This shows that what is important for Microsoft is not that the best possible software is available, but that its profits can be sustained through selling proprietary software, even if this means depriving society of potentially better software.

Microsoft recognized that the battle between proprietary and FOSS was not about competing companies or organizations, but about competing models of how to organize the development and distribution of software:

> since money is often not the (primary) motivation behind Open Source Software, understanding the nature of the threat posed requires a deep understanding of the process and motivation of Open Source development teams. In other words, to understand how to compete against OSS, we must target a process rather than a company.
>
> (Halloween document I 1998)

Some years later in 2001, Jim Allchin, President of the Platforms and Service Division at Microsoft, again emphasized the threat open source would pose to the software industry:

> Open source is an intellectual-property destroyer [. . .] I can't imagine something that could be worse than this for the software business and the intellectual-property business [. . .] I'm an American, I believe in the American Way. I worry if the government encourages open source, and I don't think we've done enough education of policy makers to understand the threat.[12]

Microsoft's CEO Steve Ballmer in 2001 called Linux a cancer: "Linux is a cancer that attaches itself in an intellectual property sense to everything it touches".[13]

These statements clearly differ from the way Microsoft presents itself as a responsible corporation. While according to Microsoft's official CSR reports, interoperability and co-operation are core values for the company, the leaked Halloween documents show that Microsoft actually considered the introduction of technical barriers for hampering the development of FOSS. According to these documents, Microsoft wants to hamper the development of the free and open software movement, despite its acknowledgment that a commons based model of software production in various respects is superior to a proprietary model. This is opposed to Microsoft's official mission of producing the best possible software solutions to help people realize their potentials.

In the second Halloween document Microsoft referred to patents and copyright legislation as a potential opportunity to combat Linux: "The effect of patents and copyright in combating Linux remains to be investigated" (Halloween Document II 1998).

Software patents

At present, Microsoft applies for more patents than ever before. Microsoft acquired its first patent in 1986.[14] In 1990 Microsoft only held eight patents.[15] During the 1990s the number of Microsoft patents started to increase rapidly: in 1995 Microsoft held around 100, and in 1999 had more than 1,000 patents.[16] Up to September 2011 Microsoft had registered 18,648 patents at the US Patent and Trademark Office.[17] A further 21,993 patent requests were pending.[18] Figure 9.1 shows that the number of patents granted to Microsoft continues to increase rapidly.

Patenting software means to monopolize ideas. A patent holder has a monopoly right on using the patented software component. This means that unless a licensing agreement is agreed other developers can no longer use the patented software for creating new programs. The view that software can be patented is not uncontested. According to US patent law abstract ideas are not patentable (Bessen and Hunt 2007, 159). As software is based on abstract mathematical formulas, the US Patent Office used to follow a restrictive policy regarding software patents. However, in the 1980s the legal climate in the US started shifting towards support of software patents (Bessen and Hunt 2007, 157). The most important step in this context probably was the decision by the US Supreme Court in 1981 that software and industrial processes are patentable (Bessen and Hunt 2007, 160). In Europe, the European Patent Convention from 1973 determines that computer programs are abstract ideas and therefore not patentable. However, in the 1980s the European Patent Office changed its guidelines. As a consequence under specific conditions it became possible to patent software.[19]

These developments have not remained unchallenged. Civil society initiatives exist, which campaign against software patents such as the Free Software Foundation's End Software Patents in the United States[20] and No Software Patents in Europe.[21]

Their main arguments against software patents include that software patents create advantages for large corporations and lead to monopolization; hinder innovation; threaten the freedom of information; create artificial scarcity; and that software consists of mathematical formulas and abstract ideas, which are not patentable.[22,23]

Software patents are usually not granted to a complete program but to its components and combinations of algorithms. If somebody is granted a patent on a software component, this means that it can no longer be used for programming other software programs, unless there is a licence agreement with the patent holder.

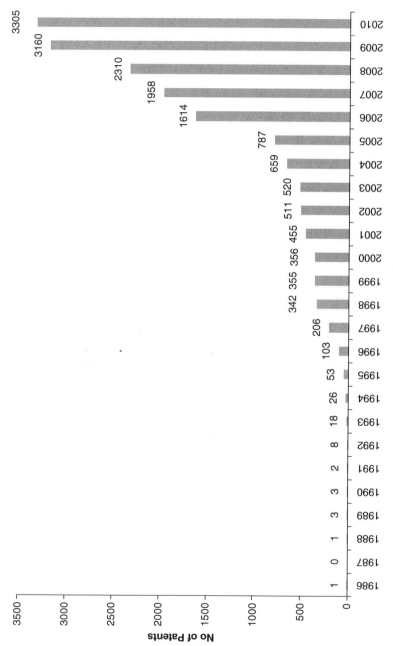

Figure 9.1 Number of Microsoft patents per year from 1986 to 2010 in the US.

Source: US Patent and Trademark Office.[1]

Note

1 U.S. Patent and Trademark Office. *List of Microsoft Patents*. Retrieved from http://patff.uspto.gov/netacgi/nph-Parser?Sect1=PTO2&Sect2=HITOFF&p=1&u=%2Fneta html%2FPTO%2Fsearch-bool.html&r=0&f=S&l=50&TERM1=microsoft&FIELD1=ASNM&co1=AND&TERM2=&FIELD2=&d=PTXT on September 28, 2011.

Thus, patenting software components restricts the development of new software. Software developers can choose between not using patented software algorithms, which might negatively affect the quality of the new program, or infringing patent law, or trying to achieve a licence agreement with the patent holder, which will most likely include a licence fee. Large corporations that themselves hold many patents will also be able to come to a cross-licensing agreement with another company, so that both company's can use the other's patents. This strengthens the power of large patent holders.

Furthermore all software development is based on previous knowledge such as mathematical rules.[24] The development of software is thus never attributable to one specific person or corporation but part of the knowledge commons of society. A patent thus takes away knowledge from society and grants exclusive usage rights to private actors.

End Software Patents and No Software Patents furthermore argue that patents threaten freedom of information and freedom of expression as they give control over important information and communication technology to patent holders. Patent holders can restrict access to this technology and thereby limit these freedoms.[25,26]

Another argument critics of software patents highlight is that software consists of knowledge, which is not consumed through usage but gets even better if it is shared. By limiting the possibility of sharing knowledge, software patents create artificial scarcity.[27]

It is not the case that Microsoft is unaware of the fact that patents are a fetter to creativity and innovation. It was Bill Gates who stressed in 1991 that patents would hamper technological innovation: "If people had understood how patents would be granted when most of today's ideas were invented, and had taken out patents, the industry would be at a complete standstill today" (Gates 1991). This is one of the most important arguments critics used against software patents. However, this insight did not make Bill Gates question software patents, but instead led him to embrace the idea of patenting software in order to secure Microsoft's market position. The fear that competitors could gain advantages through software patents for Gates allowed only one solution: "patenting as much as we can" (Gates 1991).

Also in its CSR communications Microsoft praises the importance of protecting intellectual property rights: "Our commitment to innovation also includes protecting the value of intellectual property. Microsoft believes that respect for intellectual property rights is crucial to enabling innovators to bring their ideas to market and to developing a thriving IT ecosystem" (MI_CSR 2007/2008, 4). Similar statements can be found throughout Microsoft's CSR communications. Rather than only stressing the importance of intellectual property rights for the company's business interests, Microsoft argues that patents are in the general interest of society:

Enabling IP [intellectual property] opportunity confers tremendous benefits on society: consumers benefit from innovation in the form of new products; new business and employment opportunities are created; local economic growth is enabled; productivity gains are achieved; and governments gain opportunities for increased tax revenue.

(MI_CSR 2006, 42)

On the other hand, according to Microsoft, patents foster cultural diversity: "Around the world, copyright and patent laws play a central role in fostering a diversity of cultural resources, and in promoting technological advances and economic growth. These laws are more important than ever in a global economy" (MI_CSR 2003, 13). Microsoft thus proudly reports its efforts to foster the patenting of software (MI_CSR 2004, 63).

As the above numbers (Figure 9.1) show, Microsoft has reached its goal of becoming a major holder of software patents. Microsoft is actively contributing to the monopolization of ideas and the expropriation of the knowledge commons of society for the sake of maximum private profit. It is therefore not surprising that: "For many in the open source community, the company [Microsoft] represents all that is troubling about closed source software development" (OSS Watch 2011).

In order to protest against Microsoft's proprietary software model, the Free Software Foundation runs a campaign called Microsoft's 7 sins. The Free Software Foundation criticizes Microsoft for (1) creating dependencies on Microsoft through using Microsoft products in education, (2) invading user privacy, (3) monopoly behaviour through pre-installed Microsoft programs on most computers, (4) forcing users to regularly update their versions of Windows and Office which often even forces user to switch to new hardware, (5) blocking the creation of free standards, (6) supporting digital rights management (DRM), and (7) threatening user security due to the vulnerability of Microsoft's products to viruses.[28] The Free Software Foundation argues that all these problems are inherent to proprietary software based on patents and points at the model of free software as a suitable alternative.

Microsoft's shifting approach to the open source and free software movement

While Microsoft for many years was known for its opposition to the open source and free software movement, in the mid-2000s it started to change its strategy. Microsoft initiated several projects that might be understood as the beginning of a more pragmatic, rather than a confrontational, strategy in dealing with the open source and free software movement. A 2010 statement made by the general manager of Microsoft's interoperability unit, Jan Paoli, illustrates that Microsoft's public rhetoric had changed compared to the early 2000s: "We love open source. We have worked with open source for a long time now".[29]

One of Microsoft's attempts to develop links to the open source community is the introduction of a shared source program. In 2004 Microsoft stressed in its CSR report that as part of its "responsible industry leadership" it wants to work towards expanding "Shared Source program offerings" (MI_CSR 2004, 33). The Microsoft shared software programs contains several different licences, which to different degrees allow users to view or sometimes even modify the source code. The Open Source Initiative highlights that Microsoft's Shared Source is different from open source and should be considered as a "marketing dud".[30] However, the Open Source Initiative decided that two of the Microsoft Shared Source licences qualify as open source licences (the Microsoft Public Licence and the Microsoft Reciprocal Licence).[31]

Another Microsoft initiative to make source codes available is Codeplex. On codeplex.com[32] Microsoft provides projects under licences that qualify as "free software". However, critics stress that the Codeplex projects are often add-ons to proprietary Microsoft software (OSS Watch 2011). In 2007 Microsoft became a sponsor of the Apache Software a non profit-organization of open source developers.[33] Among Apache's sponsors are several other ICT giants such as Google, Yahoo!, Facebook and HP.[34] In 2009 Microsoft started co-operating with Linux by providing device drivers under the General Public License (GPL).[35] Microsoft also runs an online directory which list all its collaborations with open source projects, most of which are connected to the Codeplex platform.[36]

However, compared to Microsoft's proprietary software products such as the Windows operating systems and Microsoft Office programs, these are marginal projects that do not affect Microsoft's core business model, which remains based on selling licences for proprietary software. Microsoft's recent interest in open source projects does not indicate a shift away from proprietary software. On the contrary Microsoft's co-operation with the open source community entails the danger that Microsoft uses ideas generated in these projects for advancing its own proprietary software products. In that case Microsoft would exploit the free labour of open source and free software developers for generating profit. The proprietary software model is still the dominant model of software production and distribution. In September 2011, Microsoft's proprietary operating system Windows had a market share of 86.57 per cent.[37] In comparison, the market share of the free software operating system Linux was only 1.04 per cent.[38]

Microsoft is continuing to expand its reach and to advance the proprietary software model. As part of its mission of contributing to "realizing human potentials" Microsoft wants to address the problem of the digital divide and lack of access to technology: "Technology is a potent force that can empower millions of people to reach their goals and realize their dreams – but for many people around the world, the Digital Divide keeps that power out of reach" (MI_CSR 2003, 23). Microsoft therefore makes a "comprehensive commitment to digital inclusion, and to help address inequities" (MI_CSR 2004, 48; see also MI_CSR 2005, 26; 2007/2008, 3). To fulfil this commitment Microsoft runs a number of programmes that provide technological infrastructure and software for free or at reduced prices to schools, libraries and community centres.

The fact that people who do not yet have access to computer technology represent millions of potential customers, suggests that Microsoft's motives for engaging in these initiatives are not primarily altruistic ones. In 2005 for example Microsoft writes that its aim is "to reach a quarter billion people who are currently underserved by technology" (MI_CSR 2005, 26; see also MI_CSR 2009, 3). As these people are potential Microsoft customers it is not surprising that Microsoft wants to introduce them to the "benefits of technology" and to provide them with skills.

Through these initiatives Microsoft is strengthening its leading market position and creating dependencies on Microsoft products. Proprietary Microsoft software is expensive and even if Microsoft provides a free starting package to schools and other organizations, it is likely that some years later they will have to buy software updates and new programs. Furthermore it is likely that Microsoft's training programmes will focus on Microsoft software and not on how to use open source systems such as for example Linux. This is particularly problematic as finding, installing and using open source solutions often requires more complex technical skills than those necessary for using proprietary software. As OSS is available for free it could present a real alternative to Microsoft for people and organizations who only have limited financial resources. Microsoft is a highly profitable company. Providing software to schools and training teachers and students in how to use Microsoft products is an investment in Microsoft's future. These initiatives not only strengthen Microsoft's market position but the proprietary software model in general.

Conclusion

Microsoft in its CSR communications tries to create an image of being a company that is aware of its global responsibility that results from its leading market position. A company that wants to provide the best possible software, whose business practices respect laws and are guided by values; that engages in charitable activities in favour of disadvantaged people all over the world; and that takes its mission of contributing to the realization of human potentials seriously. The rhetoric of Microsoft's CSR communications suggest that providing software that is beneficial for individuals and society, not profit, is the main aim of Microsoft.

Looking at media reports, court valuations and reports from the FOSS community reveals a completely different picture of the most profitable software company in the world. The way Microsoft is described by others shows it as a company that violates laws, that aims at increasing and protecting its monopoly power, that privatizes the common knowledge of society and whose ultimate aim is profit, not the best possible software for society.

Microsoft's mission is to "help people and businesses around the world realize their full potential" (MI_CSR 2011, 6). In the context of challenges posed by the FOSS movement it is doubtful that a company that makes money by providing proprietary software can fulfil these promises.

The concept of FOSS on the contrary is an important starting point towards the creation of an open and accessible commons based culture, which would provide better conditions for human creativity to thrive. However, the FOSS model is not without limitations. Both concepts do not restrict the usage of FOSS to noncommercial purposes. As a consequence companies are trying to take advantage of free and open source models. Different business models that are based on OSS are emerging. Profit is for example generated by charging money for support services or for customizing the software for the specific needs of individual customers. Another open source business model is based on a dual-licensing system in which a program is released with a proprietary as well as an open source licence. Customers that want to further develop the code but are not willing to make this modification public can then choose to purchase the program under the proprietary licence.[39,40]

One danger of these developments is that OSS developers could end up being exploited by companies that make use of OSS for generating profit. Connected to this is the danger of the emergence of new inequalities in access to software because only basic versions are available for free while users have to pay for accessing more advanced software and for receiving the necessary support services.

While Richard Stallman writes that open source misses the point of free software,[41] I argue that both open source and free software miss one crucial point: that in order to establish a thriving commons based culture and to overcome unequal access to software and exploitation of software developers, a non-commercial model of software production is inevitable. Establishing such as system would also require developing alternative models of paying software developers. Possible solutions could be connected to a guaranteed basic income or models similar to those that are being discussed in the context of the music industry such as cultural flat rate models (see for example Netanel 2003; Fischer 2004) or a cultural artistic freedom voucher (Baker 2003).

Notes

1 *Forbes Magazine.* 2011. *The World's Biggest Public Companies.* Retrieved from http://www.forbes.com/global2000/#p_1_s_acompanyRankOverall_SoftwareProgramming_All_All on June 17, 2011.
2 *The New York Times.* 2011. *Europe Approves Microsoft Purchase of Skype.* By Kevin O'Brian on October 7, 2011. Retrieved from http://www.nytimes.com/2011/10/08/technology/europe-approves-microsoft-purchase-of-skype.html?_r=1 on October 10, 2011.
3 Software Top 100. 2010. *Global Software Top 100.* Retrieved from http://www.software-top100.org/global-software-top-100-edition-2010 on October 5, 2011.
4 *Forbes Magazine.* 2011. *The World's Biggest Public Companies.* Retrieved from http://www.forbes.com/global2000/#p_1_s_acompanyRankOverall_SoftwareProgramming_All_All on June 17, 2011.
5 United States of America vs. Microsoft Corporation. 2000. *Conclusions of Law.* Retrieved from http://news.cnet.com/html/ne/Special/Microsoft/conclusions_of_law_and_order.html on October 3, 2011.
6 United States of America vs. Microsoft Corporation. 2001. *Stipulation.* Retrieved from http://cyber.law.harvard.edu/msdoj/011106-proposed-settlement.html on October 3, 2011.
7 *The Guardian.* 2006. *EU Hits Microsoft with 280.5m Antitrust Fine.* By Mark Tran on July 12, 2006. Retrieved from http://www.guardian.co.uk/business/2006/jul/12/europeanunion.digitalmedia on October 3, 2011.
8 *The Guardian.* 2006. *EU Hits Microsoft with 280.5m Antitrust Fine.* By Mark Tran on July 12, 2006. Retrieved from http://www.guardian.co.uk/business/2006/jul/12/europeanunion.digitalmedia on October 3, 2011.
9 Free Software Foundation. *The Free Software Definition.* Retrieved from http://www.gnu.org/philosophy/free-sw.html on October 4, 2011.

10 The Open Source Initiative. *The Open Source Definition*. Retrieved from http://www.opensource.org/docs/osd on October 4, 2011.

11 Richard Stallman. *Why Open Source Misses the Point of Free Software*. Retrieved from http://www.gnu.org/philosophy/open-source-misses-the-point.html on October 4, 2011.

12 Jim Allchin cited on cnet.com (see http://news.cnet.com/2100-1001-252681.html) The original article is no longer available online. Quotation thus taken from Tim O'Reilly. 2001. *A Response to Jim Allchin's Comments*. Retrieved from http://www.oreillynet.com/manila/tim/stories/storyReader$167 on September 27, 2011.

13 Steve Ballmer quoted in *The Register*. 2001. *"Linux is a Cancer"*. Retrieved from http://www.theregister.co.uk/2001/06/02/ballmer_linux_is_a_cancer/ on September 24, 2011.

14 US Patent and Trademark Office. *Patent for: "Holder for Storing and Supporting Article"*, *May 13, 1986*. Retrieved from http://patft.uspto.gov/netacgi/nph-Parser?Sect1=PTO2&Sect2=HITOFF&u=%2Fnetahtml%2FPTO%2Fsearch-adv.htm&r=18660&f=G&l=50&d=PTXT&s1=microsoft$.ASNM.&p=374&OS=an/microsoft$&RS=AN/microsoft$ on September 28, 2011.

15 US Patent and Trademark Office. *Patent for: "Holder for Storing and Supporting Article"*, *May 13, 1986*. Retrieved from http://patft.uspto.gov/netacgi/nph-Parser?Sect1=PTO2&Sect2=HITOFF&u=%2Fnetahtml%2FPTO%2Fsearch-adv.htm&r=18660&f=G&l=50&d=PTXT&s1=microsoft$.ASNM.&p=374&OS=an/microsoft$&RS=AN/microsoft$ on September 28, 2011.

16 Ars Technica. 2007. *Analysis: Microsoft's Software Patent Flip-Flop*. By Timothy B. Lee. Retrieved from http://arstechnica.com/business/news/2007/03/analysis-microsofts-software-patent-flip-flop.ars on September 28, 2011.

17 US Patent and Trademark Office. *List of Microsoft Patents*. Retrieved from http://patft.uspto.gov/netacgi/nph-Parser?Sect1=PTO2&Sect2=HITOFF&p=1&u=%2Fnetahtml%2FPTO%2Fsearch-bool.html&r=0&f=S&l=50&TERM1=microsoft&FIELD1=ASNM&co1=AND&TERM2=&FIELD2=&d=PTXT on September 28, 2011.

18 US Patent and Trademark Office. *List of Microsoft Patent Applications*. Retrieved from http://appft1.uspto.gov/netacgi/nph-Parser?Sect1=PTO2&Sect2=HITOFF&u=%2Fnetahtml%2FPTO%2Fsearch-adv.html&r=0&p=1&f=S&l=50&d=PG01&Query=an%2Fmicrosoft%24 on September 28, 2011.

19 Foundation for a Free Information Infrastructure. *Software Patents in Europe*. Retrieved from http://eupat.ffii.org/neues/intro/index.en.html on October 6, 2011.

20 http://endsoftpatents.org/

21 http://www.nosoftwarepatents.com/en/m/intro/index.html

22 End Software Patents. *Why Abolish Software Patents*. Retrieved from http://en.swpat.org/wiki/Software_patents_wiki:_home_page on October 6, 2011.

23 No Software Patents. *The Dangers*. Retrieved from http://www.nosoftwarepatents.com/en/m/dangers/index.html on October 6, 2011.

24 End Software Patents. *Software is Math*. Retrieved from http://en.swpat.org/wiki/Software_is_math on October 6, 2011.

25 End Software Patents. *Freedom of Expression*. Retrieved from http://en.swpat.org/wiki/Freedom_of_expression on October 6, 2011.

26 No Software Patents. *Freedom of Information*. Retrieved from http://www.nosoftwarepatents.com/en/m/dangers/freedom.html on October 6, 2011.

27 Open Source Initiative. *A New Argument against SWPAT*. Retrieved from http://opensource.org/node/441 on October 6, 2011.

28 The Free Software Foundation. *Microsoft's 7 Sins*. Retrieved from http://en.windows7sins.org/ on September 27, 2011.

29 Jan Paoli quoted in Network World. 2010. *Microsoft: "We Love Open Source"*. By John Brodkin on August 23, 2010. Retrieved from http://www.networkworld.com/news/2010/082310-microsoft-open-source.html?page=1 on September 28, 2011.

30 Open Source Initiative. 2007. *Who Is Behind the "Shared Source" Misinformation Campaign?* Retrieved from http://opensource.org/node/225 on October 14, 2011.

31 Open Source Initiative. 2007. *OSI Approves License Submissions.* Retrieved from http://opensource.org/node/207 on October 14, 2011.

32 http://www.codeplex.com/

33 The Apache Software Foundation. *FAQ.* Retrieved from http://www.apache.org/foundation/faq.html#what on September 27, 2011.

34 The Apache Software Foundation. *Sponsors.* Retrieved from http://www.apache.org/foundation/thanks.html on September 27, 2011.

35 Network World. 2010. *Microsoft: "We Love Open Source".* By John Brodkin on August 23, 2010. Retrieved from http://www.networkworld.com/news/2010/082310-microsoft-open-source.html?page=1 on September 28, 2011.

36 Microsoft Open Source Directory. *Project Directory.* Retrieved from http://www.microsoft.com/opensource/directory.aspx on October 14, 2011.

37 NetMarketshare. 2011. *Top Operating System Share Trend.* Retrieved from http://www.netmarketshare.com/os-market-share.aspx?qprid=9 on October 14, 2011.

38 NetMarketshare. 2011. *Top Operating System Share Trend.* Retrieved from http://www.netmarketshare.com/os-market-share.aspx?qprid=9 on October 14, 2011.

39 Open Source Watch. 2011. *Free and Open Source Software Business and Sustainability Models.* Retrieved from http://www.oss-watch.ac.uk/resources/businessandsustainability.xml#body.1_div.2 on October 6, 2011.

40 Open Source Watch. 2011. *Dual-licensing.* Retrieved from http://www.oss-watch.ac.uk/resources/duallicence2.xml on October 6, 2011.

41 Richard Stallman. *Why Open Source Misses the Point of Free Software.* Retrieved from http://www.gnu.org/philosophy/open-source-misses-the-point.html on October 14, 2011.

10 News Corporation

Consciousness industry?

Rupert Murdoch started to develop and expand News Corporation after he inherited *Adelaide News* from his father Sir Keith Murdoch in 1952 (Arsenault and Castells 2008, 491). Today, Rupert Murdoch is the 24th most powerful and the 108th richest person in the world.[1] His power and money are based on the operations of News Corp, the 149th biggest public company worldwide and the 3rd largest media content company[2] in the world.

After Rupert Murdoch took over *Adelaide News*, News Corp first expanded within Australia by acquiring the *Sunday Times* in Perth (in 1956), launching Adelaide's first TV station (in 1958), purchasing the *Daily Mirror* and the *Sunday Mirror* in Sydney (in 1960), and finally launching *The Australian* (in 1964). In 1969 News Corp entered the British market by purchasing the *Sun* and *News of the World*. In 1973 News Corp acquired the *San Antonio Express* and *San Antonio News*, expanding its operations to North America. In 1976 News Corp bought the *New York Post* in the US and in 1981 *The Times* in England. News Corp entered the film business in 1985 with the purchase of 20th Century Fox. In 1989 it launched Sky Broadcasting and one year later created the publishing house Harper Collins. In the 1990s News Corp started expanding its TV segment by entering the Asian market with Star TV in 1993, launching Fox News Channel in 1996 and Sky Italia in 2003. In 2005 News Corp purchased MySpace, but sold it again in 2011. In 2007 News Corp acquired the *Wall Street Journal*.[3]

Today, News Corp is active in most areas of the media content sector including television and radio broadcasting, print and publishing, online media and film production.[4] The company has a "truly 'global' reach" (Arsenault and Castells 2008, 489), and is active in North and South America, Europe, Asia, and Australia.[5]

CSR approach

News Corp does not publish yearly CSR reports. However, in its *Standards of Business Conduct* News Corp highlights that its commitment to the global community includes CSR:

> We take our corporate social responsibilities seriously. Specifically in the context of our business, which is news, information and entertainment, we

are always and everywhere dedicated to advancing our core values of free inquiry, free speech and free expression for all people.

(News Corp_SBC, 38)

In addition, since the launch of News Corp's Global Energy Initiative (GEI) in 2007 the company has been publishing data about its environmental impact. The goal of the initiative is to make News Corp's business operations more efficient and to reduce the company's environmental impact. In a speech in which Rupert Murdoch announced the start of the GEI to all News Corp employees around the world he stressed: "Climate change poses clear, catastrophic threats. We may not agree on the extent, but we certainly can't afford the risk of inaction".[6] The launch of this initiative and Murdoch's clear statement on the potential threats of climate change came as a surprise, as News Corp's news media until then had been known for supporting the position of climate change deniers (McKnight 2010b).

In 2010 News Corp reached its first important environmental goal: carbon neutrality. Officially News Corp has net zero carbon emissions. This was, however, achieved not only by use of renewable energy and reductions of energy consumption but also through purchasing carbon credits.[7]

According to News Corp it could reduce its total carbon footprint from 556,402 metric tons of carbon dioxide equivalent in 2006 to 532,279 metric tons of carbon dioxide equivalent in 2010. These numbers do not include energy that was purchased from green power sources.[8] News Corp's carbon footprint is higher than those of other big media companies such as Vivendi with a carbon footprint of 296,901 metric tons (CDP 2011, 72), and Time Warner with 260,618 metric tons (CDP 2011, 71). However, it is substantially lower than the carbon footprint of Disney, which amounts to 1,465,646 metric tons (CDP 2011, 739).

In 2011 News Corp received an AAA ranking in the Global Socrates database and the Carbon Disclosure project ranked News Corp A for its carbon performance and "1 in its sector" for its carbon disclosure.[9] Furthermore, in the Carbon Disclosure Project News Corp is ranked at position 93, which is the highest score of all the media content companies (CDP 2011, 23).

As part of the GEI all News Corp business units in different ways are engaging in initiatives that deal with issues of energy use and climate change. News Corp furthermore claims that it not only wants to reduce its own environmental impact, but also raise awareness of environmental issues among its partners, its audiences and its employees.[10]

The fact that it does not publish CSR reports suggests that being or at least being perceived as a socially and environmentally responsible company is not a priority for News Corp. On the other hand, the GEI can be characterized as a CSR activity and shows that the company is at some levels concerned with sustainability issues. As statements on the GEI website suggest, the initiative allows News Corp to save money by reducing its environmental impact. Murdoch writes: "Together, despite some of the toughest markets our industry has ever seen, we have saved millions of dollars by improving the energy efficiency of our day-to-day operations".[11] This resembles a reductionist approach, which highlights business benefits that result from acting responsibly. However, the limited amount of CSR material available from News Corp does not provide enough evidence for identifying a specific CSR approach.

While News Corp discloses data about its environmental impact, it does not provide any information about its social responsibility in regard to its core business activity: media content production. As I will show in the next section, watchdogs have highlighted and criticized the ideological implications of News Corp's media content, which every day reaches millions of people around the globe.

Controversies: media ideologies

One recent public controversy about News Corporation was the *News of the World* phone hacking scandal, which reached its climax in summer 2011. Two years earlier, the scandal about the phone hacking practices of *News of the World* journalists had erupted; *The Guardian* reported that the British newspaper publisher and News Corp subsidiary News International had paid 1 million GBP for a out of court settlement of legal cases in which News International journalists were accused of having hired private investigators that used illegal hacking methods in order to gain access to phone messages and other private information such tax information and bank statements for public figures.[12] What was known to close observers for some years, in 2011 turned into a public scandal. Among the targets of the hacker attacks were a number of celebrities, relatives of soldiers that were killed in Iraq or Afghanistan, and of a 13-year-old murder victim.[13] The scandal had a significant impact on News Corp: in the midst of the scandal it withdrew its bid for acquiring Sky Broadcasting,[14] and announced the closure of *News of the World* in July 2011.[15] Finally, the scandal led to the resignation of Rupert Murdoch's son James Murdoch as chairmen of News International in February 2012.[16]

These events negatively affected News Corp's reputation – the practices employed by *News of the World* journalists certainly violated journalistic, and presumably also legal standards. The phone hacking furthermore reveals how much effort the *News of the World* journalists were willing to put into stories, the news value of which mainly consisted of creating and satisfying voyeuristic appetites.

However, the scandal should not distract from looking at News Corp's regular journalistic practices. These at first sight might appear less scandalous, but have a much higher and longer-term impact on the knowledge and worldviews of millions of people around the world who are consuming News Corp's media content. Murdoch called the phone hacking a "serious wrongdoing".[17] However, he on the contrary designs and defends News Corp's day-to-day business practices, which, as I will show in the following, watchdogs consider problematic.

As one of the largest media content companies in the world, News Corp is not only an economically powerful actor, but also a main producer of media content, which is available in various world regions, and also holds significant political and cultural power. Between 2003 and 2010 News Corp's profits on average grew 12.4 per cent per year.[18] According to Arsenault and Castells, News Corp reaches around 75 per cent of the global population (Arsenault and Castells 2008, 491). News Corp generates most of its revenues in the US. However, signification portions of the company's revenues are also based on its operations in Europe, and other parts of the world, including Australia, the country from which News Corp originated (see Figure 10.1).

Rupert Murdoch is aware of the power of his transnational media empire:

> We have special powers: We can help set the agenda of political discussion. We can uncover government misdeeds and bring them to light. We can decide what television fare to offer children on a rainy Saturday morning. We can affect the culture by glorifying or demonizing certain behaviour.
>
> (Murdoch quoted in Goldman Rohm 2002, 32)

On several occasions Murdoch has made it clear that he has a concrete vision for journalism and the media business in the twenty-first century. After summarizing Murdoch's vision in the following I will highlight major criticism regarding News

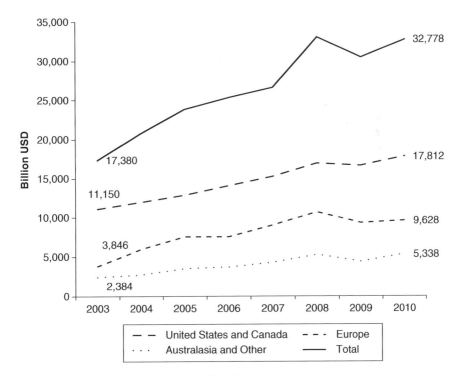

Figure 10.1 News Corp's revenues, 2003–2010.

Source: News Corp SEC filings. 10-k forms 2005–2010.

Corp's media content and discuss News Corp's commitment to fair and balanced reporting.

Rupert Murdoch's vision for media in the twenty-first century

Commentators stress that Murdoch himself exerts a great amount of vertical power over the operation of all of News Corp's media outlets (Arsenault and Castells 2008, 489; McKnight 2010a, 306; 2011, 840). Rupert Murdoch himself holds 39.7 per cent and the Murdoch family trust holds 38.4 per cent of company shares (class B common stock). This gives Murdoch almost 80 per cent of the voting power and great decision power over the activities of News Corp.[19]

According to Murdoch the success formula for media is based on: giving the audience what they want; making the audience pay for media content; and fostering deregulation of the media sector.[20,21]

Giving the audience what they want

According to Murdoch, news companies should "give their customers the news they want, when they want it, and how they want it".[22] For Murdoch the goal should not be to provide high quality journalism but to meet the expectations and preferences of a broad audience:

> I can't tell you how many papers I have visited where they have a wall of journalism prizes – and a rapidly declining circulation. This tells me the editors are producing news for themselves – instead of news that is relevant to their customers".[23]

Making the audience pay for media content

Providing news that people want might be the precondition for achieving the second requirement, which according to Murdoch is necessary for the success of news companies in the twenty-first century: making audiences pay for media content. Murdoch stresses that "The old business model based mainly on advertising is dead".[24] For Murdoch, the future of online media also needs to be based on charging people for access to media content.[25] Murdoch's idea is not to substitute the advertising based business model with a pay for access business model, but to combine both. In a letter to stockholder's in News Corp's 2009 annual report Murdoch states: "For our newspapers, this means that advertising alone will no longer have to pay all the bills. In addition to carrying advertising, successful newspapers of the future will charge for their content".[26]

In order to exploit the full profit potentials of advertising Murdoch advocates the extensive collection of data about media users.[27] He highlights that the more media companies can surveil their users the more profit they can generate: "The more we know who is watching us on television or subscribing to our papers, the more opportunity we will have to generate revenue".[28]

Fostering deregulation of the media sector

Rupert Murdoch believes in a commercial media system. He argues that the "freedom" of the press can only be guaranteed in a commercial media system in which media companies compete for profit: "It is precisely because newspapers make profits and do not depend on the government for their livelihood that they have the resources and wherewithal to hold the government accountable".[29]

Murdoch told his biographer William Shawcross that in his view newspapers are meant to be about profit:

> All newspapers are run to make profits. Full stop. I don't run anything for respectability. The moment I do I hope someone will come and fire me and get me out of the place – because that's not what newspapers are meant to be about.
>
> (Rupert Murdoch quoted in Shawcross 1992, 302)

In a speech at the Federal Trade Commission in 2009 he emphasized that government regulation of the media sector is harmful: "If we are really concerned about the survival of newspapers and other journalistic enterprises, the best thing government can do is to get rid of the arbitrary and contradictory regulations".[30]

While Murdoch opposes any regulation that hampers growth and the increase of profit, he on the other hand welcomes regulation that protects profit generation. In particular, this includes regulation that protects intellectual property rights. Murdoch states: "I fear the ability of creative companies to prosper globally could be undermined by a lack of intellectual property protection domestically".[31]

Following Murdoch's vision, News Corp has always engaged in lobbying to reduce media regulation and at many times has been successful: in 1994 after a complaint to the Federal Communications Commission (FCC) about Fox News violating the regulation according to which any foreign company is not allowed to own more than 24.9 per cent of a broadcaster, the FCC granted a waiver to Fox News (Arsenault and Castells 2008, 505). News Corp also heavily lobbied for the 1996 Telecommunications Act in the US, which made the vertical integration of Fox News, *TV Guide* and Harper Collins possible (Arsenault and Castells 2008, 499). In Britain News Corp's lobbying efforts in 2003 contributed to the passing of a communications bill that reduced the regulatory restriction on cross-ownership between television and newspapers. As the bill only benefited News Corp it was unofficially called the "Murdoch Clause" (Arsenault and Castells 2008, 505).

Murdoch's personal views not only influence the company's policies, activities and strategies but also News Corp's media content that is consumed every day by millions of people around the globe.

Media content

Various corporate watchdogs including scholars, alternative media and civil society groups have repeatedly criticized News Corp for promoting market liberal and pro-war ideologies. In particular News Corp's reporting about the Bush administration and the war in Iraq; its stance towards climate change; and its bias towards conservative and market liberal viewpoints have been under attack.

The Bush administration's "war on terror" in Iraq

It is no secret that Rupert Murdoch advocated the US attack on Iraq. Murdoch told the Australian magazine *The Bulletin* that he agreed with Bush's decision regarding Iraq: "I think Bush is acting very morally, very correctly, and I think he is going to go on with it" (Rupert Murdoch quoted in Greenslade 2003). He furthermore made clear that in his view prospects of access to oil resources justified the intervention: "Once it [Iraq] is behind us, the whole world will benefit from cheaper oil which will be a bigger stimulus than anything else" (Rupert Murdoch quoted in Greenslade 2003).

This pro-war attitude also characterized News Corp's journalism. Studies have shown that News Corp's news media outlets around the globe univocally supported the US intervention in Iraq. Research conducted by *The Guardian* journalist Roy Greenslade for example revealed that all of News Corp's 175 newspapers around the world were in support of the Iraq war (Greenslade 2003). The advocacy of the war against Iraq not only characterized New Corp's print media but also the reporting by the US TV network Fox News. The 2005 study *The State of News Media*, conducted within the Project for Excellence in Journalism found that on Fox News 38 per cent of news stories covering the war in Iraq were positive in tone while only 14 per cent were negative. In comparison, 20 per cent of CNN's stories about the Iraq war and 16 per cent of MSNBC's stories were positive, while 23 per cent of CNN's stories and 17 per cent of MSNBC's were negative (Project for Excellence in Journalism 2005).

In 2003 a study issued by the Program on International Policy Attitudes (PIPA) and Knowledge Networks revealed that misperceptions about the war in Iraq were more common among viewers of Fox News than among people who were using other media as their major news source (PIPA and Knowledge Networks 2003, 12). Sixty-seven per cent of Fox viewers believed that evidence was found that confirmed that Saddam Hussein was working closely with al-Qaeda. Thirty-three per cent of Fox viewers were convinced that weapons of mass destruction were found in Iraq. Thirty-five per cent of Fox News viewers believed that the majority of the world population favoured the US intervention in Iraq (PIPA and Knowledge Networks 2003, 13–15). In total, 80 per cent of viewers of Fox News had at least one of the three misperceptions regarding the war in Iraq. In comparison, 71 per cent of CBS viewers, 61 per cent of ABC viewers, 55 per cent of NBC as well as CNN viewers, and 23 per cent of the audience of PBS-NPR had one or more misperceptions (PIPA and Knowledge Networks 2003, 13).

Arsenault and Castells argue that Fox News' strong advocacy of the Iraq war influenced the journalistic climate in the US:

> influencing public opinion in favor of the Iraq War, not only strengthened station ties to the Bush administration, but it influenced the journalistic norms

of rival outlets in support of a similar agenda – reprogramming the television media network as a whole.

(Arsenault and Castells 2008, 501)

News Corp's contradictory policy regarding climate change

In 2007, in his speech at the launch of News Corp's GEI, Rupert Murdoch explicitly warned about the potential threats of climate change.[32] Since then News Corp has reduced its carbon emissions and in 2011 was ranked among the top disclosers within the Carbon Disclosure Project (CDP 2011, 23).

News Corp's effort to reduce its environmental impact came as a surprise since News Corp's news media had until then repeatedly provided a media platform for climate change deniers. David McKnight studied how News Corp between 1997 and 2007 dealt with climate change. He argues that News Corp's media outlets in editorials, opinion pieces and columns advanced a view of climate change as a political and not a scientific issue, described climate change sciences as orthodoxy and sceptics as dissidents, and depicted the topic as an expression of left wing "political correctness" (McKnight 2010b, 694). According to McKnight (2010b) the sceptical commentaries in News Corp's media outlets were particularly common in the US and Australia, while less frequent in the UK. In general, climate change deniers were depicted in a positive light: "The climate change deniers and sceptics, regardless of their lack of evidence and (in most cases) scientific qualifications were elevated to the status of brave dissidents against an oppressive set of beliefs" (McKnight 2010b, 703).

Murdoch's 2007 acknowledgement of the threat of climate change thus appeared to mark a significant change. However, critics point out that despite News Corp's efforts to reduce its environmental impact, its media outlets continue to spread misleading information about climate change. Kevin Knobloch, president of the Union of Concerned Scientists, has therefore called News Corps activities "environmental hypocrisy".[33] The media watchdog Media Matters highlighted that

> Fox News has done more than any other major news outlet in the United States to misrepresent climate science and sow confusion about global warming. Fox's inaccurate coverage extends across both its opinion shows and the purportedly straight news programs.[34]

In February 2011 the *Rolling Stone* ranked Rupert Murdoch the number 1 in a list of 12 politicians and corporate executives that block the fight against climate change: "No one does more to spread dangerous disinformation about global warming than Murdoch" (Goodell 2011). Fox News' TV hosts and commentators such as Brian Kilmeade, Sean Hannity, Greg Palkot, Brian Wilson, Bill Hemmer and Glenn Beck repeatedly declared in TV and radio that global warming does not exist (McKnight 2010b, 697; Media Matters 2010; Goodell 2011; Toffel and Schendler 2012, 1). Also the *Wall Street Journal* has repeatedly served as a platform for climate change sceptics (Toffel und Scehndler 2012, 1), such as for example by publishing an opinion piece entitled *No Need to Panic about Global Warming*, signed by 16 climate change sceptics in January 2012. They argued that "There's no compelling scientific argument for drastic action to 'decarbonize' the world's economy" and claim that there has been "lack of global warming for well over 10 years now".[35]

A leaked email from the managing editor of Fox News Washington, Bill Sammon, during the Copenhagen climate summit in 2009 reveals Fox's sceptical policy towards climate change. Sammon advised Fox journalists to "refrain from asserting that the planet has warmed (or cooled) in any given period without IMMEDIATELY pointing out that such theories are based upon data that critics have called into question".[36]

A study by Krosnick and MacInnis (2010) shows that viewers of Fox News tend to hold more sceptical views on climate change. Based on the nationally representative survey in the US, they found that viewers of Fox News are less likely to agree with mainstream scientists' views about global warming, while they are more likely to believe that global warming would have negative economic consequences (Krosnick and MacInnis 2010, 2).

On the website of the GEI News Corp writes that it is committed to raising awareness among its audience about environmental protection:

> We aim to inform and inspire our audiences – whether in the developed world or the developing, across a variety of media platforms – and empower them to make smart choices that will reduce the environmental impact of their own lives – and which should save them money, too.[37]

Evidence of continued climate change denial in News Corp's media, as well as Krosnick's and MacInnis' (2010) findings show that News Corp falls short in reaching this self-defined goal. Toffel and Schendler argue that the case of News Corp illustrates, that environmental rankings fail to consider a company's activism and lobbying activities (Toffel and Schendler 2012, 1). News Corp activities to reduce its own carbon emission distracts from the fact that the company fails to contribute to awareness in society about the potential threats of climate change and the need to reduce emissions not only of one company, but the whole economy. Toffel and Schendler argue: "an exclusive focus on voluntary operational greening including carbon neutrality distracts from the far greater need for climate regulation to achieve the dramatic overall reductions called for by climate science" (Toffel and Schendler 2012, 2).

News Corp's market populism

Murdoch never kept his market liberal viewpoints secret. He for example told his biographer William Shawcross that he advocates a world regulated by markets: "Today I would describe myself totally internationalist, free market, believing that most people will benefit most and the world will be a better place from heaving free markets. In ideas as well as goods" (Rupert Murdoch quoted in Shawcross 1992, 550). In October 2010 Murdoch gave a speech at the Centre of Policy Studies in London, entitled *Free Markets, Free Minds*. In this talk he argued that society needs hard working individuals who, even in times of crisis, should not expect help from governments: "In an anxious time, people naturally worry about security. When people have grown accustomed to looking to the government – for their housing, for their health care, for their retirement – the idea of looking out for themselves can seem frightening".[38] For Murdoch the financial crisis of 2008 must not lead to more regulation: "The financial crisis was a shock to the system. While the effects linger, it must not be used as an excuse by governments to roll back economic freedom".[39]

In a letter to shareholders in News Corp's 2011 annual report, Murdoch made clear that this belief in "free markets" is not only his personal viewpoint, but also guides the activities of the company. News Corp at all times would be "guided by our most fundamental belief that the combination of free speech and free markets is the most effective guarantee of a free society".[40] In this vein, News Corp's takeover of the *Wall Street Journal* was advertised with the slogan "Free markets, free people, free thinking".[41]

McKnight describes Murdoch's ideas as "market populism" (McKnight 2010a, 312). He argues that Murdoch's own ideology of "militant economic libertarianism" has "influenced the editorial direction of his key newspapers" (McKnight 2003, 347). McKnight traces how Murdoch's newspaper *The Australian* between 1975 and 1983 made an essential contribution to popularizing neo-liberal ideas in Australia (McKnight 2003, 356). Daya Thussu (2007) provides similar evidence from News Corp's activities in India, where the company's TV programmes including the news channel Star News entered the local market in the 1990s and started promoting consumerist and neo-liberal ideologies. Today the programming of commercial news networks in India is characterized by celebratory accounts of India's economic potential, infotainment and the promotion of consumerism. Thussu states: "Murdoch's channels unashamedly promote the values of free-market capitalism, with the US at its core" (Thussu 2007, 608). As Thussu notes, the market populism of commercial media networks in India undermines public debate and promotes consumerism of the Indian middle class, while marginalizing the rural poor (Thusu 2007, 608f).

The above examples of News Corps's coverage of the Iraq war and climate change, as well its market-liberal orientation show that Murdoch's company is clearly taking sides regarding contemporary political questions. Various studies cited above have confirmed a pro-war, anti-climate change and neo-liberal tendency in the reporting by News Corps media around the world.

Fair and balanced reporting

Despite this clear evidence, Murdoch still claims that his news media always report in "fair and balanced" way (Fallows 2003). According to David McKnight, for 25 years Murdoch has been accusing other news media of having a liberal bias (McKnight 2010a, 309) Similarly, the media watch group Fairness and Accuracy in Reporting (FAIR) in an analysis of Fox News' editorial policies and practices highlights that it is "the most biased name in the news" with an "extraordinary right-wing tilt" (FAIR 2001). FAIR highlights that instead of admitting this editorial focus Fox News claims to be the only news station that provides "fair and balanced" reporting, as opposed to all other news media in the US, which have a liberal bias: "Fox's entire editorial philosophy revolves around the idea that the mainstream media have a liberal bias that Fox is obligated to rectify" (FAIR 2001). The purpose behind Fox News' programme "Fox News Watch" for example is to mainly highlight a "liberal bias" in other US media (McKnight 2010a, 310). After criticism of Fox News being biased in favour of George W. Bush and his foreign policy, Murdoch, at News Corp's 2004 annual meeting in Adelaide, claimed that other TV networks are "full of Democrats and Republicans, the others only have Democrats. We don't take any position at all. We're not in the least bit biased, we're a fair and balanced company".[42] Fox News' usage of slogans such as "fair and balanced", or "we report, you decide" (Eviatar 2001) creates the impression that its reporting does not represent a particular worldview but is an objective truth.

However, in 2009 a study conducted by the Pew Research Centre showed that Americans consider Fox News more ideological then other television news networks: 47 per cent of Americans considered Fox News mostly conservative, 14 per cent considered it mostly liberal and 24 per cent regarded Fox News as neither liberal nor conservative (Pew Research Center 2009). Although Fox News is considered the most ideological of all US news networks, these results still show that a quarter of the US population believes that Fox News provides neutral and objective reporting. The study furthermore revealed that Fox viewers are more likely to consider other television news networks as liberal: 50 per cent of regular Fox viewers, but only 35 per cent of regular CNN viewers and 31 per cent of MSNBC viewers consider NBC News as mostly liberal (Pew Research Center 2009).

Apart from the fact that News Corp promotes a particular worldview while claiming to be fair and balanced, Fox News's reporting also contributes to creating misperceptions and ignorance in American society. Earlier I referred to a study that showed that 80 per cent of Fox viewers had at least one misperception regarding the Iraq war (PIPA and Knowledge Networks 2003, 13). Other studies had similar results.

Based on data from the "Biennial Media Consumption Survey" conducted by the Pew Research Center, Jonathan S. Morris compared the demographic, attitudinal and behavioural factors of viewers of US network news, CNN and Fox News. Morris found that for all years that were included in the analysis (1998, 2000, 2002, 2004) in terms of political knowledge "Fox viewers were clearly the least knowledgeable of the three audiences" (Morris 2005, 68). According to Morris' study, Fox News viewers also knew less about issues and events that were critical of their own political view (Morris 2005, 74).

A public mind poll conducted by the Fairleigh Dickinson University revealed that viewers of Fox News are less informed about current political events then people who do not watch any news at all (Fairleigh Dickinson University 2011, 1).

The results are based on a phone survey, in which 612 randomly selected adults living in the US state New Jersey were questioned about their knowledge of current events and their news sources. Compared to people that do not watch any news, Fox News viewers were 18 percentage points less likely to know about the downfall of the Egyptian government and 6 percentage points less likely to know that the Syrian revolution had not been successful (Fairleigh Dickinson University 2011, 1). These studies show that Fox News is spreading biased and misleading information about important political events that promotes a right-wing political agenda, while at the same time claiming to provide objective and balanced reporting.

Conclusion

The extensive reach of News Corp's media empire gives the company the power to influence the knowledge, viewpoints and worldviews of millions of people around the globe. Arsenault and Castells stress that this power gives News Corp a certain amount of control over the public agenda: "By burying news stories and/ or elevating others, News Corp and Murdoch are in a privileged position to decide which issues and actors are included and excluded from the space of communication" (Arsenault and Castells 2008, 504f). Manne stresses that in Australia News Corp's power to influence public opinion turns the company into an important political actor that indirectly has the power to influence political decisions:

> In contemporary Australia, a political party disagreeing with News Corporation on certain issues of fundamental ideological or material importance to it – like the invasion of Iraq, or the USA – Australian Free Trade Agreement, or the cross-media ownership laws – runs a very real, and perhaps unacceptable, political risk. The democratic implications of this single fact is profound.
>
> (Manne 2005, 97)

In the context of this high amount of power that is concentrated in the hands of one private company the question of how this power is used becomes important. Murdoch described the vision he has for journalism in the twenty-first century. This vision includes (a) producing news the audience wants to receive; (b) making the audience pay for media content; and (c) fostering the deregulation of the media sector.[43,44] All elements of Murdoch's vision are related to increasing the company's economic and social power.

Watchdogs point out that News Corp uses its power to promote particular ideologies: pro-war campaigns (Greenslade 2003; PIPA and Knowledge Networks 2003; Manne 2005, 76; Project for Excellence in Journalism 2005), climate change denial (despite initiatives to reduce the company's environmental impact) (McKnight 2010b; Krosnick and MacInnis 2010; Media Matters 2010; Goodell 2011; Toffel and Schendler 2012); and market populism (McKnight 2003; Thussu 2007).

In terms of social responsibility the primary problem is not that News Corp follows a certain editorial line. What is questionable is the particular content of this editorial line. The worldviews News Corp is promoting have implications that endanger human life, and entail particularistic values that benefit the primarily economic interests of privileged groups at the cost of the majority of people: war, climate change and economic crisis are threatening human life around the world. Thousands of people have died in wars waged by the US. According to the Eisenhower Research Project at Brown University's Watson Institute for International Studies, since 2001 the US wars in Afghanistan and Iraq up to now have killed 225,000 individuals (Eisenhower Research Project 2011, 4), left 365,000 individuals physically wounded (Eisenhower Research Project 2011, 5) and displaced more than 7.5 million people (Eisenhower Research Project 2011, 6).

Climate change is also threatening the lives of individuals, particularly in poor regions of the world. The United Nations Development Program (UNDP) estimates that by 2050 a rise of the sea level by half a metre will flood millions of square kilometres and impact 171.4 million people around the world, in particular in less developed regions in South-East Asia and the Pacific (UNDP 2011, 35f).

The economic crisis in 2008 has once again shown that the self-regulating capacities of the market are limited and that capitalism is prone to crisis. The crisis and its aftereffects have created suffering and misery for people around the world. In the US for example in 2010 alone more than 2.8 million houses, which is 1 out of every 45 housing units, were in foreclosure (National Alliance to End Homelessness and Homelessness Research Institute 2012, 32, 37). Whole states such as Greece have been heavily affected by the crisis and are now struggling to deal with high debt. The neo-liberal way of responding to the crisis caused by neo-liberal capitalism, through imposing austerity measures, is currently leading to the impoverishment of the Greek population (Ziegler 2010).

News Corp through its advocacy of war, its tendency towards climate change denial, and its unquestioned celebration of unregulated markets is supporting a worldview that has contributed to creating some of the most fundamental problems of contemporary society. The fact that News Corp is an economically powerful, integrated media conglomerate with an extensive global reach gives it the power to widely disseminate these worldviews and to influence the public agenda and political processes around the world.

Notes

1 *Forbes Magazine.* 2012. *Rupert Murdoch.* Retrieved from http://www.forbes.com/profile/rupert-murdoch/ on April 22, 2012.
2 *Forbes Magazine.* 2011. *The World's Biggest Public Companies. 2010.* Retrieved from http://www.forbes.com/global2000/#p_1_s_arank_All_All_All on June 17, 2011.
3 News Corp. *Defying Conventional Wisdom for Six Decades.* Retrieved from http://www.newscorp.com/NC_webtimeline_final.html on February 7, 2012.
4 News Corp. *Operations.* Retrieved from http://www.newscorp.com/operations/index.html on February 7, 2012.
5 News Corp. *Corporate Profile.* Retrieved from http://www.newscorp.com/investor/index.html on February 7, 2012.

6 Rupert Murdoch 2007. *Energy Initiative. Remarks by Rupert Murdoch.* Retrieved from http://www.newscorp.com/energy/full_speech.html on February 8, 2012.

7 News Corp. *Carbon Analysis.* Retrieved from http://gei.newscorp.com/carbon-analysis.html on February 8, 2012.

8 News Corp. *Carbon Analysis.* Retrieved from http://gei.newscorp.com/carbon-analysis.html on February 8, 2012.

9 News Corp. 2011. *News Corp Scores High on Carbon Disclosure Project.* Retrieved from http://gei.newscorp.com/what/2011/10/news-corp-scores-high-on-carbo.html on November 16, 2011.

10 News Corp. *Global Energy Initiative.* Strategy. Retrieved from http://gei.newscorp.com/strategy.html on February 8, 2012.

11 News Corp. *Global Energy Initiative. Letter from the Chairman.* Retrieved from http://gei.newscorp.com/letter.html on February 8, 2012.

12 *The Guardian.* 2009. *Murdoch Paper Paid £1m to Gag Phone-Hacking Victims.* By Nick Davies on July 8, 2009. Retrieved from http://www.guardian.co.uk/media/2009/jul/08/murdoch-papers-phone-hacking on February 5, 2012.

13 BBC. 2011. *Timeline. News of the World Phone Hacking Row.* Retrieved from http://www.bbc.co.uk/news/uk-politics-12253968 on February 5, 2012.

14 *The New York Times.* 2011. *Father and Son Split on Tactics in Murdoch Family Drama.* By Jeremy W. Peters on July 13, 2011. Retrieved from http://www.nytimes.com/2011/07/14/world/europe/14newscorp.html?pagewanted=all on N February 5, 2012.

15 *The New York Times.* 2011. *British Phone Hacking Scandal.* Retrieved from http://topics.nytimes.com/top/reference/timestopics/organizations/n/news_of_the_world/index.html?inline=nyt-classifier on February 5, 2012.

16 *The New York Times.* 2011. *James Murdoch Gives Up Role at British Unit.* By John F. Burns on February 29, 2012. Retrieved from http://www.nytimes.com/2012/03/01/world/europe/james-murdoch-gives-up-role-at-british-unit.html?pagewanted=all on March 1, 2012.

17 *The Guardian.* 2011. *Rupert Murdoch Says 'Sorry', in Ad Campaign.* Retrieved from http://www.guardian.co.uk/media/2011/jul/15/rupert-murdoch-sorry-ad-campaign on February 5, 2012.

18 Compound Annual Growth Rage: CAGR = (ending value/beginning value) (1/#of years) -1. Data source: News Corp SEC filings. 10-k forms 2005–2011.

19 News Corp, 2011. *Definite Proxy Statement, Form DEF 14.* Retrieved from http://investor.newscorp.com/secfiling.cfm?filingID=1193125-11-239655 on February 15, 2012.

20 Rupert Murdoch. 2009. *From Town Crier to Bloggers: How Will Journalism Survive in the Internet Age?* Retrieved from http://www.newscorp.com/news/news_435.html on February 11, 2012.

21 Rupert Murdoch. 2009. *Journalism and Freedom. Wall Street Journal*, December 8, 2009. Retrieved from http://online.wsj.com/article/SB10001424052748704107104574570191223415268.html?mod=WSJ_hpp_sections_opinion%29 on February 11, 2012.

22 Rupert Murdoch. 2009. *From Town Crier to Bloggers: How Will Journalism Survive in the Internet Age?* Retrieved from http://www.ncwscorp.com/news/news_435.html on February 11, 2012.

23 Rupert Murdoch. 2009. *From Town Crier to Bloggers: How Will Journalism Survive in the Internet Age?* Retrieved from http://www.newscorp.com/news/news_435.html on February 11, 2012.

24 Rupert Murdoch. 2009. *Journalism and Freedom. Wall Street Journal*, December 8, 2009. Retrieved from http://online.wsj.com/article/SB10001424052748704107104574570191223415268.html?mod=WSJ_hpp_sections_opinion%29 on February 11, 2012.

25 Rupert Murdoch. 2009. *Journalism and Freedom. Wall Street Journal*, December 8, 2009. Retrieved from http://online.wsj.com/article/SB10001424052748704107104 574570191223415268.html?mod=WSJ_hpp_sections_opinion%29 on February 11, 2012.

26 Rupert Murdoch 2009. *A Letter from Rupert Murdoch*. News Corp Annual Report. Retrieved from http://www.newscorp.com/Report2009/index.html on February 11, 2012.

27 Rupert Murdoch. 2009. *From Town Crier to Bloggers: How Will Journalism Survive in the Internet Age?* Retrieved from http://www.newscorp.com/news/news_435.html on February 11, 2012.

28 Rupert Murdoch 2009. *A Letter from Rupert Murdoch*. News Corp Annual Report. Retrieved from http://www.newscorp.com/Report2009/index.html on February 11, 2012.

29 Rupert Murdoch. 2009. *From Town Crier to Bloggers: How Will Journalism Survive in the Internet Age?* Retrieved from http://www.newscorp.com/news/news_435.html on February 11, 2012.

30 Rupert Murdoch. 2009. *From Town Crier to Bloggers: How Will Journalism Survive in the Internet Age?* Retrieved from http://www.newscorp.com/news/news_435.html on February 11, 2012.

31 Rupert Murdoch. 2009. *Speech at the World Media Summit in Beijing*. Retrieved from http://www.newscorp.com/news/news_431.html?source=cmailer on February 11, 2012.

32 Rupert Murdoch 2007. *Energy Initiative. Remarks by Rupert Murdoch*. Retrieved from http://www.newscorp.com/energy/full_speech.html on February 8, 2012.

33 Kevin Knobloch. 2011. *News Corp's Environmental Hypocrisy*. Retrieved from http://www.ucsusa.org/news/commentary/newscorps-environmental-hypocrisy-0509.html on February 9, 2012.

34 Media Matters. 2011. *NYT: James Murdoch Views at Odds with Fox News on Climate Change*. Retrieved from http://mediamatters.org/blog/201102190004 on February 9, 2012.

35 *Wall Street Journal*. 2012. *No Need to Panic about Global Warming. An Opinion*. Editorial by Claude Allegre et al. January 26, 2012. Retrieved from http://online.wsj.com/news/articles/SB10001424052970204301404577171531838421366 on March 3, 2012.

36 Bill Sammon quote in Media Matters 2010. *FOXLEAKS: Fox Boss Ordered Staff to Cast Doubt on Climate Science*. Retrieved from http://mediamatters.org/blog/201012150004 on February 19, 2012.

37 News Corp. *Global Energy Initiative. Reaching Our Audiences*. Retrieved from http://gei.21cf.com/strategy.html#audiences-tab on February 8, 2012.

38 Murdoch, Rupert. 2010. *Free Markets, Free Minds*. Address to the Centre of Policy Studies in London. Retrieved from http://www.newscorp.com/news/news_460.html on February 11, 2012.

39 Murdoch, Rupert. 2010. *Free Markets, Free Minds*. Address to the Centre of Policy Studies in London. Retrieved from http://www.newscorp.com/news/news_460.html on February 11, 2012.

40 Murdoch, Rupert. 2011. *Annual Report. A Letter from Rupert Murdoch*. Retrieved from http://www.newscorp.com/Report2011/letter-to-stockholders.html on February 11, 2012.

41 News Corp Advertisement. Retrieved from www.newscorp.com/free.pdf *on* February 11, 2012.

42 Rupert Murdoch quoted in *The Guardian*. 2004. *Murdoch: Fox News Does Not Favour Bush*. Retrieved from http://www.guardian.co.uk/media/2004/oct/26/newscorporation.uselections2004 on February 12, 2012.

43 Rupert Murdoch. 2009. *From Town Crier to Bloggers: How Will Journalism Survive in the Internet Age?* Retrieved from http://www.newscorp.com/news/news_435.html on February 11, 2012.

44 Rupert Murdoch. 2009. *Journalism and Freedom. Wall Street Journal,* December 8, 2009. Retrieved from http://online.wsj.com/article/SB10001424052748704107104574 570191223415268.html?mod=WSJ_hpp_sections_opinion%29 on February 11, 2012.

11 The Walt Disney Company
Nightmare factory?

Today's Walt Disney Company was founded in 1923 under the name Disney Brothers Studio. In 1966 the name was changed into The Walt Disney Company. Until the 1950s the company exclusively focused on the production of cartoons.[1] In 1955 Disney started opening theme parks around the world. The first one was Disneyland Florida, which opened in 1971, followed by Disney World in 1975, Tokyo Disneyland in 1983, Disneyland Paris in 1992, Disneyland Hong Kong in 2005 and Disneyland Shanghai which is scheduled to open in 2015. Furthermore Disney offers holidays on four different Disney cruise ships.[2] Disney launched its first TV channel in 1983 and its first radio station in 1996. Today Disney owns various TV stations, including ESPEN sports media, the Disney/ABC television group, the ABC entertainment group, ABC News, other ABC TV stations, ABC family and Disney channels worldwide.[3] In the production segment Walt Disney owns Walt Disney Studios Motion picture, Walt Disney Animation Studios, Marvel Studios, Touchstone, and Pixar Animation Studios.[4] Since 1956 Disney Music Group has been active in the music production business.[5]

The range of Disney's business activities illustrates that it is an integrated media company that is active in all areas of the media content business, offering print media, TV, radio, film and music production, distribution as well as online services. The figures and stories of Disney's media content also serve as models for books, toys, clothes, furniture, etc. that make up the company's successful consumer product segment. Disney's merchandizing products are licensed to other sellers or sold in one of the Disney theme parks and stores.

CSR approach

Disney's CSR activities started in the area of environmental protection. From 1989 until 2007 Disney published an annual *Enviroport* in which the company's activities for protecting the environment were reported. In 2008 the company published its first CSR report.

In its CSR communications The Walt Disney Company provides two justifications for engaging in CSR activities: first, that Disney is a company with a long tradition of doing good that includes social and environmental considerations in the design of its business strategies (projectionism). Second, that being a responsible company is beneficial for profit interests (reductionism).

Projectionist arguments characterize Disney's early CSR reports. To illustrate that concern for the environment is deeply embedded within Disney's basic value system and as such is inscribed into its way of doing business, it has coined the notion of "environmentality". In 2000 Kym Murphy in the preface to the *Enviroport* explained: "Environmentality; a way of thinking and acting and doing business in an environmentally conscientious way; an ethic that touches virtually every Cast Member, employee and Guest throughout our worldwide operations" (DI_ENVIRO 2000, 2 see also DI_ENVIRO 2004, 2). In 2002 "Environmentality" was described as part of a "Company-wide spirit", which is practiced "so consistently and enthusiastically throughout our Company" (DI_ENVIRO 2002, 2).

The construction of Disney as a good and ethical company is furthermore very much based on the reference to Walt Disney and his approach to conducting business (DI_ENVIRO 2001, 2; 2006, 2; 2007; DI_CSR 2008, 5). For example in the introductory letter to the 2006 *Enviroport* The Walt Disney Company's efforts to protect the environment were described as a continuation of Walt Disney's original attitude towards ecological questions "The Walt Disney Company is built upon a rich heritage of conservation that Walt Disney himself first initiated more than 60 years ago" (DI_ENVIRO 2006, 2)

This rhetoric is supplemented by a second line of argumentation, which stresses financial benefits that can result from responsible behaviour. These reductionist arguments become ever more dominant after 2002, when they first entered Disney's CSR communication. These arguments connect environmental business goals to financial advantages for the company. In 2003 Senior Vice President of Corporate Environmental Policy Kym Murphy for example points to the possibility of creating financial opportunities through acting environmentally responsible: "To the surprise of some and the delight of everyone involved (that includes you), these environmental programs and actions make sense financially and operationally more often than not" (DI_ENVIRO 2003, 2)

From 2003 onwards Disney's *Enviroports* also contain a section entitled "Fiscal Responsibility", which gives "compelling business reasons" (DI_ENVIRO 2005, 5) for acting environmentally responsible. The section details how exactly measures for protecting the environment, such as energy efficient buildings, reducing water and paper consumption, using rechargeable batteries, etc. pay off financially.

In 2004 Kym Murphy calls it a "wonder" that environmental responsibility can benefit profit interests: "The wonder of it all is that Environmentality at The Walt Disney Company not only helps the environment, but the Company's bottom line as well" (DI_ENVIRO 2004, 2). While according to Disney's *Enviroport* in 2003 it was still "to the surprise of some", in 2005 it was "not surprising" anymore that environmentally responsible actions can be beneficial for the bottom line:

> Not surprising, these well-conceived conservation initiatives that save energy and minimize GHG emissions also have a significant and positive impact on

our Company's bottom line. In this edition of *Disney's Enviroport,* you will read about specific successes that reflect millions of dollars in savings — efforts that we can all be very proud of.

(DI_ENVIRO 2005, 2)

This quotation from the introductory letter of the 2005 *Enviroport* shows that at that time Disney's rhetoric had changed to a point where reference to the bottom line became the main justification for engaging in CSR activities. Environmental policy had become so deeply integrated into financial calculations that its success was measured along criteria of reduction of expenditures. The 2006 report for example highlights:

Environmental programs and initiatives have delivered significant bottom-line savings for The Walt Disney Company (TWDC) and Cast Members continue to establish measurable goals, helping to achieve additional savings throughout businesses worldwide. From green purchasing to paper reduction strategies, environmental initiatives have saved the Company nearly $60 million in less than 10 years.

(DI_ENVIRO 2006, 3)

Environmental responsibility had been turned into part of Disney's profitability. From 2006 onwards statements that highlight benefits from CSR activities to shareholder value dominate Disney's CSR rhetoric: In 2010 CEO Robert Iger for example states: "We believe that achieving a consistently high level of corporate citizenship fundamentally adds to shareholder value, and as such is worth every bit of time and investment we put into it" (DI_CSR 2010, 2; see also DI_CSR 2008, 5).

The fact that at Disney the Chief Financial Officer is also responsible for the company's CSR activities further illustrates that Disney regards CSR primarily as a means for contributing to the achievement of financial goals:

The Chief Financial Officer at Disney is responsible not only for the company's finances, but also for our citizenship performance. There's a fundamental reason for this, one that's been core to our company since its founding: we firmly believe that our financial performance is inseparable from our performance as a corporate citizen.

(DI_CSR 2010, 3)

Looking at the development of Disney's CSR communications since the early 2000s reveals that the financial benefits of CSR have become ever more important within Disney's CSR rhetoric. In 2000 and 2001 "environmentality" was presented as an ethical obligation, as a heritage of the company's founder Walt Disney. This projectionist way of describing CSR issues was increasingly replaced by reductionist arguments that stress benefits of CSR for the bottom line.

Controversies: labour rights

The Walt Disney Company in its CSR communications prides itself as being "the world's largest licensor" of manufactured goods (DI_CSR 2008, 5; 2010, 5) as well as the largest children's book publisher (DI_CSR 2008, 5, 8). In its most recent CSR report Disney describes itself as a company that works hard in order to ensure good working conditions in its supplier factories: "Disney promotes the ethical production of Disney-branded merchandise by working to improve labor standards in facilities, testing the safety and integrity of our end product, and working to reduce the environmental footprint of our supply chain" (DI_CSR 2010, 64).

Nevertheless, during the last 15 years NGOs have continuously criticized Walt Disney for violating labour laws and its own Code of Conduct. In the following I first outline some accusations from labour activists and then discuss them in relation to Disney's CSR communication.

Violations of labour rights

In 1996, the National Labor Committee (NLC) revealed violations of labour laws and human rights in Haitian supplier factories of North American companies such as Walt Disney and Wal-Mart. In a factory licensed by Disney, workers producing "Mickey Mouse" and "Pocahontas" pyjamas were paid only 12 cents per hour, which was far below the legal minimum (NLC 1996). Furthermore the report documents that employees were forced to work overtime, that they were not paid for days off, that they were denied health care and pension benefits, exposed to an unsafe working environment and some were sexually abused (NLC 1996).

After these conditions in Disney's Haiti-based supplier factories became public, Disney not only adapted its Code of Conduct for Suppliers and established the International Labor Standards (ILS) Program, but also relocated its production to China (China Labour Watch 2010a, 6). However, violation of human rights and labour standards continued to exist. By the end of the 1990s the Hong Kong Christian Industrial Committee (CIC) reported similarly bad working conditions in Disney's supplier factories in China (CIC 1999; 2000).

From the mid-2000s onwards the non-profit organization Students and Scholars Against Corporate Misbehaviour (SACOM) as well China Labour Watch became very active in monitoring working conditions at Disney's suppliers in China (SACOM 2005; SACOM and NLC 2005; China Labour Watch 2009, 2010a, b). Several studies show that despite protests in the late 1990s, unacceptable working conditions persist in Disney's production units in China. In the following I briefly summarize the main accusations against Disney regarding working conditions in China:

- *Child labour*: In an investigation of Yiuwah Stationary Factory, which supplies Disney with books, calendars, posters, etc., China Labour Watch found that the company hired employees starting from 13 years of age (China Labour Watch 2009). In 2010 China Labour Watch again randomly selected two Disney supplier factories in China and conducted on-site undercover investigations and off-site worker interviews (China Labour Watch 2010b). In both factories – Hengtai Factory and Champion Crown Industries Ltd – the investigators found child labour (workers below 16 years of age) (China Labour Watch 2010b, 11, 19).

- *Labour contracts*: Several studies found that workers receive no or only insufficient labour contracts (SACOM 2006, 10; China Labour Watch 2009; Students Disney Watch 2009, 1f) and are often also denied health or pension insurance (SACOM and NLC 2005, 14; SACOM 2006; China Labour Watch 2010a, 1).
- *Wages*: Studies documented low wages and overtime compensations below the legal minimum (SACOM 2005, 14–19; 2006, 11–13; China Labour Watch 2010a). China Labour Watch highlighted:

> the price of the labor-intensive work is very low: workers get about $134 (900 RMB) base pay every month plus overtime compensation is at below $0.97 (6.5 RMB) per hour flat rate, regardless the dates and time when overtime work takes place.
>
> (China Labour Watch 2010b, 24)

- *Working hours*: Most studies report long working hours, compulsory overtime work (SACOM 2005, 14–19; 2006; 2010a; SACOM and NLC 2005, 7; Students Disney Watch 2009, 1f; China Labour Watch 2010b). Working time often amounts up 70 hours per week (SACOM and NLC 2005, 7; SACOM 2010a, 7; China Labour Watch 2010b, 13). In 2006 SACOM reported forced unpaid vacations during low season and compulsory and excessive unpaid overtime during high season leading to a working day between 11 and 14 hours (SACOM 2006, 12). According to a study about two Disney suppliers conducted by China Labour Watch in 2010 the average worker had to work 72 hours per week and could take off one day per month (China Labour Watch 2010b, 12).
- *Living and working conditions*: Studies report bad living conditions on factory campuses. In 2006 at three Chinese Disney suppliers for example SACOM found poor living conditions in factory dormitories with only one restroom and shower room per 180 people and a lack of personal space as well as poor canteen food (SACOM 2006, 16). Apart from unacceptable sleeping and sanitary conditions studies furthermore show that workers are constantly being pressured to work faster and are insulted by supervisors (SACOM and NLC 2005, 11). One recent study also reports restricted access to toilets during working time (SACOM 2010a). An investigative reporter from China Labour Watch described his experiences as a worker at Champion Crown Factory as follows:

> My daily agenda was eating, sleeping, and working. Life was so boring. More than that was the pressure added to my life as everyday I had to finish required production quota. We did not talk to each other, as all of us were working as fast as we could to complete or even exceed the quota.
>
> (China Labour Watch 2010b, 25)

Critics further stress that these working conditions degrade humans to machines. One of the factory investigators from China Labour Watch for example reports: "Whenever the machines were operating, some of the workers must be ready to work. They are affiliating with machines, just like a screw" (China Labour Watch 2010a, 13).

- *Safety issues*: Several studies report that workers at Disney suppliers are exposed to an unsafe working environment, chemical hazards or a high level of dust or noise without protective equipment, which leads to frequent injuries (SACOM 2005, 14–19; 2006, 16f; Students Disney Watch 2009, 1f; China Labour Watch 2010b, 12).

SACOM and NLC found an exceptionally high rate of injuries in three factories of the Disney supplier Hun Hing Printing Ltd. Workers reported health related incidents occurring almost every day (SACOM and NLC 2005, 2). One woman explained to the investigators how most injuries occur:

> While producing a book like this, many chances of injury can happen. When making this cover, we use a machine to press this edge. But there is no safety device – It depends on your carefulness. Because the book is very small, when pressing it, our hand gets very close to where the machine (It is still board) presses. When we put it in, if we are not careful, our fingers will be pressed together with this book.
>
> (SACOM and NLC 2005, 6)

One fatal incident happened on April 17, 2009 when a 17-year-old worker at Yiuwah Stationary Factory was killed while operating a paper-crushing machine (China Labour Watch 2009).

The sweatshop-like conditions of long working hours, low wages and working conditions that degrade humans to machines reveal a significant contradiction between the fantasy of a world full of joy, fun and happiness Disney creates in its shows, films and theme parks and the daily reality of Chinese factory workers.

According to Disney's Code of Conduct, the company's manufacturers have to refrain from child labour, involuntary labour, coercion and harassment of workers, and discrimination, they have to guarantee workers their right to free association, provide adequate safety at the workplace, comply with local laws regarding minimum wages and labour hours as well as environmental regulation and other laws (DI_CoC 2007).

The above investigations of labour rights clearly show violations of this Code of Conduct. Students Disney Watch thus concluded that Disney fails to meet its social responsibility: "Disney fails to comply with its social responsibilities, its code of conduct is no more than a piece of paper without realization" (Students Disney Watch 2009, 2). In the following I show how Disney responds to criticism of its CSR communications.

Disney's response to labour rights violations

In its CSR communications, Disney admits that problems with the enforcement of its Code of Conduct exist. In general, the company's reaction to accusations from labour rights activists is centred around four main themes:

- First, Disney clearly admits existing problems. It directly refers to reports from SACOM and China Labour Watch and states that further investigations have confirmed the findings of the labour right activists (DI_CSR 2008, 2010, DI_CSR online). In the 2008 CSR report, Disney for example states: "We investigated the claims immediately and confirmed that some of the factories included in the reports did indeed have compliance issues" (DI_CSR 2008, 82). Disney then stressed that as a reaction to these reports it would increase its efforts in ensuring adequate working conditions in licensed companies (DI_CSR 2008, 89).
- However, and this is the second characteristic of Disney's response to criticism, the description of how Disney aims to confront labour rights problems remains vague. The company stresses that in order to improve working conditions it is communicating with factory managers, collaborating with external stakeholders and governments, monitoring facilities and introducing reporting systems (DI_CSR 2008; 2010; DI _CSR online). Disney simply points out that efforts to improve the situation are being made, without giving any information on how the concrete measures look.

  Every year Disney investigates around 15 per cent of its manufacturing facilities. Although non-compliance rates are extremely high regarding health and safety issues (81 per cent in 2008 and 76 per cent in 2010), minimum wages (39 per cent in 2008 and 36 per cent in 2010) and overtime work (57 per cent in 2008 and 60 per cent in 2010), nowhere is it mentioned which efforts are being made in order to raise wages, reduce working hours, improve safety equipment or stop compulsory overtime. Instead, further monitoring is presented as a cornerstone of Disney's strategy towards improved working conditions.
- Third, Disney attempts to refute responsibility for bad working conditions. Disney stresses that it co-operates with vendors who manufacture Disney products that are then sold at theme parks and Disney stores on the one hand (DI_CSR 2008, 74) and licensees who have the right to produce and sell Disney branded products on the other hand (DI_CSR 2008, 74). Licensees and vendors have subcontractors and hire factories for producing the products. For this reason, Disney's influence on shaping working conditions in facilities is limited. In the 2008 report, Disney states: "we learned there are limits on our ability to ensure sustained and consistent compliance" (DI_CSR 2008, 74; see also DI_CSR 2010, 67). The limits to Disney's influence are especially evident regarding licensees: "in the case of licensing in particular, we are not selecting the factories or ordering,

importing or selling the product made in that factory. As a result, our leverage varies significantly from relationship to relationship" (DI_CSR 2008, 76). However, even if it is not Disney's business to produce, transport or sell the products, Disney financially profits from licence agreements based on intellectual property rights. Disney claims intellectual property rights over the Disney brand and income associated with these rights, but wants to yield the responsibility for how Disney branded products are produced. Furthermore, the argument that Disney has no control over the activities of subcontractors of licensees and vendors contradicts Disney's Code of Conduct for Manufacturers, which states that manufacturers need Disney's written consent before hiring subcontractors (DI_CoC 2007).

- The fourth theme concerning how Disney deals with criticism is a rhetoric of "continued efforts". In its CSR reports (DI_CSR 2008, 2010), Disney stresses that it has been working hard and will continue to work hard to improve conditions in factories. This rhetoric is based on the following logic: even if the measures taken have "still not resulted in a supply chain that meets our expectations" (DI_CSR 2008, 88), Disney will not surrender, but in the future work even harder and therefore has "committed additional resources to revising and updating the ILS program to meet the challenges of our global supply chain" (DI_CSR 2008, 88).

Despite the fact that Disney reacts to criticism, the response is insufficient because on the one hand most answers to accusations remain superficial and vague and on the other hand some essential topics are avoided. One of these neglected topics is data about issues such as wages, overtime hours and safety conditions in manufacturing factories. What Disney's CSR communications also do not say is that the company's CSO, Robert Iger, was the third highest paid chief executive in America in 2010,[6] earning around 16,500 times as much as an average worker in a Hangtai factory. According the Forbes list of *America's Highest Paid Chief Executives* in 2010 he earned 53.32 million USD.[7]

Disney, according to the 2011 Forbes 2000 list,[8] is the second largest company in media content and the 110th largest company in the world. In 2010, the work done by employees in factories that produce Disney's merchandising products contributed 2.68 billion USD to Disney's revenue (Disney SEC filings. 10-k forms 2010). The operating profit for consumer products, which is the income Disney acquired from operating this business segment, in 2010 was 677 million USD (Disney SEC filings. 10-k forms 2010). Despite these profits the wages of many of those who actually produce these consumer products remain "miserably low" as one worker told factory investigators (SACOM and NLC 2005, 9). The company could afford to spend more money on the production of its consumer products – even if this negatively affected profits.

Disney's inability to solve basic labour rights problems that have been recurring since the mid-1990s has obviously not hampered the company's economic growth. While the Walt Disney Company is flourishing, the workers who produce Disney branded consumer products still receive barely enough to cover basic expenses for housing and food. Disney's profits stem from the extreme exploitation of workers in China and other non-Western countries; the company's success is built on the misery of workers who face slave-like labour conditions.

Conclusion

The Disney brand is famous for creating exciting, joyful worlds – unfortunately for thousands of factory workers the reality cannot live up to this fantasy. Disney is aware of the fact that stories about child labour or underpaid and harassed factory workers do not fit into the company's image of fun and happiness. In the 2000 *Enviroport* Kym Murphy therefore stressed that Disney, like a few other companies, had to prove its "goodness":

> Historically speaking, most companies and their leaders are judged by their balance sheets, quarterly reports and overall profitability. Disney is, of course, subject to the same sort of scrutiny. Our Company, however, like few others, must also live up to another standard . . . its goodness. Not just the goodness of its movies, attractions and other products; but the goodness that is part of Disney's decision-making processes and the resulting actions that we take.
>
> (DI_ENVIRO 2000, 2; see also DI_CSR 2008, 5)

However, since 1995 Disney has been unsuccessful in solving major labour rights violations in its manufacturing companies. Students Disney Watch therefore concludes: "Disney strives very hard to create a theme park and culture featured with fantasy and happiness. Nevertheless, Disney does not have any interest in the well-beings of the workers who produce Mickey Mouse in the sweatshops" (Students Disney Watch 2009, 2). In fact, Disney has done well economically, while the inadequate working conditions in its supplier factories persist. Solving these problems would require bigger commitments from Disney than just monitoring factories, installing working groups, communicating with stakeholders and writing reports. These measures might contribute to creating a positive image for the company, but they do not really help workers who are suffering from low wages and long working hours. Solving these problems would require financial commitments from Disney that are likely to run counter to the company's profit interests.

Disney's CSR approach has become increasingly instrumental. CSR initiatives are worthwhile for the company only if they pay off financially. Based on such an approach, it is doubtful that CSR programmes will change anything about the situation of Disney's factory workers in China.

A look at working conditions in Disney's manufacturing factories reveals that the "wonder", as Kym Murphy once called it (DI_ENVIR 2004, 2), of bringing together profit and responsible business practices is more of a flimflam than actual magic.

Notes

1 Disney. *Disney History*. Retrieved from http://thewaltdisneycompany.com/about-disney/disney-history on September 3, 2011.
2 Disney. *Parks and Resorts*. Retrieved from http://thewaltdisneycompany.com/disney-companies/parks-and-resorts on September 3, 2011.
3 Disney. *Media Networks*. Retrieved from http://thewaltdisneycompany.com/disney-companies/media-networks on September 3, 2011.
4 Disney. *The Walt Disney Studios*. Retrieved from http://thewaltdisneycompany.com/disney-companies/studio-entertainment on September 3, 2011.
5 Disney. *Disney Music Group*. Retrieved from http://thewaltdisneycompany.com/disney-companies/studio-entertainment on September 3, 2011.
6 *Forbes Magazine*. 2011. *America's Highest Paid Chief Executives*. Retrieved from http://www.forbes.com/lists/2011/12/ceo-compensation-11_rank.html on September 2, 2011.
7 This income consists of 2 million USD salary, 13.46 million USD bonus, 21.18 million USD stock and 16.67 million from other income sources. Source: *Forbes Magazine*. 2011. *America's Highest Paid Chief Executives*. Retrieved from http://www.forbes.com/lists/2011/12/ceo-compensation-11_rank.html on September 2, 2011.
8 *Forbes Magazine*. 2011. *The World's Biggest Public Companies*. Retrieved from http://www.forbes.com/global2000/#p_1_s_acompanyRankOverall_BroadcastingCable_All_All on June 17, 2011.

12 Vivendi

Corporate pirates?

Vivendi is a French media corporation that in the 2011 Forbes 2000 ranking was the 149th largest company and the 3rd largest media company in the world.[1] The company was founded as a water supply company in 1853 named Compagnie Génerale des Eaux. The name of the company was changed into Vivendi in 1998.

On December 8, 2000 Vivendi acquired Canal Plus and The Seagram Company Ltd, the owner of Universal Studios including Universal Music Group, and changed its name to Vivendi Universal (Vivendi Annual Report 2000, 9). Furthermore Vivendi started giving up its water and waste business by spinning it off into Vivendi Environment. In 2002 Vivendi started to focus fully on its media business. It reduced its share of Vivendi Environment to 20.4 per cent (Vivendi Annual Report 2002, 17), which in 2003 changed its name into Veolia Environment (Vivendi Annual Report 2002, i). After having sold parts of Universal Entertainment to General Electric in 2004, in 2006 the company changed its name back into Vivendi (Vivendi Annual Report 2006, 20).

Under the label "Activation Blizzard" Vivendi operates in the computer game business with successful games such as "World of Warcraft" and "Call of Duty" (VI_CSR 2010, 4) and owns Universal Music Group, the world's leading music company (VI_CSR 2010, 28). The company is also active in the telecommunications sector and owns the French telecom operator SFR, which controls 33.1 per cent of French telephone, and 23 per cent of the French Internet market (Vivendi Annual Report 2010, 33), Maroc Telecom Group which has around 25.8 million customers (VI_CSR 2010, 4), and the Brazilian telecom operator GVT which has a market share of about 22.2 per cent in the 97 Brazilian cities in which it operates (Vivendi Annual Report 2010, 44). Vivendi furthermore owns the leading French Pay TV company Canal+, which has about 12.7 million subscribers (VI_CSR 2010, 5).

CSR approach

Vivendi started reporting on CSR issues related to its communications business in 2000. Up till 2007 Vivendi published an annual *Sustainable Development Report* that focused on social, environmental and economic sustainability. In 2008 Vivendi started to produce a combined *Activity and Sustainable Development Report*. The report is then divided into a first part, which presents the group's profile and reports about its business activities, and a second part, which deals with Vivendi's sustainability strategy.

The company's CSR communications contain some dualist, but mostly reductionist arguments.

In 2002 Vivendi went through a major financial crisis – the company's losses amounted to 23.3 billion EUR (Vivendi Annual Report 2003). Consequently, the opening message from the CEO in Vivendi's 2002 sustainability report primarily focused on the company's financial difficulties and strategies for recovery:

> For Vivendi Universal, 2002 will be remembered as a year of tremendous transformation and upheaval in the wake of serious financial difficulties. In these highly testing conditions, we have had to take radical action to restore our financial health and regain market confidence.
>
> (VI_CSR 2002, 1)

In the following year Vivendi put forward a dualist idea of sustainable development that simultaneously included social and environmental aspects on the one hand and economic growth on the other hand. Vivendi stated that it understands sustainable development as a "commitment to incorporating social and environmental considerations in the growth of its activities" (VI_CSR 2003, 9). This statement shows that Vivendi aims to consider social and environmental factors in its business operations without having to compromise its economic growth goals.

Vivendi lists a number of "values" on which it wants to focus its sustainable development strategy. Among them are non-economic goals such as fostering cultural diversity, respecting ethical standards and meeting the social responsibility of behaving as a good corporate citizen (VI_CSR 2003, 9). Some other values are directly related to Vivendi's business operations: focusing on consumers in order to build consumer loyalty and supporting teamwork (VI_CSR 2003, 9). Finally also the financial "value" of "value creation" is included in the list: "We must deliver consistent revenue and earnings growth, in order to provide our shareholders with true value creation. Our objective is to outperform our competitors", encouraging creativity which would "drive our continued innovation and growth" (VI_CSR 2003, 9). This is a highly dualist notion of sustainable development, which assumes that economic and social goals can be achieved simultaneously without ever considering how they affect each other.

Despite this dualist conceptualization of sustainable development, reductionist statements that stress the benefits of CSR for the bottom line dominate Vivendi's CSR communications throughout the following years. Vivendi's CEO Jean-Bernard Lévy in the introductory letter to the 2004/2005 report for example argues that sustainable development is beneficial for the company's business relations, its capacity to innovate, its risk management and efficiency: "This sustainable development approach is beneficial to the Group because it enriches the quality of our internal and external exchanges and sustains the company's ability to innovate, to contribute to counteracting risks, and consequently, to become more efficient" (VI_CSR 2004/2005, 1).

Michel Bourgeois, Vivendi's Executive Vice President of Communication and Public Affairs, in the same report further highlights positive effects for the company's reputation: the "integration of the sustainable development process in the Group's strategy" is "all the more necessary in that it contributes to countering risks to the Group's reputation which is one of its major assets, and to opening up new opportunities in regards to innovation, skills, and markets" (VI_CSR 2004/2005, 3; see also VI_CSR 2005/2006, 4). In 2010 Vivendi's Chief Financial Officer Philippe Capron in a similar manner explains how far sustainable development policies are relevant for the company's financial performance: "A company's financial performance also relies on its sustainable development policy, which enables it to understand its extrafinancial risks as well as create opportunities. Vivendi is particularly exposed to reputation risks" (VI_CSR 2010, 59).

These statements exemplify a reductionist rhetoric that stresses the financial benefits of CSR. Another example that illustrates Vivendi's reductionist understanding of CSR can be found in its 2006/2007 report. Here Vivendi lists so-called "sustainable development key figures", which exclusively focus on achievements that are directly related to the company's growth oriented business goals. Examples are: "more than 2 billion dollars invested in content", "4 million music titles downloaded on the SFR music platform", "more than 700 game titles in the Vivendi Games catalogue", "4,000 artists under contract with the universal music group", etc. (VI_CSR 2006/2007, 3). The fact that Vivendi presents its business achievements as sustainability achievements, illustrates that sustained economic growth is the essential component of the company's notion of sustainable development.

Some passages of Vivendi's CSR communications highlight that as leading media company it has the responsibility to protect minors, to promote cultural diversity, to raise awareness regarding sustainable development, to foster access to ICTs and to share knowledge (VI_CSR 2004/2005, 2; 2005/2006, 3; 2006/2007, 43; 2008, 59; 2009, 12; 2010, 52). In 2010 Vivendi summarizes its media-related responsibilities as follows: "The Group has an obligation to promote pluralism of content, encourage dialogue between cultures, facilitate access to the information and communication technologies and raise public awareness of sustainable development issues" (VI_CSR 2010, 15). However, these goals are not described as ends in themselves but reduced to means for creating business advantages. Vivendi highlights: "the fact that we have positioned culture and intercultural dialogue among our priorities enables us to win market shares and gives us legitimacy in the eyes of civil society, the public authorities, and the younger generations" (VI_CSR 2010, 59). This statement clearly reveals a reductionist rationale behind Vivendi's commitment to being a socially responsible media company.

A strategy Vivendi employs throughout its sustainability reports is quoting statements of various investment consultants, which illustrate that sustainability issues are increasingly influencing company assessments and investment decisions and therefore are essential for a company's economic success: in 2003 Vivendi's sustainability report for example quotes an analyst from ISIS Asset Management:

In our assessment methods, we give very positive marks to companies where social responsibility is dealt with at the level of the Board of Directors either through a Code of Conduct or the support of an Ethics Committee. We also positively evaluate companies where these issues are dealt with at top management level.

> (ISIS Asset Management quoted in VI_CSR 2003, 10)

The 2006/2007 contains a quote from Jean-Michel Bonamy and Marc Fox from Global Investment Research at Goldman Sachs International, who stress that how a company scores regarding the Environmental, Social, and Corporate Governance (ESG) framework is an important category in its assessment of companies:

> The Goldman Sachs Media ESG framework (February 2006) is a proxy for overall management quality to identify companies best positioned for long-term performance in the sector. The ESG framework is designed to quantify performance on environmental, social and governance criteria, thematic leadership, and cash returns on investment. Given that two-thirds of the sector's asset base is comprised of intangibles, and almost half of the costs relate to human and intellectual capital, we view leadership on ESG issues simply as superior management of company assets.
>
> (Jean-Michel Bonamy and Marc Fox quoted in VI_CSR 2006/2007, 11; see also VI_CSR 2008, 62 and VI_CSR 2009, 51 for similar quotes)

Overall, Vivendi's CSR communications are based on a dualist notion of sustainability that defines social and environmental responsibility and economic growth as parallel company goals. Despite this dualist definition in a majority of statements Vivendi privileges sustained economic growth over social and environmental responsibility.

Based on such an approach to CSR it is likely that Vivendi's commitments to social responsibility are not fully realized in its actual business practices. In the following I will investigate this further by looking at Vivendi's approach to music file-sharing and discuss how it relates to the company's CSR communications.

Controversies: music file-sharing

With the acquisition of Universal Music Group (UMG) Vivendi on December 8, 2000 entered the music market. (vivendi annual report 2000, 9). From 2000 until 2006 Vivendi owned 92 per cent of UMG. On February 6, 2006 Vivendi acquired the remaining shares from Matushita Electric Industrial Co Ltd and from then on owned 100 per cent of UMG (Vivendi Annual Report 2006, 29). According to Music and Copyright (2011), UMG is the largest recording-music company worldwide. In 2010 UMG controlled 28.7 per cent of digital and physical music sales, followed by Sony Music Entertainment (SME) with a market share of 23 per cent (Music and Copyright 2011).

As a major player in the music business UMG has been active in the fight against illegal music file-sharing. In the following I will outline Vivendi's efforts to confront online music file-sharing, give an overview of how Vivendi frames this issue in its CSR communications and point out potential alternative ways for music distribution.

Vivendi's fight against music file-sharing

In 2000 UMG was heavily involved in the lawsuit against the popular file-sharing platform Napster: UMG's subsidiaries A&M records, Geffen records, Interscope Records, MCA Records, Island Records and Motown Records were listed as plaintiffs in the district courts lawsuit[2] as well as the on the federal court appeal.[3] The decisions of a US federal appeals court in February 2001, which confirmed that Napster had been infringing copyrights,[4] was the starting point for a long lasting offensive by the recording industry against file-sharing.

During the last 10 years UMG has been involved in a number of lawsuits against several file-sharing platforms. As a member of the *Recording Industry Association of America* (RIAA), UMG participated in lawsuits against Puretunes. com[5] and LimeWire.[6] Represented by the International Federation of the Phonographic Industry (IFPI), Vivendi was involved in lawsuits against OiNK[7] and The Pirate Bay.[8] In 2006 UMG furthermore sued the video sharing websites Bolt.com and Grouper,[9] and was involved in the lawsuit against the file-sharing platform Kazaa.[10] In 2007, UMG pressed charges against the video and music file-sharing site Veoh.[11]

In addition to these lawsuits against providers of file-sharing applications, as a member of the RIAA UMG has also been involved in lawsuits against thousands of individuals. Between 2003 and 2008, the RIAA sued more than 30,000 people: "The targets include the elderly, students, children and even the dead".[12] The RIAA's attack against file-sharers was first and foremost intended to delegitimize file-sharing in public opinion. The RIAA euphemistically described it as an "education program":

> The program was designed to educate fans about the law, the consequences of breaking the law, and raise awareness about all the great legal sites in the music marketplace. Like any tough decision, there are trade offs. On balance, the legal marketplace is far better off because of the program.[13]

The majority of the lawsuits were settled out of court.[14] The main reason for that is that potential fines for violations of the US Copyright Act can amount to up to $150,000 USD per music track.[15] Most of the people the RIAA accused of copyright violations could not afford a lawyer and therefore were afraid of going to court. They thus agreed to pay a few thousand dollars settlement in order to avoid even higher charges.[16]

As part of its "education program", between February 2007 and February 2008 the RIAA sent pre-lawsuit letters to 5,404 students at universities throughout the

US, accusing them of copyright violations and threatening them with a lawsuit.[17] In order to avoid a lawsuit, students could admit copyright infringements and pay a settlement – approximately 3,000 USD (EFF 2008, 8) – to the RIAA. The letters the students received from the RIAA were solely based on suspicions and did not have any legal grounding. Many students thus paid money to the RIAA without any legal charges ever being raised against them. The money from the settlements was then used to finance further lawsuits, and not to remunerate artists.[18,19]

In 2008 the RIAA announced that it wanted to stop the lawsuits and instead cooperate with ISPs, which should, after warnings, cut off the Internet connection of copyrights infringers.[20] In the UK the legal basis for this strategy was established through the Digital Economy Act, which came into effect in June 2010. According to this act, ISPs should send warning letters to users that are suspected of illegal downloads of music or films. In the case of repeated infringements ISPs have to provide information to copyright owners about the violations of their copyrights, so that they can then take legal steps.[21]

File-sharing and copyrights in Vivendi's CSR communications

In Vivendi's CSR communications the topic of illegal file-sharing first appeared in 2002. The issue is most extensively discussed in Vivendi's *Sustainable Development Reports* 2003, 2004/2005 and 2005/2006, those years when Vivendi's profits from operating the music business reached their 10-year minimum, amounting to 70 million EUR, compared to 719 million EUR in 2001 an 471 million EUR in 2010 (Vivendi Annual Reports 2001–2010).

Vivendi describes "piracy" as a major economic threat to the whole media industry as it undermines intellectual property: "Unauthorized copying and piracy are major issues in the media industry as they seriously undermine a cornerstone of economic development: intellectual property" (VI_CSR 2003, 12). Vivendi stresses that "piracy" is a problem for all its business sectors including music, computer games, pay TV and telecommunications (VI_CSR 2003, 12; 2004/2005, 13; 2005/2006, 23). It therefore is one of Vivendi's major priorities: "to ensure respect for intellectual property, which is a wellspring of the economic development of the group and its different business activities (music, films, programming, game software, etc.)" (VI_CSR 2006/2007, 24).

As profit in the music industry is largely based on strong intellectual property rights it is not surprising that Vivendi describes the protection of intellectual property as one of its economic responsibilities (VI_CSR 2002, 9; 2003, 12; 2004/2005, 13; 2005/2006, 23; 2006/2007, 24; 2008, 65; 2009, 55; 2010, 58). In the 2004/2005 *Sustainable Development Report*, for example, Vivendi wrote:

> Universal Music Group's priorities are to maintain its position as market leader, to fight piracy, to continue to promote legal digital alternatives and exploit new opportunities for sales such as musical products for mobile telephony (ring tones, videos and images, wait tones), and development in emerging markets.
>
> (VI_CSR 2004/2005, 10)

In the years 2003, 2004/2005 and 2005/2006, the company outlined its strategy of how to fight illegal music file-sharing. It focused on four main measures: the development of legal pay-music download applications (VI_CSR 2003, 12; 2004/2005, 13; 2005/2006, 23), lobbying governments to strengthen intellectual property rights and anti-piracy regulations (VI_CSR 2003, 12; 2005/2006, 23), informing the public about the "dangers of piracy" (VI_CSR 2003, 12; 2004/2005, 14), and suing copyright infringers (VI_CSR 2003, 12; 2004/2005, 14).

In recent years, the attention Vivendi's sustainability reports pay to the topic of "piracy" has decreased. The main reasons for this might be that over time legal pay-music services have been established and music downloads have turned into an important source of income for Vivendi. In the 2006/2007 report the company's CEO Jean-Bernard Lévy says that: "The group's efforts have kept piracy in check, and the burgeoning of online offerings, which may have seemed like a threat before, is now an opportunity" (VI_CSR 2006/2007, 24). However, the protection of intellectual property remains an important topic. In 2009 and 2010 in its sustainability report Vivendi stressed that ensuring the protection of intellectual property rights is still a priority of the group (VI_CSR 2009 55f; 2010, 58).

Vivendi's focus on protecting and enforcing intellectual property rights shows a major contradiction in the companies CSR reporting: Vivendi regards the protection of intellectual property as one of its major economic responsibilities, while at the same time defining the fight against cultural exclusion as one of its social responsibilities. In 2002 Vivendi stressed that it wanted to fight the digital divide, as it would lead to social exclusion (VI_CSR 2002, 18). In the 2005/2006 sustainability report Vivendi defined "sharing knowledge" as one of the company's media-related responsibilities to society (VI_CSR 2005/2006, 3; see also VI_CSR 2006/2007, 52; 2008, 59; 2009, 75). The company stresses that it wants to encourage a "spirit of openness" regarding digital technologies: "Vivendi works to facilitate access to knowledge, close the digital gap, and encourage the expression of talent, participation in cultural life and a spirit of openness" (VI_CSR 2008, 96). In 2010 Vivendi stated that it aimed to help disadvantaged groups to access ICTs and media content: "Vivendi is committed to facilitating access to information and communication technologies (ICTs) and to content so that groups in isolation due to their place of residence, age, or financial situation can share in the benefits of the digital revolution" (VI_CSR 2010, 80).

Measures Vivendi takes for promoting access to ICTs for example include donating money to NGOs that support access to ICTs in Africa (VI_CSR 2002, 18; 2004/2005, 28); running a programme for helping visually impaired and deaf people to access ICTs (VI_CSR 2002, 18; 2004/2005, 28; 2008, 95; 2009, 75; 2010, 81); providing its services at reduced prices to schools and universities (VI_CSR 2008, 94; 2009, 75; 2010, 80f); and offering training programmes to improve media and ICT literacy (VI_CSR 2002, 18; 2010, 81).

These measures focus on easing access to ICTs for people living in remote areas, for disabled people and youths. What Vivendi neglects is that its business model is based on charging people for accessing ICTs, knowledge and information, which always excludes those who cannot afford it. The commitment to fostering an open and accessible digital culture contradicts Vivendi's actual business practices, which, apart from excluding people from TV, Internet and telecommunications through charging fees, also include imposing intellectual property rights on cultural products and suing those who try to make them publicly accessible through sharing them freely on the Internet. In contrast to Vivendi's rhetoric of openness and accessibility, its actual practices regarding intellectual property are essentially based on an anti-access and anti-openness policy.

Vivendi recognizes that as a provider of media products it has a social responsibility of making ICTs, knowledge and information accessible. However, as a media company its profits rest on excluding those who do not pay for these products from accessing them. This shows that there exists a fundamental contradiction between the company's social responsibility and what Vivendi conceives as its economic responsibility, that is, being a profitable, market-leading player in the media business. The company's economic interest of profiting from restricted access to media products outweighs Vivendi's concern for access and openness.

However, according to Vivendi online peer-to-peer file-sharing is not only a threat to the media business, but to music and film production in general. Art and artists are presented as the victims of file-sharing: "Illegal file sharing via the Internet of musical, movie and video game content jeopardizes artistic creation and cultural industries" (VI_CSR 2003, 12). If songs and movies are shared freely on the web then, the argument goes, not enough money would be available for producing new music and films (VI_CSR 2003, 12). "Free music" would therefore be unsustainable: "'free music' is not sustainable, that cultural diversity and creation are endangered if the sector as a whole is unbalanced and that certain players, deprived of the payment they are entitled to, will disappear" (VI_CSR 2003, 13).

The record companies' attempt to construct an alliance between them and musicians can be contested. Despite the recording companies' claim, deals between musicians and labels are often not mutually beneficial.

Alterative models of music distribution

Critics have calculated that traditionally recording companies benefit more from the sale of recorded music than artists in financial terms: Courtney Love in the early 2000s accused recording companies of stealing from artists and therefore called them, instead of file-sharers, the real pirates. In 2000 Love started her talk at the Digital Hollywood Online Entertainment Conference with the following words:

> Today I want to talk about piracy and music. What is piracy? Piracy is the act of stealing an artist's work without any intention of paying for it. I'm not talking about Napster-type software. I'm talking about major label recording contracts.
>
> (Love 2000)

Love calculates that even if a band signs a record deal with a relatively high royalty rate of 20 per cent and sells 1 million copies of its record, the band will earn around 180,000 USD; while the recording company makes around 6.6 million USD profit (Love 2000).

Connolly and Krueger showed that record sales never were a lucrative source of income for artists: the top 35 bands worldwide in 2003 earned 7.5 times more from touring than they did from the sale of their records (Connolly and Krueger 2006, 670) – despite the fact that in 2003 recording sales amounted to 11.8 billion USD, while total concert ticket sales was only 2.1 billion USD (Connolly and Krueger 2006, 673). This means that while the total amount of money earned from the sale of records is much higher than the income from ticket sales, the latter make up for a much larger part of an artist's income. Matthew David highlights that the "a royalty-based system of paying artists has never been successful at rewarding and securing any but the tiniest number of artists" (David 2010, 146). He therefore concludes: "The claim that 'pirates' are robbing artists of their rewards better describes the practices of major record labels than it does the actions of file-sharers" (David 2010, 143).

Alternative models of music distribution that benefit artists rather than record companies are possible. Some starting points already exist today:

- Bands have started to bypass recording companies and to provide their music as downloads on the Internet. Radiohead for example in 2007 released its album "In Rainbows" for download on the Internet. Users could decide whether and how much they wanted to pay for the download. Within three weeks the album had been downloaded 1.2 million times. Thirty-eight per cent of those who downloaded the album were willing to pay. The average payment was $6 USD (David 2010, 152). Another example is Amanda Palmer, who provided her album "Amanda Palmer Performs the Popular Hits of Radiohead on Her Magical Ukulele" on her website for a minimum payment per album of $1 USD.[22]
- Jamendo.com is a platform that enables artists to publish their music under a creative commons licence.[23]
- Another model for ending the criminalization of file-sharers while at the same time ensuring the remuneration of artists is the concept of a cultural flat rate. There exist various models of a cultural flat rate, which are based on the idea of legalizing peer-to-peer file-sharing on the Internet, while artists are paid through charging a "non-commercial use levy" on products connected to file-sharing such as MP3players, copying devices or Internet access (Netanel 2003) or charging all Internet users a monthly fee (Fischer 2004). Similarly the Electronic Frontier Foundation's concept of "Voluntary Collective Licensing of Music Filesharing" suggests that file sharers pay a monthly fee of about $5–10 USD to newly installed collecting societies. After paying this fee users would be entitled to download music using any technical device they wanted to, while the collecting societies distributed the money between artists.[24] Dean Baker (2003) has proposed a slightly different model of an artistic freedom voucher: "The AFV would allow each

individual to contribute a refundable tax credit of approximately $100 to a creative worker of their choice, or to an intermediary who passes funds along to creative workers" (Baker 2003).

These examples show that free sharing of music on the Internet might kill the profits of recording companies, but will not kill music.

We have seen that the majority of musicians never benefited financially from record sales. Furthermore, alternative ways of music distribution that are not based on intellectual property rights and at the same time ensure the remuneration of artists are possible. These alternative models also open up music culture as they allow unknown artist to publish their music without being dependent on getting a record deal.

However, the described models of sharing music on the Internet run counter to the profit interest of music companies. Like UMG, the large players in the music business keep fighting against online music sharing. For example from 2008 until 2011, in the US alone, UMG spent more than 10 million USD on lobbying issues.[25]

The actions of UMG and other recording companies are not against the law, but can nevertheless be questioned from a social and cultural point of view. Laws always exist and are created within a certain social context, as critical legal scholars have highlighted: "law and society are mutually constituting" (Trubek 1984, 609). A legal order is connected to dominant worldviews and provides legitimacy for certain social relations: "the world views embedded in legal consciousness 'legitimate' unjust social relations by making these relations seem either necessary or desirable: (Trubek 1984, 597).

The current copyright jurisdiction supports the commercialization of products of intellectual and cultural production. Through privatizing cultural products by imposing intellectual property rights on them, they can be turned into commodities. It needs to be questioned whether treating the results of cultural and intellectual production as commodities is best for the development of human society and culture. Cultural products are not scarce as they can be used without being consumed. This means that no matter how often a song is listened to, an item of information is consumed, a piece of art is looked at, a movie is watched, etc. it does not lose any of its qualities. It is therefore not necessary to restrict access to using cultural products.

Conclusion

Vivendi's approach to CSR is based on the concept of sustainable development. However, it seems that Vivendi understands sustainability more in terms of the company's private profit rather than in terms of social and environmental aspects. For Vivendi acting socially and environmentally responsible remains subordinate to achieving maximum economic growth.

The original idea of sustainable development on the contrary was based on the insight that unreflected and unconditional growth is unsustainable. The idea of sustainable development emerged out of the concern regarding the existence of certain "limits to growth" (Meadows et al. 1972). In the 30-year update of *Limits to Growth* Meadows, Randers and Meadows stress that "a sustainable society would be interested in qualitative development, not physical expansion" (Meadows, Randers and Meadows 2004, 22).

Vivendi aims at sustained quantitative growth of its business. Reaching this goal depends on strong intellectual property rights. The example of file-sharing shows how Vivendi tries to reinforce exclusion in the realm of culture. While the company sees the protection of intellectual property rights as one of its main economic responsibilities, it defines the promotion of access to media content and ICTs as one of its social responsibilities. Intellectual property rights are a means of excluding people from culture and information products and hinder the establishment of an accessible and inclusive media system and culture. Vivendi talks about meeting its responsibility of "sharing knowledge", but it seems that what it actually means is "selling knowledge" in order to make profit.

The Internet makes it much easier to challenge the corporate media model. The case of online peer-to-peer music file-sharing gives an idea of how non-commodified culture could look. However, together with other media corporations, Vivendi has been actively trying to stop this development and demanded the establishment and enforcement of strict copyright regulations. Arguably this is the most rational reaction from the perspective of sustaining corporate profits, but probably not the most responsible one in terms of the flourishing of human society and culture.

Notes

1 *Forbes Magazine.* 2011. *The World's Biggest Public Companies.* Retrieved from http://www.forbes.com/global2000/ on June 17, 2011.
2 United States District Court Northern District of California. 2000. Retrieved from http://news.cnet.com/News/Pages/Special/Napster/napster_patel.html on September 16, 2011.
3 United States Court of Appeals. 2000. Retrieved from http://bulk.resource.org/courts.gov/c/F3/239/239.F3d.1004.00-16403.00-16401.html on September 16, 2011.
4 *The New York Times.* 2001. *The Napster Decision.* By Matt Richtel on February 13, 2011. Retrieved from http://www.nytimes.com/2001/02/13/business/napster-decision-overview-appellate-judges-back-limitations-copying-music.html?scp=2&sq=napster&st=nyt on September 16, 2011.
5 RIAA. 2004. *Puretunes.com Settles Record Companies' Copyright Infringement Lawsuit.* Retrieved from http://www.riaa.com/newsitem.php?content_selector=newsandviews&news_month_filter=10&news_year_filter=2004&id=EB080FF5-4C4F-6292-65C5-BE297977FDE8&searchterms=%20Universal%20Music%20Group&terminclude=&termexact= on September 16, 2011.
6 *Wired Magazine.* 2006. *Music Industry Squeezes LimeWire.* Retrieved from http://www.wired.com/techbiz/media/news/2006/08/71545 on September 16, 2011.
7 *The Guardian.* 2008. *UK File-Sharers Arrested.* By Rosie Swash on June 3, 2008. Retrieved from http://www.guardian.co.uk/music/2008/jun/03/news.rosieswash?INTCMP=SRCH on September 16, 2011.

8 *The Guardian.* 2009. *The Pirate Bay Trial: Guilty Verdict.* April 17, 2009. Retrieved from http://www.guardian.co.uk/technology/2009/apr/17/the-pirate-bay-trial-guilty-verdict on September 16, 2011.

9 Electronic Frontier Foundation. 2006. *Universal Sues Video Sharing Sites Grouper and Bolt.com* Retrieved from http://www.eff.org/deeplinks/2006/10/universal-sues-video-sharing-sites-grouper-and-bolt-com on September 16, 2011.

10 CNET News. 2006. *With Settlement, Kazaa Casts off its Pirate Garb.* Retrieved from http://news.cnet.com/With-settlement%2C-Kazaa-casts-off-its-pirate-garb/2100-1027_3-6099064.html?tag=lia;rcol on September 16, 2011.

11 *Wired Magazine.* 2007. *Universal Sues Video-Sharer Veoh, Alleging Copyright Violations.* By David Kravets on September 6, 2007. Retrieved from http://www.wired.com/politics/onlinerights/news/2007/09/veoh_lawsuit?currentPage=2 on September 16, 2011.

12 *Wired Magazine.* 2008. *File Sharing Lawsuits at a Crossroads, After 5 Years of RIAA Litigation.* By David Kravets on September 4, 2008. Retrieved from http://www.wired.com/threatlevel/2008/09/proving-file-sh/ on September 16, 2011.

13 RIAA. *FAQ.* Retrieved from http://www.riaa.com/faq.php on September 16, 2011.

14 The first file-sharing case that went to trial was against single mother Jamie Thomas. In 2007 she was sentenced to pay $222,000 USD for sharing 24 songs. The RIAA used this opportunity to fuel fear among those accused of illegal file-sharing: *Wired Magazine* quotes RIAA attorney Richard Gabriel, who after the verdict said to the press: "This is what can happen if you don't settle" (*Wired Magazine.* 2007. *RIAA Jury Finds Minnesota Women Liable for Piracy, Awards $ 222.000.* By David Kravets on October 4, 2007 Retrieved from http://www.wired.com/threatlevel/2007/10/riaa-jury-finds/ on September 16, 2011).

   However, the verdict was vacated only one year later, after judge Michael Davis granted a new trial because wrong instructions had been given to the jury (United States Districts Court. District of Minnesota. 2008. Civil File No. 06-1497 (MJD/RLE) Retrieved from http://www.wired.com/images_blogs/threatlevel/files/riaathomasbrief.pdf on September 16, 2011).

15 *Wired Magazine.* 2008. *RIAA to Stop Music Fans, Cut Them Off Instead.* By Elliot Van Buskirk on December 19, 2007. Retrieved from http://www.wired.com/epicenter/2008/12/riaa-says-it-pl/ on September 16, 2011.

16 *Wired Magazine.* 2008. *File Sharing Lawsuits at a Crossroads, After 5 Years of RIAA Litigation.* By David Kravets on September 4, 2008. Retrieved from http://www.wired.com/threatlevel/2008/09/proving-file-sh/ on September 16, 2011.

17 RIAA. 2008. *RIAA Sends More Pre-Lawsuit Letters to Colleges One Year into Campaign.* Retrieved from http://www.riaa.com/newsitem.php?content_selector=newsandviews&news_month_filter=2&news_year_filter=2008&id=B0FAEEC1-A56A-0F04-D999-94A807ADAA6E&searchterms=23%20New%20Schools%20to%20Receive%20Latest%20Round%20of%20RIAA%20Pre-Lawsuit%20Letters%20&terminclude=&termexact= on September 16, 2011.

18 *Wired Magazine.* 2007. *Universal Sues Video-Sharer Veoh, Alleging Copyright Violations.* By David Kravets on September 6, 2007. Retrieved from http://www.wired.com/politics/onlinerights/news/2007/09/veoh_lawsuit?currentPage=2 on September 16, 2011.

19 *The Guardian.* 2009. *Behind the Music: Mystery of the Filesharing Windfalls.* By Heilenne Lindvall on July 30, 2009. Retrieved from http://www.guardian.co.uk/music/musicblog/2009/jul/30/filesharing-music-industry-windfalls?INTCMP=SRCH on September 16, 2011.

20 *Wired Magazine. 2008. RIAA to Stop Suing Music Fans, Cut Them Off Instead.* By Elliot Van Buskirk. Retrieved from http://www.wired.com/epicenter/2008/12/riaa-says-it-pl/ on September 16, 2011.

21 *The Guardian.* 2012. *Ofcom Outlines New Anti-Piracy Rules.* by Mark Sweeny on June 26, 2012. Retrieved from http://www.guardian.co.uk/technology/2012/jun/26/ofcom-outlines-anti-piracy-rules on June 2, 2010.

22 Amanda Palmer. Retrieved from http://music.amandapalmer.net/album/amanda-palmer-performs-the-popular-hits-of-radiohead-on-her-magical-ukulele on September 21, 2011.
23 Jamendo.com Retrieved from http://www.jamendo.com/en/ on September 21, 2011.
24 Electronic Frontier Foundation. 2008. *A Better Way Forward: Voluntary Collective Licensing of Music File Sharing*. Retrieved from https://www.eff.org/wp/better-way-forward-voluntary-collective-licensing-music-file-sharing/ on September 21, 2011.
25 Center for Responsive Politics. 2011. *Lobbying Universal Music Group*. Retrieved from http://www.opensecrets.org/lobby/firmsum.php?id=D000019159&year=2000 on September 21, 2011.

13 Social (ir)responsibility in the media and communication system

In the following sections I will provide answers to the research questions that guided the empirical study of CSR in the media and communication industries. The questions relate to CSR approaches, CSR practices and CSR challenges. I conclude with a general interpretation of the results.

CSR approaches

One main goal of this study was to identify the arguments and justifications media and communication companies are using for explaining their commitment to CSR.

For this purpose I conducted critical content analysis of the CSR reports of selected media and communication companies. The coding categories were "no CSR rhetoric", "reductionist rhetoric", "projectionist rhetoric", "dualist rhetoric" and "dialectical rhetoric". These categories describe the different ways of how a CSR theory or the CSR approach of a company relates economic goals on the one hand and social and environmental responsibilities on the other hand. A reductionist view establishes an instrumental relation in which engaging in CSR activities is regarded as a means for achieving profit goals. A projectionist rhetoric argues that profit generation should be subordinated to a concern for the common good. A dualist approach separates profit goals and CSR goals from each other and argues that both can be achieved at the same time. The dialectical view regards the relation of profit goals on the one hand and social and environmental responsibility on the other hand as antagonistic. From this perspective profit goals and social responsibility goals mutually shape each other. Profit generation is considered to have socially irresponsible outcomes, while acting socially responsible hampers the achievement of profit goals.

The empirical analysis shows that two of the studied companies – News Corp and Apple – have no elaborated CSR approach. News Corp does not publish any regular CSR or similar reports. A brief statement of commitment to CSR in News Corp's *Standards of Business Conduct* is all the company has officially published on this topic. In this document News Corp states:

> We take our corporate social responsibilities seriously. Specifically in the context of our business, which is news, information and entertainment, we

are always and everywhere dedicated to advancing our core values of free inquiry, free speech and free expression for all people.

(New Corp_SBC 2011, 38)

Since 2006 Apple has published a yearly supplier audit report. However, these documents only describe audit results and do not contain any CSR rhetoric or justification of why the company engages in CSR activities. Apple basically uses one phrase to express its commitment to CSR:

> Apple is committed to the highest standard of social responsibility in every-thing we do. We are dedicated to ensuring that working conditions are safe, the environment is protected, and employees are treated with respect and dig-nity wherever Apple products are made.
>
> (Apple_SR 2006, 4)

These findings suggest that appearing as socially responsible is not a priority for Apple or News Corp.

On their websites the remaining six companies provide extensive information about their CSR approach and activities. While Vivendi, HP, Microsoft, AT&T and Disney regularly publish CSR, sustainability or environmental reports, Google follows a different strategy. It has thus far not published any CSR report. However, Google's company website contains a variety of information about the company's values and business principles. Based on this information it was pos-sible to evaluate how Google presents its view of the company's role in society and the relation between its economic activities and other responsibilities.

The analysis showed that similar arguments to CSR theory are also present in company CSR reports. However, most of the studied companies do not follow a consistent CSR approach, but employ different arguments. AT&T, HP, Google and Disney use a mixed rhetoric in their CSR communications, while AT&T, HP, Vivendi and Google use different justifications for CSR in parallel. Disney changed its rhetoric over time, and Microsoft's CSR communications basically focus on only one CSR approach.

- *AT&T*: In AT&T's CSR communication dualist as well as reductionist arguments are present at the same time. The company switches between these two lines of argument both within one report and between differ-ent years. Passages that contain dualist arguments often focus on the idea of creating both a better company and a better society, such as "we work to build a better company [. . .] and create a better world and more sustainable future" (AT&T_CSR 2007/2008, 5). Other statements within AT&T's CSR communications, however, contain reductionist arguments that point out how CSR can be used in an instrumental way for achieving business goals. AT&T for example highlights "good citizenship spurs growth, creates stability and triggers new opportunities to help the world communicate" (AT&T_CSR 2007, 3).

- *HP*: HP uses projectionist, dualist and reductionist arguments. Projectionist statements highlight that HP wants to "improve the lives of people through-out the world" (HP_CSR 2001, 1), to "improve society" (HP_CSR 2010a, 7) and to "create a better world" (HP_CSR 2010a, 5). In dualist passages HP argues that it wants to be a "world leader" both in terms of economic success and its citizenship activities (HP_CSR 2007, 4). Statements like this stress the intention of simultaneously achieving economic and social responsibility goals, without relating them to each other, and can therefore be characterized as dualist. Other passages contain reductionist arguments. HP for example argues that corporate responsibility would be "a prime business opportunity to grow our company in new ways" (HP_CSR 2004, 5). Here CSR in a reduc-tionist manner is described as a means for creating business advantages.
- *Google*: Google's strategy is different from all other companies in the sample. The fact that it does not publish a separate CSR report but provides infor-mation about how its practices are responsible throughout its corporate web-pages, illustrates that Google presents itself as a new type of company that from its very foundation is built on ethical principles. Google's *Code of Con-duct* starts with the phrase "Don't be evil".[1] This illustrates a values-based, projectionist approach. Google claims that all its practices are based on this commitment. Following this rhetoric Google's main aim is presented as doing something good for individuals and society, rather than simply maximizing profits. Google at the same time also uses a dualist rhetoric when highlighting its philanthropic activities that are based on the idea of giving part of the rev-enue generated by the company's business operations back to society.[2]
- *The Walt Disney Company*: Within Disney's CSR communications rhetorical changes can be observed over time. Disney switched from a projectionist to a reductionist CSR rhetoric. In its early *Enviroports* Disney put forward a pro-jectionist rhetoric that described the concept of environmentality as a set of values that affects the whole way of doing business, as a "company-wide spirit" (DI_ENVIRO 2000, 2). According to these passages the generation of profits is subordinated to a certain mentality, a spirit, a whole way of thinking that guides all corporate practices. Disney's rhetoric changed quickly: in its 2005 report Disney highlighted that CSR activities resulted in financial benefits for the company: "In this edition of *Disney's Enviroport*, you will read about spe-cific successes that reflect millions of dollars in savings—efforts that we can all be very proud of" (DI_ENVIR 2005, 2). In later years economic rather than ethical values were used as the justification for CSR activities. Finally the 2010 report leaves no doubt that the company's primary motivation for engaging in CSR activities are of a financial nature: "We believe that achieving a con-sistently high level of corporate citizenship fundamentally adds to shareholder value, and as such is worth every bit of time and investment we put into it" (DI_CSR 2010, 2).
- *Microsoft*: Microsoft's CSR rhetoric is based on projectionist arguments. These arguments present the company as an organization that is primarily driven by values and a desire to contribute to the common good. Following

a projectionist rhetoric profit generation is still legitimate but only based on certain values or a concern for society and/or the environment. In this manner Microsoft describes itself as "a values-driven company, motivated by its mission to help people and business realize their potential" (MI_CSR 2004, 74).

- *Vivendi*: Vivendi combines a dualist and a reductionist CSR rhetoric. The company's CSR reports are based on a dualist notion of sustainable development that puts forward the goal of acting socially and environmentally responsible without compromising economic growth goals (VI_CSR 2003, 9). Other passages contain a reductionist rhetoric that points out how CSR activities can benefit the company's profit goals. In its 2010 report Vivendi for example points out that CSR activities can create business opportunities: "A company's financial performance also relies on its sustainable development policy, which enables it to understand its extrafinancial risks as well as create opportunities" (VI_CSR 2010, 59). In reductionist manner Vivendi commits to meeting its media specific responsibilities such as sharing knowledge and facilitating access to ICTs and media content, while at the same time revealing an instrumental rationale behind this commitment: "the fact that we have positioned culture and intercultural dialogue among our priorities enables us to win market shares and gives us legitimacy in the eyes of civil society, the public authorities, and the younger generations" (VI_CSR 2010, 59).

Table 13.1 summarizes which CSR approaches the companies that were included in this study are using.

Table 13.1 CSR rhetoric of media and communication companies

	No CSR approach	Reductionist rhetoric (profit generation through responsible behaviour)	Projectionist rhetoric (responsible behaviour guides profit generation)	Dualist rhetoric (profit generation and responsible behaviour)	Dialectical rhetoric (profit generation conflicts with responsible behaviour)
Apple	X				
AT&T		X		X	
Google			X	X	
HP		X	X	X	
Microsoft			X		
News Corp	X				
The Walt Disney Company		X	X		
Vivendi		X		X	

The fact that some companies simultaneously apply different CSR approaches shows that the identified justifications for engaging in CSR activities are not mutually exclusive. The types of CSR rhetoric presented seem to be suitable for addressing different types of audiences. A company might use a reductionist rhetoric for attracting investors and shareholders, which have financial interests in the company. The usage of dualist and especially projectionist arguments might on the other hand aim at targeting readers that are more interested in the company's values and its social performance, such as ethical consumers, NGOs, or the media.

None of the companies, however, problematizes the relationship between generating profit and meeting social responsibility goals (dialectical CSR rhetoric). The CSR reports of the companies studied thus are based on the premise that it is possible to reconcile profit and social responsibility.

CSR practices

To discuss how the business practices of the companies studied relate to their CSR rhetoric I analysed the companies' financial performances, criticism of corporate practices raised by watchdog organizations as well as companies' responses to the criticism.

Financial performance

The first 10 years of the twenty-first century were a financially successful decade for the media and communication companies that were included in this study. All companies managed to substantially increase their profits and revenues, as well as their assets. Figures 13.1 to 13.6 show the development of these key financial indicators for each company.

As these figures show, AT&T is the economically most successful company within the sample. A look at the Forbes 2000 ranking shows that the media distribution (telecommunications) sector in general is the most profitable media sector. Figure 13.7 illustrates that the largest share of media and communication companies that are included in the Forbes 2000 ranking are telecommunications companies (in total 63). Nine media distribution companies are within the top 100 of the Forbes ranking, while the top 100 only contain three media hardware, one media software as well as one online media company, and no media content companies.

However, in terms of compound annual growth rates (CAGR), Google is the leading company within the sample[3]: between 2000 and 2010 Google's revenues grew 108 per cent per year and its total assets increased by 104 per cent per year. The first year in which Google was profitable was 2001, since then the company has multiplied its profits on average by 103 per cent per year. This means that during a period of 10 years every year Google more than doubled its profits, revenues and assets. Google has by far the highest CAGR among the companies in the sample. The second fastest growing company is Apple. On average the company's revenues grew by 23 per cent, its profits by 33 per cent and its assets by 27 per cent each year from 2000 to 2010. Average annual profit growth rates for the remaining companies are high as well. They mostly range at around 10 per cent

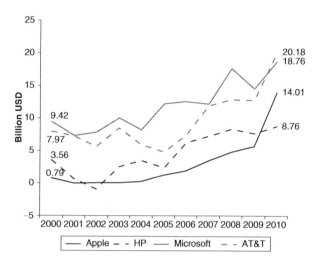

Figure 13.1 Profit development: Apple, HP, Microsoft and AT&T.

Source: Own figure based on the SEC filings of each company.[1]

Note

1 Data based on SEC filings 10-k forms, as available in the Edgar database: http://www.sec.gov/edgar/searchedgar/companysearch.html

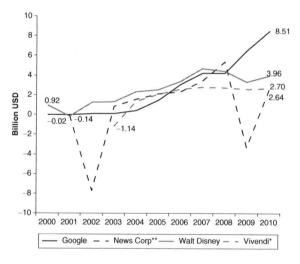

Figure 13.2 Profit development: Google, News Corp, Walt Disney and Vivendi.

Source: Own figure based on the SEC filings of each company, for Vivendi, data is based on official financial reports.[1]

Notes

1 Data based on SEC filings 10-k forms, as available in the Edgar database: http://www.sec.gov/edgar/searchedgar/companysearch.html. Data for Vivendi is based on the company's official financial reports: http://www.vivendi.com/vivendi/Financial-Reports

  * Data are available for Vivendi from 2003.

** Data are available for News Corp from 2001.

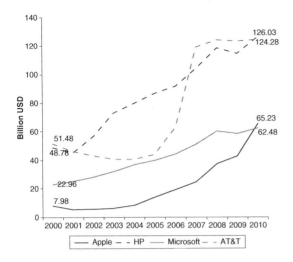

Figure 13.3 Revenue development: Apple, HP, Microsoft and AT&T.

Source: Own figure based on SEC filings of each company.[1]

Note

1 Data based on SEC filings 10-k forms, as available in the EDGAR database: http://www.sec.gov/
edgar/searchedgar/companysearch.html

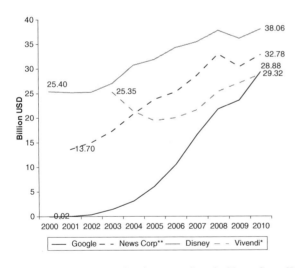

Figure 13.4 Revenue development: Google, News Corp, Walt Disney and Vivendi.

Source: Own figure based on the SEC filings of each company; for Vivendi, data is based on official
financial reports.[1]

Notes

1 Data based on SEC filings 10-k forms, as available in the EDGAR database: http://www.sec.
gov/edgar/searchedgar/companysearch.html, data for Vivendi is based on the company's official
financial reports: http://www.vivendi.com/vivendi/Financial-Reports

  * Data are available for Vivendi from 2003.
** Data are available for News Corp from 2001.

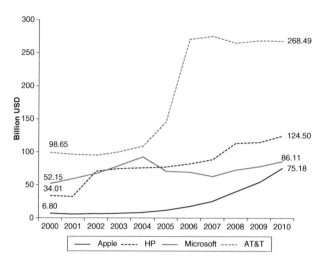

Figure 13.5 Asset development: Apple, HP, Microsoft and AT&T.

Source: Own figure based on the SEC filings of each company.[1]

Note

1 Data based on SEC filings as available in the EDGAR database: http://www.sec.gov/edgar/searchedgar/companysearch.html

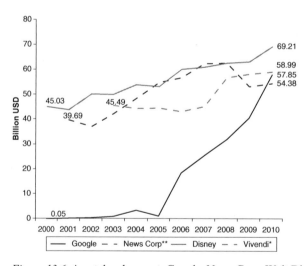

Figure 13.6 Asset development: Google, News Corp, Walt Disney and Vivendi.

Source: Own figure based on the SEC filings of each company; for Vivendi, data is based on official financial reports.[1]

Notes

1 Data based on SEC filings as available in the EDGAR database: http://www.sec.gov/edgar/searchedgar/companysearch.html
  Data for Vivendi is based on the company's official financial reports: http://www.vivendi.com/vivendi/Financial-Reports
 * Data are available for Vivendi from 2003.
** Data are available for News Corp from 2001.

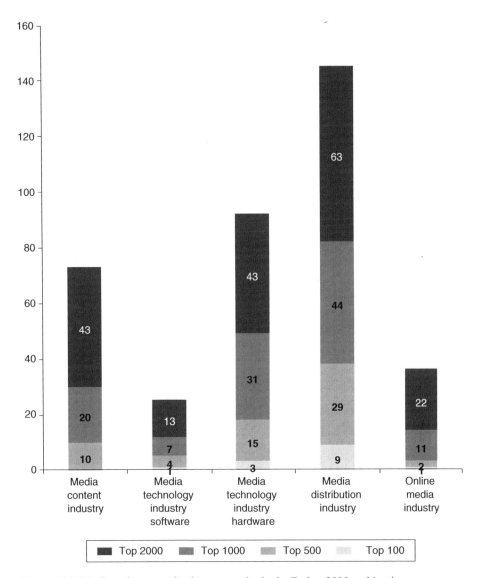

Figure 13.7 Media and communication companies in the Forbes 2000 ranking.[1]

Source: Calculation based on Forbes 2000.[2]

Notes
1 The sectors included in this figure are comprised of the following Forbes industries: Media content sector (Broadcasting and Cable; Print and Publishing); Media software sector (Software and Programming); Online media sector (Computer Services); Media distribution sector (Telecommunication Services); Media hardware sector (Communication Equipment, Computer Hardware, Computer Storage Devices, Consumer Electronics).
2 *Forbes Magazine*. 2011. The World's Biggest Public Companies. April 2011. Retrieved from http://www.forbes.com/global2000/list/ on June 17, 2011.

or more: Disney's profits between 2000 and 2010 grew by 15 per cent every year; News Corp's profits annually grew 12 per cent between 2003 and 2010; between 2004 and 2010 Vivendi increased its profits by 10 per cent every year. The annual growth of HP's and AT&T's profits between 2000 and 2010 was around 9 per cent, and Microsoft's profits in the same time period increased by average 7 per cent each year.

These figures show that the first decade of the twenty-first century was a period of profitable growth for the media companies included in the sample. This economic success was accompanied by strong criticism from corporate watchdogs that raised doubts regarding the social responsibility of Apple, AT&T, Google, HP, Microsoft, News Corp, The Walt Disney Company and Vivendi.

Watchdog criticism

The studied companies represent different business models in the media and communication sector. In order to study their CSR practices, for each company I selected one CSR area that seemed the most relevant in terms of the company's business model (see Chapter 4 for details). Based on information provided by corporate watchdogs, I identified main points of criticism related to each company's business practices.

The issue selected for the analysis of Apple CSR practices was working conditions in the supply chain. Among the main critics of Apple's supply chain business practices are China Labour Watch and SACOM as well as member organizations of the European project makeITfair, which have investigated and criticized working conditions in Apple's supplier factories. Common problems at Apple's supplier factories are:

- compulsory and excessive overtime (SOMO 2007, 22; FinnWatch, SACOM and SOMO 2009, 37; SACOM 2011b, 5f)
- low wages that are barely enough to cover basic living expenses such as food and housing (SOMO 2005b, 27; 2007a, 21; FinnWatch, SACOM and SOMO 2009, 44; SACOM 2011b, 4)
- lack of health protection equipment (SOMO 2007, 23; SACOM 2011a, 14), exposure of workers to hazardous substances that resulted in poisoning (SACOM 2010b, 2; 2011a, 14; 2011b, 7), as well as insufficient information supplied to workers about the chemicals they were using (SACOM 2011a, 14)
- harsh management style, strict disciplinary measures and harassment of workers (FinnWatch, SACOM and SOMO 2009, 38; SACOM 2011a, 16)
- high work pressure (FinnWatch, SACOM and SOMO 2011, 30) and social isolation of workers (FinnWatch, SACOM and SOMO 2011, 30; SACOM 2011a, 12f).

I studied AT&T's sense of social responsibility in regard to the topic of net neutrality. The media watchdog group Free Press together with members of the Save the Internet Campaign strongly criticized AT&T's lobbying efforts to abolish net neutrality. They argue that abolishing net neutrality would:

- destroy the openness and egalitarian technical structure of the Internet and reinforce inequality online[4]
- reinforce tendencies of monopolization (Turner 2009, 9)
- threaten free speech, participation and the public sphere on the Internet[5]
- disadvantage those organizations and individuals that have less financial resources available (often non-commercial initiatives, individuals and civil society groups)[6]
- privilege corporate content providers, who are likely to have more financial resources in order to pay for prioritization and therefore foster the commercialization of the Internet (Lessig and McChesney 2006)
- create artificial scarcity of bandwidth capacity (Turner 2009, 3).

The CSR area that I selected for the in-depth analysis of Google's business practices is online privacy. The corporate watchdogs that are criticizing Google's business practices are Privacy International, Google-watch.com, Corporate Watch, Google Monitor and Privacy Rights Clearinghouse. Furthermore the way Google deals with user privacy during the last years has been subject to various critical academic studies (e.g. Maurer et al. 2007; Tene 2008; Tatli 2008; Blackman 2008; Vaidhyanathan 2011; Fuchs 2011b). These watchdogs have particularly criticized that Google's business model of selling user data to advertisers for creating personalized advertisements would:

- constitute a fundamental invasion of user privacy, which can have negative impacts on the lives of individual users[7,8,9,10,11]
- be based on the exploitation of users and the commodification of user data and increase the commercialization of the Internet (Fuchs 2010).

To study HP's business practices I focused on the topic of e-waste. Watchdogs that pointed to the wrongdoings of HP in this area are Greenpeace and the BAN Action Network. Major points of criticism are:

- High concentration of toxic substances in HP products (Greenpeace 2006b, 109).
- Untrue claims about the elimination of certain flame-retardant PDBE chemicals.[12]
- Insufficient take-back programmes, especially in developing countries (Greenpeace 2011b, 1).
- HP products found at waste dumps in developing countries (BAN 2005, 37; Greenpeace 2007).

In order to investigate to what extent Microsoft's business practices are socially responsible I discussed the topic of software patents. Microsoft's critics are the Open Source Initiative, Open Source Watch, the Free Software Foundation as well as the civil society initiative No Software Patents. According to these critics, a business model of selling proprietary software, which is based on software patents would[13,14,15,16]

- create advantages for large companies and lead to monopolization
- threaten the freedom of information
- restrict creativity and further advancement of knowledge
- fetter human creativity and innovative capacity
- privatize the commons of society and create artificial scarcity.

Microsoft has not only been criticized but also criminally convicted in the US[17] as well as Europe[18] for violating anti-trust laws while attempting to secure its monopoly position.

The focus area for the analysis of News Corp's social responsibility was media content. Among News Corp's major critics are civil society groups such as Media Matters (2010), the Project for Excellence in Journalism (2005), the Pew Research Center (2009) and Fairness and Accuracy in Reporting (FAIR 2001) as well as journalists (e.g. Greenslade 2003) and academics (e.g. McKnight 2003, 2010a, b, 2011; Manne 2005; Morris 2005, 68; Thussu 2007; Arsenault and Castells 2008; Fairleigh Dickinson University 2011). These watchdogs have shown that News Corp:

- pushes a specific ideology while at the same time claims to be fair and balanced. Studies found biased reporting practices in particular in regard to the US war on terror (Greenslade 2003; Project for Excellence in Journalism 2005; Arsenault and Castells 2008, 501) and climate change (McKnight 2010b, Media Matters 2010; Goodell 2011; Toffel and Schendler 2012, 1). Furthermore critics argue that News Corp is promoting a neo-liberal and market populist worldview (McKnight 2003, 2010a; Thussu 2007)
- diminishes diversity by enforcing a uniform editorial line throughout its media outlets around the world (Greenslade 2003; Manne 2005)
- creates misperception among its audience regarding important issues such as climate change or the US war in Iraq (PIPA and Knowledge Networks 2003; Goodell 2011), and leaves its audience uninformed about current political events (Morris 2005, 68; Fairleigh Dickinson University 2011, 1).

The focus area that I selected for The Walt Disney Company was working conditions in the supply chain. Watchdogs, such as the Institute for Global Labour and Human Rights, formerly called the National Labour Committee; China Labour Watch; Student and Scholars Against Corporate Misbehaviour; Christian Industrial Committee (CIC); and Students Disney Watch report sweatshop-like working conditions in Disney's supplier factories. The detected problems relate to:

- non-compliance with minimum wage regulations (SACOM 2005, 14–19; 2006, 11–13; China Labour Watch 2010a)
- excessive and compulsory overtime work (SACOM 2005, 14–19; 2006; 2010a; SACOM and NLC 2005, 7; Students Disney Watch 2009, 1f; China Labour Watch 2010b)
- poor living conditions in factory dormitories (SACOM 2006, 16)
- high work pressure (SACOM and NLC 2005, 11)

- unsafe working environments, chemical hazards, high level of dust or noise without protective equipment and frequent injuries (SACOM 2005, 6–13; SACOM 2005, 14–19; 2006, 16f; Students Disney Watch 2009, 1f; China Labour Watch 2009, 2; 2010b, 12).

I analysed the social responsibility of Vivendi's business practices by focusing on the topic of peer-to-peer music file-sharing. Critics of Vivendi's business practices in this area are the Electronic Frontier Foundation, the alternative online medium consumerist.org, and artists such as Courtney Love. These critics highlight that:

- as an individual company and as member of the RIAA and IFPI Vivendi contributed to the criminalization and prosecution of thousands of individuals[19]
- the company is using dubious methods for pushing file-sharers, particularly students, into agreeing to settlements and pay a settlement fees of approximately \$3,000 USD (EFF 2008, 8)
- Vivendi's royalties based model benefits the company rather than artists. Critics thus stress that record labels are the "real pirates" who are stealing from artists (Love 2000; David 2010, 143).

The points of criticism mentioned here are described at length in Chapters 5–12. This summary illustrates that for all companies included in this study, watchdogs have highlighted major wrongdoings that question the social responsibility of these companies. The next section discusses the companies' responses to this criticism.

Response to criticism

In the CSR communications of the media and communication companies studied I identified four different response strategies to criticism raised by corporate watchdogs:

- The first corporate strategy is to refer to criticism in the CSR report, to acknowledge some of the main points raised by critics and to promise to take steps to solve the problem. Here companies admit that certain problems exist and commit to finding a solution. In the following I call this a *strategy of admit, downplay and promise solutions*. It characterizes Disney's, HP's and Apple's responses to watchdog criticism.
- A second way of how the companies studied deal with critique is to provide a completely different description of the same issue without ever referring to the watchdogs' arguments. Here huge gaps exist between assessments made by corporate watchdogs on the one hand and corporations on the other hand. This way of dealing with criticism can be called *a strategy of redefinition*. It describes the way Vivendi, Google and partly also Microsoft respond to criticism.

- A third strategy is using criticism raised by watchdogs for developing new ways of capital accumulation. Here, criticism is undermined by incorporating it. This *strategy of incorporation* describes a recent development in the way Microsoft deals with criticism.
- Finally, a fourth way of responding to criticism is to completely ignore the issue in CSR communications. Companies using this strategy might in various ways respond to the criticism or deal with the issue in other documents and statements but never mention it in any CSR document. In the following I refer to this strategy as a *strategy of ignorance*. It characterises AT&T's response to criticism.

The strategy of admit, downplay and promise solutions can be found in the CSR communications of Apple, HP and Disney. Apple for example in its *Supplier Audit Reports* acknowledges that sometimes labour rights violations occur in its supply chain. Apple started to report on CSR as a response to watchdog criticism. Its first supplier responsibility report starts with the sentence: "In the summer of 2006, we were concerned by reports in the press alleging poor working and living conditions at one of our iPod final assembly suppliers in China" (Apple_SR 2006, 1). Similarly Disney also admits shortcomings in regard to the protection of labour rights. As a response to criticism Disney states: "We investigated the claims immediately and confirmed that some of the factories included in the reports did indeed have compliance issues" (DI_CSR 2008, 82). In its CSR reports HP also directly referred to criticism from Greenpeace (HP_CSR 2010a, 12).

These companies not only admit that problems exist but furthermore promise to work towards a solution. After a number of suicides at one of Apple's supplier factories in Shenzhen, China, and subsequent public criticism, in early 2012 Apple was the first electronics company to join the Fair Labour Association and publish a list of its suppliers. After being confronted with criticism Disney also promised to review its practices: "In response to a 2009 public report alleging labor standards violation at a facility in China [. . .] we recognized the importance of reviewing our approach to health and safety compliance in light of the current labour standards environment" (DI_CSR 2008, 89). As a response to criticism HP pointed out that it cooperates with NGOs such as Greenpeace and the World Wide Fund for Nature (WWF) in order to improve its CSR performance (HP_CSR 2009a, 12; HP_CSR 2010a, 11f).

Apple, HP and Disney furthermore highlight that they have adopted codes that are intended to prevent irresponsible practices. Disney and Apple point out that their code of conduct for suppliers requires suppliers to meet certain labour rights standards. Similarly HP has a policy that forbids the export of waste to developing countries (HP_CSR 2010a, 79). However, as investigations by corporate watchdogs show problems exist despite these codes.

While companies that follow this strategy do not deny the existence of problems, they tend to downplay them and point out that their responsibility is limited. Apple for example after its first supplier audit wrote:

The overwhelming majority of employees interviewed were pleased with the work environment and how they were treated. We also heard a lot of positive comments about amenities offered by these suppliers, including educational opportunities, the quality of food in dining halls, Internet access, recreational options such as gymnasiums and sports leagues, talentshows, TV rooms and movies.

(Apple_SR 2006, 2)

In summary companies that follow the strategy of *admit, downplay and promise solutions* acknowledge the existence criticism, admit that problems exist, promise to work towards solutions and highlight improvements, while at the same time they tend to downplay the extent of the problem.

In the cases of Vivendi, Google and Microsoft, the differences between company and watchdog assessments are more fundamental. These companies employ a *strategy of redefinition*. This means that one and the same topic is described and discussed in two opposing ways by companies on the one hand and corporate watchdogs on the other hand: while watchdogs point out that certain corporate practices are harmful for society, the companies stress that the same practices are socially responsible

Vivendi for example stresses that "piracy" is a major problem for the media industry in general and the music industry in particular and stresses that the protection of intellectual property is one of the main economic responsibilities of the company (VI_CSR 2002, 9; 2003, 12; 2004/2005, 13; 2005/2006, 23; 2006/2007, 24; 2008, 65; 2009, 55; 2010, 58). However, Vivendi does not only argue that enforcing intellectual property is economically important, but that it is necessary for protecting cultural diversity and fostering creativity: Vivendi for example argues that "'free music' is not sustainable, that cultural diversity and creation are endangered if the sector as a whole is unbalanced and that certain players, deprived of the payment they are entitled to, will disappear" (VI_CSR 2003, 13). Contrary to these arguments critics point out that the company contributes to the criminalization of thousands of individuals and that the current royalty based system for paying artists actually only benefits record companies, instead of musicians. Therefore they stress that recording companies, such as Vivendi's UMG, are the real pirates that are stealing from musicians. From this critical perspective file-sharing can be viewed as an act of resistance against the corporate system of music distribution and a way to bypass recording companies. While watchdogs argue that recording companies steal from artists, Vivendi redefines this issue and argues that a commercial music model secures creative production and diversity and therefore is socially responsible.

This *strategy of redefinition* also characterizes Google's response to critics. The company describes its business model as beneficial for both advertisers and users. Advertisers benefit from personalized marketing opportunities while users receive relevant ads: "We give advertisers the opportunity to place clearly-marked ads alongside our search results. We strive to help people find ads that are relevant and useful, just like our results".[20] Google considers advertising as "a valuable form of information in their own right".[21] Google and watchdogs describe one and the same issue – personalized advertising – in two opposing ways. While for watchdogs personalizing advertisements entails a major threat to user privacy, commodify personal data and exploiting users, Google argues that users benefit from receiving tailored ads that match their interests.

Another company that uses the *strategy of redefinition* is Microsoft. Similar to Vivendi, Microsoft also describes intellectual property rights as necessary for the company and beneficial for society. In its 2003 CSR report for example Microsoft argued that businesses and society benefit from intellectual property rights:

> Enabling IP opportunity confers tremendous benefits on society: consumers benefit from innovation in the form of new products; new business and employment opportunities are created; local economic growth is enabled; productivity gains are achieved; and governments gain opportunities for increased tax revenue.
>
> (MI_CSR 2006, 42)

Microsoft ignores the objections from advocates of the free and open source movement according to which patents privatize common knowledge, hamper the further advancement of software, create artificial scarcity and foster digital inequality. The company redefines the whole issue, arguing that a model in which software is private property that is traded on the market is socially responsible

However, from around 2006 onwards Microsoft started to change the way it dealt with the challenge of free and open source. While in 2001 Microsoft's CEO Steve Ballmer called Linux a cancer,[22] the tone had changed fundamentally in 2010 when the general manager of Microsoft's interoperability unit Jan Paoli announced: "We love open source".[23] The change in Microsoft's strategy can be described as a shift from the *strategy of redefinition* to a *strategy of incorporation*. From around 2006 onwards Microsoft started to highlight collaborations with the open source community in its CSR reports (MI_CSR 2009, 12; 2010, 33), ranging from open source licences[24] to the sponsoring of open source initiatives,[25] to licensing agreements (MI_CSR 2007/2008, 4).

None of this means that Microsoft gave up its support for strong intellectual property rights. Statements that stress that patents are beneficial for society can still be found in the latest editions of Microsoft's CSR reports. According to the rhetoric that marks the shift to a *strategy of incorporation* Microsoft is no longer a responsible company because it respects intellectual property rights but because it respects intellectual property rights and co-operates with the open source community. This co-operation, however, is not without benefit for Microsoft. The benefits for Microsoft from co-operating with the open source community range from the appeasement of its worst critics, to benefits from knowledge exchange with developers from the open source community, to enlarged functionality of Microsoft's products. Microsoft's co-operation with open source does not challenge the proprietary software model. On the contrary, a danger is that Microsoft exploits the open source community in order to strengthen its market position.

Microsoft has not made the source code of any of its successful software packages available. On Microsoft open source platform codeplex.com open source developers present their software ideas. Microsoft can steal their ideas by imitating or rebuilding certain components and turning them into proprietary software. As the source code of Microsoft's software is closed, it is hard to determine which codes and components are included in a software package. Microsoft has found a way to capitalize on open source. The way Microsoft deals with open source is not a strategy of real co-operation but rather of incorporation as it makes open source work for Microsoft and for proprietary software.

Finally, a fourth corporate strategy of dealing with criticism is to ignore the criticized issue altogether. Among the companies included in this study, only AT&T is using this *strategy of ignorance*. Companies that use this strategy do not mention the criticized issue and do not try to justify their behaviour in their CSR communications. AT&T never mentions the topic of net neutrality in its CSR communications. However, outside its CSR reports, such as AT&T's public policy blog, internal memos, as well as lobbying letters to the FCC, AT&T has made it clear that it strongly opposes net neutrality. The fact that AT&T does not mention the topic in its CSR reports suggests that net neutrality is nothing AT&T wants to discuss while describing itself as socially responsible.

News Corp is the only company within the sample that does not publish regular CSR reports. It is therefore not possible to identify a response strategy for News Corp. However, Rupert Murdoch has responded elsewhere to the criticism that News Corp's reporting is biased towards a market liberal, pro-war and anti-climate change ideology. His response is to refute criticism by launching a counter-attack towards the company's critics: Murdoch, at News Corp's 2004 annual meeting in Adelaide, for example claimed that other TV networks are "full of Democrats and Republicans, the others only have Democrats. We don't take any position at all. We're not in the least bit biased, we're a fair and balanced company".[26]

Table 13.2 summarizes the described response strategies.

The biggest difference between these responses is the one between admit, downplay and promise solutions and all the other strategies. Only in the case of the admit downplay and promise solutions strategy does some kind of agreement between companies and watchdogs exist: companies acknowledge that their business practices create certain social and environmental problems. Companies that use any of the other strategies on the contrary do not agree with any of the criticisms corporate watchdogs are raising. They either redefine the criticized issue and describe the same business practices that watchdogs characterize as irresponsible as socially responsible (strategy of redefinition), or they ignore the criticized issue altogether (strategy of ignorance), or try to find ways of how to address the criticized issue in a way that benefits their business goals (strategy of incorporation).

The difference between companies that acknowledge criticism and those that do not might be due to the fact that they are confronted with different types of criticism: companies that acknowledge social and environmental threats resulting from their business practices (strategy of admit, downplay and promise solutions) are HP, Apple and Disney. They are criticized for threatening human health and the environment (HP) or for failing to ensure adequate working conditions in their supply chain (Disney, Apple). Watchdogs criticizing these companies highlight a number of negative effects of corporate practices such as the use of toxic substances and insufficient take-back programmes in the case of HP and low wages, excessive

Table 13.2 Summary of response strategies

Strategies	Main characteristics		Companies
Admit, downplay and promise solutions	Direct reference to watchdog reports/criticism	Yes	HP, Disney, Apple
	Response to the criticized issue	• Admit that the problem exists • Downplay the extent of the problem or the extent of responsibility for the problem • Promise to work towards a solution	
Redefinition	Direct reference to watchdog reports/criticism	No	Vivendi, Microsoft, Google
	Response to the criticized issue	• Discussion of the criticized issue in the CSR communication but in a way that is opposed to the way watchdogs frame the issue	
Incorporation	Direct reference to watchdog reports/criticism	No	Microsoft
	Response to the criticized issue	• Incorporation of the criticized issue for the development of new capital accumulation models	
Ignorance	Direct reference to watchdog reports/criticism	No	AT&T
	Response to the criticized issue	• The criticized issue is ignored in the CSR communication; the criticized issue might be addressed in other documents, such as internal documents, lobbying documents, company blog entries, talks, interviews etc.	

Note: News Corp was excluded from this summary as it does not publish regular CSR reports. Therefore no response strategy could be identified.

overtime, lack of safety protection, etc. in the cases of Disney and Apple. These points of criticism suggest concrete possibilities for improvement: watchdogs urge HP to minimize the use of substances in its products and to expand its take-back programmes; they demand from Apple and Disney the payment of higher wages, compliance with regulation regarding maximum working hours, and a guarantee that their workers have the right to free association, etc. These demands do not draw the business model of the respective companies into question. In these cases, companies can confront the watchdog's criticism by demonstrating willingness to correct the symptoms and to improve in certain specific areas.

Companies that use one of the other strategies on the contrary are confronted with a much more fundamental criticism, which calls into question the legitimacy of their business models: the profit of Vivendi's UMG presupposes copyright protection of musical products that allow turning music into a tradable commodity; Microsoft's income is based on selling patented software; Google's profit is entirely based on advertising and the sale of user data; and the more AT&T is able to control Internet traffic, the more it can increase its income.

The criticisms raised by watchdogs highlight that that these business models are illegitimate in terms of social responsibility: watchdogs highlight that it is against the common good to copyright music, to patent software, to sell user data and to restrict and control Internet traffic. If Vivendi, Microsoft, Google and AT&T agreed with this critique they would admit that their business practices are socially irresponsible. In order to present themselves as responsible companies, they thus either redefine the issue and describe their practices as socially responsible (Vivendi, Google, early Microsoft); try to adapt their business models (late Microsoft); or ignore the issue altogether (AT&T).

In summary, Apple, Disney and HP are confronted with a critique of symptoms, while Vivendi, Google, Microsoft and AT&T are confronted with a critique of their business models. The former criticism leaves companies room for highlighting their willingness and ability to improve. The latter criticism is more radical. As it questions the legitimacy of business models it becomes impossible for companies to acknowledge it, without simultaneously admitting that their business practices are socially irresponsible.

The criticism raised by watchdogs and the inability of companies to offer adequate solutions to the issues points to the existence of fundamental challenges for the concept of CSR in the media and communication sector.

CSR challenges

The CSR areas that were considered in this study were working conditions in the supply chain (Apple and Disney), net neutrality (AT&T), user privacy (Google), e-waste (HP), open source and free software (Microsoft), media content (News Corp) and illegal peer-to-peer file-sharing (Vivendi). In all of these areas the comparison of corporate self-descriptions and watchdog descriptions revealed business practices that favour profit maximization over the common good. These business practices thus contradict a socially responsible media and communication system.

In the following I will discuss each of these issues and thereby highlight main challenges for media and communication companies in the twenty-first century.

Apple and The Walt Disney Company – alienated, precarious labour vs self-determined knowledge work

Disney and Apple represent two different companies within the media and communication business: Disney is mainly known as a media content company, while Apple is active in the media hardware sector. Nevertheless the situation in their supply chains is quite similar. Both companies are major clients of large manufacturing companies, often based in China. Corporate watchdogs have investigated working conditions in Disney's as well as Apple's supplier factories and repeatedly found violations of labour rights.

Working conditions in Disney's and Apple's supply chain are in stark contrast to the commodities produced. Workers in Disney's supplier factories are producing toys, books, clothes and furniture. These merchandizing products for Disney's children's programme, family movies, TV show, and series symbolize a world of fun, joy, fantasy and happy endings. It is a sad irony that the day-to-day working reality of the mostly young workers in Disney's factories is in stark contrast to the joyful fantasy worlds Disney creates in its TV and film productions.

In the case of Apple the goods produced – iPhones, Macs, iPads, iPods – are a symbol of modern twenty-first century lifestyle and progress. The conditions under which these products are produced on the contrary resemble the early days of industrial capitalism. The fact that for example an iPhone costs at least twice or even three times as much as an average monthly salary of a worker in the electronics supply chain reveals a deep separation between workers and the fruits of their labour.

Computer technology has the potential to alleviate work, to increase productivity and to reduce the amount of necessary labour time. It entails the potential that unqualified, monotonous, repetitive and mechanical assembly line labour in particular, which reduces workers to extensions of machines without human intellect or creativity, could in the future be increasingly taken over by machines. The way computers are produced today, however, contradicts this potential. Furthermore the computer industry illustrates the separation of today's global workforce: the low-qualified manual labour of producing computer products on the one hand creates the technological basis for today's high-qualified knowledge labour on the other hand. While the former is mainly carried out in factory halls in the global south and is characterized by repetitive manual labour, harsh discipline and low status, the latter takes place office buildings in the global north, is based on creativity, teamwork, flexible working hours and high status. Although different in many respects, both are often characterized by precarious work contracts, high work pressure and stress.

Apple as well as Disney are among the biggest media companies in the world. Both companies could afford to pay workers higher wages for less working hours, provide proper housing and training and ensure adequate safety protection. However, low wages and excessive working hours enable the meeting of high production targets and the achievement of high profit margins.

The bigger the misery of workers, the higher the corporate profits. Such business practices conflict with the common good; economic success requires the misery of workers and thus hampers the emergence of decent work and self-determined knowledge work.

AT&T – digital inequality vs an egalitarian Internet

During the last few years AT&T has undertaken numerous lobbying efforts in order to influence the FCC's net neutrality regulation. Net neutrality ensures that at the technical level all online content is delivered to users at the same speed, irrespective of whether it is provided by government entities, corporations, protest groups, individuals, etc. AT&T's goal is the abolition of net neutrality. Without net neutrality AT&T could extend its control over Internet traffic.

AT&T has partly been successful – net neutrality regulation has been weakened. NGOs point out that AT&T's business interest in abolishing net neutrality contradicts the common good. Net neutrality advocates such as Free Press highlight that selling Internet delivery speed as a commodity would create new digital inequalities. Paid prioritization models would privilege economically powerful actors and make it difficult for non-profit actors to distribute content online. This would threaten free speech, increase the commercialization of the Internet and further reduce the possibility of civil society and oppositional groups to make alternative, non-commercial content visible online.

AT&T has not responded to this criticism in its CSR communications. However, in lobbying documents, talks, internal documents and on its public policy blog the company has made it clear that it will continue its fight against net neutrality. In its CSR communications AT&T claims that it provides "technologies that empower others" (AT&T_CSR 2010, 4). The company argues, that its "vision is to connect people with their world" (AT&T_CSR 2008, 27). AT&T's business practices, however, contradict these claims: its stance towards net neutrality reveals a conflict between its business interests and the establishment of an open, inclusive and accessible Internet.

Google – data commodity vs public online infrastructure

Google.com is the most frequently accessed website on the Internet. Users can access all its services free of charge. Google's business model consists of selling user data to advertisers to create personalized advertisements. Thus, access to Google's services only at the first sight appears to be free – it comes at the cost of the commodification of personal information. The sale of user data as a commodity entails the threat of surveillance and an invasion of the rights of Internet users. The use of user data for advertising purposes requires the creation of large searchable databases that allow the combining of information about Internet users in different ways in order to identify different consumer groups that might be susceptible to certain consumer products. For Internet users it becomes impossible to determine which of their data is stored in which databases and to whom it is accessible.

Google's philosophy is based on the principle of not being evil. The inventor of this famous motto, Paul Buchheit, stressed in an interview that this slogan was intended to demarcate Google from its competitors which "were kind of exploiting the users to some extent" (Buchheit 2008, 170). However, Google's business model is also based on the exploitation of users as it turns data, which Google users produce while using their services, into its property that is then sold as a commodity to advertisers. Furthermore through the sale of user data Google invades the privacy of Internet users. Google provides services that are highly valued by the online community. However, if they want to use these services they have no other choice than to consent to Google's terms of service and the usage of their data for advertising purposes. This gives Google a high amount of power over deciding about how user data are used and to whom they are made available. The free accessibility of Google's services thus comes at high cost: the renunciation of the right to determine the use of personal information.

HP – the threat of e-waste vs green IT

HP generates profits through the sale of computer hardware. Computer products often contain various toxic substances that threaten human health and the environment. HP is no exception. Insufficient take-back programmes increase the likelihood that HP products are inadequately disposed of and end up as part of (illegal) e-waste exports to developing countries. The recycling of e-waste without the use of proper protective equipment in the informal sector can have devastating effects on human health and the environment.

One important measure to reduce these dangers is to avoid the production of waste. HP is one of the largest hardware companies in the world. In order to generate profit it needs to continuously sell computer hardware. Short lifespans and fast obsolescence of computer products allows an increase in sales numbers. Most computers today are built in a way that makes the exchange of individual parts difficult. The difficulty of exchanging individual computer parts combined with high prices for repair services force many computer users to replace their devices as soon as one part of it breaks. Advertising and rapid introduction of new product versions that promise increased functionality and improved optical design, albeit often containing little technological innovation, further contribute to the creation of a throw-away culture.

HP has the power to decide how computer products should be designed. They could be built in an environmentally friendly way. Important measures would be to foster innovation that enables the reduction of the amount of hazardous products to an absolute minimum, to construct robust products with long lifespans and exchangeable parts, to build refillable ink cartridges, etc.

In its CSR communications HP commits to environmental protection: "Environmental protection is a complex undertaking, but the laws of nature are simple. We will provide leadership on the journey to an environmentally sustainable future, with efficient products and creative recycling systems" (HP_CSR 2001,1). HP's goal regarding waste is to increase the total amount of recycled products (HP_CSR 2010a, 119).

However, an absolute increase in the amount of recycled products does not necessarily indicate an improvement. Only if the total number of products sold remains the same or is reduced would this mean a reduction of inadequately disposed waste. HP, however, does not aim at increasing product lifespans or reducing the amount of products sold to users. At a some point every computer product will need to be disposed of. The shorter the product lifespan, the more products can HP sell and the more waste that will be produced. Short product life cycles thus benefit the profit interests of HP, but increase the amount of e-waste, which threatens the environment and human health, particularly in developing countries in which HP's take-back programmes are insufficient, and to which e-waste continues to be (illegally) exported.

Microsoft – knowledge monopoly vs collective knowledge resources

Microsoft is the largest software company in the world. People around the globe are using Microsoft's proprietary software. Microsoft has been convicted both in Europe and the US for violations of antitrust principles. Software patents are at the heart of Microsoft's business model. Only the exclusive right over knowledge allows Microsoft to sell software licences to computer users.

Software is a form of knowledge, its development requires certain skills and previous knowledge ranging from mathematical rules to specific programming languages. Microsoft's software thus contains previous knowledge and through patenting software Microsoft exploits the common stock of the knowledge of society for creating private property. Based on this privatization Microsoft is able to prevent others from accessing this knowledge. Microsoft does not want anybody to know what the source code of its software products looks like because then they could be reproduced and improved, which would impede Microsoft's ability to sell licences and to generate profit. Microsoft's business practices thus deprive society from the best possible software. Making all software source code publicly available would allow other programmers to further adapt, develop and improve software. Collectively, the chances are higher that software is developed that matches the various needs of individuals and society.

Patenting software makes software scarce. It creates access barriers and thus fosters digital exclusion. In its CSR communications Microsoft, however, repeatedly makes a "comprehensive commitment to digital inclusion, and to help address inequities" (MI_CSR 2004, 48). Microsoft initiated programmes that are intended to confront the digital divide, such as the Unlimited Potential programme in which Microsoft makes donations to community centre libraries and schools in developing countries (MI_CSR 2003, 23).

Such programmes do not change the fact that proprietary software as such hampers access to software and fosters exclusion. Quite on the contrary Microsoft's programmes strengthen the dependence on Microsoft's products. Pupils and students acquire the skills for using Microsoft's software, instead of being trained how to use the available open source alternatives. These initiatives thus help Microsoft to establish new markets for its proprietary software. Microsoft's supposed attempt to reduce digital inequality further promotes it.

Microsoft's business interests conflict with the common good: instead of allowing the collective capabilities of the human intellect to develop the best possible software for society and making it universally accessible, Microsoft patents software and monopolizes access to software and source code in order to create the highest possible profits for the company.

News Corp – media as instruments of ideologies vs media as critical public watchdogs

For News Corp the production of news is a profitable business. Arsenault and Castells calculate that News Corp reaches 75 per cent of the global population (Arsenault and Castells 2008, 491). In the media content sector, economic power is inherently connected to cultural power. Economically successful media companies can distribute their content to a large number of people. As critics highlight, News Corp exploits this power to promote a destructive worldview: war, the destruction of nature, and social inequality pose a threat to individuals and society and are not desirable. When arguing for the necessity of war, downplaying the threats of climate change and advocating neo-liberal policies News Corp is presenting the particular interest of some individuals who benefit from war, environmental destruction and neo-liberalism as the general interest of society. News Corp instrumentalizes its media power to distribute ideologies. Furthermore News Corp's reporting creates disinformation and ignorance in society: studies show that its audience is often less informed than people who do not consume any news at all (Morris 2005, 68; Fairleigh Dickinson University 2011, 1).

News Corp's practices contradict the potential of the media to provide information, to foster education, enlightenment, critical thinking and debate in society. Quite on the contrary the company instrumentalizes its power for promoting destructive and anti-humanist ideologies that present the particular interests of privileged groups as the general interest of society.

Vivendi – cultural enclosures vs an open and accessible culture

Vivendi is the owner of UMG, the largest recoding company in the world. The business of music recording companies during the last decade has increasingly been challenged through peer-to-peer file-sharing. The development of digital technologies and the Internet reduced reproduction cost and simplified music distribution. Music is not scarce; it can be used without being consumed. The number of people who can simultaneously listen to the same piece of music is unlimited. These qualities make music easy to share. In order to maintain a business model that is based on the sale of music, recording companies need to enforce intellectual property rights both through legal and technical means. In order to maintain their profits, recording companies such as UMG are commodifying music and thereby destroying its accessibility and creating cultural enclosures. Critics, however, highlight that music is part of the collective cultural resources of society. Access to music is an important element of cultural participation. The more open and accessible culture is, the more it can flourish.

The production of music is inspired by other cultural products, and listening to music can inspire new forms of musical or other creative forms.

For the sake of its profit Vivendi introduces artificial scarcity and tries to create an exclusive, restricted and inaccessible music culture. It thus hampers the flourishing of the cultural resources of society. Nevertheless, in its CSR communications Vivendi claims that it wants to foster an open culture. "Sharing knowledge" is presented as one of the company's main media-related responsibilities to society (VI_CSR 2005/2006, 3; 2006/2007, 52; 2008, 59; 2009, 75; 2010, 80). The company highlights that it wants to contribute to minimizing the digital divide, which it describes as a "new form of social exclusion": "Today, the gap is widening between those who can use these new tools effectively and those who cannot. This digital divide is a new form of social exclusion" (VI_CSR 2002, 18).

Vivendi neglects to mention that its own business practices based on copyrighted music foster cultural exclusion. Its business interests suppress the creation of an open and accessible culture that allows culture to flourish, to be freely shared, to inspire human creativity and to benefit all members of society.

Conclusion

Table 13.3 summarizes the social responsibility challenges described above.

At a more abstract level the contradictions that were identified in this study illustrate one basic antagonism of capitalist society: the contradiction between productive forces and relations of production. In Marxist theory the notion of productive forces describes labour power, raw materials and means of production, while the concept of relations of production refers to the social relations through which production, distribution and consumption are organized. Marx described the unfolding of an antagonism between productive forces and relations of production:

> At a certain stage of development, the material productive forces of society come into conflict with the existing relations of production or – this merely expresses the same thing in legal terms – with the property relations within the framework of which they have operated hitherto.
>
> (Marx 1859/1994, 211)

Table 13.3 Challenges for media and communication in the twenty-first century

Apple & Disney	Alienated, precarious labour vs self-determined knowledge work
AT&T	Digital inequality vs an egalitarian Internet
HP	The threat of e-waste vs green IT
Google	Data commodity vs public online infrastructure
Microsoft	Knowledge monopoly vs collective knowledge resources
News Corp	Media as instruments of ideologies vs. media as critical public watchdogs
Vivendi	Cultural enclosures vs an open and accessible culture

The examples studied here illustrate this antagonism in the contemporary media and communication system. Today's productive forces in the realm of media and communication could enable self-determined knowledge work, the development of green IT products, the creation of an open and accessible culture, of collective knowledge resources, the functioning of media as critical public watchdogs, the creation of a free online infrastructure and an egalitarian Internet. However, the realization of these potentials that are arising from the development of productive forces is constrained by the capitalist relations of production, which depend on and produce the exploitation of labour power and nature, the creation of cultural enclosures and knowledge monopolies, the media as instruments of ideology and commodification, and inequality.

The contradictions that are summarized in Table 13.3 not only describe challenges for media and communication today, but furthermore challenge the idea of CSR: the companies included in this case study all call themselves socially responsible – most of them provide regular CSR reports, and even News Corp, which does not report on CSR issues, has made a commitment to CSR. However, the results presented here show that, despite CSR, the business practices of media and communication companies often conflict with the common good. The largest media companies in the world create an exclusive, non-accessible media culture and digital inequality, monopolize knowledge, promote conformity and uncritical media content, commodify user data, threaten the environment and human health through large amounts of e-waste, and take advantage of precarious working conditions. Through their practices these companies are suppressing the possibilities for creating decent working conditions and self-determined knowledge work, green IT, an open, accessible media culture and digital equality, collective knowledge resources, a media system in which media can function as critical public watchdogs, and free online infrastructure.

Notes

1 Google. *Code of Conduct*. Retrieved from http://investor.google.com/corporate/code-of-conduct.html on November 18, 2011.
2 Google. *Corporate Social Responsibility*. Retrieved from http://www.google.com/intl/zh-CN/corporate/responsibility_en.html on November 20, 2011.
3 Data is based on the companies' official SEC filings as available in the Edgar database http://www.sec.gov/edgar/searchedgar/companysearch.html
   For Vivendi data is based on official financial reports as available on the company homepage: http://www.vivendi.com/vivendi/Financial-Reports
   For details of financial data and data sources for each company see also the detailed company case for each company in Chapters 5–12.
   CAGR is calculated as follows: CAGR = (ending value/beginning value) (1/#of years) - 1.
4 Free Press. *Saving the Internet. A History*. Retrieved from http://www.savetheinternet.com/timeline on December 12, 2011.
5 Free Press. 2009. *Seven Reasons: Why We Need Net Neutrality Now*. Retrieved from http://www.savetheinternet.com/blog/09/08/03/seven-reasons-why-we-need-net-neutrality-now on October 28, 2013.
6 Free Press. *Frequently Asked Questions*. Retrieved from http://www.savetheinternet.com/faq on December 4, 2011.
7 Privacy International. 2007. *Consultation Report. Race to the Bottom?* Retrieved from http://www.privacyinternational.org/issues/internet/interimrankings.pdf on January 21, 2012.

8   Google-watch.com *And Then We Were Four*. Retrieved from http://www.google-watch. org/bigbro.html on January 21, 2012.

9   Privacy Rights Clearinghouse. 2004. *Google's New Email Service, Gmail, Under Fire for Privacy Concerns*. Retrieved from https://www.privacyrights.org/ar/GmailAGadvisory. htm on January 21, 2012.

10 Corporate Watch. 2008. *Google's New Spy*. Retrieved from http://www.corporatewatch. org/?lid=3134 on January 21, 2012.

11 Google Monitor. 2011. *Google's No Privacy by Design Business Model*. Retrieved from http://googlemonitor.com/2011/googles-no-privacy-by-design-business-model/ on January 21, 2012.

12 Greenpeace. 2006. *Toxic Substances in Laptops: Greenpeace study exposes HP's lie*. Retrieved from http://www.greenpeace.org/international/en/press/releases/toxic-substances-in-laptops-g/ on November 3, 2011.

13 End Soft Patents. *Why Abolish Software Patents*. Retrieved from http://en.swpat.org/ wiki/Arguments#Arguments_specific_to_software_patents on October 6, 2011.

14 No Software Patents. *The Dangers*. Retrieved from http://www.nosoftwarepatents. com/en/m/dangers/index.html on October 6, 2011.

15 The Free Software Foundation. *Microsoft's 7 Sins*. Retrieved from http://en.windows7sins. org/ on September 27, 2011.

16 Open Source Initiative. 2009. *A New Argument Against SWAPT*. Retrieved from http:// opensource.org/node/441 on October 16, 2011.

17 United States of America vs Microsoft Corporation. 2001. *Stipulation*. Retrieved from http://cyber.law.harvard.edu/msdoj/011106-proposed-settlement.html on October 3, 2011.

18 *The Guardian*. 2006. *EU Hits Microsoft 280.5m Antitrust Fine*. By Mark Tran on July 12, 2006. Retrieved from http://www.guardian.co.uk/business/2006/jul/12/europeanunion. digitalmedia on October 3, 2011.

19 *Wired Magazine*. 2008. *File Sharing Lawsuits at a Crossroads, After 5 Years of RIAA Litigation*. By David Kravets on September 4, 2008. Retrieved from http://www.wired. com/threatlevel/2008/09/proving-file-sh/ on September 16, 2011.

20 Google. *Competition. About Ads*. Retrieved from http://www.google.com/competition/ howgoogleadswork.html on November 18, 2011.

21 Google. *Company Information*. Retrieved from http://www.google.com/intl/en/about/ corporate/company/ on November 17, 2011.

22 Steve Ballmer quoted in *The Register*. 2001. *"Linux is a Cancer"*. Retrieved from http:// www.theregister.co.uk/2001/06/02/ballmer_linux_is_a_cancer/ on September 24, 2011.

23 Jan Paoli quoted in *Network World*. 2010. *Microsoft: "We Love Open Source"*. By John Brodkin on August 23, 2010. Retrieved from http://www.networkworld.com/ news/2010/082310-microsoft-open-source.html?page=1 on September 28, 2011.

24 Open Source Initiative. 2007. *OSI Approves License Submissions*. Retrieved from http://opensource.org/node/207 on October 14, 2011.

25 The Apache Software Foundation. *FAQ*. Retrieved from http://www.apache.org/foundation/ faq.html#what on September 27, 2011.

26 Rupert Murdoch quoted in *The Guardian*. 2004. *Murdoch: Fox News Does Not Favour Bush*. Retrieved from http://www.guardian.co.uk/media/2004/oct/26/newscorporation. uselections2004 on February 12, 2012.

14 The logic of property and the logic of the common in the media system

The results of this study show that the self-descriptions of media and communication companies do not correspond to their actual business practices. While Apple, AT&T, Google, HP, Microsoft, News Corp, Vivendi and The Walt Disney company claim that they are socially responsible, corporate watchdogs have documented irresponsible business practices throughout the media and communication sector. I will argue in the following that the reason why CSR cannot fulfil its promises is that it does not transcend the logic of property. The negative actuality, which watchdogs have documented, is an expression of the logic of property that dominates the media and communication system. Realizing the full potentials of media and communication in the twenty-first century requires a shift towards the logic of the common. Before I elaborate this argument in greater detail I will describe these two logics based on recent literature that has theorized the common. Subsequently I show how the companies studied exhibit the logic of property and point out potential alternatives that are based on the logic of the common.

Conceptualizing the logic of property and the logic of the common

Hardt and Negri argue that the concept of property and its defence are "the foundation of every modern political constitution" (Hardt and Negri 2009, 15). This is what they call the "republic of property" (Hardt and Negri 2009, 8). This republic of property can "determine and dictate the conditions of possibility of social life in all its facets and phases" (Hardt and Negri 2009, 8). Opposed to the logic of property is the logic of the common. Property belongs to individual owners that engage in the purchase and sale of commodities. The exchange of commodities thus lies at the centre of the logic of property. Nick Dyer-Witheford argues that the common on the contrary is not sold, but shared (Dyer-Witheford 2010a, 82). Similarly David Harvey points out that the common is collective and non-commodified:

> At the heart of the practice of communing lies the principle that the relation between the social group and that aspect of the environment being treated

as common shall be both collective and non-commodified – off limits to the logic of market exchange an market valuations.

(Harvey 2012, 73)

Nick Dyer-Witheford stresses that commons are shared among collectivities: "The notion of a commodity, a good produced for sale, presupposes private owners between whom this exchange occurs. The notion of the common pre-supposes collectivities – associations and assemblies – within which sharing is organized" (Dyer-Witheford 2010a, 82). He highlights that in the circuit of capital money is used to produce commodities which are then turned into more money (M – C[ommodity] – M'). In the circuit of the common on the contrary, associations organize collective resources in order to produce more commons that can then be used to build more associations (A – C[ommon] – A') (Dyer Witheford 2010b). Nick Dyer-Witheford distinguishes different moments in the circuit of the common (Dyer-Witheford 2010b): eco-social commons as collective planning institutions for internal and external health; labour commons as the "democratized organization of productive and reproductive work"; and networked commons referring to networks as collective infrastructure. In the circulation of the common these different moments reinforce each other and enable the production of common goods and services, a "commonwealth" (Dyer-Witheford 2010b).

Contemporary capitalist society is based on the logic of property, while the logic of the common transcends it. The logic of the common thus points towards a different organization of society in which goods are shared as commons among collectivities. However, within capitalist society certain goods also exist that contradict and tend to resist capitalist command and exhibit the logic of the common. These are goods that are either part of nature such as air or water, or goods that are collectively produced by all members of society. According to Hardt and Negri, commons on the one hand are "the common wealth of the material world" (Hardt and Negri 2009, viii). On the other hand commons are the "results of social production that are necessary for social interaction and further production such as knowledge, languages, codes, information, affects, and so forth" (Hardt and Negri 2009, viii). Similarly David Harvey (2012) argues that apart from the commons of nature, cultural and intellectual commons also exist. The latter differ from the former as they are not constrained by scarcity (Harvey 2012, 72). Harvey furthermore identifies urban commons, which constitute the city as a collectively produced social space (Harvey 2012). Likewise Slavoj Žižek distinguishes between the commons of culture such as language and education as well as important social infrastructure, and the commons of internal and external nature (Žižek 2009, 91).

The logic of the common points towards a society that transcends capitalism and the logic of property. At the same time traces of the common can be found within a capitalist society. As Hardt and Negri argue, despite an "ideological aversion" capital always depended on the commons and increasingly does so (Hardt and Negri 2009, 153). Capital thus opposes and at the same time needs the common. Massimo De Angelis therefore calls the relationship between capitalism and the commons schizophrenic:

On the one hand, capital is a social force that requires continuous enclosures; that is, the destruction and commodification of non-commodified common spaces and resources. However, there is also an extent to which capital has to accept the non-commodified and *contribute to its constitution*.

(De Angelis 2009, 33)

Hardt and Negri argue that "contemporary forms of capitalist production and accumulation in fact, despite their continuing drive to privatize resources and wealth, paradoxically make possible and even require expansion of the common" (Hardt and Negri 2009, ix). In Hardt's and Negri's view this is due to the increased importance of information and knowledge as well as innovation and creativity for capitalist production. Therefore, "capitalist production by addressing its own needs is opening up the possibility of and creating the bases for a social and economic order grounded in the common" (Hardt and Negri 2009, x).

Capital seeks to exploit the productive capacity of the commons by privatizing them: "capitalist society seems driven to eliminate or mask the common by privatizing the means of production and indeed all aspects of social life" (Hardt and Negri 2009, 153). While attempting to control the commons, however, capital at the same time limits their productive capacity (Hardt and Negri 2009, 288). This illustrates how the logic of the common shines through within the logic of property and thereby challenges and contradicts it.

In order to better understand the logic of property and the logic of the common, it is necessary to describe both in a more systematic way: Hofkirchner and Fuchs (2003) argue that society consists of the system of economy, the system of politics and the system of culture. The economy is the system that organizes the production, distribution and consumption of resources. The central power in this area thus is the possession of ownership rights (Hofkirchner and Fuchs 2003, 5). The system of politics is concerned with making collective decisions regarding all aspects of social life. Power in this system is related to the ability to participate in decision-making processes (Hofkirchner and Fuchs 2003, 6). The system of culture deals with the rules of society. Power in this system means the power to define rules, norms, values and morals (Hofkirchner and Fuchs 2003, 6). In summary the three subsystems of society regulate ownership rights, decision power, and the rules and norms of society. The logic of the common and the logic of property differ regarding each of these three aspects:

- *The logic of the common*: In the logic of the common the economy is organized based on the principle of common ownership of means of production. Production is collectively organized. The commons are shared among collectivities. The main principle that guides the sphere of politics is participatory democracy. Every member of society has the power to participate in decisions concerning all important aspects of social life including the economy. According to the cultural logic of the common achieving the common good requires universal values that support economic and political participation such as solidarity, equality, inclusion, sharing and co-operation.

- *The logic of property*: Following the logic of property, the means of production belong to individual property holders. Production is privately organized and individual property holders exchange commodities among each other. Decision power in the logic of property is concentrated in the hands of political and economic elites. Elected representatives decide on the rules of society. Economic life is largely excluded from democratic decision making. Within a certain legal framework the owners of means of production have the right to decide how to employ them to produce whichever good in whichever way. Following the cultural logic of property the common good can be realized based on particularistic values that support economic and political elitism such as self-interest, profit maximization and competition.

To sum up: the logic of the common is based on common ownership, participatory decision power and universal values; the logic of private property is based on private ownership, elitist decision power and particularistic values.

Critique: the logic of property in the media and communication system

At these three levels – economy, politics and culture – the business practices of the companies included in this study exhibit the logic of private property.

Economy

The companies studied are privately owned corporations that produce commodities that are exchanged on the market. Their business practices require the commodification and appropriation of commons. This commodification affects all moments of the circuit of the common: eco-social commons, labour commons, networked commons (Dyer-Witheford 2010b).

- *Commodification of eco-social commons*: HP is an example of the appropriation of eco-social commons. Products with short lifespans increase HP's sales numbers and at the same time increase the amount of e-waste that can potentially destroy the environment and threaten human health. Sustainable IT products with high quality and long lifespans would reduce profit margins as they are more expensive to produce and at the same time would reduce sales numbers, as sustainable products can be used for longer time periods. HP's business model on the contrary allows generating high profits while threatening human health, and nature.
- *Commodification of labour commons*: The example of Disney and Apple illustrates that the logic of property depends on the commodification of labour power. Millions of workers who do not have anything else to sell but their labour power are forced to work in factories in order to be able to make a living. The conditions under which workers in China and other low-cost production countries are working today resemble nineteenth century capitalism.

Low wages combined with excessive working hours allow companies such as Apple or Disney to lower production costs and increase profit margins, while threatening the physical and mental health of workers. These companies exploit the human propensity to work in order to maximize private profit.

- *Commodification of networked commons*: The examples of Vivendi, Microsoft, AT&T, News Corp and Google illustrate the appropriation of networked commons through the logic of property. In order to realize profit Vivendi and Microsoft depend on intellectual property rights that turn cultural and knowledge products into scarce commodities. Instead of allowing an open and accessible culture to flourish, they introduce access restrictions that hamper creativity and knowledge production while fostering cultural inequality.

AT&T's business model is based on commodifying access to the technological infrastructure of the Internet. Like other infrastructure such as roads, bridges, or canals, the Internet has become an essential means for connecting people and enabling communication and co-operation between them. Being excluded from the Internet means being excluded from many aspects of social life and culture. The Internet also provides important infrastructure for the joint creation of knowledge and culture. The more accessible the Internet is, the more people engage in communication and co-operation online, the richer the culture and knowledge produced becomes. An accessible Internet infrastructure thus benefits society in general, while access restrictions satisfy AT&T's profit interest.

Google provides free access to its services for all Internet users. This universal access contradicts the logic of property. Nevertheless to be able to generate profit Google depends on the sale of a different commodity: user data. In the logic of property free access on the one hand comes with further commodification on the other hand. Google's services make the Internet searchable and online content accessible and thus form important web infrastructure. However, Google's business interests prevent this infrastructure from becoming common and collective as its usage comes at the cost of the commodification of personal information, which enforces the logic of property.

News Corp generates profit through selling space for advertisements as well as restricting access to media content. For News Corp news, information and other media content is a means to generate profit. Its success in generating profit through producing media content has allowed the company to expand its reach and to gain high symbolic power, which News Corp uses for promoting the values of the logic of property. Instead of being a collective knowledge and information resource, News Corp turns media content into a means for both generating profit and promoting particularistic values that ideologically support the imperative of profit maximization.

Politics

At the political level the companies studied also illustrate the logic of property. As they are private companies the decision power over the companies' activities is concentrated in the hands of their owners. Other actors who are either directly or indirectly affected by a company's activities such as workers or local communities have no influence on the company's decisions. The only way society can influence the activities of corporations is indirectly, via government regulation. Their economic power gives the owners of the companies studied the power over decisions that affect all members of society. The private organization of the media and communication system gives companies the power to decide which hardware products are produced and how, how they are designed, which music is "worth" producing, how software is designed, which topics are worth reporting, how and who receives access to the Internet at which speed, and which user data is stored and who can access them.

Culture

All the companies studied have been financially successful during the last decade (see Chapter 13). Generating profit is their main purpose of existence. However, all companies commit to the concept of CSR or to certain values that go beyond the mere pursuit of profit. In their CSR communications the companies studied highlight that they do not exclusively focus on the particularistic value of individual profit maximization, but care about how business practices affect the common good. CSR policies and reports draw on values of the logic of the common in order to provide greater legitimacy to corporate behaviour. However, research conducted by corporate watchdogs reveals that despite commitments to CSR, corporate practices in many respects are socially irresponsible. During the last 10 years the companies studied increased their profits while at the same time created miserable working conditions, exploited human labour power, threatened human health and the environment, promoted destructive ideologies and restricted access to culture, knowledge and important technological infrastructure. This shows that CSR reports make use of universal values, which characterize the logic of the common, while actual corporate practices privilege profit maximization over the common good. The concept of CSR instrumentalizes the cultural logic of the common as it strategically refers to universal values for generating legitimacy for corporate practices that follow the logic of property and the particularistic values of profit maximization.

To sum up: the business activities of the media and communication companies studied are based on the logic of property. They commodify the commons of society, rely on undemocratic decision making, and are guided by the particular value of profit maximization. The concept of CSR promises a shift towards more universal values that aims at the common good. Research conducted by corporate watchdogs, however, reveals that the shift towards the values of the logic of the common is merely rhetorical while actual practices remain based on the logic of the property. In principle, the media and communication companies studied produce goods and provide services that are beneficial for society: computer hardware, software, news and entertainment, music, movies, online search infrastructure, telecommunications infrastructure. However, through subordinating the production and distribution of media and communication products under the logic of property, these support the profit interests of shareholders but cannot unfold their full benefits for society. The way hardware, software, music, news and entertainment, Internet and telecommunications infrastructure are produced under the logic of property have negative side effects for individuals, society and the environment. Identifying starting points for a media and communication system that helps to achieve the common good requires looking at alternatives that anticipate the logic of the common.

Alternatives: the logic of the common in the media and communication system

There exist attempts to build alternatives to the private media model that reject the logic of property and are instead based on the logic of the common. These alternatives attempt to organize the provision of media products and services in a way that is based on sharing media and communication products as commons (economy), participatory decision making (politics) and universal values (culture). Such projects are, however, often constrained and threatened by the social predominance of the logic of property, which they try to resist.

- *Worker owned cooperatives as alternative to precarious and alienated labour*:
  Creating alternatives to alienated and precarious labour requires overcoming private ownership of means of production. Only as long as some are excluded from access to means of production, those who own the latter can exploit the former. Worker-owned co-operatives are one possibility for overcoming this class division of owners and dependent employees. In a worker-owned co-operative the means of production are common resources that equally belong to everybody engaged in the production process. Common ownership also changes the politics of the economy as it requires democratic decision making throughout all economic operations. Today worker-owned co-operatives are the exception. However, examples can be found in most economic industries including media and communication sectors such as publishing (e.g. The Toolbox for Education and Social Action – TESA[1]) or programming and web design (e.g. Ronin Tech Collective[2]; Quilted[3]).

  A barrier to creating worker-owned co-operatives in the hardware segment is that it requires high-technological equipment, which is expensive and thus difficult to afford for most co-operatives. One attempt to make means of production more accessible is the development of 3D printers, for example a printer called RepRap, described by its developers as "humanity's first general-purpose self-replicating manufacturing machine".[4] RepRap is a desktop printer that is able to print 3D plastic objects. As the RepRap itself consists largely of plastic parts it is able to replicate itself. Thus, with a RepRap printer and some additional parts that can be bought in a regular hardware store it is possible to print another RepRap printer.[5]

  At the current stage of development, creating and using a RepRap requires certain skills and technical knowledge. Furthermore the only material that the current version of RepRap is able to print is plastic, which reduces the range of printable objects. However, the developers of RepRap are working on increasing the range of printable materials including electrical conductors.[6] Despite the early stage in the development of open source 3D printers, the decisive point that RepRap illustrates is that hardware production can be organized along the principles of open source. With the help of a 3D printer physical products can become downloadable from the Internet, similar to informational goods (Söderberg and Daoud 2012). Furthermore, the fact that the 3D printer is based on open source makes it a common means of production that eludes the logic of property.

Today worker-owned co-operatives are islands in a sea of privately owned corporations. The fact that they have to compete with capitalist corporations creates performance and work pressure. Worker-owned co-operatives today can realize common ownership of means of production but cannot escape the logic of property. They still depend on the exchange of commodities in order to produce their products and to generate income. Creating a commons based economy, in which collective resources are used for producing commons that are freely shared, requires structural transformations that go beyond and enable changes at the level of individual organizations. Nevertheless strengthening worker-owned co-operatives as an alternative to alienated and precarious employment relations seems crucial. Starting points for this might be the introduction of public support systems for and support networks between worker-owned organizations.

- *Eco-friendly computers as alternative to short-lived toxic products*: Reducing the negative environmental impact of computer products requires the consideration of the entire product life cycle from production to usage to the disposal of a product. Threats to the environment and human health result from the usage of toxic products in production, short product lifespans, and improper disposal. One attempt to create an eco-friendly computer is the Recompute desktop computer, that was developed by an industrial design student at the University of Houston.[7] The Recompute PC is based on the principle of Full Life Cycle Design that tries to find sustainable solutions for manufacturing, usage and product disposal.[8] The entire Recompute case is made from corrugated cardboard that is glued together and treated with a non-toxic flame retardant. This significantly reduces the materials used for the computer case as well as the energy necessary for producing it. At the usage level Recompute PCs support personal customization by allowing users to easily add and reuse existing hardware. All parts are exchangeable, which makes it possible to repair instead of disposing of the entire computer if parts of it break down. Due to the fact that the case is made of cardboard a Recompute PC can be easily disassembled, which makes the dismantling and thus the recycling of the parts much easier. As the computer uses regular circuit boards it still contains toxic substances. However, the easy dismantling increases the likelihood that the computer components will be reused and/or recycled.[9] The environmental impact of Recompute PC could still be improved for example through using components without toxic substances and those with longer lifespans; however, it is more eco-friendly than most available computers.

- *Shared art as alternative to copyrighted music*: The Internet provides artists with the opportunity to self-publish their music. Some singers and bands such as for example Amanda Palmer, Radiohead, or the Nine Inch Nails have already started to self-release some of their work online as downloads. Online platforms such as Jamendo.com have specialized in providing music under a creative commons licence. However, the need to earn money in order to be able to make a living makes it difficult for artists to provide all of their work as a gift to the public. The question therefore arises how to remunerate artists. One way for musicians to self-publish their work and still earn some money is to ask for (voluntary) payments. Amanda Palmer for example required downloaders to pay a minimum of $1 USD for the download of her album "Amanda Palmer Performs the Popular Hits of Radiohead on Her Magical Ukulele".[10] Another option is online platforms such as magnatune.com that require users to buy a subscription for accessing music available on the platform, which then in part is used to pay artists. These options allow the bypassing of recording companies while still providing an income to artists. However, in these cases music is still sold as a commodity. For music to become a freely shared common it is necessary to find more structural alternatives for remunerating artists. Ideas that point in this direction for example are the concept of a "non-commercial use levy" on products connected to file-sharing such as MP3players, copying devices or Internet access (Netanel 2003), the concept of an "artistic freedom voucher" (Baker 2003), or the Electronic Frontier Foundation's idea of "Voluntary Collective Licensing of Music Filesharing".[11] Society could furthermore facilitate the free sharing of cultural products through providing all cultural producers with a publicly funded guaranteed income. These are different options that could be used for gradually moving towards a commons based cultural system that poses a fundamental alternative to the contemporary predominantly commercial culture.

- *Free and open source software as alternative to proprietary software*: The FOSS community challenges the proprietary software model. Proprietary software restricts access to the source code and allows users neither to modify nor to redistribute a program. This grants the owners of proprietary software a monopoly on the knowledge included in the software and the right to charge licence fees to everybody who wants to use it. The Free Software Foundation as well as the Open Source Initiative oppose the proprietary software model and have developed alternative software licences. Both free software and open source licences have in common that they require the source code of software to be accessible and modifiable but do not prohibit commercial uses of a program: "'Free software' does not mean 'noncommercial'. A free program must be available for commercial use, commercial development, and commercial distribution".[12] Similarly the Open Source Initiative stresses: "All Open Source software can be used for commercial purposes".[13] Some free software and open source licences even allow turning software that was originally released under a free software or open source licence into proprietary software. The principle of copyleft prohibits this. A copyleft licence requires that all versions and modifications of a program are redistributed under the same licence as the original product and thus cannot be turned into proprietary software. One of the most important copyleft licences is the GNU General Public License.[14,15] However, non-copyleft software can also qualify as free and/or open source software. Non-copyleft software licences allow copies or modified versions of a program to be redistributed as proprietary software.[16,17]

The free software and open source movements want to challenge access to knowledge restrictions. Their critique of proprietary software relates to the fact that it limits the opportunities for using, studying, modifying and redistributing software. Neither of them, however, questions the commodity logic. By permitting commercial use of free and open source software, both movements tolerate the fact that private profit is generated based on the free and collective labour of software developers. Turning collectively developed FOSS into a (proprietary) commodity is an exploitation of all the developers that spend hours of unpaid work for creating software. The principle of open source and free software has the potential to challenge the logic of property through negating commodification. In order to establish a thriving commons based culture and to overcome unequal access to software as well as the exploitation of software developers, a non-commercial commons based model of software production is needed.

• *Critical media as an alternative to commercialized media*: In principle, everybody can become a producer of media content. This can range from producing simple leaflets, to self-printed newspapers, to pirate or community radio or TV stations. Through the Internet the possibilities of producing media content have further expanded. However, most independent media producers suffer from a lack of resources, which makes it difficult for them to compete with commercial media companies. Financial resources are necessary to continuously produce media content, for employing staff, for purchasing and maintaining technical equipment, as well as for promotion and advertising. Examples of alternative critical journalism are manifold. However, often alternative media remain small scale and marginal. Among the more popular examples are Democracy Now, Adbusters, Mother Jones, Indymedia, or Le Monde Diplomatique. All of them provide critical journalism that questions domination, considers social phenomena in their wider context and as complex, dynamic and changeable, and keeps alive the vision of potential social alternatives that can be achieved through social struggles. Their critical journalism covers issues and provides viewpoints that are largely neglected by corporate media. Democracy Now for example highlights "Democracy Now!'s War and Peace Report provides our audience with access to people and perspectives rarely heard in the U.S. corporate-sponsored media".[18] To acquire the necessary income for producing critical media content, alternative media projects depend on public support and individual donations. Some of them have also chosen to sell space for advertisements. However, it is often difficult for alternative media that are critical of consumer culture and capitalism to attract advertisers. Furthermore this entails the danger of becoming dependent on advertisers and losing their independence. Reviewing access statistics on the Internet shows that alternative media receive much less attention than corporate media. Democracynow.org for examples is ranked at 20,854[19] on the Alexa Traffic Ranking, while News Corp's Foxnews. com is ranked at 187.[20] Similarly News Corp's Wsj.com is ranked at 224[21] while Motherjones.com is ranked at 7,727.[22]

Public funding models for journalism would help alternative projects to overcome financial insecurity and to fully focus on the production and distribution of critical media content. Strengthening alternative projects is important in order to challenge the dominance of corporate media that accept and promote the worldviews and interests of a global corporate elite of which they themselves are an essential part.

- *Non-commercial search engines as alternative to the online data commodity*: Creating a common online search infrastructure requires non-commercial initiatives that ensure that search results are not biased because of commercial interests, that do not commodify user data and that protect the privacy of Internet users. Such non-commercial alternatives are rare. One subversive example of how to bypass Google's data collection is the non-commercial project Scroogle[23] that used Google search while blocking Google's cookies, which hinders Google from collecting any information. In early 2012 the project had to be discontinued because Google blocked Scroogle through throttling its servers.[24] Users, however, can use legal ad-block software in order to prevent Google from displaying advertisements to them. This has the potential to undermine Google's business model.

  Furthermore non-commercial alternatives to Google exist. Metager for example is a meta-search engine project, run by the Leibniz University Hannover and the non-profit association SuMa-eV.[25] Metager does not store any user information or displays advertisements or sponsored links. Thus far non-commercial search engines are not only the exception, but furthermore not very well-known. In Alexa Traffic Ranking Metager.de is ranked at 110,143[26] and Metager2.de is ranked at 1,732,295,[27] while Google.com is ranked first as the most widely used website,[28] and Google.de is ranked at 24.[29]

  Strengthening non-commercial search engines is important for providing alternatives to advertising-funded commercial projects that force users to constantly view advertisements and that collect and sell massive amounts of user data. In times in which the vast majority of the collective knowledge of society is stored online, dedicating public money to creating a common infrastructure that makes these collective knowledge resources accessible and searchable seems crucial.

- *Community WiFi as alternative to Internet access restrictions*: Community WiFi projects are based on the idea of sharing Internet access. Around the world various projects exist that aim at making Internet access available in public spaces and for underserved communities. NYCWireless, a New York based NGO, for example has built free public wireless Internet networks in parks and underserved neighbourhoods in New York City.[30] In Germany, the non-commercial initiative Freifunk[31] aims at facilitating community Internet access. Free and open community networks according to Freifunk include: "public accessibility (open for everybody) non-commercial (not part of an enterprise business strategy) communityowned (not owned by a single person/organization) uncensored" (Freifunk 2006). To enable the creation of such networks, Freifunk has developed the FeifunkFirmware (FFF) that can be installed on WiFi routers in order to set up and run Freifunk community networks (Freifunk 2006). The association Free Networks supports the creation of free network access worldwide. In its directory Free Networks lists numerous community wireless projects around the globe.[32] All of these projects are run by non-commercial organizations or dedicated individuals who envision a shared and universally accessible Internet.

The alternatives described in this chapter anticipate in different ways the logic of the common. They establish collective ownership of means of production, foster participation and democratic decision making, support the free sharing of commons, the protection of nature, and equal access to all knowledge resources of society. However, their development is hampered because they are surrounded by a social environment that is based on the logic of property. The logic of property continuously attempts to encroach upon them: alternative projects that anticipate the logic of the common, such as the idea of free software and open source, critical alternative media, worker-owned co-operatives, free music file-sharing, community WiFi projects, or non-commercial search engines, are threatened to be either exploited by the logic of property or to be marginalized or destroyed. Furthermore alternative projects often suffer from a lack of resources and therefore depend on the unpaid work of volunteers and often remain marginal (Sandoval and Fuchs 2010; Sandoval 2011).

It is an important task for progressive political reforms to improve the conditions under which alternative projects are operating for example through employing redistributive measures in order to provide financial support to alternative projects. Strengthening such alternatives is crucial for overcoming the social irresponsibility of a commercial media system and increasing the prospects of creating a commons based, socially responsible media culture.

Notes

1 The Toolbox for Education and Social Action. See: http://toolboxfored.org/
2 Ronin Tech Collective. See: http://www.ronin.coop/
3 Quilted. See: http://quilted.coop/
4 RepRap. Retrieved from http://reprap.org/wiki/RepRap on July 31, 2012.
5 RepRap. Retrieved from http://reprap.org/wiki/RepRap on July 31, 2012.
6 RepRap. Video introduction to RepRap. Retrieved from http://vimeo.com/5202148 on July 31, 3012.
7 Recomputer. *Sustainable Cardboard Computer*. Retrieved from http://www.recomputepc.com/ on July 30, 2012.
8 Recomputer. *About. Philosophy*. Retrieved from http://recomputepc.com/index.php/about/about-philosophy on July 30, 2012.

9   Recomputer. *About. Philosophy.* Retrieved from http://recomputepc.com/index.php/about/about-philosophy on July 30, 2012.

10 Amanda Palmer. Retrieved from http://music.amandapalmer.net/album/amanda-palmer-performs-the-popular-hits-of-radiohead-on-her-magical-ukulele on September 21, 2011.

11 Electronic Frontier Foundation. 2008. *A Better Way Forward: Voluntary Collective Licensing of Music File Sharing.* Retrieved from https://www.eff.org/wp/better-way-forward-voluntary-collective-licensing-music-file-sharing/ on September 21, 2011.

12 The Free Software Foundation. *Philosophy.* Retrieved from http://www.gnu.org/philosophy/free-sw.en.htmlon July 29, 2012.

13 The Open Source Initiative. *FAQs.* Retrieved from http://opensource.org/faq#commercial on July 29, 2012.

14 The Free Software Foundation. *Philosophy.* Retrieved from http://www.gnu.org/philosophy/categories.en.html on July 29, 2012.

15 The Open Source Initiative. *FAQs.* Retrieved from http://opensource.org/faq#copyleft on July 29, 2012.

16 The Free Software Foundation. *Philosophy.* Retrieved from http://www.gnu.org/philosophy/categories.en.html on July 29, 2012.

17 The Open Source Initiative. *FAQs.* Retrieved from http://opensource.org/faq#copyleft on July 29, 2012.

18 Democracy Now. *About.* Retrieved from http://www.democracynow.org/about on July 29, 2012.

19 Alexa Traffic Ranking. *Democracynow.org.* Retrieved from http://www.alexa.com/siteinfo/democracynow.org on July 29, 2012.

20 Alexa Traffic Ranking. *Foxnews.com.* Retrieved from http://www.alexa.com/siteinfo/foxnews.com on July 29, 2012.

21 Alexa Traffic Ranking. *Wsj.com.* Retrieved from http://www.alexa.com/siteinfo/wsj.com on July 29, 2012.

22 Alexa Traffic Ranking. *Motherjones.com.* Retrieved from http://www.alexa.com/siteinfo/motherjones.com on July 29, 2011.

23 http://www.scroogle.org/

24 Scroogle. *So Sorry . . .* Retrieved from http://www.scroogle.org/sucks.html on July 30, 2012.

25 Metager2. *Support.* Retrieved from http://metager2.de/support.php on July 29, 2012.

26 Alexa Traffic Ranking. *Metager.de.* Retrieved from http://www.alexa.com/siteinfo/metager.de on July 19, 2013.

27 Alexa Traffic Ranking. *Metager2.de.* Retrieved from http://www.alexa.com/siteinfo/metager2.de on July 19, 2013.

28 Alexa Traffic Ranking. *Google.com.* Retrieved from http://www.alexa.com/siteinfo/google.com on July 19, 2013.

29 Alexa Traffic Ranking. *Google.de.* Retrieved from http://www.alexa.com/siteinfo/google.de on July 19, 2013.

30 NYCWireless. *About.* Retrieved from http://nycwireless.net/about-us/ on July 26, 2012.

31 Freifunk. See: http://start.freifunk.net/

32 FreeNetworks. *Directory.* Retrieved from http://freenetworks.org/freenetworks-members-affiliates.shtml on July 26th, 2012.

15 Conclusion
Social media as commons based media

In order to conclude the study at hand, I will first provide answers to the research questions posed in the introduction (Chapter 1). Based on this presentation of results I will subsequently discuss whether contemporary media and communication companies have monstrous features, introduce a counter-concept to CSR and identify strategies for emancipatory social transformation.

CSR: from corporate to social media?

The main concern of this book was to study the theory and practices of CSR in the media and communication industries and to assess to what extent these two aspects contribute to achieving a socially responsible media and communication system.

Chapter 2 discussed the role and responsibilities of individual corporations. I argued that the question of CSR relates to the purpose of the corporation and thereby raises new questions regarding the relation between the corporate and the social.

Based on Wolfgang Hofkirchner's (2002, 2003) distinction of ways of thinking, I identified four ways of how CSR theories relate profit and social goals of the corporation: reductionism, projectionism, dualism and dialectics.

- Reductionist approaches (see Chapter 2, "Reductionism – instrumentalizing the social") reduce CSR to a means for advancing corporate profit goals. They describe CSR as a business opportunity in so far as it helps finding and entering new markets and creating competitive advantages through building a good image and reputation. From this perspective, a socially responsible corporation is a corporation that maximizes profits and turns social problems into business opportunities.
- Projectionist approaches (see Chapter 2, "Projectionism – idealizing the corporate") argue that in order to be socially responsible the business goals of corporations should be guided by values or a special concern for society and the environment. The profit motive becomes subordinated to the greater goal of acting socially responsible. According to this view, a socially responsible corporation subjects its profit goals to ethical norms, or the expectations of society, or regulation, or a social and environmental consciousness.

- Dualist approaches (see Chapter 2, "Dualism – separating the corporate and the social") separate the social goals and the profit goals of the corporation from each other. Being profitable and acting socially responsible are perceived as two separate goals of the corporation. Following this perspective, a socially responsible corporation maximizes profits and gives back to society through philanthropic giving or other social activities.
- Dialectical approaches (see Chapter 2, "Dialetics – problematizing the relation between the corporate and the social") problematize the relation between profit goals and social responsibility. Based on a dialectical perspective, it becomes possible to observe how pursuing its profit goals shapes the social performance of a corporation and how acting socially responsible influences the corporation's profit goals.

Reductionist, projectionist, as well as dualist approaches never question the profit motive. The superiority of capitalism thus remains unquestioned. By failing to reflect on their own normative foundations, these approaches take the existence of capitalist social relations for granted and thereby contribute to the naturalization of capitalism, which makes it appear fixed and unchangeable. Dialectical approaches on the contrary emerge out of a critique of other CSR theories. They argue that the fact that corporations in some cases act "socially responsible" should not distract from looking at the broader picture that reveals that many of the problems humanity is facing today have been and will continue to be created through the exploitative, expansive, competitive and profit-maximizing logic of capitalism. According to this perspective, the fundamental contradiction between profit and social responsibility can only be sublated by an alternative mode of economic and social organization that is radically democratic at the economic and political level.

Departing from this typology of ways of thinking about CSR, in the next chapter (Chapter 3) I discussed different approaches to CSR in media and communication industries. I first suggested a systematic model of the media and communication industries that includes media production, distribution, consumption, and, as a feature of online media industries, prosumption (see Figure 3.1). This model on the one hand shows how media content circulates through these different stages, and on the other hand illustrates which industries are involved in making these communication flows possible. The industries I identified are: the media content industry; the media technology industry which consists of the media hardware and the media software; the media distribution industry; and the online media industry.

After having clarified the definition of the media and communication industries, I applied the typology of CSR approaches to theories of the social responsibility of media companies:

- Reductionist approaches stress that media and communication companies should employ CSR strategically in order to be able to exploit competitive advantages (see Chapter 3, "Reductionism – social responsibility as strategic advantage").

- Projectionist approaches argue that media, despite their commercial organization, should fulfil the expectations of society. Following this perspective, socially responsible media resist commercial pressures towards irresponsible behaviour by basing their operations on ethical principles and guidelines (see Chapter 3, "Projectionism – ethics in a commercial media system").

- Dualist approaches separate business goals and social responsibility and argue that both can be achieved independently from each other. This approach for example characterizes theories that consider media and journalism as two distinct areas, whereby media are supposed to be economically successful, while journalism is supposed to be ethical and socially responsible (see Chapter 3, "Dualism – commercial success and ethical behaviour").

- Dialectical approaches focus on how the profit goals and social responsibilities of the media mutually shape each other. From this perspective, the economic success and profitability of media companies have consequences that impair their social responsibility. On the other hand, socially responsible media that resist commercial mechanisms and market pressures are likely to suffer from a lack of resources and visibility. The idea of public broadcasting is based on a dialectical approach to the social responsibility of the media as it recognizes that in order to fulfil their social responsibility media need to be freed from the pressure to be profitable (see Chapter 3, "Dialectics – the social irresponsibility of commercial media").

However, in times of neo-liberal privatization and deregulation this model has been substantially weakened. With the decline of the public service broadcasting model the success of the commercial media has become complete. The questions of how commercial mechanisms affect the social responsibilities of the media in their everyday operations, and how this shapes media and communication in the twenty-first century thus becomes ever more important

I therefore argued that a dialectical perspective is the most promising for empirically researching the social responsibilities of media and communication in the context of contemporary capitalism: such an approach allows the identification and study of areas of conflict between the private interest of companies and the public good in the information age.

In Chapter 4 I suggested a critical content analysis that compares corporate self-descriptions to assessments made by corporate watchdogs in order to critically analyse CSR approaches, CSR practices, and CSR challenges of eight of the biggest media and communication companies: Apple, AT&T, Google, HP, Microsoft, News Corp, Vivendi, and The Walt Disney Company.

In Chapters 5–12 I presented the analysis of the CSR approaches and practices of eight of the biggest media and communication companies: Apple, AT&T, Google, HP, Microsoft, News Corp, The Walt Disney Company and Vivendi. The analysis focused on a variety of social responsibility topics that shape media and communication industries in the twenty-first century: software patents (Microsoft), media ideologies (News Cop), user privacy and commodification of data

(Google), net neutrality (AT&T), peer-to-peer file-sharing (Vivendi), working conditions in the supply chain (Apple and Disney) and e-waste (HP).

The study results that I summarized and evaluated in Chapter 13 show that although the amount of CSR information provided varies considerably between companies, all of them describe themselves as socially responsible (see "CSR approaches"). Looking at concrete corporate practices however reveals a different picture (see "CSR practices"). Economic indicators showed that in financial terms the first decade of the twenty-first century was highly successful for the media and communication companies studied. Google is the fastest growing company within the sample. Between 2001 and 2010 its profit grew on average by 103 per cent every year. Apple follows Google with a compound annual profit growth rate of 33 per cent between 2000 and 2010. Likewise, the remaining companies have high average annual profit growth rates ranging between 7 and 15 per cent (see Table 15.1)

While the companies studied were successful in terms of profit, they did not succeed in meeting their social responsibilities. For all the companies studied, watchdog criticism revealed a number of corporate social irresponsibilities such as labour rights violations (Apple, Disney), threats to human health and the environment through e-waste (HP), the monopolization of knowledge through software patents (Microsoft), the creation of cultural enclosures through music copyrights (Vivendi), the promotion of destructive ideologies (News Corp), the commodification of user data and the surveillance of Internet users (Google) and the promotion of digital inequality (AT&T).

Based on the analysis of how companies react to this criticism in their CSR communications, I identified four response strategies: HP, Disney and Apple acknowledge that their business practices create certain social and environmental problems, while they at the same time downplay the extent of the problem

Table 15.1 Compound annual growth rates of media and communication companies

Company	Years	Compound annual growth rate (percentage)
Google	2001–2010	103
Apple	2000–2010	33
Walt Disney	2000–2010	15
News Corp	2003–2010	12
Vivendi	2004–2010	10
HP	2000–2010	9
AT&T	2000–2010	9
Microsoft	2000–2010	7

Source: SEC filings and company reports.[1]

Notes
1 Data is based on the companies' official SEC filings as available in the Edgar database: http:// www.sec.gov/edgar/searchedgar/companysearch.html

For Vivendi data is based on official financial reports as available on the company homepage: http:// www.vivendi.com/vivendi/Financial-Reports

CAGR is calculated as follows: CAGR = (ending value/beginning value) (1/#of years) -1.

and promise solutions (strategy of admit, downplay and promise solutions). Here some degree of agreement between companies and watchdogs exists. Companies that use any of the three other strategies on the contrary do not agree with the criticism raised by corporate watchdogs. They either redefine the criticized issue and describe the same business practices that watchdogs characterize as irresponsible as socially responsible (strategy of redefinition, for example Microsoft, Vivendi and Google), or they ignore the criticized issue altogether (strategy of ignorance, for example AT&T), or try to find how to address the criticized issue in a way that benefits their profit goals (strategy of incorporation, for example Microsoft).

The criticism raised by watchdogs and the inability of companies to offer adequate solutions to the issues points to the existence of fundamental challenges for the concept of CSR in the media and communication sector and in general. Based on the comparison of watchdog criticisms and corporate self-descriptions regarding the issues studied, I identified seven social responsibility challenges for media and communication in the twenty-first century (see "CSR challenges"):

- alienated, precarious labour vs self-determined knowledge work (Apple & Disney)
- digital inequality vs an egalitarian Internet (AT&T)
- the threat of e-waste vs green IT (HP)
- data commodification vs public online infrastructure (Google)
- knowledge monopoly vs collective knowledge resources (Microsoft)
- media as instruments of ideologies vs media as critical public watchdogs (News Corp)
- cultural enclosures vs an open and accessible culture (Vivendi).

These results illustrate the existence of an antagonism between productive forces and relations of production (Marx 1859/1994, 211) in the contemporary media and communication system. Today's productive forces in the realm of media and communication could enable self-managed knowledge work, the development of green IT products, the creation of an open and accessible culture, collective knowledge resources, the functioning of media as critical public watchdogs, the creation of a free online infrastructure and an egalitarian Internet. However, the realization of these potentials that arise from the development of the productive forces is constrained by the capitalist relations of production that depend on and produce the exploitation of labour power and nature, the creation of cultural enclosures and knowledge monopolies, and the media as instruments of ideology, commodification and inequality.

In interpreting these empirical results (Chapter 14) I argued that the contemporary media and communication system is characterized by a contradiction between the logic of property and the logic of the common. The logic of the common is based on common ownership (economy), participatory decision power (politics) and universal values (culture); while the logic of private property is based on private ownership (economy), elitist decision power (politics), and particularist values (culture) (see "Conceptualizing the logic of property and the logic of the common").

The results of this study illustrate that media and communication companies on all these levels exhibit the logic of property (see "Critique: the logic of property in the media and communication system"): economically they exploit the labour commons, destroy the eco-social commons and appropriate the network common. Politically the companies studied monopolize decision power about how media and communication should be organized. Culturally in their CSR reports the companies studied refer to universal values that characterize the logic of the common, while actual corporate practices privilege profit maximization over the common good.

The concept of CSR serves as an ideology that creates legitimacy for corporate practices that follow the logic of property and the particularist value of profit maximization. Despite CSR a commercial media system remains an essentially private media system that privileges private profit interests over social needs. I argued that fostering a truly socially responsible media and communication system for the twenty-first century requires strengthening the logic of the common (see "Alternatives: the logic of the common in the media and communication system") and proposed several starting points for establishing alternatives:

- worker owned co-operatives as alternative to precarious and alienated labour
- eco-friendly computers as an alternative to short-lived toxic products
- shared art as alternative to copyrighted music
- FOSS as an alternative to proprietary software
- critical media as alternative to commercialized media
- non-commercial search engines as alternative to the online data commodity
- community WiFi as alternative to Internet access restrictions.

Despite the fact that these alternatives exist, their development is nonetheless hampered as they are surrounded by a social environment that is based on the logic of property. The logic of property continuously attempts to encroach upon them: alternative projects that anticipate the logic of the common are threatened to either be exploited by the logic of property or to be marginalized or destroyed.

Based on these results it is now possible to answer the main research question of this study:

> What do the theory and practice of corporate social responsibility look like in the media and communication industries and to what extent can these two aspects contribute to achieving a socially responsible media and communication system?

All the media and communication companies studied claim that their business practices are socially responsible. Their approaches to CSR are based on the assumption that profit goals and social responsibilities are reconcilable. They employ a reductionist, projectionist and/or dualist CSR rhetoric according to which acting responsibly is beneficial for profit goals (reductionism); requires responsible profit generation that is guided by values or a concern for society and the environment (projectionism); or can be realized in parallel to achieving profit goals (dualism). Unsurprisingly, none of the companies studied takes a dialectical perspective and considers the potential conflicts between profit goals and social responsibilities. Despite CSR, the legitimacy of the profit motive as such and thus the legitimacy of a commercial media model remain unquestioned.

The study of the actual business practices of the media and communication companies revealed that while the companies were successful in reaching their profit goals, at the same time they failed to act socially responsible. The analysis presented here shows that, despite CSR, the business practices of media and communication companies often conflict with the common good.

These results indicate that the way media and communication companies understand and practice CSR today does not contribute to the creation of a genuinely social media system as a socially responsible media system. The business practices of the companies studied are restricting access to media and communication and thus fostering an unequal media culture, hampering the solidary sharing of information and communication resources, and restricting freedom of social participation. They furthermore design and produce technologies in a way that benefits their profit goals by creating inhumane working conditions and destructive impacts on nature.

Boltanski and Chiapello argue that

> the persistence of capitalism, as a mode of co-ordinating action and a lived world, cannot be understood without considering the ideologies which, in justifying and conferring a meaning on it, help to elicit the good will of those on whom it is based, and ensure their engagement.
>
> (Boltanski and Chiapello 2007, 12)

They call these justifying ideologies the "spirit of capitalism" (Boltanski and Chiapello 2007, 8). CSR can be described as such an ideology that provides a moral justification for capitalism and as a part of the contemporary spirit of capitalism. The increased talk about CSR thus needs to be viewed in connection with the transformation of capitalism since the 1970s and the emergence of post-Fordist capitalism (see for example Hanlon and Fleming 2009, 943). CSR matches the logic of contemporary capitalism: in the context of globalization and neo-liberal deregulation, which created regulatory gaps, the idea of socially responsible corporations for example is used as an argument to legitimize deregulation and voluntary corporate self-regulation (Shamir 2004, 677; Sklair and Miller 2010, 491). In the context of the diversification of commodities and the rising importance of brands (Klein 2000, 3; Lash and Lury 2007, 6), CSR furthermore becomes a necessary component of corporate image and reputation management. In addition, rising socio-economic inequality, economic crisis and critique raised by protest movements create the need to sustain the legitimacy of corporations and capitalism. Thus CSR fits well into the logic of the contemporary phase of capitalism, rather than posing a challenge to it.

However, using CSR as a legitimating ideology at the same time requires companies to justify to what extent their practices are socially responsible and to publish CSR reports. Thereby companies also provide information based on which they can be held accountable. Through comparing these corporate self-descriptions to context information and assessments by independent watchdog organizations I showed that CSR serves as an ideology that diverts attention away from actual existing corporate social irresponsibilities and thereby strengthens the legitimacy of capitalism. Despite its reference to universal social values, current theories and practices of CSR as such do not promote a socially responsible media system and a shift from corporate to social media.

Monster media?

Rather than contributing to a social media system, the companies studied are appropriating the eco-social, labour and network commons of society in order to generate private profit. The metaphor of the monster is thus still valid for describing informational capitalism: like Dracula, who feeds on human blood, media and communication companies are feeding on the commons of society. They feed on the network commons by privatizing them, on the labour commons by exploiting them and on the eco-social commons by destructing them: for the sake of profit, the media and communication companies studied privatize the network commons, create artificial scarcity and thereby hamper their development; they exploit human labour power often under conditions that resemble nineteenth century capitalism that Marx (1867/1990) described; they threaten the eco-social commons through products that have destructive effects on human health and the environment.

But contemporary media and communication companies are not only like Dracula, they furthermore also resemble the story of Frankenstein and his monster. Moretti highlights:

> On the one hand, the scientist cannot but create the monster [. . .] On the other hand, he is immediately afraid of it and wants to kill it, because he realizes he has given life to a creature stronger than himself and of which he cannot henceforth be free.
>
> (Moretti 1982, 69)

Frankenstein's monster is commonly interpreted to represent the proletariat (Moretti 1982, 1999; Montag 2000). However, it could also represent the commons. Media and communication organizations cannot but produce the commons. All knowledge and information depends on previous knowledge; it is collectively produced by all members of society. In this context Marx argued that all "scientific work, all discovery and invention" is "universal labour", which "is brought about partly by the cooperation of men now living, but partly also by building on earlier work" (Marx 1894/1991, 199). Thus, all knowledge and information, including the products media companies are producing, depend on the collective cultural and knowledge resources of society and therefore are always part of the commons. Like Frankenstein could not but create the monster, media and communication companies cannot but contribute to the production of the commons. At the same time, the commons also pose a threat to media companies, like the monster threatened Frankenstein.

In respect to Frankenstein, Morretti argues: "The fear aroused by the monster, in other words, is the fear of one who is afraid of having 'produced his own grave-diggers'" (Moretti 1982, 69). Media and communication companies experience the same fear in regard to the commons. On the one hand they need the commons, on the other hand the logic of the commons threatens them as it contradicts their profit goals. To accumulate profit, most media and communication companies produce knowledge, information and cultural products. Such products are not scarce as they are not consumed during usage and they can be easily shared. These qualities contradict the logic of exchanging commodities; they exhibit the logic of sharing commons. In order to confront that threat and to protect their profits, after producing the commons, media companies must immediately capture them through patents, property rights and access restrictions. These practices benefit the goal of corporate profit, but at the same time hamper the creation of an open, accessible and flourishing media and communication culture.

Frankenstein's creation became monstrous because Frankenstein abandoned him, leaving him isolated with no chance to socialize. Frankenstein's monster addresses his creator: "Believe me, Frankenstein: I was benevolent; my soul glowed with love and humanity: but am I not alone, miserably alone?" (Shelley 1818/2000, 94). Frankenstein felt threatened by his creation and thus abandoned it; media and communication companies feel threatened by the products on which their profit is based, and thus capture them through imposing on them property rights and access restrictions. In different ways, both Frankenstein's monster and media and communication products are kept from becoming social, but instead remain individualized, private, and thus monstrous.

The contemporary media and communication landscape thus represent both archetypical monsters of modern Western literature – Dracula and Frankenstein's monster. The capitalist media landscape is shaped by an antagonism between Dracula and Frankenstein's monster – media and communication companies and the communication commons.

From CSR to RSC

The results of this study show that CSR cannot fulfil its promises, it cannot wipe off the monstrous features of capital, it cannot make corporate media social. Nonetheless, the increased quest for CSR reveals a desire for an economy that ensures social and environmental responsibility. CSR reflects the desire to make profit compatible with the common good, to make profit more social.

254 *Conclusion: commons based media*

Karl Marx once argued:

> Reason has always existed but not always in rational form. The critic, there-
> fore, can start with any form of theoretical and practical consciousness and
> develop the true actuality out of the forms inherent in existing actuality as its
> ought-to-be and goal.

(Marx 1843/1997, 213)

The concept of CSR is an ideology. But this ideology entails, as Marx described, a rational element. It entails the desire for a socially responsible economy. However, the way CSR is understood and practiced today does not contribute to this goal. CSR proposes making profit social through either extending its reach (reductionism), taming it through imposing values upon it (projectionism), or balancing it through supporting social projects (dualism). As this study has shown, none of these approaches can succeed in turning profit socially responsible.

In order to realize the rational element entailed in CSR, it is necessary to go beyond CSR. For that purpose one can employ a technique that Marx suggested for discovering the "rational kernel" in Hegel's idealist understanding of dialectics. Marx argued that Hegel's dialectics "is standing on its head. It must be inverted, in order to discover the rational kernel within the mystical shell" (Marx 1867/1990, 103). The same holds true for CSR. In order to discover its "rational kernel" within the "mystical shell", CSR must be turned from its head to its feet. Turned from its head to its feet, corporate social responsibility (CSR) turns into the responsibility to socialize corporations (RSC).

RSC is the logical continuation of a dialectical perspective on CSR that considers conflicts between the profit motive and social responsibility: in order to become truly social, capitalist corporations need to be socialized, so that private wealth turns into common wealth. Private profit is based on the principle of feeding on the common resources of society (labour power, natural resources, knowledge resources, etc.) and turning them into private property. Generating profit thus means that private wealth is maximized at the cost of general social well-being. Thus, only if the creation of economic wealth no longer takes on the form of private profit, that is, only if general economic wealth supersedes private profit, can the conflict between economic goals and social responsibility be resolved. This requires the socialization of the societal logic from private property to common property, from elitist decision making to participatory decision making and from particularistic values to universal values.

Freed from the need to accumulate and maximize private profits, media and communication companies could realize their full potentials and contribute to the common good: socializing media and communication companies, turning them into genuinely social media, would allow them to transform private profit into common value by realizing self-managed knowledge work, developing green IT products, creating an open and accessible culture, collective knowledge resources, establishing media as critical public watchdogs, creating free online infrastructure and an egalitarian Internet.

Radical reformism as a strategy of social transformation

The quest for RSC as a means for making the economy truly social and contributing to the realization of a global sustainable information society (Hofkirchner et al. 2007), raises the question of how to promote emancipatory social transformations. Eric Olin Wright argues that emancipatory social transformation requires social empowerment in the form of democratic control over the state and the "subordination of economic power to social power" (Olin Wright 2010, 367f), which according to him means "that private ownership of the means of production ceases to govern the allocation and use of productive resources" (Olin Wright 2010, 368).

Olin Wright distinguishes three models of transformation: ruptural, interstitial and symbiotic (Olin Wright 2010, 304). He argues that ruptural transformations aim at immediate revolutionary transformations "through direct confrontation and struggle" (Olin Wright 2010, 303). Interstitial transformations aim at building alternatives "in the niches and margins of capitalist society" without posing a direct threat to the dominant system (Olin Wright 2010, 303f). Symbiotic transformations aim at reforms that simultaneously contribute to social empowerment and also are in the interest of dominant classes as they help to solve the practical problems of capitalism (Olin Wright 2010, 305). According to Olin Wright, these three approaches correspond to revolutionary (ruptural), anarchist (interstitial) and social democratic (symbiotic) traditions of conceptualizing social transformations (Olin Wright 2010, 305).

The approaches that Olin Wright describes either opt for immediate revolutionary transformation, the creation of non-capitalist alternatives within capitalism, or immanent reforms. However, there is also a fourth option that is based on a dialectics of reform and revolution. Such a perspective advocates a gradual transformation through reforms that increase social empowerment over the state and the economy and thus at the same time improve the conditions for a more radical social transformation. Radical reforms thus want to achieve immediate improvements and social empowerment and through these improvements also open up spaces for advancing the long-term goal of a social alternative. Radical reformism can thereby employ social movement activism as well as party politics. Adding a revolutionary perspective could expand the prospects of both anarchist counter-projects and social democratic reformism and create synergy effects between them. It adds an expansive element to anarchist projects, in such a way that they no longer limit themselves to being small-scale counter-projects but become expanding social alternatives. At the same time party politics and political reforms that do not confine themselves to immanent improvements, but take a transcendent perspective, could help to improve the objective conditions for such an expansion of alternative projects.

In Chapter 13, I proposed starting points for alternative, civil society projects that strengthen the logic of the common, such as building worker owned media and communication co-operatives; developing eco-friendly computers; sharing art; supporting non-commercial FOSS; creating alternative critical media; non-commercial search engines; and community WiFi projects.

However, these alternatives, like most non-commercial projects, often suffer from a lack of financial resources, which makes it difficult for them to compete with commercial companies. These problems are related to the fact that alternative projects cannot operate outside the logic of capitalism. Non-commercial projects face difficulties in acquiring the money that is necessary for paying employees, acquiring necessary production resources, regularly producing their products, maintaining their services, advertising them and so on. It is therefore necessary to provide structural support for alternative projects and to initiate political reforms to improve the conditions for their development and expansion. In Chapter 2, I suggested starting points for radical reforms that:

- strengthen democracy (e.g. through public funding of civil society groups and social movements, more direct forms of political decision making, freely accessible political education, etc.)
- democratize the workplace (e.g. through guaranteeing workers the right to participate in corporate decision-making processes including decisions about wages and working hours and to support worker unions and worker-owned co-operatives)
- reduce poverty and socio-economic inequality (e.g. through the redistribution of wealth through fiscal policies, the introduction of a guaranteed basic income, worldwide legal minimum wages, worldwide laws against child labour, the reduction of the working week, anti-discrimination laws, abolition of laws that restrict migration, the full cancellation of third world debts, public provision of health care, pensions, education and infrastructure including access to media, ICTs and the Internet)
- restrict corporate power (e.g. through economic regulations, control of capital flows, nationalization of the banking system, public funding of civil society watchdog organizations and alternative media that report about corporate crimes and wrongdoings around the world, etc.) and
- strengthen those tendencies that entail the potential of going beyond capitalism and contradict the capitalist private property logic and are based on the idea of the common (e.g. through the abolition of intellectual property rights and the support of initiatives that strengthen the common such as the open source movement, file-sharing, or Wikipedia).

A radical reformism that combines social movement activism, bottom-up alternative projects and structural reforms could help to realize RSC, the responsibility to socialize corporations. Theories of CSR largely remain within the boundaries of corporate capitalism. In practice, CSR cannot fulfil its promise of ensuring social responsibility within the confines of a private media industry. The idea of RSC adds a transcendent perspective to the debate on social responsibility and insists on the real possibility of alternative forms of economic and social organizations. RSC highlights that freeing the media from their monstrous appearance and creating a socially responsible media system requires non-commercial alternatives. Moving from corporate to social media thus means replacing the privately owned and controlled commercial media system with a commonly owned and controlled commons based media system. This, however, is a long-term, indeterminate political process that is subject to social struggles.

References

Abbott, Walter F. and R. Joseph Monsen. 1979. On the measurement of corporate social responsibility: self-reported disclosure as a method of measuring corporate social investment. *The Academy of Management Journal* 22(3), 501–515.

Adams, Carol A., Hill, Wan-Ying and Clare B. Roberts. 1998. Corporate social reporting practices in Western Europe: legitimating corporate behaviour? *British Accounting Journal* 30, 1–21.

Adorno, Theodor W. 1957/1976. Sociology and empirical research. In *The Positivist Dispute in German Sociology*, 68–86. London: Heinemann.

Adorno, Theodor W. 1962/1976. On the logics of the social sciences. In *The Positivist Dispute in German Sociology*, 105–122. London: Heinemann.

Adorno, Theodor W. 1963/2000. *Problems of Moral Philosophy*. Oxford: Polity.

Adorno, Theodor W. 1968/2002. *Introduction to Sociology. Lectures*. Cambridge: Polity.

Adorno, Theodor W. 1969/1976. Introduction. In *The Positivist Dispute in German Sociology*, 1–67. London: Heinemann.

Adorno, Theodor W. 1972. Ideology. In *Aspects of Sociology*. Boston: Bacon Press.

Adorno, Theodor W. 1972/1995. Gesellschaftstheorie und empirische Forschung. In Theodor W. Adorno. *Soziologische Schriften*, 538–546. Frankfurt: Suhrkamp.

Albarran, Alan B. 2010. *The Media Economy*. New York: Routledge.

Allmer, Thomas. 2012. Critical Internet surveillance studies and economic surveillance. In *Internet and Surveillance*, 124–143, edited by Christian Fuchs, Kees Bursma, Anders Albrechtslund and Marisol Sandoval. New York: Routledge

Almeder, Robert. 1980. The ethics of profits: reflections on corporate social responsibility. *Business and Society* 19(2), 7–14.

Altmeppen, Dieter. 2011. Journalistische Berichterstattung und die Verantwortung von Medienunternehmen: Über die doppelte Verantwortung von Medienunternehmen. In *Handbuch CSR*, 247–266, edited by Juliana Raupp, Stefan Jarolimek and Friederike Schultz. Wiesbaden: VS.

American Society of Newspaper Editors. 1923. *Codes of Ethics or Canons of Journalism*. Retrieved from http://ethics.iit.edu/indexOfCodes-2.php?key=18_113_1262 on March 6, 2011.

Arsenault, Amelia. 2011. The structure and dynamics of communications business networks. Mapping the global networks of the information business. In *The Political Economies of Media*, edited by Dwayne Winseck and Dal Yong Jin, 101–120. London: Bloomsbury.

Arsenault, Amelia and Manuel Castells. 2008. Switching power: Rupert Murdoch and the global business of media politics: A sociological analysis. *International Sociology* 23(4), 488–513.

Atkinson, Paul and Amanda Coffey. 2004. Analysing documentary realities. In *Qualitative Research. Theory, Method and Practice*. 2nd edition. Edited by David Silverman, 56–75. London: Sage.

AT&T. 2010. *Letter to the FCC*. Retrieved from http://fjallfoss.fcc.gov/ecfs2/document/view.action?id=7020910395 on December 12, 2011.

Babbie, Earl. 2010. *The Practice of Social Research*. 12th edition. Belmont: Wadsworth.

Backman, J. 1975. *Social Responsibility and Accountability*. Reston: Reston Publishing.

Baker, Dean. 2003. *The Artistic Freedom Voucher: An Internet Age Alternative to Copyrights. Center for Economic and Policy Research Briefing Paper*. Retrieved from http://www.cepr.net/documents/publications/ip_2003_11.pdf on September 23, 2011.

BAN. 2005. *The Digital Dump. Exporting Re-Use and Abuse to Africa*. Retrieved from http://www.ban.org/BANreports/10-24-05/documents/TheDigitalDump.pdf on November 6, 2011.

BAN and SVTC. 2002. *Exporting Harm. The High-Tech Trashing of Asia*. Retrieved from http://www.ban.org/E-waste/technotrashfinalcomp.pdf on November 6, 2011.

Banerjee, Subhabrata Bobby. 2007. *Corporate Social Responsibility. The Good the Bad and the Ugly*. Cheltenham: Edward Elgar.

Banerjee, Subhabrata Bobby. 2008. Corporate social responsibility. The good the bad and the ugly. *Critical Sociology* 34(1), 51–79.

Bardoel Jo and Leen d'Haenens. 2004. Media meet the citizen. Beyond market mechanisms and government regulations. *European Journal of Communication* 19(2), 165–194.

Bartkus, Barbara R. and Myron Glassman. 2008. Do firms practice what they preach? The relationship between mission statements and stakeholder management. *Journal of Business Ethics* 83, 207–216.

Bell, Elizabeth, Lynda Haas and Laura Sells (eds). 1995. *From Mouse to Mermaid. The Politics of Film, Gender and Culture*. Bloomington: Indiana University Press.

Belsey, Andrew and Ruth Chadwick. 1992. Preface. In *Ethical Issues in Journalism and the Media*, edited by Andrew Belsey and Ruth Chadwick, xi–xii. London: Routledge

Benhabib, Seyla (1984): The Marxian method of critique: normative presuppositions. *PRAXIS International* 3, 284–298.

Berg, Bruce L. 2001. *Qualitative Research Methods for the Social Sciences*. Needham Heights: Abacom.

Bessen, James and Robert M. Hunt. 2007. An empirical look at software patents. *Journal of Economics and Management Strategy* 16(1), 157–189.

Blackman, Josh. 2008. Omniveillance, Google, privacy in public and the right to your digital identity. *Santa Clara Law Review* 49, 313–392.

Bloch, Ernst 1972. *Subjekt-Objekt. Erläuterungen zu Hegel*. Frankfurt a. Main: Suhrkamp.

Boeyink, David E. 1994. How effective are codes of ethics? A look at three newsrooms. *Journalism and Mass Communication Quarterly* 71, 893–904.

Boje, David M. 2008. Contributions of critical theory ethics for business and public administration. In *Critical Theory Ethics for Business and Public Administration*, 3–28, edited by David M. Boje. Charlotte: Information Age Publishing.

Boltanski, Luc and Eve Chiapello. 2007. *The New Spirit of Capitalism*. London: Verso.

Bowen, Howard. 1953. *Social Responsibilities of the Businessman*. New York: Harper.

boyd, danah. 2009. Social media is here to stay . . . Now what? *Microsoft Research Tech Fest*, Redmond, Washington, February 26. http://www.danah.org/papers/talks/MSRTechFest2009.html

Böhme, Gernot and Nico Stehr. 1986. *The Knowledge Society: The Growing Impact of Knowledge on Social Relations*. Dordrecht: Springer Netherlands.

Brode, Douglas. 2005. *Multiculturalism and the Mouse. Race and Sex in Disney Entertainment.* Austin: University of Texas Press

Bruns, Axel. 2007. Produsage, generation C, and their effects on the democratic process. In *Media in Transition 5.* Retrieved from http://eprints.qut.edu.au/7521/ on September 14, 2009.

Bruun, Lars. 1979. *Professional Codes in Journalism.* Vienna, Austria: International Organization of Journalists.

Buchheit, Paul. 2008. Interview (interviewed by Jessica Livingston). In *Founders at Work: Stories of Startups' Early Days*, 161–172, edited by Jessica Livingston. New York: Springer.

Burke, Lee and Jeanne M. Logsdon. 1996. How corporate social responsibility pays off. *Long Range Planning* 29(4), 495–502.

Byrne, Eleanor and Martin McQuillan. 1999. *Deconstructing Disney.* London: Pluto.

Callinicos, Alex. 2003. *An Anti-Capitalist Manifesto.* Cambridge: Polity.

Carasco, Emily F. and Jang B. Singh. 2003. The content and focus of the codes of ethics of the world's largest transnational corporations. *Business and Society Review* 108(1), 71–94.

Carnegie, Andrew. 1889. Wealth. *The North American Review* 148(391), 653–665.

Carroll, Archie B. 1979. A three-dimensional conceptual model of corporate social performance. *Academy of Management Review* 4, 497–505.

Carroll, Archie B. 1991. The pyramid of corporate social responsibility: towards the moral management of organizational stakeholders. *Business Horizons* 34(4), 39–48.

Carroll, Archie B. 1999. Corporate social responsibility: evolution of a definitional construct. *Business and Society* 38, 268–295.

Castelló, Itziar and Josep M. Lozano. 2011. Searching for new forms of legitimacy through corporate responsibility rhetoric. *Journal of Business Ethics* 100, 11–29.

Castells, Manuel. 1996. *The Rise of the Network Society.* Malden: Blackwell.

Caves, Richard E. 2000. *Creative Industries.* Cambridge: Harvard University Press.

CDP. 2011. *Global 500 Report.* Retrieved from https://www.cdproject.net/CDPResults/CDP-G500-2011-Report.pdf on March 3, 2011.

Charters, Darren. 2002. Electronic monitoring and privacy issues in business-marketing: the ethics of the DoubleClick experience. *Journal of Business Ethics* 35, 243–254.

Chaudhri, Vidhi and Jian Wang. 2007. Communicating corporate social responsibility on the Internet: a case study of the top 100 information technology companies in India. *Management Communication Quarterly* 21, 232–247.

Cheng, Hsing Kenneth, Subhajyoti Bandyopadhyay and Hong Guo. 2011. The debate on net neutrality. A policy perspective. *Information Systems Research* 22(1), 60–82.

Cerf, Vinton. 2009. The open Internet. What it is, and why it matters. *Telecommunication Journal of Australia* 59(2), 18.1–18.10.

China Labour Watch. 2009. *Shattered Dreams: Underage Worker Death at Factory Supplying to Disney, Other International Brands.* Retrieved from http://chinalaborwatch.org/pro/proshow-106.htmlon August 29, 2011.

China Labour Watch. 2010a. *Code of Conduct is No More than False Advertising. Disney Suppliers Continue Exploiting Chinese Workers.* Retrieved from http://www.chinalaborwatch.org/upfile/2011_1_19/2011119143318163.pdf on August 29, 2011.

China Labour Watch 2010b. *Investigation Report of Two Walt Disney Factories.* Retrieved from www.chinalaborwatch.org/investigations/2010_11_10/C00403E.pdf on August 29, 2011.

China Labour Watch. 2010c. *"We are extremely tired, with tremendous pressure", A follow-up investigation of Foxconn.* Retrieved from http://www.chinalaborwatch.org/pro/proshow-100.html on October 20, 2011

Chon, Boom Soo, Junho H. Choi, George A. Barnett, James A. Danowski and Sung-Hee Joo. 2003. A structural analysis of media convergence: cross-industry merger and acquisitions in the information industries. *Journal of Media Economics* 16(3), 141–157.

Christians, Clifford G., Mark Fackler, Kim B. Rotzoll and Kathy Brittain McKee. 2001. *Media Ethics*. 6th edition. New York: Longman.

CIC. 1999. *Mulan's Sisters. Working for Disney is not Fairy-Tale*. Retrieved from http://www.cleanclothes.org/news/4-companies/910-mulans-sisters-working-for-disney-is-no-fairy-tale on September 1, 2011.

CIC. 2000. *Labour Rights Violations at 12 Chinese Factories*. Retrieved from http://www.cleanclothes.org/news/4-companies/912-labour-rights-violations-at-12-china-factorie on September 1, 2011.

CITI. 2011a. *Wireline Local Market Concentration*. Retrieved from http://www4.gsb.columbia.edu/null/download?&exclusive=filemgr.download&file_id=739241 on December 15, 2011.

CITI. 2011b. *Mobile Wireless Market Concentration*. Retrieved from http://www4.gsb.columbia.edu/null/download?&exclusive=filemgr.download&file_id=739253 on December 15, 2011.

Clarkson, Max B.E. 1995. A stakeholder framework for analyzing and evaluating corporate social performance. *Academy of Management Review* 20(1), 92–117.

Cochran, Philip L. and Robert A. Wood. 1984. Social responsibility and financial performance. *The Academy of Management Journal* 27(1), 42–56.

Cogman, David and Jeremy M. Oppenheim. 2002. Controversy incorporated. *The McKinsey Quarterly 4*, 57–65.

Commission on Freedom of the Press. 1947. *A Free and Responsible Press*. Retrieved from http://www.archive.org/stream/freeandresponsib029216mbp/freeandresponsib029216mbp_djvu.txt on March 6, 2011.

Compaine, Benjamin M and Douglas Gomery. 2000. *Who Owns the Media*. 3rd edition. Mahwah: Lawrence Erlbaum.

Connolly, Marie and Alan B. Krueger. 2006. Rockonomics: the economics of popular music. In *Handbook of the Economics of Art and Culture*, edited by Victor A. Ginsburgh and David Throsby. Amsterdam: Elsevier.

Corlett, Angelo J. 1998. A Marxist approach to business ethics. *Journal of Business Ethics* 17, 99–103.

Croteau, David and William Hoynes. 2000. *Media Society. Industries, Images, and Audiences*. 2nd edition. Thousand Oaks: Sage.

Croteau, David and William Hoynes. 2006. *The Business of Media. Corporate Media and the Public Interest*. 2nd edition Thousand Oaks: Pine Forge Press.

DanWatch. 2011. *What a Waste. How Your Computer Causes Health Problems in Ghana*. Retrieved from http://makeitfair.org/de/en/the-facts/reports/what-a-waste on December 12, 2011.

David, Matthew. 2010. *Peer to Peer and the Music Industry. The Criminalization of Sharing*. Los Angeles: Sage.

Davis, Ian. 2005. What is the business of business? *The McKinsey Quarterly* 3, 105–113.

Davis, Keith and R.L. Blomstrom.1966. *Business and Its Environment*. New York: McGraw Hill.

Dawson, Michael and John Bellamy Foster. 1998. Virtual capitalism. In *Capitalism and the Information Age*, 1–67, edited by Robert W. McChesney, Eileen Meiksins Wood and Jon Bellamy Foster. New York: Monthly Review Press.

DCMS. 1998. *Creative Industries Mapping Document*. Retrieved from http://webarchive. nationalarchives.gov.uk/+/http://www.culture.gov.uk/reference_library/publications/ 4740.aspx on March 5, 2011.

DCMS. 2001. *Creative Industries Mapping Document*. Retrieved from http://webarchive. nationalarchives.gov.uk/+/http://www.culture.gov.uk/reference_library/publications/ 4632.aspx/ on March 5, 2011.

De Angelis, Massimo. 2009. The tragedy of capitalist commons. In *Turbulence* 5, 32–33. Retrieved from http://turbulence.org.uk/wp-content/uploads/2009/11/turbulence_05. pdf on June 4, 2012.

Dean, Jodi. 2012. *The Communist Horizon*. New York: Verso.

Dickson, Marsha A. and Molly Eckman. 2008. Media portrayal of voluntary public reporting about corporate social responsibility performance: does coverage encourage or discourage ethical management. *Journal of Business Ethics* 83, 725–743.

Dorfman, Arial and Armand Mattelart. 1975. *How to Read Donald Duck. Imperialist Ideology in the Disney Comic*. New York: International General.

Douzinas, Costas and Slavoj Žižek. (eds) 2010. *The Idea of Communism*. London: Verso.

Drucker, Peter. 1984. The new meaning of corporate social responsibility. *California Management Review* 16(2), 53–63.

Dundes, Allen 2002. *Bloody Mary in the Mirror. Essays in Psychoanalytic Folkloristics*. Jackson: University Press of Mississippi.

Dyck, Alexander and Luigi Zingales. 2002. *The Corporate Governance Role of the Media*. Retrieved from http://papers.ssrn.com/sol3/Delivery.cfm/SSRN_ID335602_ code021101510.pdf?abstractid=335602&mirid=1 on March 12, 2011.

Dyer-Witheford, Nick. 2010a. *Commonism*. Turbulence 1, 81–87. Retrieved from http:// turbulence.org.uk/wp-content/uploads/2008/07/turbulence_jrnl.pdf on June 28, 2012.

Dyer-Witheford, Nick. 2010b. *The Circulation of the Common. Talk at the University of Minnesota*. Retrieved from http://www.globalproject.info/it/in_movimento/nick-dyer-witheford-the-circulation-of-the-common/4797 on June 4, 2012.

Eagelton, Terry. 2007. *Ideology: An Introduction*. London: Verso.

Economides, Nicholas. 2001. *The Microsoft Antitrust Case*. Retrieved from http://www. stern.nyu.edu/networks/Microsoft_Antitrust.Rejoinder.pdf on October 13, 2011.

EFF (Electronic Frontier Foundation). 2008. *Electronic Frontier Foundation. RIAA vs. The People: Five Year Later*. Retrieved from http://www.eff.org/files/eff-riaa-whitepaper. pdf16 on September 20, 2011.

Eisenhower Research Project. 2011. *The Costs of War since 2001: Iraq, Afghanistan, and Pakistan*. Executive Summary. Retrieved from http://costsofwar.org/sites/default/ files/Executive%20Report%20Costs%20of%20War%20December%202011.docx on February 25, 2012.

Elliott-Boyle, Deni. 1985/1986. A conceptual analysis of ethics codes. *Journal of Mass Media Ethics* 1(1), 22–26.

Engels, Friedrich. 1892/2009. *The Condition of the Working Class in England*. London: Penguin.

Epstein, Edward M. 1987. The corporate social policy process: beyond business ethics, corporate social responsibility, and corporate social responsiveness. *California Management Review* 24(3), 99–114.

Epstein, Edward M. 2007. The good company. Rhetoric or reality? Corporate social responsibility and business ethics redux. *American Business Law Journal* 44(2), 207–222.

Esty, Daniel C. and Andrew Winston. 2009. *Green to Gold: How Smart Companies use Environmental Strategy to Innovate, Create Value, and Build Competitive Advantage*. Chichester: John Wiley and Sons.

European Commission 2001. *Green Paper. Promoting a European Framework for Corporate Social Responsibility. COM(2001) 366.* Retrieved from http://eur-lex.europa.eu/LexUriServ/LexUriServ.do?uri=COM:2001:0366:FIN:en:PDF on September 5, 2012.

European Commission 2002. *Communication from the Commission. Corporate Social Responsibility: A Business contribution to Sustainable Development. COM(2002) 347.* Retrieved from http://eur-lex.europa.eu/LexUriServ/LexUriServ.do?uri=COM:2002:0347:FIN:en:PDF on September 5, 2012.

European Commission. 2003. *Directive 2002/96/EC of the European Parliament and of the Council of 27 January 2003 on Waste Electrical and Electronic Equipment (WEEE).* Retrieved from http://eur-lex.europa.eu/LexUriServ/LexUriServ.do?uri=OJ:L:2003:03 7:0024:0038:EN:PDF on November 6, 2011.

European Commission 2006. *Communication from the Commission Concerning Corporate Social Responsibility. Implementing the Partnership for Growth and Jobs: Making Europe a Pole of Excellence on CSR. COM(2006) 136.* Retrieved from http://eur-lex.europa.eu/LexUriServ/LexUriServ.do?uri=COM:2006:0136:FIN:EN:PDF on May 15, 2008.

European Commission 2011. *Communication from the Commission. A Renewed Strategy 2011-2014 for Corporate Social Responsibility.* Retrieved from http://eur-lex.europa.eu/LexUriServ/LexUriServ.do?uri=COM:2011:0681:FIN:EN:PDF on September 5, 2012.

European Council 2000. *Presidency Conclusions. Lisbon European Council 23 and 24 March 2000.* Retrieved from http://ue.eu.int/ueDocs/cms_Data/docs/pressdata/en/ec/00100-r1.en0.htm on May 15, 2008.

Eviatar, Daphne. 2001. Murdoch's Fox News. *The Nation* February 22, 2001. Retrieved from http://www.thenation.com/article/murdochs-fox-news on February 14, 2012.

FAIR. 2001. *The Most Biased Name in the News.* Retrieved from http://www.fair.org/index.php?page=1067 on February 23, 2012.

Fairclough, Norman and Ruth Wodak. 1997. Critical discourse analysis. In *Discourse as Social Interaction,* 258–284, edited by Teun A. Van Dijk. London, Thousand Oaks, New Delhi: Sage.

Fairleigh Dickinson University. 2011. *Public Mind Poll. Some News Leaves People Knowing Less.* November 21, 2011. Retrieved from http://publicmind.fdu.edu/2011/knowless/final.pdf *on February 23, 2011.*

Falck, Oliver and Stephan Heblich. 2007. Corporate social responsibility: doing well by doing good. *Business Horizons* 50, 247–254.

Fallows, James. 2003. *The Age of Murdoch. The Atlantic.* Retrieved from http://www.theatlantic.com/magazine/archive/2003/09/the-age-of-murdoch/2777/ on February 12, 2012.

FCC (Federal Communication Commission). 2009. *Notice of Proposed Rulemaking FCC 09-93.* Retrieved from http://hraunfoss.fcc.gov/edocs_public/attachmatch/FCC-09-93A1.pdf on December 11, 2011.

FCC (Federal Communication Commission). 2010. *Report and Order FCC 10-201.* Retrieved from http://hraunfoss.fcc.gov/edocs_public/attachmatch/FCC-10-201A1.pdf on December 11, 2011.

Fink, Conrad. 1995. *Media Ethics.* Boston: Allyn & Bacon.

FinnWatch, SACOM and SOMO. 2009. *Playing With Labour Rights.* Retrieved from http://makeitfair.org/the-facts/reports/playing-with-labour-rights/at_download/file on October 19, 2011.

FinnWatch, SACOM and SOMO. 2011. *Game Console and Music Player Production in China.* Retrieved from http://makeitfair.org/the-facts/reports/game-console-and-music-player-production-in-china on October 18, 2011.

Fischer, William. 2004. *Promises to Keep. Technology, Law, and the Future of Entertainment.* Palo Alto: Stanford University Press.

FLA. 2012. *Independent Investigation of Apple Supplier, Foxconn.* Retrieved from http://www.fairlabor.org/sites/default/files/documents/reports/foxconn_investigation_report.pdf on April 10, 2012.

Fleming, Peter and Marc Jones. 2013. *The End of Corporate Social Responsibility.* London: Sage.

Flew, Terry. 2011. *The Creative Industries. Culture and Policy.* London: Sage.

Frederick, William. 1960. The growing concern over business responsibility. *California Management Review* 2, 54–61.

Freeman, Edward. 1984. *Strategic Management. A Stakeholder Approach.* Marshfield/London: Pietman.

Freeman, Edward. 1994. The politics of stakeholder theory. Some future directions. *Business Ethics Quarterly* 4(4), 409–421.

Freeman, Edward. 1999. Response: divergent stakeholder theory. *The Academy of Management Review* 24(2), 233–236.

Freeman, Edward and Robert A. Phillips. 2002. Stakeholder theory: a libertarian defense. *Business Ethics Quarterly* 12(3), 331–349.

Freifunk. 2006. *Freifunk.net – A Successful Do-It-Yourself Approach for Building Wireless Community Networks in Germany.* Retrieved from http://start.freifunk.net/files/freifunk-presentation_engl_0.pdf on July 28, 2012.

Friedman, Milton. 1962/1982. *Capitalism and Freedom.* Chicago: University of Chicago Press.

Friedman, Milton. 1970/2009. The social responsibility of business is to increase its profits. In *Business Ethics. Case Studies and Selected Readings,* 75–80, edited by Marianne M. Jennings. Mason: South Western.

Fuchs, Christian. 2008. *Internet and Society. Social Theory in the Information Age.* New York: Routledge.

Fuchs, Christian. 2009a. A contribution to the critique of the political economy of the Internet. *European Journal of Communication* 24(1), 69–87.

Fuchs, Christian. 2009b. *Social Networking Sites and the Surveillance Society.* Salzburg/Vienna: Unified Theory of Information Research Group.

Fuchs, Christian. 2010. Labor in informational capitalism and on the Internet. *The Information Society* 26(3), 179–196.

Fuchs, Christian. 2011a. *Foundations of Critical Media and Information Studies.* New York: Routledge.

Fuchs, Christian. 2011b. A contribution to the critique of the political economy of Google. *Fast Capitalism* 8(1).

Gandy, Oscar. 1993. *The Panoptic Sort. A Political Economy of Personal Information.* Boulder: Westview Press.

Gandy, Oscar H. 1997. The political economy approach: a critical challenge. In *The Political Economy of the Media Volume 1,* 87–106, edited by Peter Golding and Graham, Murdock. Cheltenham/Brookfield: Elgar.

Garnham, Nicholas. 1983. Public service versus the market. *Screen* 24(1), 6–27.

Garnham, Nicholas 1986/2006: Contribution to a political economy of mass-communication. In *Media and Cultural Studies. KeyWorks* edited by Meenakshi Gigi Durham and Douglas Kellner, 201–229, Malden, Oxford, Carlton: Blackwell.

Garnham, Nicholas. 1987/1997. Concepts of culture. Public policy and the cultural industries. In *Studying Culture,* edited by Anne Gray and Jim McGuigan, 54–61. London, New York: Arnold.

Garnham, Nicholas. 1998. Political economy and cultural studies: reconciliation or divorce. In *Cultural Theory and Popular Culture*. A Reader, John Sorey, 600–612. Edinburgh: Pearson.

Garnham, Nicholas. 2006. From cultural to creative industries. *International Journal of Cultural Policy* 11(1), 15–29.

Garriga, Elisabet and Domènec Melé. 2004. Corporate social responsibility theories: mapping the territory. *Journal of Business Ethics 53*, 51–71.

Gates, Bill. 1991. *Challenges and Strategy*. May 16, 1991. Retrieved from http://www.std.com/obi/Bill.Gates/Challenges.and.Strategy September 28, 2011.

Gates, Bill. 2000. *Global Foundation Address*. Retrieved from http://www.gatesfoundation.org/speeches-commentary/Pages/bill-gates-2000-global-foundation.aspx on August 4, 2012.

Gauntlett, David. 2011. *Making is Connecting. The Social Meaning of Creativity, from DIY and Knitting to YouTube and Web 2.0*. Cambridge: Polity.

Geisst, Charles R. 2006. *Encyclopedia of American Business History*. New York: Facts on File.

Girard, Bernard. 2009. *The Google Wa*y. San Francisco: No Starch Press.

Giroux, Henry and Grace Pollock. 2010. *The Mouse that Roared. Disney and the End of Innocence*. Plymouth: Rowman and Littlefield.

Golding, Peter and Graham Murdock. 1973. For a political economy of mass communication. In *The Socialist Register 1973*, 205–234, edited by Ralph Miliband and John Saville. London: Merlin.

Goldman Rohm, Wendy. 2002. *The Murdoch Mission. The Digital Transformation of a Media Empire*. New York: John Wiley.

Golob, Ursa and Jennifer L. Bartlett. 2007. Communicating about corporate social responsibility. *Public Relations Review* 33(1), 1–9.

Goodell, Jeff. 2011. Who's to blame. 12 politicians and excess blocking progress on global warming. *The Rolling Stone*, February 2, 2011. Retrieved from http://www.rollingstone.com/politics/lists/whos-to-blame-12-politicians-and-execs-blocking-progress-on-global-warming-20110119 on February 2, 2012.

Gray, Rob, Reza Kouhy and Simon Lavers. 1995. Corporate social and environmental reporting. *Accounting, Auditing & Accountability Journal* 8(2), 47–77.

Grayson, David. 2009. *Corporate Responsibility and the Media*. Doughty Centre for Corporate Responsibility and Centre for Corporate Citizenship Germany. Retrieved from http://www.som.cranfield.ac.uk/som/dinamic-content/research/doughty/crandthemediafinal.pdf on February 22, 2011.

Greenpeace. 2005a. *Hewlett Packard in Global Toxic Trouble*. Retrieved from http://www.greenpeace.org/international/en/news/features/hewlett-packard-toxic-trouble-111/ on November 12, 2011.

Greenpeace. 2005b. *E-waste Wave Sweeps the Globe*. Retrieved from http://www.greenpeace.org/eastasia/news/stories/toxics/2005/20050523-e-waste-wave/ on November 13, 2011

Greenpeace. 2006a. *Toxic Chemicals in Computers Exposed*. Retrieved from http://www.greenpeace.org/international/Global/international/planet-2/report/2006/9/toxic-chemicals-in-computers.pdf on November 3, 2011.

Greenpeace. 2006b. *Toxic Substances in Laptops: Greenpeace Study Exposes HP's Lie*. Retrieved from http://www.greenpeace.org/international/en/press/releases/toxic-substances-in-laptops-g/ on November 3, 2011.

Greenpeace. 2007. *Toxic Tea Party*. Retrieved from http://www.greenpeace.org/international/en/news/features/e-waste-china-toxic-pollution-230707/ on November 4, 2011.

Greenpeace. 2008. *Toxic Tech: Not in Our Backyard*. Retrieved from http://www.greenpeace. org/international/Global/international/planet-2/report/2008/2/not-in-our-backyard.pdf on November 6, 2011.

Greenpeace. 2009. *Guide to Greener Electronics*. Version 11. Retrieved from http://www. greenpeace.org/usa/Global/usa/report/2009/3/guide-to-greener-electronics-11.pdf   on November 3, 2011.

Greenpeace. 2011a. *How Dirty is Your Data*. Retrieved from http://www.greenpeace.org/ international/Global/international/publications/climate/2011/Cool%20IT/dirty-data-report-greenpeace.pdf on November 13, 2011.

Greenpeace. 2011b. *Guide to Greener Electronics*. HP. Retrieved from http://www.green-peace.org/international/Global/international/publications/climate/2011/Cool%20IT/ greener-guide-nov-2011/hp.pdf on November 13, 2011.

Greenslade, Roy. 2003. *Their Master's Voice. The Guardian*, February 17, 2003. Retrieved from http://www.guardian.co.uk/media/2003/feb/17/mondaymediasection. iraq on November 6, 2012.

Gulyás, Ágnes. 2009. Corporate social responsibility in the British media industry. *Media Culture and Society* 31(4), 657–668.

Habermas, Jürgen. 1968/1971. *Knowledge and Human Interest*. Boston: Beacon Press.

Hall, Stuart. 1973/2006. Encoding/decoding. *Media and Cultural Studies. KeyWorks* edited by Meenakshi Gigi Durham and Douglas Kellner, 163–173, Malden, Oxford, Carlton: Blackwell.

Halloween Document I. 1998. *Open Source Software: A (New?) Development Methodology.* Retrieved from http://www.catb.org/~esr/halloween/halloween1.html on October 2, 1011.

Halloween Document II. 1998. *Linux OS Competitive Analysis: The Next Java VM?* Retrieved from http://www.catb.org/~esr/halloween/halloween2.html on October 2, 2011.

Hamilton, James T. 2003. *Media Coverage of Corporate Social Responsibility*. Work-ing Paper Series of the Joan Shorenstein Center on Press, Politics and Public Policy. Retrieved from   http://www.hks.harvard.edu/presspol/publications/papers/working_ papers/2003_03_hamilton.pdf on March 14, 2011.

Hanlon, Gerard. 2008. Rethinking corporate social responsibility and the role of the firm. In *The Oxford Handbook of Corporate Social Responsibility*, 156–172, edited by Andrew Crane, Abagail McWilliams, Dirk Matten, Jeremy Moon and Donald S. Siegel. Oxford: Oxford University Press.

Hanlon, Gerard and Peter Fleming. 2009. Updating the critical perspective on corporate social responsibility. *Sociology Compass* 3(6), 937–948.

Hardt, Michael and Antonio Negri. 2009. *Commonwealth*. Cambridge, London: Belknap Press.

Harman, Chris 2011. *Zombie Capitalism. Global Crisis and the Relevance of Marx*. Chicago: Haymarket Books.

Harris, Nigel. 1992. Codes of conduct for journalists. In *Ethical Issues in Journalism and the Media*, 62–76, edited by Andrew Belsey and Ruth Chadwick. London: Routledge.

Harrison, Teresa M. and Brea Barthel. 2009. Wielding new media in web 2.0: exploring the history of engagement with the collaborative construction of media products. *New Media & Society* 11(1), 155–178.

Hartley, John. 2005. Creative industries. In *Creative Industries*, 1–39, edited by John Hartley. Malden: Blackwell.

Hartman, Laura P., Robert S. Rubin and K. Kathy Dhanda. 2007. The communication of corporate social responsibility: United States and European Union multinational corpo-rations. *Journal of Business Ethics* 74, 373–389.

Harvey, David. 2010. *The Enigma of Capital and the Crises of Capitalism*. London: Profile Books.

Harvey, David. 2012. *Rebel Cities*. London: Verso

Haug, Wolfgang Fritz. 2003. *High-Tech-Kapitalismus*. Hamburg: Argument.

Hayek, Friedrich August. 1978. *New Studies in Philosophy, Politics, Economics and the History of Ideas*. London: Routledge.

Hayek, Friedrich August. 1982. *Law Legislation and Liberty. A New Statement of the Liberal Principles of Justice and Political Economy*. London: Routledge.

Hayek, Friedrich August. 1990. *The Fatal Conceit. The Errors of Socialism*. London: Routledge.

Heal, Geoffrey. 2008. *When Principles Pay: Corporate Social Responsibility and the Bottom Line*. New York: Columbia University Press

Herkommer, Sebastian. 2005. Zur Aktualität marxistischer Ideologietheorie. In *Kritische Wissenschaften im Neoliberalismus*, 31–50, edited by Christina Kaindl. Marburg: BdWi.

Herman, Edward S. and Noam Chomsky. 1988. *Manufacturing Consent. The Political Economy of the Mass Media*. London: Vintage Books.

Herman, Edward S. and Robert McChesney. 1997. *The Global Media. The New Missionaries of Global Capitalism*. London, Washington: Cassell.

Herman, Paul R. 2010. *The HIP Investor: Make Bigger Profits by Building a Better World*. Chichester: John Wiley and Sons.

Hesmondhalgh, David. 2007. *The Cultural Industries*. 2nd edition. London: Sage

Hesmondhalgh, David and Andy C. Pratt. 2006. Cultural industries and cultural policies. *International Journal of Cultural Policy* 11(1), 1–13.

Himelboim, Itai and Yehiel Limor. 2011. Media institutions, news organizations, and the journalistic social role worldwide: a cross-national and cross-organizational study of codes of ethics. *Mass Communication and Society* 14(1), 71–92.

Hodgson, Damian E. 2004. Project work: the legacy of bureaucratic control in the post-bureaucratic organization. *Organization* 11(1), 81–100.

Hofkirchner, Wolfgang. 2002. *Projekt eine Welt. Kognition – Kommunikation – Kooperation. Versuch über die Selbstorganisation der Informationsgesellschaft*. Münster, Hamburg, London: LIT.

Hofkirchner, Wolfgang. 2003. A new way of thinking and a new world view. On the philosophy of self-organisation I. In *Causality, Emergence, Self-Organisation*, 131–149, edited by Arshinov, Vladimir and Christian Fuchs. Moskau: NIA-Parioda.

Hofkirchner, Wolfgang and Christian Fuchs. 2003. The Architecture of the Information Society. In *Proceedings of the 47th Annual Conference of the International Society for the Systems Sciences (ISSS)*, edited by Jennifter Wilby and Jenet K. Allen. Retrieved from http://fuchs.uti.at/wp-content/uploads/ArchitectureInformationSociety.pdf on June 14, 2012.

Hofkirchner, Wolfgang, Christian Fuchs, Celina Raffl, Matthias Schafranek, Marisol Sandoval and Robert Bichler. 2007. *ICTs and Society: The Salzburg Approach. Towards a Theory For, About, and By Means of the Information Society*. Salzburg. ICT&S Center Research Paper Series.

Holloway, John 2003. Where is class struggle? In *Anti-Capitalism. A Marxist Introduction*, 224–234, edited by Alfred Saad-Filho. London: Pluto Press.

Horkheimer, Max. 1930/1995. A new concept of ideology? In *Between Philosophy and Social Science*. Boston: MIT Press.

Horkheimer, Max 1937/2002a. Traditional and critical theory. In *Critical Theory Selected Essays. Max Horheimer*, 188–243, New York: Continuum.

Horkheimer, Max 1937/2002b. Traditional and critical theory. Postscript. In *Critical Theory Selected Essays. Max Horheimer*, 244–252, New York: Continuum.

Horkheimer, Max. 1947/2004. *Eclipse of Reason*. London, New York: Continuum.

Horkheimer, Max and Theodor W. Adorno. 1947/1997. *Dialectic of Enlightenment*. London, New York: Verso.

Hou, Jiran and Bryan H. Reber. 2011. Dimensions of disclosures: CSR reporting by media companies. *Public Relations Review* 37(2), 166–168.

Hsieh, Hsiu-Fang and Sarah E. Shannon. 2005. Three approaches to qualitative content analysis. *Qualitative Health Research* 15, 1277–1288.

ICO, FinnWatch and ECA. 2005. *Day and Night at the Factory*. Retrieved from http://www.corporatejustice.org/IMG/pdf/en_kiina-raportti.pdf on October 19, 2011.

Imhof, Kurt, Roger Blum, Heinz Bonfadelli and Otfried Jarren. 2004. *Mediengesellschaft. Strukturen, Merkmale, Entwicklungsdynamiken*. Wiesbaden: VS Verlag für Sozialwissenschaften.

Jarvis, Jeff. 2009. *What Would Google Do?* New York: HarperCollins.

Jones, Clement. 1980. *Mass Media Codes of Ethics and Councils. A Comparative International Study of Professional Standards*. UNESCO Reports and Papers on Mass Communication. Paris: UNESCO Press.

Jones, Thomas M. 1995. Instrumental stakeholder theory: a synthesis of ethics and economics. *Academy of Management Review* 20(2), 402–437.

Jose, Anita and Shang-Mei Lee. 2007. Environmental reporting of global corporations: content analysis based on websites disclosures. *Journal of Business Ethics* 72, 307–321.

Julien, Heidi. 2008. Content analysis. In *The Sage Encyclopaedia of Qualitative Research Methods*, 120–121, edited by Lisa M. Given. Los Angeles: Sage.

Jupp, Victor. 2006. Documents and critical research. In *Data Collection and Analysis*, 272–290, edited by Roger Sapsford and Victor Rupp. 2nd edition. London: Sage.

Kaptein, Muel. 2004. Business codes of multinational firms: what do they say? *Journal of Business Ethics* 50, 13–31.

Keynes, John Maynard 1936/1967. *The General Theory of Employment Interest and Money*. London: MacMillan

Kieran, Matthew. 1998. Objectivity, impartiality and good journalism. In *Media Ethics*, 23–36, edited by Matthew Kieran. London: Routledge

Kjonstad, Bjorn and Hugh Willmott. 1995. Business ethics: restrictive or empowering. *Journal of Business Ethics* 14, 445–464.

Klein, Naomi. 2000. *No Logo*. London: Flamingo.

Knoche, Manfred. 1999. Das Kapital als Strukturwandler der Medienindustrie – und der Staat als sein Agent? In *Strukturwandel der Medienwirtschaft im Zeitalter Digitaler Kommunikation*, 149–193, edited by Manfred Knoche and Gabriele Siegert. München: Fischer.

Knoche, Manfred. 2002. Kommunikationswissenschaftliche Medienökonomie als Kritik der Politischen Ökonomie der Medien. In *Medienökonomie in der Kommunikationswissenschaft. Bedeutung, Grundfragen und Entwicklungsperspektiven. Manfred Knoche zum 60. Geburtstag*, 102–109, edited by Gabriele Siegert. Münster: Lit.

Knoche, Manfred. 2005. Entwicklung von Medientechniken als "Neue Medie" aus der Sicht einer Kritik der Politischen Ökonomie der Medien. In Alte Medien – Neue Medien, 40–62, edited by Klaus Arnold and Christoph Neuberger. Wiesbaden: Verlag für Sozialwissenschaften.

KPMG. 2011. *KPMG International Survey of Corporate Responsibility Reporting*. Retrieved from http://www.kpmg.com/Global/en/IssuesAndInsights/ArticlesPublications/corporate-responsibility/Documents/2011-survey.pdf on August 2, 2012.

Kracauer, Siegfried. 1952/1953. The challenge of qualitative content analysis. *The Public Opinion Quarterly* 6(4), 631–642.

Kraemer, Kenneth L, Greg Linden and Jason Dedrick. 2011. *Capturing Value in Global Networks: Apple's iPad and iPhone.* Retrieved from http://pcic.merage.uci.edu/papers/2011/Value_iPad_iPhone.pdf on May 14, 2012.

Krippendorff, Klaus. 2004. *Content Analysis. An Introduction to its Methodology.* Thousand Oaks: Sage.

Krosnick, Jon A and Bo MacInnis. 2010. *Frequent Viewers of Fox News Are Less Likely to Accept Scientist's Views of Global Warming.* Retrieved from http://woods.stanford.edu/docs/surveys/Global-Warming-Fox-News.pdf on February 10, 2012.

Krugman, Paul. 2007. *The Conscience of a Liberal.* New York, London: W. W. Norton & Company

Krugman, Paul. 2008. *The Return of Depression Economics and the Crisis of 2008.* New York, London: W. W. Norton & Company

Laitila, Tiina. 1995. Journalistic codes of ethics in Europe. *European Journal of Communication* 10(4), 527–544

Lash, Scott and Celia Lury. 2007. *Global Culture Industry: The Mediation of Things.* Cambridge: Polity

Lee, Ming-Dong Paul. 2008. A review of the theories of corporate social responsibility: its evolutionary path and the road ahead. *International Journal of Management Reviews* 10(1), 53–73.

Lessig, Laurence and Robert McChesney. 2006. No tolls on the Internet. *The Washington Post.* Retrieved from http://www.washingtonpost.com/wp-dyn/content/article/2006/06/07/AR2006060702108.html on December 17, 2011.

Linzmayer, Owen W. 2004. *Apple Confidential 2.0: The Definitive History of the World's Most Colourful Company.* San Francisco: No Starch Press.

Love, Courtney. 2000. *Speech at the Digital Hollywood Online Entertainment Conference.* New York. Retrieved from http://www.gerryhemingway.com/piracy.html on September 20, 2011.

Lukács, Georg. 1923/1971. *History Class Consciousness.* London: Merlin Press.

Lyon, David. 2003. Surveillance as social sorting. Computer codes and mobile bodies. In *Surveillance as Social Sorting. Privacy, Risks, and Digital Discrimination*, 13–30, edited by David Lyon. London: Routledge.

Macey, David. 2000. *The Penguin Dictionary of Critical Theory.* London: Penguin.

Maignan, Isabelle and David. A. Ralston. 2002. Corporate social responsibility in Europe and the U.S.: insights from businesses' self-presentations. *Journal of International Business Studies* 33(3), 497–514.

Manne, Robert. 2005. Murdoch and the war on Iraq. In *Do Not Disturb: Is the Media Failing Australia?* 76–97, edited by Robert Manne. Melbourne: Black Inc.

Mannheim, Karl. 1929/2002. *Ideology and Utopia. Collected Works of Karl Mannheim.* London: Routledge.

Maravelias, Christian. 2003. Post-bureaucracy – control through professional freedom. *Journal of Organizational Change Management* 16(5), 547–566.

Marcuse, Herbert. 1936/1988. The concept of essence. In *Negations. Essays in Critical Theory*, 43–87. London: Free Associations Books.

Marcuse, Herbert. 1937/1989. Philosophy and critical theory. In *Negations. Essays in Critical Theory*, 134–158. London: Free Associations Books.

Marcuse, Herbert. 1962/1978. Über das Ideologieproblem in der hochentwickelten Industriegesellschaft. In *Ideologie. Ideologiekritik und Wissenssoziologie*, 320–341, edited by Kurt Lenk. Darmstadt: Luchterhand.

Margolis, Joshua D. and James P. Walsh. 2003. Misery loves companies: rethinking social initiatives by business. *Administrative Science Quarterly* 48(2), 268–305.

Martin, William J. 1995. *The Global Information Society*. Brookfield: Gower.

Marx, Karl. 1842/1976. Debatten über Preßfreiheit und Publikation der Landständischen Verhandlungen. *MEW Volume 1*, 28–77. Berlin: Dietz.

Marx, Karl. 1843/1997. Letters from the Deutsch-Französische Jahrbücher. A letter to Ruge in September 1843. In *Writings of the Young Marx on Philosophy and Society*, 203–215, edited by Loyd D. Easton and Kurt H. Guddat. Indianapolis: Hackett Publishing.

Marx, Karl 1844/2007a. Contribution to the critique of Hegel's philosophy of right. In *The Portable Atheists. Essential Readings for the Nonbeliever*, 64–74, edited by Christopher Hitchens. Philadelphia: Da Capo Press.

Marx, Karl. 1844/2007b. *Economic Philosophic Manuscripts*. Mineola, New York: Dover Publications.

Marx, Karl. 1846/2004. The German ideology. In *The German Ideology. Part One with Selections from Parts Two and Three and Supplementary Texts*, 37–120, edited by Christopher Johann Arthur. New York: International Publishers.

Marx, Karl. 1849/1959. Der erste Preßprozess der "Neuen Rheinischen Zeitung". In *MEW Volume 6*, 223–239. Berlin: Dietz.

Marx, Karl. 1857/2004. Introduction to a critique of the political economy. In *The German Ideology. Part One with Selections from Parts Two and Three and Supplementary Texts*, 124–152, edited by Christopher Johann Arthur. New York: International Publishers.

Marx, Karl. 1859/1994. A contribution to the critique of political economy. Preface. *Karl Marx. Selected Writings*, 209–213, edited by Lawrence H. Simon. Indianapolis: Hackett Publishing.

Marx, Karl 1864/2001. Inaugural address for the International Working Man's Association. In *Poverty, Inequality and Health in Britain. A Reader*, 89–96, edited by Davey Smith, Daniel Dorling and Mary Shaw. Bristol: The Policy Press.

Marx, Karl. 1867/1990. *Capital Volume I*. London: Penguin.

Marx Karl. 1885/1992. *Capital Volume II*. London: Penguin

Marx, Karl. 1894/1991. *Capital Volume III*. London: Penguin

Mathiesen, Thomas. 1997. The viewer society: Michel Foucault's panopticon revisited. *Theoretical Criminology* 1, 215–237.

Maurer, Hermann, Tilo Balke, Frank Kappe, Narayanan Kulathuramaiyer, Stefan Weber and Bilal Zaka. 2007. *Report on Dangers and Opportunities Posed by Large Search Engines, Particularly Google*. Retrieved from http://www.iicm.tugraz.at:8080/Ressourcen/Papers/dangers_google.pdf on January 21, 2012.

Maxwell, Richard and Toby Miller. 2012. *Greening the Media*. Oxford: Oxford University Press.

Mayring, Philipp. 2000. Qualitative Inhaltsanalyse. *Forum Qualitative Sozialforschung* 1(2), 1–10.

Mayring, Philipp. 2004. Qualitative content analysis. In *A Companion to Qualitative Research*, 266–269, edited by Uwe Flick, Ernst von Kardoff and Ines Steinke. London: Sage.

Mayring, Philipp. 2010. *Qualitative Inhaltsanalyse*. Weinheim/Basel: Beltz.

McChesney. 1997. The Mythology of Commercial Broadcasting and the Contemporary Crisis of Public Broadcasting. The 1997 Spry Memorial Lecture. Retrieved from http://www.ratical.com/co-globalize/RMmythCB.html on March 8, 2011.

McChesney, Robert W. 2004. *The Problem of the Media. U.S. Communication Politics in the 21st Century*. New York: Monthly Review Press.

McElhaney, Kellie A. 2008. *Just Good Business: The Strategic Guide to Aligning Corporate Social Responsibility and Brand*. San Francisco: Berrett-Koehler.

McGuire, James W. 1963. *Business and Society*. New York: McGraw-Hill.

McInerney, Thomas 2007. Putting regulation before responsibility: towards binding norms of corporate social responsibility. *Cornell International Law Journal* 40, 171–200.

McKnight, David. 2003. A world hungry for a new philosophy: Rupert Murdoch and the rise of neoliberalism. *Journalism Studies* 4(3), 347–358.

McKnight, David. 2010a. Rupert Murdoch's News Corporation: a media institution with a mission. *Historical Journal of Film, Radio and Television* 30(3), 303–316.

McKnight, David. 2010b. A change in climate? The journalism of opinion at News Corporation. *Journalism* 11(6), 693–706.

McKnight, David. 2011. "You're all a bunch of pinkos": Rupert Murdoch and the politics of HarperCollins. *Media Culture and Society* 33(6), 835–850.

McManus, John H. 1997. Who's responsible for journalism? *Journal of Mass Media Ethics* 12(1), 5–17.

McNally, David. 2011. *Monsters of the Market. Zombies, Vampires and Global Capitalism*. Leiden: Brill.

McQuail, Dennis. 1997. Accountability of media to society: principles and means. *European Journal of Communication* 12(4), 511–529.

McQuail, Dennis. 2010. *Mass Communication Theory*. 6th edition. London: Sage.

Meadows, Donella, Dennis Meadows, Jorgen Randers and William W. Behrens. 1972. *Limits to Growth*. New York: Universe Books.

Meadows, Donella, Jorgen Randers and Dennis Meadows. 2004. *A Synopsis. Limits to Growth. The 30-Year Update*. Retrieved from http://www.sustainer.org/pubs/limits togrowth.pdf on September 25, 2011.

Media CSR Forum. 2008. *Mapping the Landscape. CSR Issues for the Media Sector*. Retrieved from http://mediacsrforum.org/downloadDocumentFile.php?document=68 on February 22, 2011.

Media Matters 2010. *News Corp's Support for Combating Climate Change Undermined by Deniers at Fox News, WSJ*. Retrieved from http://mediamatters.org/research/201001220027 on February 10, 2012.

Melton, Gordon. 2011. Preface: what is a vampire? In *The Vampire Book. The Encyclopedia of the Undead*, xxix–xxxiii, edited by Gordon Melton. Canton: Visible Ink Books.

Mertens, Donna M. 2010. *Research and Evaluation in Education and Psychology*. Thousand Oaks: Sage.

Merton, Robert K. 1976. The ambivalence of organizational leaders. In *Sociological Ambivalence and Other Essays*. New York: Macmillan.

Mettler-Meibom, Barbara. 1994. *Kommunikation in der Mediengesellschaft. Tendenzen, Gefährdungen, Orientierungen*. Berlin: Edition Sigma.

Miles, Matthew B. and A. Michael Huberman. 1994. *Qualitative Data Analysis*. Thousand Oaks: Sage.

Miège, Bernard. 2011. Theorizing the cultural industries: persistent specificities and reconsiderations. In *The Handbook of Political Economy of Communication*, edited by Janet Wasko, Graham Murdock and Helena Sousa. Malden: Blackwell.

Montag, Warren. 2000. The "workshop of filthy creation": a Marxist reading of Frankenstein. In *Mary Shelley Frankenstein*, 384–395, edited by Johanna M. Smith. Boston: Bedford/St. Martins.

Moretti, Franco 1982. The dialectic of fear. *New Left Review* 136, 67–85.

Moretti, Franco. 1999. Dracula and capitalism In *Dracula. Contemporary Critical Text-books*, 43–54, edited by Glennis Byron. New York: St. Martin's Press.

Morgan, David L. 2008. Random Sampling. In *The Sage Encyclopedia of Qualitative Research Methods*, 725, edited by Lisa M. Given. Los Angeles: Sage.

Morhardt, Emil J. 2009. Corporate social responsibility reporting on the Internet. *Business Strategy and the Environment,* 19, 436–452.

Morris, Jonathan S. 2005. The Fox News factor. *The Harvard International Journal of Press/Politics* 10(3), 56–79.

Mosco, Vincent. 1988. Introduction: information in the pay-per society. In *The Political Economy of Information*, 3–26, edited by Vincent Mosco and Janet Wasko. Madison: The University of Wisconsin Press.

Mosco, Vincent. 1994. The political economy of communication. Lessons from the found-ers. In *Information and Communication in Economics*, 105–124, edited by Robert E. Babe. Norwell: Kluwer.

Mosco, Vincent. 2004. *The Digital Sublime: Myth, Power and Cyberspace.* Cambridge: MIT Press.

Mosco, Vincent. 2009. *The Political Economy of Communication.* London: Sage.

Münch, Richard. 1995. *Dynamik der Kommunikationsgesellschaft.* Frankfurt a. Main: Suhrkamp.

Murdock, Graham. 1997. Base notes: the conditions of cultural practice. In *Cultural Studies in Question*, 86–101, edited by Marjorie Ferguson and Peter Golding. London: Sage.

Murdock, Graham and Peter Golding. 1997. For a political economy of mass communica-tion. In *The Political Economy of the Media Volume I*, 3–32, edited by Peter Golding and Graham Murdock. Cheltenham, Brookfield: Elgar.

Murdock, Graham and Peter Golding. 1999. Common markets: corporate ambitions and com-munication trends in the UK and Europe. *Journal of Media Economics* 12(2), 117–132.

Murdock, Graham and Peter Golding. 2002. Digital possibilities, market realities: the con-tradictions of market convergence. *Socialist Register* 38, 111–129.

Murdock, Graham and Peter Golding. 2005. Culture, communications and political econ-omy. In *Mass Media and Society*, 60–82, edited by James Curran and Michael Gurevitch. London: Hodder.

Music and Copyright. 2011. *Universal Music Group Reasserts its Recorded-Music Domi-nance in* 2010. March 23, 2011. Retrieved from http://musicandcopyright.wordpress. com/2011/03/23/universal-music-group-reasserts-its-recorded-music-dominance-in-2010/on September 15, 2011.

National Alliance to End Homelessness and Homelessness Research Institute. 2012. *The State of Homelessness in America 2012*. Retrieved from http://www.endhomelessness. org/content/article/detail/4361 on February 25, 2012.

Neocleous, Mark. 2003. The political economy of the dead: Marx's vampires. *History of Politcal Thought* XXIV(4), 669–684.

Netanel, Neil W. 2003. Impose a non-commercial use levy to allow free peer-to-peer file sharing. *Harvard Journal of Law and Technology* 17(1), 1–84.

Newitz, Annalee. 2006. *Pretend We're Dead. Capitalist Monsters in American Pop Cul-ture.* Stanford: Duke University Press.

Nielsen, Anne Ellerup and Christina Thomsen. 2007. Reporting CSR – what and how to say it? *Corporate Communications: An International Journal* 12(1), 25–40.

NLC. 1996. *The U.S. in Haiti. How to get Rich on 11 Cents an Hour.* Retrieved from http:// www.globallabourrights.org/reports?id=0178 on September 1, 2011.

Noam, Eli M. 2009. *Media Ownership and Concentration in America*. New York: Oxford University Press.

O'Leary, Zina. 2004. *The Essential Guide to Doing Research*. London: Sage.

Olin Wright, Eric. 2010. *Envisioning Real Utopias*. London: Verso

O'Reilly, Tim. 2005. *What is Web 2.0. Design Patterns and Business Models for the Next Generation of Software*. Retrieved from http://oreilly.com/web2/archive/what-is-web-20.html on September 14, 2009.

Orlitzky, Marc, Frank L. Schmidt and Sara L. Rynes. 2003. Corporate social and financial performance: a meta-analysis. *Organizational Studies* 24, 403–411.

OSS Watch 2011. *Microsoft: An End to Open Hostility*. Retrieved from http://www.oss-watch.ac.uk/resources/microsoft.xml on September 27, 2011.

Patton, Michael Quinn. 2002. *Qualitative Research and Evaluation Methods*. 3rd edition. Thousand Oaks: Sage.

Perrini, Francesco. 2005. Building a European portrait of corporate social responsibility reporting. *European Management Journal* 23(6), 611–627.

Pew Research Center. 2009. *Fox News Viewed as Most Ideological Network*. Retrieved from http://www.people-press.org/2009/10/29/fox-news-viewed-as-most-ideological-network/ on February 23, 2012.

PIPA and Knowledge Networks. 2003. *Misperceptions, the Media and the Iraq War*. Retrieved from http://www.worldpublicopinion.org/pipa/pdf/oct03/IraqMedia_Oct03_rpt.pdf on February 24, 2012

Plaisance, Patrick Lee. 2009. *Media Ethics. Key Principles for Responsible Practice*. Thousand Oaks: Sage.

Pratt, Andy C. 2006. Cultural policies and public policy. *International Journal of Cultural Policy* 11(1), 31–44.

Preston, Lee E. 1975. Corporation and society: the search for a paradigm. *Journal of Economic Literature* 13(2), 434–453.

Preston, Lee E. and Douglas P. O'Bannon. 1997. The corporate-financial performance relationship: a typology and analysis. *Business and Society* 36, 419–429.

Prior, Lindsay. 2003. *Using Documents in Social Research*. London: Sage.

Prior, Lindsay. 2004. Doing things with documents. In *Qualitative Research. Theory, Method and Practice*, 76–94, edited by David Silverman. 2nd edition. London: Sage.

Prior, Lindsay 2008. Document analysis. In *The Sage Encyclopedia of Qualitative Research Methods*, 230–231, edited by Lisa M. Given. Los Angeles: Sage.

Project for Excellence in Journalism. 2005. *The State of News Media*. Retrieved from http://stateofthemedia.org/2005/cable-tv-intro/content-analysis/ on February 23, 2012.

Pross, Harry. 1972. *Medienforschung. Film, Funk, Presse, Fernsehen*. Darmstadt: Habel.

Punch, Keith F. 2005. *Introduction to Social Research*. 2nd edition. Los Angeles: Sage.

Rasmussen, David 1996. Critical theory and philosophy. In *Handbook of Critical Theory*, 11–38, edited by David Rasmussen. Cambridge: Blackwell.

Rehmann, Jan. 2008. *Einführung in die Ideologietheorie*. Hamburg: Argument Verlag.

Richards, Ian. 2004. Stakeholders vs shareholders: journalism, business and ethics. *Journal of Mass Media Ethics* 19(2), 119–129.

Ritsert, Jürgen. 1972. *Inhaltsanalyse und Idelogiekritik. Ein Versuch über kritische Sozialforschung*. Frankfurt am Main: Fischer

Roberts, John. 2003. The manufacture of corporate social responsibility: constructing corporate sensibility. *Organization* 10(2), 249–265.

Robins, Kevin and Frank Webster. 1988. Cybernetic capitalism: information, technology, everyday life. In *The Political Economy of Information*, 44–75, edited by Vincent Mosco, Vincent and Janet Wasko. Madison: University of Wisconsin Press.

Röttgers, Kurt 1975. *Kritik und Praxis*. Berlin, New York: de Gruyter.

Saad-Filho, Alfred (ed.). 2003. *Anti-Capitalism. A Marxist Introduction*. London: Pluto Press.

SACOM. 2005. *Looking for Mickey Mouse's Conscience – A Survey of the Working Conditions of Disney's Supplier Factories in China*. Retrieved from *sacom.hk/wp-content/uploads/2008/07/disney.pdf on September 1, 2011*.

SACOM. 2006. *A Second Attempt in Looking for Mickey Mouse's Conscience – A Survey of the Working Conditions of Disney's Supplier Factories in China*. Retrieved from http://sacom.hk/wp-content/uploads/2008/09/7-disney-research-2006.pdf on September 1, 2011.

SACOM. 2010a. *Disney, Walmart and ICTI Together Make Workers Rights Violations Normal and Sustainable*. Retrieved from http://sacom.hk/wp-content/uploads/2010/10/report-on-disney-walmart-and-icti.pdf on September 1, 2011.

SACOM. 2010b. *Apple Owes Workers and Public a Response over the Poisoning*. Retrieved from http://sacom.hk/wp-content/uploads/2010/05/apple-owes-workers-and-public-a-response-over-the-poisonings.pdf on October 16, 2011.

SACOM. 2011a. *Foxconn and Apple Fail to Fulfil Promises: Predicaments of Workers after the Suicides*. Retrieved from http://sacom.hk/wp-content/uploads/2011/05/2011-05-06_foxconn-and-apple-fail-to-fulfill-promises1.pdf on October 20, 2011.

SACOM. 2011b. *iSlave behind the iPhone. Foxconn Workers in Central China*. Retrieved from http://sacom.hk/wp-content/uploads/2011/09/20110924-islave-behind-the-iphone.pdf on October 20, 2011.

SACOM and NLC. 2005. *Disney's Children's Books Made with the Blood, Sweat and Tears of Young People in China*. Retrieved from http://www.woek-web.de/web/cms/upload/pdf/aktion_fair_spielt/publikation/sacom_national_labor_committee_2005_disneys_childrens_books.pdf on October 15, 2013.

Sandoval, Marisol. 2011. Warum es and der Zeit ist den Begriff der Alternativmedien neu zu definieren. In *Handbuch der Alternativmedien 2011/2012*, 24–36, edited by Bernd Hüttner, Christiane Leidinger and Gottfried Oy. Neu-Ulm: AG-Spak.

Sandoval, Marisol. 2012. Consumer surveillance on web 2.0. In *Internet and Surveillance*, 147–169, edited by Christian Fuchs, Kees Bursma, Anders Albrechtslund and Marisol Sandoval, New York: Routledge

Sandoval, Marisol and Christian Fuchs. 2010. Towards a critical theory of alternative media. *Telematics and Informatics* (special issue on community media, edited by Nico Carpentier and Salvatore Scifo) 27(2), 141–150.

Sardar, Ziauddin. 1996. Walt Disney and the double victimization of Pocahontas. *Third Text*, 10(37), 17–26.

Scherer, A. G. and Palazzo, G. 2007. Toward a political conception of corporate responsibility. Business and society seen from a Habermasian perspective. *Academy of Management Review* 32, 1096–1120

Schiller, Dan. 2000. *Digital Capitalism*. Cambridge: MIT Press.

Schiller, Herbert. 1997. Manipulation and the packaged consciousness. In *The Political Economy of the Media Volume I*, 423–437, edited by Peter Golding and Graham Murdock. Cheltenham, Brookfield: Elgar.

Schiller, Herbert and Schiller Anita. 1988. Libraries, public access to information, and commerce. In *The Political Economy of Information*, 146–166, edited by Vincent Mosco and Janet Wasko. Madison: The University of Wisconsin Press.

Seaton, Jean. 2003. Broadcasting history. In *Power Without Responsibility*, 6th edition, 107–234, edited by James Curran and Jean Seaton. London: Routledge.

Secchi, Davide. 2007. Utilitarian, managerial and relational theories of corporate social responsibility. *International Journal of Management Reviews* 9(4). 347–373.

Seneviratne, Kalinga. 2006. Definition and history of public broadcasting. In *Public service Broadcasting in the Age of Globalization*, 9–58, edited by Indrajit Bnerjee and Kalinga Seneviratne. Nanyang: Asian Media Information and Communication Centre.

Servaes, Jan. 2003. *The European Information Society*. Bristol: Intellect Books.

Sevignani, Sebastian. 2009. *Ideologie – Kulturindustrie und Hegemonie*. Master Thesis. Salzburg.

Shamir, Ronen. 2004. The de-radicalization of corporate social responsibility. *Critical Sociology* 30(3), 669–689.

Shawcross, William. 1992. *Rupert Murdoch. Ringmaster of the Information Circus*. London: Chatto & Windus.

Shelley, Mary. 1818/2000. *Frankenstein or The Modern Prometheus*. In *Mary Shelley Frankenstein* 19–189, edited by Johanna M. Smith. Boston: Bedford/St. Martins.

Shirky, Clay. 2008. *Here Comes Everybody*. London: Penguin.

Siebert, Fred S., Theodore Peterson and Wilbur Schramm. 1956. *Four Theories of the Press*. Urbana: University of Illinois Press.

Sklair, Leslie. 2001. *The Transnational Capitalist Class*. Oxford: Blackwell.

Sklair, Leslie and David Miller. 2010. Capitalist globalization, corporate social responsibility and social policy. *Critical Social Policy* 30(4), 472–495.

Smith Adam. 1759/1976. Theory of moral sentiments. In *The Glasgow Edition of the Works and Correspondence of Adam Smith*, edited by D.D. Raphael and A.L. Macfie. Indianapolis: Oxford University Press.

Smith, Adam. 1776/1976. An inquiry into the nature and the causes of the wealth of nations Vol I and II. In *The Glasgow Edition of the Works and Correspondence of Adam Smith*, edited by R.H. Campbell and A.S. Skinner. Indianapolis: Oxford University Press.

Smythe, Dallas W. 1977/1997: Communications: blindspots of western Marxism. In *The Political Economy of the Media Volume I*, 438–464, edited by Peter Golding and Graham Murdock. Cheltenham, Brookfield: Elgar.

Söderberg, Johan and Adel Daoud. 2012. Atoms want to be free too! Expanding the critique of intellectual property to physical goods. *TripleC Journal for a Global Sustainable Information Society* 10(1), 66–76.

Sohn, Howard F. 1982. Prevailing rationales in the corporate social responsibility debate. *Journal of Business Ethics* 1, 139–144.

SOMO. 2005a. *CSR Issues in the ICT Hardware Manufacturing Sector*. Retrieved from http://somo.nl/publications-nl/Publication_476-nl/at_download/fullfile on October 17, 2011.

SOMO. 2005b. *ICT Hardware Sector in China and Corporate Social Responsibility Issues*. Retrieved from http://somo.nl/publications-en/Publication_624/at_download/fullfile on October 16, 2011.

SOMO. 2007. *Apple. CSR Company Profile*. Retrieved from http://somo.nl/publications-en/Publication_1963/at_download/fullfile on October 17, 2011.

Sparks, Collin. 1995. The future of public broadcasting in Great Britain. *Critical Studies in Mass Communication* 12, 325–341.

Spence, Crawford. 2007. Social and environmental reporting and hegemonic discourse. *Accounting, Auditing and Accountability Journal* 20(6), 855–882.

Stiglitz, Joseph E. 1994. *Whither Socialism*. Cambridge, London: MIT Press.

Stiglitz, Joseph E. 2010. *The Stiglitz Report. Reforming the International Monetary and Financial System in the Wake of the Global Crisis*. New York, London: The New Press.

Stoker, Bram. 1879. *Dracula. A Mystery Story*. 1897 edition for Amazon Kindle.

Stross, Randall. 2008. *Planet Google*. New York: Free Press.

Students Disney Watch. 2009. *Mickey Mouse is No Longer Lovely*. Retrieved from http://sacom.hk/wp-content/uploads/2009/12/sdw-labour-report_summary.pdf on August 31, 2011

Sun, William, Jim Stewart and David Pollard. 2010. Reframing corporate social responsibility. In *Reframing Corporate Social Responsibility: Lessons from the Global Financial Crisis*, 3–19, edited by William Sun, Jim Stewart and David Pollard. Bingley: Emerald.

SustainAbility and WWF. 2004. *Through the Looking Glass. Corporate Social Responsibility in the Media and Entertainment Sector*. A Discussion Paper by the WWF and SustainAbility. Retrieved from http://www.wwf.org.uk/filelibrary/pdf/looking_glass_0105.pdf on March 14, 2011.

SustainAbility, UNEP and Ketchum. 2002. *Good News & Bad. The Media, Corporate Social Responsibility and Sustainable Development*. Retrieved from http://www.sustainability.com/library/good-news-bad#.T2d3tY7FL0M on March 11, 2011.

Svales, George S. 1988. Another look at the president's letter to stockholders. *Financial Analyst Journal* 44(2), 71–73.

Tatli, Emin Islam. 2008. Privacy in danger. Let's Google your privacy. In *IFIP International Federation for Information Processing, Volume 262; The Future of Identity in the Information Society*, 51–59, edited by Simone Fischer-Hübner, Penny Duquenoy, Albin Zuccato and Leonardo Martucci. Boston: Springer.

Teddlie, Charles and Abbas Tashakkori. 2009. Foundations of Mixed Methods Research. Thousand Oaks: Sage.

Tench, Ralph, Ryan Bowd and Brian Jones. 2007. Perceptions and perspectives: corporate social responsibility and the media. *Journal of Communication Management* 11(4), 348–370.

Tene, Omar. 2008. *What Google Knows: Privacy and Internet Search Engines*. Retrieved from http://works.bepress.com/omer_tene/2 on January 21, 2012.

Terranova, Tiziana and Joan Donovan. 2013. Occupy social networks. The paradoxes of corporate social media for networked social movements. In *Unlike Us Reader. Social Media Monopolies and Their Alternatives*, 296-311, edited by Geert Lovink and Miriam Rasch. Amsterdam: Institute of Network Cultures.

Thussu, Daya Kishan. 2007. The "Murdochization" of news? The case of Star TV in India. *Media Culture and Society* 29(49): 593–611.

Tjaden, Karl Hermann. 2006. Voraussetzung, Gegenstand und Ziel kritischer Gesellschaftswissenschaft. In *Soziologie als Gesellschaftskritik. Wider den Verlust einer aktuellen Tradition*, 71–90, edited by Stephan Moebius and Gerhard Schäfer. Hamburg: VSA.

Toffel, Michael and Auden Schendler. 2012. *Where Green Corporate Ratings Fail. Harvard Business School Working Knowledge*. Retrieved from http://hbswk.hbs.edu/pdf/item/6906.pdf on March 5, 2012.

Toffler, Alvin. 1980. *The Third Wave*. London: Collins.

Trommershausen, Anke. 2011. *Corporate Responsibility in Medienunternehmen*. Köln: Halem.

Trubek, David M. 1984. Where the action is: critical legal studies and empiricism. *Stanford Law Review* 36 (1/2), 575–622.

Turner, Derek S. 2009. *Digital Déjà Vu: Old Myths in the Network Neutrality Debate.* Retrieved from http://freepress.net/files/dejavu.pdf on December 12, 2011.

UNDP. 2011. *Human Development Report.* Retrieved from http://hdr.undp.org/en/reports/global/hdr2011/download/ on May 14, 2012.

UNEP. 2009a. *Recycling – From E-Waste to Resources.* Retrieved from http://ewasteguide.info/files/UNEP_2009_eW2R.PDF on November 6, 2011.

UNEP. 2009b. *Reducing Emissions from Private Cars: Incentive Measures for Behavioural Change.* Retrieved from http://www.unep.ch/etb/publications/Green%20Economy/Reducing%20emissions/UNEP%20Reducing%20emissions%20from%20private%20cars.pdf on November 11, 2011.

Urip, Sri. 2010. *CSR Strategies: Corporate Social Responsibility for a Competitive Edge in Emerging Markets.* Chichester: John Wiley and Sons.

Vaidhyanathan, Siva. 2011. *The Googlization of Everything (And Why We Should Worry).* Berkeley: University of California Press.

Van Dijck, José. 2009. Users like you? Theorizing agency in user-generated content. *Media, Culture & Society* 31(1), 41–58.

Van Dijck, José. 2013. *The Culture of Connectivity. A Critical History of Social Media.* Oxford: Oxford University Press.

Vise, David A. 2005. *The Google Story.* London: Pan Mac Millan.

Ward, Annalee R. 2002. *Mouse Morality. The Rhetoric of Disney Animated Film.* Austin: University of Texas Press.

Wartick, Steven L. and Philip L. Cochran. 1985. The evolution of the corporate social performance model. *The Academy of Management Review* 10(4), 758–769.

Wasko, Janet. 2001. *Understanding Disney.* Cambridge: Polity.

Wilmshurst, Trevor D. and Geoffrey Frost. 2000. Corporate environmental reporting. A test of legitimacy theory. *Accounting, Auditing & Accountability Journal* 13(1), 10–26.

Windsor, Duane. 2006. Corporate social responsibility: three key approaches. *Journal of Management Studies* 43(1), 93–114.

Winseck, Dwayne. 2011. The political economies of media and the transformation of the global media industries. In *The Political Economies of Media*, 3–48, edited by Dwayne Winseck and Dal Yong Jin. London: Bloomsbury.

Winter, Carsten. 2006. TIME-Konvergenz als Herausforderung für Management und Medienentwhicklung. In *Konvergenzmenagement und Medienwirtschaft*, 13–51, edited by Matthias Karmasin und Karsten Winter. München: Fink.

Wolff, Stephan. 2004. Analysis of documents and records. In *A Companion to Qualitative Research*, 284–289, edited by Uwe Flick, Ernst von Kardoff and Ines Steinke. London: Sage.

World Radio and Television Council. 2001. *Public Broadcasting. Why? How? UNESCO Sector of Communication and Information Division of Communication Development and Conseil Mondial de la Radiotélévision.* Retrieved from http://unesdoc.unesco.org/images/0012/001240/124058eo.pdf on March 6, 2011.

Wright, Charles Robert. 1986. *Mass Communication: A Sociological Perspective.* 3rd edition. New York: Random House.

Ziegler, Jean. 2010. *Europe is Playing Along with the IMF and Multinationals.* Retrieved from http://humaniteinenglish.com/spip.php?article1527 on May 14, 2012.

Zimmer, Michael. 2008. The externalities of search 2.0. The emerging privacy threats when the drive for the perfect search engine meets web 2.0. *First Monday* 13(3).

Žižek, Slavoj. 2006. Nobody has to be vile. *London Review of Books* 28(7). Retrieved from http://www.lrb.co.uk/v28/n07/slavoj-zizek/nobody-has-to-be-vile on May 7, 2011.

Žižek, Slavoj. 2009. *First as Tragedy Then as Farce.* London: Verso.

Company CSR reports

Apple

Apple_SR 2006. *Final Assembly Supplier Audit Report.* Retrieved from http://images. apple.com/supplierresponsibility/pdf/Apple_SR_2007_Progress_Report.pdf on October 18, 2011.

Apple_SR 2007. *Driving Change. Supplier Responsibility Progress Report.* Retrieved from http://images.apple.com/supplierresponsibility/pdf/Apple_SR_2008_Progress_ Report.pdf on October 18, 2011.

Apple_SR 2008. *Supplier Responsibility. Progress Report.* Retrieved from http://images. apple.com/supplierresponsibility/pdf/Apple_SR_2009_Progress_Report.pdf on October 18, 2011.

Apple_SR 2009. *Supplier Responsibility. Progress Report.* Retrieved from http://images. apple.com/supplierresponsibility/pdf/Apple_SR_2010_Progress_Report.pdf on October 18, 2011.

Apple_SR 2010. *Apple Supplier Responsibility. Progress Report.* Retrieved from http:// images.apple.com/supplierresponsibility/pdf/Apple_SR_2011_Progress_Report.pdf on October 18, 2011.

AT&T

AT&T_CSR 2006. *Social Responsibility Report.* Retrieved from http://www.att.com/gen/ landing-pages?pid=7735 on December 2, 2011.

AT&T_CSR 2007. *Connecting with People, Everywhere They Live and Work – AT&T's Corporate Citizenship Commitment.* Retrieved from http://www.att.com/gen/landing-pages?pid=7735 on December 2, 2011.

AT&T_CSR 2007/2008. *AT&T Citizenship and Sustainability Report. Connecting for a Sustainable Future.* Retrieved from http://www.att.com/gen/landing-pages?pid=7735 on December 2, 2011.

AT&T_CSR 2008. *AT&T Citizenship and Sustainability Report. Connecting for a Sustainable Future.* Retrieved from http://www.att.com/gen/landing-pages?pid=7735 on December 2, 2011.

AT&T_CSR 2009. *AT&T Citizenship and Sustainability Report. Connecting for a Sustainable Future.* Retrieved from http://www.att.com/gen/landing-pages?pid=7735 on December 2, 2011.

AT&T_CSR 2010. *Meet the Possibility Economy - 2010 AT&T Sustainability Report.* Retrieved from http://www.att.com/gen/landing-pages?pid=7735 on December 2, 2011.

Google

Google company website (see respective footnotes).

HP

HP_CSR 2001. *Social and Environmental Responsibility Report.* Retrieved from http://www. hp.com/hpinfo/globalcitizenship/08gcreport/pdf/hp_csr_full_hi.pdf on October 18, 2011.

HP_CSR 2002. *Global Citizenship Report.* Retrieved from http://www.hp.com/hpinfo/ globalcitizenship/08gcreport/pdf/hpgcr_2003highres.pdf on October 18, 2011.

HP_CSR 2003. *Global Citizenship Report.* Retrieved from http://www.hp.com/hpinfo/globalcitizenship/08gcreport/pdf/2004gcreport.pdf on November 1, 2011.

HP_CSR 2004. *Global Citizenship Report.* Retrieved from http://www.hp.com/hpinfo/globalcitizenship/08gcreport/pdf/hp2005gcreport.pdf on October 18, 2011.

HP_CSR 2005. *Global Citizenship Report.* Retrieved from http://www.hp.com/hpinfo/globalcitizenship/08gcreport/pdf/hp2006gcreport.pdf on October 18, 2011.

HP_CSR 2006. *Global Citizenship Report.* Retrieved from http://www.hp.com/hpinfo/globalcitizenship/08gcreport/pdf/hp_fy06_gcr.pdf on October 18, 2011.

HP_CSR 2007. *Global Citizenship Report.* Retrieved from http://www.hp.com/hpinfo/globalcitizenship/07gcreport/pdf/hp_fy07_gcr.pdf on October 18, 2011.

HP_CSR 2008. *Global Citizenship Report.* Retrieved from http://www.hp.com/hpinfo/globalcitizenship/08gcreport/printminipdf_window.html on October 18, 2011.

HP_CSR 2009a. *Global Citizenship Report.* Retrieved from http://www.hp.com/hpinfo/globalcitizenship/09gcreport/pdf/fy09_fullreport.pdf on October 18, 2011.

HP_CSR 2009b. *Changing the Equation - The Impact of Global Citizenship in 2009 and Beyond.* Retrieved from http://www.hp.com/hpinfo/globalcitizenship/09gcreport/pdf/fy09_brochure.pdf on October 18, 2011.

HP_CSR 2010a. *A Connected World - The Impact of HP Global Citizenship in 2010 and Beyond.* Retrieved from http://www.hp.com/hpinfo/globalcitizenship/pdf/hp_fy10_gcr.pdf on October 18, 2011.

HP_CSR 2010b. *A Connected World - The Impact of HP Global Citizenship in 2010 and Beyond.* Retrieved from http://www.hp.com/hpinfo/globalcitizenship/fy10_brochure.pdf on October 18, 2011.

Microsoft

MI_CSR 2003. *Citizenship Report.* Retrieved from http://www.microsoft.com/about/corporatecitizenship/en-us/reporting/ on September 26, 2011.

MI_CSR 2004. *Global Citizenship Report.* Retrieved from http://www.microsoft.com/about/corporatecitizenship/en-us/reporting/ on September 26, 2011.

MI_CSR 2005. *Citizenship Report.* Retrieved from http://www.microsoft.com/about/corporatecitizenship/en-us/reporting/ on September 26, 2011.

MI_CSR 2006. *Partners in Innovation - Citizenship Report.* Retrieved from http://www.microsoft.com/about/corporatecitizenship/en-us/reporting/ on September 26, 2011.

MI_CSR 2007/2008. *Citizenship @ Microsoft.* Retrieved from http://www.microsoft.com/about/corporatecitizenship/en-us/reporting/ on September 26, 2011.

MI_CSR 2009. *Corporate Citizenship @ Microsoft - Addressing Societal Needs in the Global Community.* Retrieved from http://www.microsoft.com/about/corporatecitizenship/en-us/reporting/ on September 26, 2011.

MI_CSR 2010. *Citizenship Report.* Retrieved from http://www.microsoft.com/about/corporatecitizenship/en-us/reporting/ on September 26, 2011.

MI_CSR 2011. *Citizenship Report.* Retrieved from http://www.microsoft.com/about/corporatecitizenship/en-us/reporting/ on September 26, 2011.

News Corp

News Corp_SBC. 2011. *Standards of Business Conduct.* Retrieved from http://www.newscorp.com/PDF/StdBusinessConduct_2011.pdf on February 8, 2012.

The Walt Disney Company

DI_ENVIRO 2000. *Enviroport*. Retrieved from http://disney.go.com/disneyhand/ environmentality/enviroport_2000_web.pdf on September 1, 2011.

DI_ENVIRO 2001. *Enviroport*. Retrieved from http://corporate.disney.go.com/media/ environmentality/enviroports/enviroport_2001_web.pdf on September 1, 2011.

DI_ENVIRO 2002. *Enviroport*. Retrieved from http://corporate.disney.go.com/media/ environmentality/enviroports/enviroport_2002_web.pdf on September 1, 2011.

DI_ENVIRO 2003. *Enviroport*. Retrieved from http://corporate.disney.go.com/media/ environmentality/enviroports/enviroport_2003_web.pdf on September 1, 2011.

DI_ENVIRO 2004. *Enviroport*. Retrieved from http://corporate.disney.go.com/media/ environmentality/enviroports/enviroport_2004_web.pdf on September 1, 2011.

DI_ENVIRO 2005. *Enviroport*. Retrieved from http://amedia.disney.go.com/environmentality/ enviroports/twdc_2005_enviroreport_a.pdf on September 1, 2011.

DI_ENVIRO 2006. *Enviroport*. Retrieved from http://amedia.disney.go.com/environmentality/ enviroports/twdc_2006_enviroreport_a.pdf on September 1, 2011.

DI_ENVIRO 2007. *Enviroport*. Retrieved from http://corporate.disney.go.com/environmentality/ enviroport/2007/index.html on September 1, 2011.

DI_CSR 2008. *Corporate Responsibility Report*. Retrieved from http://corporate.disney. go.com/files/FINAL_Disney_CR_Report_2008.pdf on September 1, 2011.

DI_CSR 2010. *Corporate Citizenship Report*. Retrieved from http://corporate.disney. go.com/citizenship2010/downloads/ on September 1, 2011.

DI_CoC 2007. *Code of Conduct for Manufacturers*. Retrieved from http://corporate. disney.go.com/citizenship/codeofconduct.html on September 1, 2011.

DI_CSR online. *Labor Standards FAQ*. Retrieved from http://corporate.disney.go.com/ citizenship/faq.html on September 1, 2011.

Vivendi

VI_CSR 2002. *Report – Our Economic, Social and Environmental Responsibility*. Retrieved from http://www.corporateregister.com/a10723/vu02-ens-fr.pdf on August 21, 2011.

VI_CSR 2003. *Sustainable Development Report*. Retrieved from http://www.justmeans. com/download_report_info?repofile=Vml2ZW5kaS1TdXN0YWluYWJsZS1EZXZlb G9wbWVudC1SZXBvcnQtMjAwMy5wZGY=&reponame=U3VzdGFpbmFibGUgR GV2ZWxvcG1lbnQgUmVwb3J0IDIwMDM= on August 21, 2011.

VI_CSR 2004/2005. *Sustainable Development Report*. Retrieved from http://www. justmeans.com/download_report_info?repofile=Vml2ZW5kaS0yMDA0LTIwMDUtU 3VzdGFpbmFibGUtRGV2ZWxvcG1lbnQtUmVwb3J0LnBkZg==&reponame=MjA wNC0yMDA1IFN1c3RhaW5hYmxlIERldmVsb3BtZW50IFJlcG9ydA== on August 21, 2011.

VI_CSR 2005/2006. *Sustainable Development Report*. Retrieved from http://www.just- means.com/download_report_info?repofile=Vml2ZW5kaS0yMDA1LTIwMDYtU3V zdGFpbmFibGUtRGV2ZWxvcG1lbnQtUmVwb3J0LnBkZg==&reponame=MjAwN S0yMDA2IFN1c3RhaW5hYmxlIERldmVsb3BtZW50IFJlcG9ydA== on August 21, 2011.

VI_CSR 2006/2007. *Sustainable Development Report*. Retrieved from http://www.vivendi. com/wp-content/uploads/2008/09/20070711-sustainable-development-report.pdf on August 21, 2011.

VI_CSR 2008. *Activity and Sustainable Development Report*. Retrieved from http://www.vivendi.com/wp-content/uploads/2009/05/radd-vivendi-va-190509.pdf on August 21, 2011.

VI_CSR 2009. *Activity and Sustainable Development Report*. Retrieved from http://www.vivendi.com/wp-content/uploads/2010/05/20100527-radd-ang-version-finale-25-mai-2010.pdf on August 21, 2011.

VI_CSR 2010. *Activity and Sustainable Development Report*. Retrieved from http://www.vivendi.com/wp-content/uploads/2011/05/201-05-23-radd-uk-2010-2.pdf on August 21, 2011.

Company SEC filings and financial reports

Apple

Apple SEC filings. 10-k forms 1994–2012. In Edgar database. Retrieved from http://www.sec.gov/cgi-bin/browse-edgar?action=getcompany&CIK=0000320193&type=10-k&dateb=&owner=exclude&count=40 on February 14, 2013.

AT&T

AT&T SEC filings. 10-k forms 1993–2010. In Edgar Database. Retrieved from http://www.sec.gov/cgi-bin/browse-edgar?action=getcompany&CIK=0000732717&type=10-k&dateb=&owner=exclude&count=40 on October 15, 2013.

Google

Google SEC filings. 10-k forms 2004–2010. In Edgar Database. Retrieved from http://www.sec.gov/cgi-bin/browse-edgar?action=getcompany&CIK=0001288776&type=10-k&dateb=&owner=exclude&count=40 on January 16, 2011.

HP

HP SEC filings. 10-k forms 1993–2010. In Edgar database. Retrieved from http://www.sec.gov/cgi-bin/browse-edgar?action=getcompany&CIK=0000047217&type=10-k&dateb=&owner=exclude&count=40 on November 13, 2011.

Microsoft

Microsoft SEC filings. 10-k forms 1994–2011. In Edgar Database. Retrieved from http://www.sec.gov/cgi-bin/browse-edgar?action=getcompany&CIK=0000789019&type=10-k&dateb=&owner=exclude&count=40 on October 5, 2011.

News Corp

News Corp SEC filings. 10-k forms 2005–2011. In Edgar Database. Retrieved from http://www.sec.gov/cgi-bin/browse-edgar?action=getcompany&CIK=0001308161&type=10-k&dateb=&owner=exclude&count=40 on February 15, 2012.

The Walt Disney Company

Disney SEC filings. 10-k forms. 1997–2010. In Edgar Database. Retrieved from http://www.sec.gov/cgi-bin/browse-edgar?action=getcompany&CIK=0001001039&type=10-k&dateb=&owner=exclude&count=40 on September 5, 2011.

Vivendi

Vivendi Annual Reports. 2001–2010. Retrieved from http://www.vivendi.com/vivendi/Annual-Reports,4975 on September 12, 2011.

Index